Spicer's
Practical Auditing

Spicer's Practical Auditing

Eighteenth Edition

Spicer and Oppenheim
Chartered Accountants

Amyas Mascarenhas
Director of Audit and Accounting Research
Spicer and Oppenheim

Stuart Turley
Senior Lecturer, Department of Accounting and Finance
University of Manchester

Butterworths
London, Edinburgh
1990

United Kingdom	Butterworth & Co (Publishers) Ltd, 88 Kingsway, LONDON WC2B 6AB and 4 Hill Street, EDINBURGH EH2 3JZ
Australia	Butterworths Pty Ltd, SYDNEY, MELBOURNE, BRISBANE, ADELAIDE, PERTH, CANBERRA and HOBART
Canada	Butterworths Canada Ltd, TORONTO and VANCOUVER
Ireland	Butterworth (Ireland) Ltd, DUBLIN
Malaysia	Malayan Law Journal Sdn Bhd, KUALA LUMPUR
New Zealand	Butterworths of New Zealand Ltd, WELLINGTON and AUCKLAND
Puerto Rico	Equity de Puerto Rico, Inc, HATO REY
Singapore	Malayan Law Journal Pte Ltd, SINGAPORE
USA	Butterworth Legal Publishers, AUSTIN, Texas; BOSTON, Massachusetts; CLEARWATER, Florida (D & S Publishers); ORFORD, New Hampshire (Equity Publishing); ST PAUL, Minnesota; and SEATTLE, Washington

A CIP Catalogue record for this book is available from the British Library.

ISBN 0 406 12300 4

Typeset by Kerrypress Ltd, Luton, Beds.
Printed by Billings Book Plan, Worcester.

Preface

In the first years of this century, in response to pressure from fellow auditors and students of auditing, the authors of the original edition of this book set out to provide 'a textbook on the subject of auditing, which should be at once practical and comprehensive'. Sadly, in today's world of diverse and specialised audits, it is no longer possible to be comprehensive to the same level of detail in a work of this size. But the principles discussed and the audit approach suggested in this edition should apply to all audits. Our main aim in preparing this work is that it should continue to provide a practical guide of the highest standard for practising auditors and students alike.

The role and regulation of auditors is coming under increasing scrutiny around the world and it is important that the practice of auditing is seen in its economic and regulatory context. In a new Part I of the book, we provide an overview of some of the important background and environmental factors which determine the role and nature of the modern audit. Auditor independence and the liability of auditors are two topics discussed in this section which will be of particular interest to both students and practitioners.

Part 2 sets out a practical approach to an audit. It reflects the heavy emphasis that today's auditor gives to audit planning and risk analysis to ensure that audit effort is properly directed so as to maximise efficiency and effectiveness. In this Part, we use a description of the internal control structure applicable to all audits, large and small, which is now employed by most, if not all, leading firms of auditors and has been formalised in the latest auditing standards issued in the United States, though not yet in the United Kingdom. In our detailed discussion of going concern issues, we suggest a path that auditors should tread, given the potential repercussions of recent insolvency legislation. Management letters are being given increasing attention by auditors, as they provide a medium for giving to the audit client a greater return from the audit, for relatively little additional effort. We devote a separate chapter to this topic.

Part 3 sets out suggested audit procedures applicable to specific account balances in the form of easily accessible checklists, with a number of specimen standard letters.

The detailed procedural guidance in this book is closely based on Spicer & Oppenheim's internal audit manual. We are grateful to Spicer & Oppenheim for permission to make use of this material. References to 'the Institute' in this book are to the Institute of Chartered Accountants in England & Wales. We are grateful for permission to make use of quotations and extracts from Auditing Standards and Guidelines and other pronouncements issued by the Institute.

Amyas Mascarenhas
Stuart Turley
November 1989

Contents

Preface   v

Part One: Auditing in perspective   1
Introduction to Part One   3

1   **What is an audit?**   5
  1.1 Auditing defined   5
  1.2   Key components   5
      1.2.1   Entity   5
      1.2.2   Performance, position and information   6
      1.2.3   Competent, independent person   6
      1.2.4   The collection and evaluation of evidence   6
      1.2.5   Established criteria   6
      1.2.6   Reporting an opinion   7
  1.3   Auditing and information   7
  1.4   Types of audit   9
      1.4.1   Financial statements audits   9
      1.4.2   Regularity audits   9
      1.4.3   Management and operational audits   9
      1.4.4   Social audits   10
      1.4.5   Internal audits and external audits   10
  1.5   Summary   10

2   **Why audit? — the auditing environment**   12
  2.1   Demand and supply   12
  2.2   Accountability   12
      2.2.1   Stewardship relationships   12
      2.2.2   Other interests   13
  2.3   Economic explanations for auditing   13
      2.3.1   Agency contracts   14
      2.3.2   Information for decisions   14
      2.3.3   Auditing as insurance   14
  2.4   The auditing environment   15
      2.4.1   Audit firms   16
      2.4.2   Parliament, the law and regulatory agencies   16
      2.4.3   The professional bodies   17
      2.4.4   The courts and professional liability   20
  2.5   The statutory audit requirement   20
      2.5.1   Auditing provisions in company law   21
      2.5.2   The historical development of the statutory audit   22
      2.5.3   The auditor's responsibility for fraud   24
  2.6   Summary   25

3   **Auditor behaviour — independence and ethics**   26
  3.1   Introduction   26
  3.2   The importance of independence   26
  3.3   What is auditor independence?   27
  3.4   Factors strengthening independence   27
      3.4.1   Company law   27
      3.4.2   Professional recommendations   28
      3.4.3   Individual firms' rules   29

Contents

3.5 Factors threatening independence 30
    3.5.1 Fees 30
    3.5.2 Services 30
    3.5.3 Appointment 30
    3.5.4 Competition between audit firms 30
    3.5.5 Incorporation 30
3.6 Further suggestions for strengthening independence 31
3.7 Monitoring proposals 31
    3.7.1 Professional rules 31
    3.7.2 Legal regulations 31
    3.7.3 Disclosure of information 31
    3.7.4 Audit committees 32
3.8 Structural proposals 32
    3.8.1 changing the tenure of audit appointments 32
    3.8.2 Separation of auditing from other services 32
    3.8.3 A regulatory agency 32
3.9 Other ethical considerations 33
    3.9.1 Confidentiality 33
    3.9.2 Obtaining work, publicity and advertising 33
    3.9.3 Changes in appointment 33
3.10 Summary 33

4 **Liability and the duty of care** 35
4.1 Introduction 35
4.2 Conditions for liability 35
4.3 What standard of care? 35
    4.3.1 Guidance from cases 36
    4.3.2 Audit risk, audit failure and business failure 37
4.4 To whom is the auditor liable? 37
    4.4.1 Privity 37
    4.4.2 Proximity 38
4.5 Cases on third party liability 38
    4.5.1 *Candler v Crane Christmas* 38
    4.5.2 *Hedley Byrne v Heller* 38
    4.5.3 *Scott Group v McFarlane* 39
    4.5.4 *JEB Fasteners v Marks, Bloom* 39
    4.5.5 *Twomax v Dickson, McFarlane & Robinson* 39
    4.5.6 *Lloyd Cheyham v Littlejohn* 40
    4.5.7 *Caparo Industries v Dickman* 40
    4.5.8 *Al Saudi Banque v Clark Pixley* 41
4.6 Summary 41

5 **Collecting audit evidence** 43
5.1 The need for evidence 43
5.2 Sources of evidence 43
    5.2.1 Internal evidence 43
    5.2.2 External evidence 44
    5.2.3 Auditor-generated evidence 44
5.3 Types of evidence 44
    5.3.1 Observation and physical examination 44
    5.3.2 Documentary testing 45
    5.3.3 Reperformance 45
    5.3.4 Enquiry and confirmation 45
    5.3.5 Analytical procedures 45
5.4 Desired qualities of audit evidence 46
    5.4.1 Relevance 46
    5.4.2 Reliability 46

Contents

　　　　5.4.3　Objectivity　47
　　　　5.4.4　Conclusiveness　47
　　　　5.4.5　Comprehensiveness　47
　　　　5.4.6　Efficiency　48
　　5.5　Problems in using audit evidence　48
　　　　5.5.1　Availability　48
　　　　5.5.2　Quantity v quality　48
　　　　5.5.3　Inappropriate reliance　48
　　　　5.5.4　Aggregation　49
　　5.6　Audit objectives　49
　　　　5.6.1　Existence or occurrence　49
　　　　5.6.2　Completeness　49
　　　　5.6.3　Rights and obligations　49
　　　　5.6.4　Valuation and allocation　50
　　　　5.6.5　Presentation and disclosure　50
　　5.7　The audit process　50
　　5.8　Planning　51
　　　　5.8.1　Understanding the business　51
　　　　5.8.2　Assessing risk and materiality　51
　　　　5.8.3　Understanding and evaluating internal control　52
　　　　5.8.4　Determining audit approach and procedures　52
　　　　5.8.5　Segmenting the audit process　53
　　5.9　Collection of evidence　53
　　　　5.9.1　Tests of controls　53
　　　　5.9.2　Substantive testing　53
　　5.10　Forming an opinion　54
　　　　5.10.1　Aggregating evidence　54
　　　　5.10.2　Overall review of financial statements　54
　　　　5.10.3　Deciding an opinion　54
　　5.11　Summary　54

6　**Reporting an audit opinion**　56
　　6.1　Introduction　56
　　6.2　Objectives of audit reporting　56
　　6.3　A judgemental opinion　57
　　6.4　Readership of audit reports　57
　　6.5　Standardised reports　57
　　6.6　The elements of the audit report　58
　　　　6.6.1　The formal lines of communication　58
　　　　6.6.2　The scope of the report　58
　　　　6.6.3　The basis of the auditor's report　58
　　　　6.6.4　The content of the opinion　59
　　6.7　Truth and fairness　60
　　　　6.7.1　The meaning of true and fair　60
　　　　6.7.2　An overriding requirement　60
　　　　6.7.3　Establishing truth and fairness　60
　　　　6.7.4　The influence of accounting standards　61
　　6.8　Types of opinion　61
　　　　6.8.1　Unqualified opinions　61
　　　　6.8.2　Reports giving other than an unqualified opinion　62
　　　　6.8.3　Material v fundamental　62
　　6.9　Other reports　63
　　6.10　Summary　63
　　References and further reading　64

Contents

Part Two: A practical approach to an audit   65
Introduction to Part Two   67

7   Planning and audit objectives   69
   7.1   Why the auditor must plan the audit   69
   7.2   Who should perform the planning   69
   7.3   Scope and nature of audit planning   69
   7.4   Phases of planning   70
   7.5   Determining the objectives of the engagement   70
   7.6   Engagement letters   71
Appendices
   7.1   Specimen memorandum of terms of engagement for a company client   72

8   Understanding the client's business   77
   8.1   Why an auditor needs to understand the client's business   77
   8.2   What an auditor needs to know   77
      8.2.1   Introduction   77
      8.2.2   The nature of the business   77
      8.2.3   Organisation and operating characteristics   79
      8.2.4   The business strategy   80
   8.3   Learning about the client's business   80
      8.3.1   Planning the information gathering exercise   80
      8.3.2   Sources of information   81
      8.3.3   Recording and assimilating the information   83
Appendices
   8.1   Understanding the client's business — checklist   84

9   Audit risk and materiality   89
   9.1   Introduction   89
   9.2   Nature of audit risk   89
   9.3   Nature of materiality   90
   9.4   Assessment of audit risk   91
      9.4.1   Overall assessment at the financial statement level   91
      9.4.2   Assessment at the account balance or class-of-transactions level   91
   9.5   Consideration of materiality   92
      9.5.1   Planning materiality   92
      9.5.2   Keeping track of errors   95
      9.5.3   Materiality at the account balance or class-of-transactions level   96
   9.6   Forming an audit opinion   96
      9.6.1   Degree of estimation   97
      9.6.2   Critical points   97
      9.6.3   Accounting policies   97
      9.6.4   Separate disclosures   98

10 Inherent and internal control risk   99
   10.1 Introduction   99
      10.1.1 What this chapter is about   99
      10.1.2 Requirement to understand the internal control structure   100
      10.1.3 Computerised and manual systems   100
   10.2 The control environment   100
      10.2.1 Importance of the control environment   100
      10.2.2 Effect of dominant individual   103
   10.3 Accounting system   103
      10.3.1 Importance of the accounting system   103
      10.3.2 Legal requirements   105

Contents

10.4 Control procedures 106
    10.4.1 Types of control procedure 106
    10.4.2 General controls 106
    10.4.3 Application controls 108
    10.4.4 Controls over assets 108
    10.4.5 Security of data 109
    10.4.6 Identifying and assessing controls 109
    10.4.7 Detect v prevent controls 109
    10.4.8 Focus on completeness 110
    10.4.9 Outside service centre 110
10.5 Documenting the internal control structure 111
10.6 Walk-throughs 112
10.7 Assessing inherent and control risk 112
    10.7.1 General principles 112
    10.7.2 Preliminary assessment of inherent and control risk 113
    10.7.3 Further reduction in assessed level of inherent and control risk 114
Appendices
10.1 Checklist of environmental inherent and control risk factors 115
10.2 Checklist of common control procedures 118

11 Other influences on audit planning 123
11.1 Preliminary analytical procedures 123
    11.1.1 Nature of analytical procedures 123
    11.1.2 Analytical procedures in audit planning 124
    11.1.3 Examples of financial information and ratios 125
    11.1.4 Documenting preliminary analytical procedures 126
11.2 Involvement of other auditors 126
11.3 Use of internal auditors 127
11.4 Use of the work of specialists 128

12 Developing an audit strategy and audit programme 130
12.1 Strategy and detailed planning 130
12.2 Decision levels in an audit strategy 130
12.3 Developing an audit strategy 131
12.4 Examples of strategies 133
12.5 Communicating the audit plan 136
12.6 Developing audit programmes 139
Appendices
12.1 Audit planning memorandum — checklist 141

13 Work scheduling and staffing the audit 142
13.1 Introduction 142
13.2 Work scheduling 142
13.3 Staffing 143
    13.3.1 The main influences on staff allocation 143
    13.3.2 Scope, complexity and risks 143
    13.3.3 Timing factors 144
    13.3.4 Client's assistance 144
13.4 Preparing audit time budgets 145
Appendices
13.1 The audit team 146

14 Tests of controls 149
14.1 Introduction 149
14.2 Objective of tests of controls 149
14.3 Types of tests of controls 150
    14.3.1 Observation 150

Contents

14.3.2 Enquiry 150
14.3.3 Inspection 151
14.3.4 Reperformance 151
14.4 Extent of tests of controls 151
14.4.1 Assurance provided by evidence 151
14.4.2 Evidence from prior audits 152
14.4.3 Evidence obtained at an interim visit 152
14.4.4 Consistency of evidence 153
14.4.5 Sufficiency of evidence 153
14.5 Documentation 154

15 Substantive tests 155
15.1 Types of testing 155
15.2 Tests of details 155
15.2.1 Inspection of documents 155
15.2.2 Inspection of assets 156
15.2.3 Direct confirmation 156
15.2.4 Reperformance of computations and reconciliations 156
15.2.5 Other procedures 157
15.3 Selective tests of details 158
15.4 Timing of tests of details 158
15.4.1 Factors to consider 159
15.4.2 Extending audit conclusions to the year end 159
15.5 Analytical procedures as substantive tests 160
15.6 When to use analytical procedures 160
15.6.1 The financial statement item or assertion 161
15.6.2 Plausibility and predictability of the relationship 162
15.6.3 Availability and reliability of data 162
15.6.4 Precision of the expectation 163
15.7 Identifying and investigating significant differences 164
15.8 Documentation of analytical procedures 165
15.9 Dealing with errors 166
15.9.1 Nature of errors 166
15.9.2 Kinds of error 166
15.9.3 Other discrepancies 166
15.9.4 Dealing with individual errors 167
15.9.5 Keeping track of errors 168
15.9.6 Prior period errors 169
15.9.7 Aspects of materiality judgments 169
15.9.8 Risk of further undetected error 170
15.9.9 Resolving material differences 170

16 Audit sampling 171
16.1 Introduction 171
16.2 Background to audit sampling 171
16.2.1 Meaning of sampling 171
16.2.2 Sampling risk 172
16.2.3 Non-sampling risk 172
16.2.4 Substantive tests and tests of controls 172
16.3 When to sample 172
16.4 How to design a substantive sample test 173
16.4.1 Objective of the test and error definition 173
16.4.2 Defining the population and sampling unit 173
16.4.3 Completeness of population 173
16.4.4 Determining sample size 174
16.4.5 Sample selection 178
16.5 Evaluation of sample results 180
16.5.1 Projection of errors 181

Contents

16.5.2 Comparison of projected error to tolerable error and consideration of sampling risk 181
16.5.3 Investigation of cause and implications of errors 182
16.6 Tests of controls 182

17 Auditing accounting estimates 185
17.1 Introduction 185
17.2 Developing accounting estimates 186
17.3 Internal control structure related to accounting estimates 186
17.4 Evaluating accounting estimates 187

18 Computer-assisted audit techniques 189
18.1 Introduction 189
18.2 Computer audit software 190
18.3 General purpose software 192
18.4 Special audit packages 192
18.5 Miscellaneous computer audit techniques 193
18.5.1 Audit test data 193
18.5.2 Test data generator 194
18.5.3 Integrated test facility 195
18.5.4 Embedded audit facilities 195
18.5.5 Utility programs 195
18.5.6 Program comparison 196
18.5.7 Program code analysis 196
18.5.8 System activity file interrogation 196
18.5.9 Flowcharting 196

19 Execution and control 198
19.1 Execution 198
19.1.1 Introduction 198
19.1.2 Briefing and supervision 198
19.1.3 Review of working papers 199
19.2 Communication 200
19.3 Documentation 201
19.3.1 The need for working papers 201
19.3.2 Working paper files 201
19.3.3 'Lead-schedule-and-pyramid' filing 202
19.3.4 Content of working papers 204
19.3.5 Preparation of working papers 204
19.3.6 Ownership and confidentiality of working papers 205
19.4 Time control 206
Appendices
19.1 Development and documentation of computer models 207

20 Completion reviews 209
20.1 Review of post balance sheet events 209
20.2 Types of post balance sheet events 209
20.2.1 Definitions 209
20.2.2 Examples 209
20.2.3 Window dressing 211
20.2.4 Infringement of borrowing powers 212
20.3 Audit procedures 212
20.3.1 General 212
20.3.2 Timing of procedures 213
20.3.3 Management representations 213
20.3.4 Consolidated groups 214

Contents

20.4 Subsequent discovery of errors in issued reports 214
20.5 Overall review of financial statements 215
    20.5.1 Objectives of the overall review 215
    20.5.2 Compliance with generally accepted accounting principles 215
    20.5.3 Adequacy of disclosures 215
    20.5.4 Compatibility with knowledge of the business 216
Appendices
20.1 Key ratios 217

21 Audit clearance procedures 220
21.1 Objectives 220
21.2 Points for partner attention 221
21.3 Points forward 222
21.4 Sign-off checklist 223
21.5 Letters of representation 223
    21.5.1 Requirement for written confirmation 223
    21.5.2 Contents of the letter 223
    21.5.3 Groups 224
21.6 Engagement administration 224
    21.6.1 Permanent files 225
    21.6.2 Time and cost summaries 225
21.7 Preliminary announcements 226
    21.7.1 Introduction 226
    21.7.2 Client categories 226
    21.7.3 Audit timetable 227
21.8 Release of accounts 227
    21.8.1 Final clearance of accounts 227
    21.8.2 No release to third parties before signature 227
Appendices
21.1 Sign-off checklist 228
21.2 Examples of representations by management 230
21.3 Preliminary announcements — audit clearance 232

22 Management letters 233
22.1 Introduction 233
22.2 Structure and content 233
    22.2.1 Importance of good structure and content 233
    22.2.2 Introductory paragraphs 234
    22.2.3 The body of the letter 234
    22.2.4 Restriction on distribution 236
    22.2.5 Concluding paragraphs 236
22.3 Collection of material for inclusion 237
22.4 Input from the client 238
22.5 Other matters 238
    22.5.1 Addressee 238
    22.5.2 Other recipients 239
    22.5.3 Multiple letters 239
    22.5.4 Timing and follow-up 239
Appendices
22.1 Examples of management letters 240

23 Going concern 246
23.1 Introduction 246
23.2 Identification of going concern problems 246
    23.2.1 Red flags 246
    23.2.2 Infringement of borrowing limits 247

Contents

23.3 Audit procedures 247
    23.3.1 Preliminary enquiries 247
    23.3.2 Consideration of management's plans 247
    23.3.3 Disagreement with directors 249
    23.3.4 Bank and other facilities 249
    23.3.5 Group support 249
    23.3.6 Letters of subordination 251
23.4 Disclosures 252
    23.4.1 Accounting adjustments 252
    23.4.2 Disclosure in financial statements 253
    23.4.3 Going concern audit report references 253
    23.4.4 Directors and shadow directors — statutory penalties 254
23.5 Checklist of procedures 255

Appendices
23.1 Suggested wording for requesting audit confirmation of a letter of support 257
23.2 Specimen letter informing directors of statutory penalties 258

24 Consolidated financial statements 259
24.1 Introduction 259
24.2 Planning 260
    24.2.1 Why the auditor should plan the group audit 260
    24.2.2 The stages in planning 260
    24.2.3 Group structure 260
    24.2.4 Assessing group audit risk and group materiality 261
    24.2.5 Identification of areas of high risk, audit difficulty or accounting complexity 261
    24.2.6 Identification of group audit requirements 262
    24.2.7 Feedback on work done 262
    24.2.8 Integrity, independence and competence 263
    24.2.9 Documenting and communicating the auditor's requirements 263
24.3 Conducting the consolidation audit 264
    24.3.1 Review of working papers 265
    24.3.2 Review of questionnaire responses and other returns 265
    24.3.3 Signed financial statements 266
    24.3.4 Events subsequent to the balance sheet date 266
    24.3.5 Checking the validity of consolidation calculations and the completeness and accuracy of consolidation adjustments 266
24.4 Completing the consolidation audit 269
    24.4.1 Overall review of financial statements 269
    24.4.2 Group points for partner attention 270
    24.4.3 Sign-off checklist 270
24.5 Checklist of illustrative substantive procedures 270

25 The new audit 273
25.1 Introduction 273
25.2 Administrative aspects of the new appointment as auditors 273
    25.2.1 Obtaining clearance from the previous auditors 273
    25.2.2 Independence 273
25.3 Particular audit considerations in a new engagement 274
    25.3.1 Background information 274
    25.3.2 Closing figures 274
    25.3.3 Accounting policies and financial statement presentation 275
25.4 Retirement or resignation as auditors 275
    25.4.1 Giving formal written notice of resignation 275
    25.4.2 Communication with the proposed successor 275

Contents

Appendices
    25.1 Specimen letters — changes in appointment   277

Part Three: Suggested procedures for specific account balances   279
Introduction to Part Three   281

Tangible fixed assets   283
Intangible fixed assets   285
Investments   287
Stock and work in progress   290
Contract work in progress   295
Trade debtors   299
Prepayments and other debtors   303
Cash and bank balances   304
Group and associated undertakings   306
Trade creditors   309
Other current liabilities   312
Taxes   314
Borrowings   319
Provisions for liabilities, financial commitments and contingencies   321
Dividends, earnings per share, capital and reserves   323
Income   325
Expenditure   326
Directors, minutes, directors' reports   329
Funds' statements   331
Trial balance, accounting records and the financial statements   332

Index   333

Part One
Auditing in Perspective

INTRODUCTION TO PART 1

Auditing is continually changing and developing to meet the needs of the business environment it serves. Accompanying this development there has been increasing public visibility of what auditors do. The role of auditing and the nature of audit work have attracted comment on the front pages of national newspapers, rather than in just the financial pages and have even led on occasions to questions and statements in Parliament. This coverage has not always been good news for the auditing profession, but it does indicate a heightened awareness in society of the potential importance of what auditors do. It also reflects the way in which auditing practice and the activities of audit firms have developed and expanded to include new areas of considerable public interest, perhaps particularly in relation to financial services, the financial markets, and the public sector. While at one time auditing was generally regarded as a procedural activity involving the application of mechanical techniques, there is now greater realisation that both the purpose and the execution of an audit are far from simple matters.

This book is primarily about the practical execution of an audit. Part 2 provides a full description of one way of structuring and carrying out an audit in order to arrive at a reporting conclusion. This is supported in Part 3 by suggestions of individual substantive audit tests applicable to specific account balances. However, any approach to the procedural aspects of conducting an audit — structuring the process, setting test objectives, and deciding on the nature and amount of evidence required — has to be based on some understanding of what the auditor is supposed to be doing — what qualities the auditor should possess, on whose behalf the work is being carried out, and what kind of output from the audit is desired. In other words, the auditor must have some view about what is expected by the intended audit beneficiaries.

The first part of the book provides a short overview of some of the important background and environmental factors which determine the role and nature of the modern audit. It gives a brief introduction to auditing theory and shows how auditing activity is located in a more general framework where the nature and expectations of the audit can be seen in relation to other business relationships and means of monitoring business performance. The subjects covered in this section are set out in Figure 1.

The framework in Figure 1 reflects how auditing theory relies on considerations in three major areas:

- the circumstances and relationships which create the need for, or provide *justification* for, having an audit;

- the *behavioural* qualities required of those who perform audit services on behalf of others;

- the *functional* aspects of executing an audit in a manner which satisfies the role set for it.

Within this part of the book there is only scope to introduce these aspects of auditing theory briefly. Each subject is discussed in outline terms in order to give a basic understanding of the theoretical considerations which apply to auditing and provide a context for the more procedural and practice-oriented elements of carrying out an audit which are included in Parts 2 and 3. Those with a more general interest in the basis and background of auditing should consider consulting some of the additional reading which is referred to at the end of this first part.

Figure 1 Components of Auditing Theory

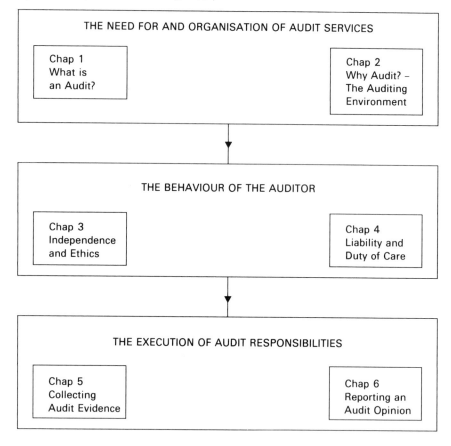

CHAPTER 1   WHAT IS AN AUDIT?

1.1   AUDITING DEFINED

In the United Kingdom, the most commonly quoted definition of auditing is that stated by the professional accountancy bodies in specifying the applicability of Auditing Standards and Guidelines:

> "An audit is the independent examination of, and expression of an opinion on, the financial statements of an enterprise" (APC, 1989).

A number of limitations are immediately apparent in this definition. It describes auditing only in terms of financial information contained in prepared statements; the criteria to be used in forming and phrasing an opinion are not referred to; and there is little indication of what an audit should consist of, other than the word 'examination'. In order to discuss the main background and conceptual aspects of auditing activity, it will be more helpful to start from the following somewhat wider and more generalised definition:

> 'Auditing involves the collection and evaluation of evidence about the performance and position of an entity or about information on that performance and position, by a competent independent person, with a view to reporting an opinion on the quality of that performance, position or information as measured by established criteria.'

Working from this broad definition, which covers a wide range of possible activities, the question of 'what is an audit?' is discussed below in three stages:

- by looking at the key components in the definition;
- by considering in particular the relationship between auditing and information; and
- by outlining some of the different types of audit which are consistent with the definition.

1.2   KEY COMPONENTS

There are six key components in the above general definition of auditing (see Table 1.1):

1.2.1   *Entity*

In any audit engagement it is important that the scope of the audit is clearly understood and that the auditor can identify the boundaries between what is being audited and what is outside his or her consideration. Normally the scope of the audit is defined with reference to a particular economic entity, which will most likely also be an identifiable legal entity, and to a specific time period. This would be the case in the audit of the annual financial statements of a limited company for example. In some situations these parameters might vary, however, as for example in the internal audit of a branch or outlet which may not be a separate legal unit, or in the audit of an information system, which is not necessarily an economic entity or constrained to a particular period of time. The general rule is that the entity being audited, or the scope of the audit should be clear.

5

1.2.2 *Performance, Position and Information*

Most types of audit involve the evaluation of information which has been prepared by an entity's management to represent its performance and position. The statutory audit of a limited company, for example, involves an assessment of the representations contained in the financial statements which it is the directors' responsibility to prepare. So, typically, the auditor is involved in examining the propriety of representations made by others. In some types of audit, however, the auditor's task involves generating new information rather than simply commenting on reports prepared by others. For example, a value for money audit of a public sector body might involve the auditor in devising and applying measures of efficiency and effectiveness and thus generating new information about performance and position. Similarly in a social audit the auditor can create and report information which otherwise would not exist.

1.2.3 *Competent, Independent Person*

A third key component in the definition quoted earlier relates to the qualifications of the persons carrying out the audit. The first quality that is required is that the auditor should be technically competent. This quality involves the ability to collect the appropriate evidence and to understand the criteria against which evidence should be judged. It refers to the question — 'if something is wrong does the auditor have the necessary skill to make its discovery likely?' The need for this quality is often recognised by limiting the categories of individual who are legally allowed to take up an appointment as auditor for certain types of organisation.

Technical competence is not the only quality looked for in an auditor. In addition, it will be expected that the auditor will follow certain standards of behaviour. The most obvious such standard is that the auditor should be independent in his or her approach to an assignment and that the way in which the audit is planned, executed and reported should not be affected by outside influences or pressures. Other behavioural, or 'ethical' standards might also be expected of an auditor, for example the need to carry out work with 'due care'.

1.2.4 *The Collection and Evaluation of Evidence*

The main substance of an audit, in terms of activity, is the process of collecting and evaluating audit evidence. Evidence is the basis on which the auditor can discharge his or her responsibility to report an opinion. Without evidence the audit report cannot be seen as the result of a rational process of investigation. Evidence can take many forms — oral, documentary or physical; it can come from a variety of sources — from the organisation and its management, from third parties, and from the auditor's own work; and it should possess certain qualities of relevance and reliability. The questions of how much and what types of evidence should be collected are critical to the conduct of each audit and it is to these questions that most of the analysis in this book is directed.

1.2.5 *Established Criteria*

On the basis of the evidence collected, the representation or information being audited must be assessed against established standards or criteria. In many types of organisation the overriding criterion applied in forming an audit opinion is the notion of the 'truth and fairness' of the information being reported. In public sector organisations there may also be criteria of economy, efficiency and effectiveness which the auditor has to apply in evaluating performance. These criteria determine the objectives of the audit investigation. Criteria such as fairness or efficiency are not well defined and will depend to a considerable extent on the judgement of the individual auditor. In order to apply these overall standards auditors will develop more detailed objectives and decision rules for the evaluation of information, for example whether it is complete and represents valid transactions which have been properly measured and disclosed in the appropriate way.

The existence of established criteria is important in order that the consumers of audit services can interpret what the result of an audit means. The auditor should attempt to apply established criteria in a way which is consistent with the evaluations that would be made by those on whose behalf the audit is being carried out.

1.2.6 *Reporting an Opinion*

The final component of our definition of auditing, and the final stage in the audit process, is the reporting of an opinion. The audit report is the means by which the auditor communicates the findings and conclusions drawn in the audit to those who have a legitimate interest in them. It should refer to the particular responsibilities or aspects of performance and accountability which are within the scope of the audit.

As noted earlier, that report might contain new information or, more usually, offer an opinion on the quality of information prepared by others. The general purpose of an audit opinion is to comment on the correspondence between the reported information on the performance and position of the entity and the established criteria for reporting. In many cases the structure and content of the audit report follow standard codes of words which have evolved in response to the need to ensure consistency between the messages communicated in reports on different organisations.

In summary, the discussion above has outlined six key components, decisions and judgements which will determine the nature of any particular type of audit. These are reiterated in Table 1.1 together with an indication of their importance to the underlying question of 'what is an audit?'

Table 1.1 Key Elements of an Audit

Element		Significance
The entity	–	The scope of the audit
Performance, position and information	–	The subject of the audit
Competent, independent person	–	The auditor's qualification to audit
Collection and evaluation of evidence	–	The method of auditing
Established criteria	–	The objectives of audit investigation
Reporting an opinion	–	The output of the audit

1.3 AUDITING AND INFORMATION

It has already been stated that while auditing is normally limited to commenting on information which has been prepared by the management of an entity, in some circumstances the auditor might actually produce and report new information. For example, if an organisation had chosen to depart from an accounting standard the auditor might not only comment on this departure but generate and report alternative calculations quantifying its effect. In situations other than financial statements audits the auditor might also generate new information, for example in management audits and systems audits. Whether commenting on or providing information the auditor is trying to help fill an information gap between the organisation and those interested in its activities. The way in which this gap can arise is shown in Figure 1.1.

Figure 1.1 The Information Gap in External Reporting by Organisations

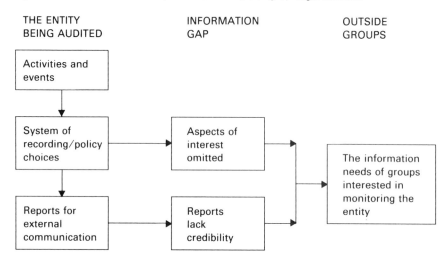

THE ENTITY   INFORMATION   OUTSIDE
BEING AUDITED   GAP   GROUPS

Groups and individuals external to an entity may be interested in making judgements about the activities and events within the entity and their results. In the absence of the ability to observe these activities and results directly these external parties are reliant on information. An information gap may arise for two reasons:

- because reports produced by the entity omit information of interest to the external parties; and

- because these reports lack credibility as a reliable basis for making judgements or decisions about the entity as they are produced by management who may wish to portray events in a manner which serves their own interests rather than those of the external parties.

An auditor may be appointed in order to help reduce this gap. The most common situation, and that which is assumed as the basis of the practices described later in this book, is where the auditor's role is concentrated on the second aspect of the information gap. The primary role of the audit in this situation is to enhance the credibility of reported information by commenting on its quality.

In the context of financial reporting and auditing, the role of the audit is as illustrated in Figure 1.2.

Figure 1.2 Financial Information and its Audit

The system of recording financial information about economic events and the selection of policies for communicating this information in the annual financial statements may result in certain gaps from the point of view of external users. To a large extent, however, these will not be considered by the auditor, who is concerned primarily with the credibility of what is reported. Thus, for example, the auditor would not be concerned about the failure to include segmental information in a company's financial statements, even though it might be of interest to investors, unless accounting regulations and the criteria for financial reporting specified that this information should be disclosed. The decision whether or not such disclosures should be required in regulations is essentially an accounting rather than an auditing problem. Accounting is the process of measuring, classifying, recording and summarising economic events as a basis for providing financial reports to assist judgements and decisions about an entity. Auditing financial reports involves evaluating whether they reflect the economic events in a manner which is in accordance with generally accepted accounting rules.

1.4 TYPES OF AUDIT

It may be useful at this stage to outline briefly some of the principal comparative features of different categories of audit.

1.4.1 *Financial Statements Audits*

The term 'auditing' is usually interpreted as referring to the audit of financial statements. This type of audit is undertaken in order to determine and report whether the information contained in a set of financial statements is in accordance with certain criteria which have been set for that organisation, such as truth and fairness and compliance with accepted accounting standards. The audit will usually cover the balance sheet, income statement, funds flow statement and the related notes. The subject of the audit is therefore these reports, not the management or the organisation itself or any particular aspect of its performance. The auditor's focus is simply the correspondence between the relevant statements and the underlying performance, irrespective of its quality.

1.4.2 *Regularity Audits*

A regularity, or compliance, audit is one where the principal objective is to establish whether particular policies, procedures or rules of operation laid down for an organisation have in fact been followed. For example, in a public sector organisation there may be established rules governing the way in which available contracts must be advertised, put out to tender and ultimately awarded. Part of the audit of such an enterprise could involve checking that these procedures have been complied with during the period covered by the audit, or that the organisation's activities have been 'regular' in the sense of following the relevant regulations. The subject of the audit in this case is principally the method of working of the enterprise and its personnel. In many situations this type of audit will be carried out at the request of management itself, who will be the recipient of the audit report. In other circumstances the audit may be performed on behalf of a supervisory authority, perhaps that with responsibility for specifying the operating rules in the first place.

1.4.3 *Management and Operational Audits*

While financial statement audits are concerned primarily with the agreement between reported and actual performance and position and regularity audits with the degree of observance of laid down rules and policies in the organisation being audited, management or operational audits focus on performance in more qualitative terms. For example, the criteria of economy, efficiency and effectiveness, which are covered by the more general notion of value for money, are commonly applied in audit assessments of the quality of performance of public sector enterprises. More generally, there are obviously very many types of criteria which could be applied in such performance based audits. Equally there are many areas of management decision-making where agreed external standards may be difficult to identify and apply and where the audit therefore involves a much more subjective review. The scope of activities which may be audited obviously goes beyond purely accounting functions.

Auditing firms have for many years provided management with comments on the efficiency and effectiveness of control systems as a by-product of the financial statement audit. More recently a number of firms have sought to promote the idea of using the statutory audit as an opportunity to offer other operational reviews on a greater scale, looking at, for example, performance in investment appraisal or working capital management.

In theory there is no reason why the concept of a management audit should not extend to the highest levels of management, but in practice most operational reviews are undertaken over lower levels and reported to top management. The main exception to this situation is the public sector where, as already noted, assessing value for money is part of the external auditor's responsibility.

1.4.4 *Social Audits*

A particular aspect of performance review which has developed into an identifiable separate form of auditing is that of social performance. In this area the 'audit' generally involves the collection and publication of a considerable volume of 'social accounting' information which is not otherwise available, rather than simply commenting on the quality of information already provided by the organisation's management. The aspects of performance included in a social audit could include pollution and other environmental considerations, community activities and relationships, employment policies and consumer interests. Often social audits are carried out by groups with a particular interest in an organisation's activities rather than by an appointed independent auditor.

1.4.5 *Internal Audits and External Audits*

All of the above classes of audit relate to differences in the subject of the audit — information, procedure and performance. The final classification point we shall recognise here concerns the groups being served by the audit rather than its subject. The distinction between internal and external auditing is that the former takes place within an organisation at the request and initiation of top management, and on their behalf, whereas the latter involves responsibilities and reporting to groups outside the organisation. Additionally, the internal auditor is an employee of the organisation itself and so for at least some functions is less independent than the external auditor who is appointed from outside.

There may be some interaction between the internal and external audits of an organisation. The presence of an internal audit function may influence the direction and amount of work undertaken by the external auditor, as it can provide evidence of the strength of management control over the organisations activities and the external auditor may be able to request or use work by the internal auditor, but it is unlikely to remove the need for an external audit. Internal and external auditing are concerned essentially with different levels of accountability.

It is possible for both internal and external audits to cover any of the subjects referred to already — the financial statements, compliance with procedures and rules, the efficiency of operations and management and even social performance. Traditionally, internal auditing was seen as involving mainly regularity and compliance type considerations, such as the detailed operations of controls and systems and the accuracy of processing of financial information. More recently, however, its role has expanded to involve much greater advisory and operational review type activities, where it is seen as contributing to general goals of management efficiency and effectiveness rather than simply to control objectives.

1.5 SUMMARY

The purpose of this chapter has been to provide a general introduction to the concept of audit. By defining auditing in very broad terms it has been possible to identify the main generalised components of auditing as a societal activity. In order to understand the role served by auditing it is important to identify the scope of the audit, its subject, who should be considered qualified to audit, the general method of work involved in the audit, criteria or rules against which the subject of the audit can be evaluated and the output expected from the audit. The role of auditing with respect to the provision of information on organisational performance and position has been shown, and a variety of types of audit which fall within the broad definition applied in this chapter have been briefly introduced.

It is important to recognise the diversity of possible activities which can be regarded as auditing, but against this general background it is necessary to specify the limits within which the practices and procedures developed in this book apply. First, the considerations and methods which are described in subsequent chapters are largely limited to the audit of financial statements. Second, although much of the material is relevant to the audit of many different types of enterprise, the organisational model which is used is that of a limited liability company. The principal subject of this book, therefore, is the statutory requirement in Company Law for the audit of the annual financial statements of limited liability companies. In the remainder of Part 1 general concepts of auditing are discussed mainly in terms of their application to this type of audit and the approach developed in Part 2 is designed for the execution of audit responsibilities in that context.

CHAPTER 2 WHY AUDIT? — THE AUDITING ENVIRONMENT

2.1 DEMAND AND SUPPLY

Auditing improves the information available to parties interested in the activities of an organisation, usually by commenting on the quality of management reports, thus enhancing their credibility. However, not all situations where interest groups could benefit from such an enhancement of information result in a legal requirement for an audit. In this chapter the factors in the environment which determine the demand and supply of auditing services are examined in more detail.

This examination has three strands. First, different perspectives which have been used to construct theoretical rationalisations for company audits are reviewed, focusing on two main themes: accountability, that is explanations of auditing derived from the concept of accountability; and economic incentives, that is attempts which have been made to create a theory of auditing based on the economic motivations of the parties to the audit.

Second, the way in which the supply of audit services is organised and regulated in the current audit environment is described. Finally, the responsibilities that are placed on the auditor by the statutory audit requirement for limited companies, and how these have developed through time are reviewed.

2.2 ACCOUNTABILITY

Attempts to provide a rationale for the circumstances in which the need for an audit may arise often refer to its role in the accountability process. Although it is not a simple notion to define, accountability has two main elements: the recognition that a responsibility or duty is owed by one party to one or more other parties; and the idea that it should be possible to monitor the way in which that responsibility has been discharged through the provision of some information, explanation or report on its performance. Auditing is seen as a control mechanism which aids the process of monitoring performance and thus ensures or promotes accountability. To be effective, accountability requires information on performance. That information should possess qualities of relevance and reliability, and by enhancing reliability auditing can facilitate accountability and accountable relationships. The audit can be seen as just one such mechanism in the general context of corporate regulation.

If the concept of accountability is to be relied on to understand why there are audits, it is important to consider in what circumstances this duty should be recognised.

2.2.1 Stewardship Relationships

A duty of accountability is generally accepted where one party acts on behalf of another, or in what might be called 'stewardship' situations. Most commonly these involve financial relationships, as for example when shareholders provide capital to the management of an enterprise who then have a responsibility to report back on their stewardship of those resources. However, there are often situations in which groups or individuals have an interest in the performance of an organisation without having any financial stewardship relationship with its management. Can duties of accountability be held without a financial link?

2.2.2 *Other Interests*

Other relationships than those arising from financial stewardship are sometimes recognised as involving accountability and giving rise to a need for audit. For example, in some countries the role of auditing is seen as linked to the need for certification of accounts for taxation purposes.

The Corporate Report (ASSC 1975), a review of the purposes and structure of corporate reporting sponsored by the Accounting Standards Steering Committee, suggested that a duty to report information could arise in circumstances where the activities of an organisation 'impinge on the interests' of a group. More generally, notions of social accountability hold that organisations should be accountable to the society or community which hosts their operations for such aspects of performance as pollution of the environment and impact on the society. Employees do not directly provide financial resources to an enterprise but it is sometimes argued that they are owed a duty of accountability by management because of the potential impact of management decisions on their current welfare and future prospects. In some European countries, for example Belgium, the workforce has a say in the appointment of the auditor.

The purpose of this discussion is not to identify exactly where the boundaries of accountability lie. Rather it is to point to the fact that these boundaries are sometimes problematic and that they can involve more than simply financial relationships. Accountability is dependent on the standards that society expects and is prepared to enforce at any particular time. These standards change and, as we shall see later, the kind of role and responsibility that has been given to the audit function within the accountability process has also changed.

The concept of accountability thus gives rise to the need for an audit on the grounds that certain duties to report in a credible and reliable manner are associated with business activity. A legal requirement is seen as necessary on the assumptions that otherwise these duties could not be enforced in a consistent way and that the interests of those to whom a duty of accountability is to be held must be given legal protection because of the inability of some or all of those groups or individuals to enforce their own interests through market transactions.

While auditing has continually developed to reflect changing notions of accountability, it must also be stated that there are many circumstances where no audit requirement exists even though it could be argued that a duty of accountability is present, including many which would fall within the heading of 'other interests' above. The statutory requirement for companies to have an audit has been established with reference to specific management duties of accountability recognised in law. Traditionally, this has been seen as mainly in the area of financial and fiduciary relationships. Thus, an auditor of a limited liability company reports to the shareholders, although he or she may take certain wider aspects of accountability into consideration when assessing the financial statements, for example the needs of creditors and prospective shareholders. It is possible that the courts may take a somewhat wider view of the auditor's responsibilities but the formal legal duty is defined in terms of commenting to shareholders on management reports.

While in the public sector there has been some move away from simply recognising stewardship objectives to including wider notions of efficiency and effectiveness within the auditor's contribution to the accountability process, this broadening has not yet found its way into the regulation of private sector corporate activity.

2.3   ECONOMIC EXPLANATIONS FOR AUDITING

Another approach to identifying a rationale for auditing is to look at economic interpretations of what it involves. This approach starts from the question: if the statutory

the professional accountancy bodies and the courts. The functions served by each of these are described below, but first some comments are made on the actual suppliers of audits, the audit firms.

2.4.1 *Audit Firms*

Audit firms range in size from one person in practice individually to those which are large multinational organisations involving thousands of staff and partners, generating world-wide fees amounting to billions of pounds. While there are several thousand audit firms or sole practitioners in the UK in total, the vast majority of the audits of the largest companies are undertaken by a relatively small number of firms. The eight leading firms at the beginning of 1989 were responsible for the audits of 767 of the 'Times' top 1000 United Kingdom companies. When the value of these audits, in terms of fees, is taken into account this proportionate share is even larger. For example, in 1985 it was estimated that these same firms accounted for 82% of the audit business of companies included in the 'Financial Times' 500 index when measured by fees, but only 66% in number. The next seven firms audited only a further 9% in value.

Other than in one person practices, auditors have adopted partnerships as their form of business organisation. In part this was due to the fact that company law did not allow an incorporated body to act as auditor. This situation will change as a result of the Companies Act 1989 which contains a provision that companies as well as partnerships and individuals may be recognised as auditors. There is however a statutory condition that the majority of voting rights in any such company should be held by recognised auditors, and the professional bodies may require more stringent conditions to be met.

Traditionally, the most common categories of audit firm which have been recognised are the top eight or nine firms (the 'big eight'), a second tier of other national and international firms, and the smaller regional and local practices. The composition of these groupings changes frequently however as separate firms merge with one another. The merger phenomenon is apparent at all levels of audit firm size but attracts particular attention when it involves the largest firms. The likelihood that within the foreseeable future the big eight will become the big four or five is significant because it could lead to an oligopolistic structure in the market for audit services.

While smaller firms tend to have smaller clients where the audit may be hard to separate from some other services provided, all firms provide a wide range of services to clients in addition to auditing. These include taxation services, management consultancy, information systems, bookkeeping and receivership and insolvency, as well as more novel functions, from monitoring election ballots to gathering official statistics for the Olympic Games. In recent years, most firms have experienced a growth in the proportion of fees coming from consultancy-based services relative to the more traditional areas such as audit. This reflects both a buoyant demand for consultancy and also the fact that since the mid 1970s competition over audit business has become more intense. While at one time firms argued that they tended to compete on other than price grounds, the evidence of price competition has increased as management have shown greater willingness to review audit appointments, obtain competitive tenders and put pressure on audit fees.

2.4.2 *Parliament, The Law and Regulatory Agencies*

The most authoritative sources of regulation of auditing are Parliament which enacts the appropriate legislation and the regulatory agencies which are given responsibility for ensuring these laws are followed. By introducing legal requirements, the government of the day and Parliament more generally attempt to represent an interpretation of what is the societal value of auditing. The relevant provisions should reflect public expectations of the need for and desired contribution of an audit. These values change over time and consequently legislation must continually change to provide new standards.

Legislation within the United Kingdom is also influenced by policies determined at a European level, and the development of company law in recent years has been significantly affected by the Directives adopted by the European Community. Member states of the Community are obliged to implement these Directives in national legislation.

The basic statutory requirement that the annual financial statements of every company, irrespective of its size, must be audited is contained in the Companies Act 1985. The Act sets certain standards regarding the objectives of the audit and what it should contain, by specifying the auditor's reporting responsibilities. It also contains a number of provisions which specify certain controls on the way in which an audit can be organised, for example who is entitled to audit, rules governing the appointment and dismissal of an auditor, and the disclosure of audit fees. The requirements of the Act are described in more detail in a later section.

The law may explicitly or implictly delegate certain aspects of regulation to other agencies. For example, historically the Companies Acts have recognised members of certain professional bodies as suitable to be appointed as auditors but have left the control of membership qualifications to be determined by those bodies. This situation has changed with the 1989 Act however in that, while authority will still be delegated to recognised qualifying and recognised supervisory bodies, the law now contains much more explicit conditions about the rules and practices such bodies must apply to be granted recognised status.

The arm of government responsible for the enforcement of business and audit regulations is the Department of Trade. The Department has the power, for example, to appoint Inspectors to conduct an investigation of a company's affairs where there is the suggestion that there has been some irregularity in the running of the company. An investigation is intended to collect evidence and report it to the Department and may result in legal proceedings. Department of Trade investigations are part of the broad framework for the regulation of business activity. In some cases the inspectors have commented on auditing matters, often critically, and these comments have influenced developments in the auditing profession.

For example, auditors have been criticised in inspectors' reports for failure to detect error, failure to collect specific pieces of evidence, not acting on evidence which had been collected, inadequate reporting and forming erroneous judgements on accounting treatments adopted by companies. While inspectors have never directly accused auditors of not being independent, they have sometimes been critical of the ease with which dominant individuals within company management have been able to mislead auditors. A spate of reports in the mid 1970s, many including criticisms of auditors, resulted eventually in the setting up in 1979 of the Joint Disciplinary Scheme which is operated by the Institute of Chartered Accountants in England and Wales, the Institute of Chartered Accountants of Scotland and the Chartered Association of Certified Accountants.

2.4.3 *The Professional Bodies*

The professional accountancy bodies whose members perform audits have had an important role in educating and training auditors, through the process of qualifying for membership, in making recommendations about standards of audit practice and auditor behaviour and in taking disciplinary action when these standards are not met. The Companies Act 1989 has introduced some changes to the position of the professional bodies and placed greater responsibilities upon them for regulation of audit activity.

Previously the members of four accountancy bodies were recognised in company law as qualified for appointment as auditor:

The Chartered Association of Certified Accountants

The Institute of Chartered Accountants of England and Wales

The Institute of Chartered Accountants in Ireland

The Institute of Chartered Accountants in Scotland

The position will change under the 1989 Act which restricts eligibility for appointment as a statutory auditor to individuals holding an appropriate accountancy qualification who are members of a recognised supervisory body. Qualifying bodies will be recognised for the purposes of educating and training suitably qualified auditors. The supervisory bodies will maintain a register of individuals eligible to carry out UK company audits and make certain information publicly available about firms eligible under their rules. Individuals will have to be registered as auditors through these bodies and use the title 'registered auditor' when signing audit reports. It is intended that the four bodies mentioned above will become recognised supervisory and qualifying bodies. In order to achieve this status, however, the bodies will have to apply to the Secretary of State and will have to satisfy a number of criteria, including having rules and practices to ensure that, for example, adequate technical standards are established and applied by members, having effective monitoring and enforcement and ensuring that audit work is carried out properly with integrity, independence and the avoidance of conflicts of interest.

The recognition of a limited number of qualifying bodies reflects the need to ensure that those authorised to undertake audits have the necessary technical competence. Competence is controlled through the education and training, entry and continuing professional education structure of the professional bodies. Controls over competence are increasingly important in an environment where audits are affected by the increasing complexity of information technology, by the growing volume and complexity of accounting regulations and by the potential scarcity of skilled personnel.

The professional bodies have acted to influence audit practice through issuing recommendations about audit procedures and the conduct of the audit. Since 1980 these recommendations have been in the form of Auditing Standards and Guidelines which are prepared by the Auditing Practices Committee (APC) and issued by the individual professional bodies. Five bodies collaborate in the APC — the four already referred to plus the Chartered Institute of Public Finance and Accountancy. APC's constitution allows for a membership of up to 17. At 1 September 1989, the two standards and 32 guidelines which are listed in Table 2.1 were in force. The status of these regulations is made clear in the Explanatory Foreword to Auditing Standards and Guidelines. Auditing Standards are mandatory in that they are expected to be applied whenever an audit is carried out and the bodies may take disciplinary action against members who fail to do so. Guidelines, in contrast, are intended to be persuasive but not prescriptive and are non-mandatory. It is likely that in a court of law both Standards and Guidelines would be regarded as indicative of good practice, so departures from Guidelines should be carefully justified.

Table 2.1 Auditing Standards & Guidelines - 1 September 1989

Explanatory foreword

Auditing Standards

The auditor's operational standard

The audit report

Auditing Guidelines - Operational

Planning, controlling and recording

Accounting systems

Audit evidence

Internal controls

Review of financial statements

Auditing Guidelines – Industries

Charities

Building societies in the United Kingdom

Trade unions and employers' associations

Housing associations

The impact of regulations on public sector audits

Pension schemes in the United Kingdom

Banks in the United Kingdom

Auditing Guidelines – Detailed operational

Bank reports for audit purposes

Events after the balance sheet date

Amounts derived from the preceding financial statements

Representations by management

Attendance at stocktaking

Engagement letters

Auditing in a computer environment

Reliance on internal audit

Quality control

The auditor's considerations in respect of going concern

Financial information issued with audited financial statements

Prospectuses and the reporting accountant

Reliance on other specialists

Reports to management

Group financial statements — reliance on the work of other auditors

Applicability to the public sector of auditing standards and guidelines

Analytical review

Auditing Guidelines – Audit Reports

Auditors' reports and SSAP16 'Current cost accounting'

Reports by auditors under company legislation in the United Kingdom

Reports by auditors under Company legislation in the Republic of Ireland

In addition to trying to influence the practical aspects of conducting an audit through standards and guidelines the individual professional bodies have also sought to establish ethical guidelines concerning various aspects of audit behaviour and auditor-client

19

relationships. This guidance tries to ensure that appropriate standards of professional behaviour are followed in order to maintain public confidence in auditors and refers to issues such as accepting appointments, obtaining work and conflicts of interest. Ethical behaviour is discussed more fully in Chapter 3.

A final aspect of the role fulfilled by the professional bodies has been in disciplining members for inadequate performance or behaviour. As noted earlier, a Joint Disciplinary Scheme has been operated by the English and Welsh, Scottish and Certified bodies. This scheme has tended to deal with instances where direct complaints have been made about auditors or where evidence of inadequate behaviour has been alleged, and has not been very visible publicly. Following the Companies Act 1989 the supervisory responsibilities of a recognised body will be much more rigorous reflecting an emphasis on active supervision rather than simply response to complaint. For example, it is likely that inspection of audit firms' practices will be necessary in order to establish their suitability for registration as auditors.

2.4.4 *The Courts and Professional Liability*

Auditing is also regulated through the fact that a court of law might hold an auditor liable for his or her behaviour if it is held to fall short of the standards required. The courts attempt to interpret and define the nature and extent of the auditor's statutory and other responsibilities.

Liability under the law can arise from two sources:

- statute law which creates liability for both civil and criminal offences. For example it is a criminal offence to publish, or concur in publishing, a report known to be misleading or deceptive (Theft Act, 1968) and make false or misleading statements to induce investments (Financial Services Act, 1986).

- common law, which is concerned mainly with the circumstances under which a liability for negligent behaviour might be held.

Most legal cases and allegations of inadequate auditing concern the auditor's common law responsibilities for the quality of his or her work and opinion. There is a duty to carry out statutory or contractual responsibilities with due care, honesty and integrity. If someone believes that the auditor's behaviour falls short of the required standards then a civil action can be brought for damages for negligence. The courts seek to define the boundaries of liability for negligence, both by specifying the standards of behaviour which are consistent with the duty of care, and by determining the type of relationship between auditors and other parties where the duty of care applies. The extent of the auditor's liability for negligence is described in a later chapter.

The existence of liability has led auditors to obtain professional indemnity insurance. This in turn has meant that in practice there is often a tendency to settle claims out of court, with the agreement of the insurers, rather than incur the costs and risks associated with a court hearing. Some would argue that the resultant lack of decided cases establishing precedents has simply increased the uncertainty concerning auditor liability and that defending more cases in court would provide a better response to the issue of liability than seeking protection through costly insurance.

2.5 THE STATUTORY AUDIT REQUIREMENT

A key element in the environment around which the supply of auditing services is organised is the formal legal requirement for companies to have their accounts audited (the 'statutory audit'). In this section the main auditing provisions of the Companies Acts are summarised, together with how they have evolved and developed over time.

2.5.1 *Auditing Provisions in Company Law*

Reference has already been made to changes in the legal framework surrounding auditing introduced through the Companies Act 1989. These changes are concerned mainly with the regulatory structure for auditing and the status and role of the professional bodies and their rules for qualifying, members' behaviour and practice rather than the legal requirements for an individual audit. The latter will remain largely unchanged from the Companies Act 1985, which consolidated the provisions of previous statutes regarding the audit. Many of these provisions are commented on elsewhere, for example in the chapters dealing with auditor independence and audit reports, and so are considered only briefly here. Unless otherwise stated, the provisions referred to below are contained in the Companies Act 1985.

(i) Appointment, removal and resignation

The 1985 Act required that every company appoint an auditor at each annual general meeting to hold office until the next such meeting. In the case of first time appointment or where there is a casual vacancy, the directors may appoint the auditor. Following the 1989 Act, the shareholders of a private company will be able to dispense with the annual reappointment of the auditor. To remove an auditor before completion of the term of office requires an ordinary resolution of the company. Special notice is required of any resolutions to change or remove the auditor. The auditor can resign during office by giving a resignation notice which either states that there are no circumstances connected to the resignation which should be disclosed to members or creditors or indicates such circumstances. The 1989 Act has extended the requirement for such a statement to all cases where the auditor ceases to hold office.

(ii) Qualifications

As noted in the previous section, the 1985 Act named four professional accountancy bodies whose members could act as statutory auditors. The changes in the 1989 Act require auditors to possess a professional qualification from a recognised qualifying body and to be subject to the monitoring rules of a recognised supervisory body.

(iii) Remuneration

The auditor's remuneration, which includes expenses, is to be fixed by whoever makes the appointment, although in practice the directors will generally be given the power to do this. The amount paid must be disclosed in the accounts and following the 1989 Act fees for non-audit work will also be required.

(iv) Duties

The auditor's principal duty is to report to members on the truth and fairness of the balance sheet and profit and loss account, and whether these annual financial statements have been prepared in accordance with the provisions of the 1985 Act. In addition, the auditor has a responsibility to report when the following conditions do not hold true, that proper accounting records have been maintained; that the accounts agree with those records; that all information and explanations required for the purposes of the audit have been received; and the consistency between information in the directors' report and the financial statements. There are also responsibilities to report certain information, mainly concerning directors' emoluments and loans to officers, if it is not disclosed in the financial statements, and to report when a small company is producing modified accounts.

(v) Rights

The rights of the auditor which are embodied in law are concerned with two main aspects: gathering information and communicating with members. The auditor has a right of access to all records and documents which might be required for the audit, and the right to require whatever information and explanations are necessary from officers of the company. For communication with members, the auditor has the right to attend and to be heard at all general meetings on any matters concerning him or her as auditor. Additionally, the auditor can have representations circularised to members before any meeting at which there is a proposal for his or her removal.

2.5.2 *The Historical Development of the Statutory Audit*

The first compulsory audit for companies was introduced in the Joint Stock Companies Act 1844, which required that an auditor was to be appointed to report on the company's solvency to creditors. Interestingly the Act included no requirements concerning the qualifications or status of appointed auditors, and the main practice of the day was for a shareholder to be chosen as auditor by the other members.

This legal requirement was relatively short-lived in that the 1856 Joint Stock Companies Act removed the compulsory audit and it was not reintroduced for all companies until 1900. However, it would be wrong to believe that there was no auditing between 1856 and 1900. Although there was no legal requirement for an audit, the model Articles of Association in the 1856 Act included voluntary provisions for an audit to report on the 'truth and correctness' of the balance sheet. Legislation covering the specific industries of railways and banking did include audit requirements and even outside these industries many companies continued with voluntary shareholder audits. During this period the main focus of the audit moved from the issue of solvency to the detection and even prevention of fraud and error. A number of legal cases of the time attempted to define the auditor's responsibility in this area, including the much quoted judgement by Lopes LJ in *re Kingston Cotton Mill Co (No 2)* [1896] 2 Ch 279) that the auditor was a 'watchdog' not a 'bloodhound'.

By the time the compulsory audit requirement was reintroduced in 1900, fraud detection was firmly established as the primary objective of the audit followed by verification of the accuracy of accounting records. As regards who could be appointed as an auditor, there was still no requirement for any professional qualification although it may have been expected that companies would appoint professional accountants. However it was laid down that the auditor could not be a director or officer of the company, thus recognising the need for independence from management. This requirement reflects a view of the audit as primarily dealing with the relationship between management and shareholder rather than between company and creditor. The 1900 Act also included provisions that the auditor should give a written certificate that all the auditing requirements of the Act had been complied with and make a report to Shareholders on the 'truth and correctness' of the balance sheet. The latter report only had to be read out at the general meeting and often would not accompany the published balance sheet. Another development in the 1900 Act was that the auditor was given the right of access to all the company's books and records for the purposes of the audit.

The next major change in the direction of the statutory audit involved the movement away from the primacy of fraud detection to the giving of an opinion on the credibilty of the financial statements, but this process took over forty years to complete. The Companies Act of 1929 did little to change existing audit requirements and it was not until 1948 that new objectives were given formal statutory recognition. The change in audit objectives reflected a number of factors in the general business environment. There was greater recognition of the role of financial statements in economic decision-making, particularly regarding investment, and of the need for the information to be reliable for this purpose. Detection of fraud and error came to be seen as an area of management responsibility. The growth in the size and complexity of business organisations also meant that it was no longer practicable, because of the volume of transactions and the time and cost constraints on the audit, to see fraud detection as the main audit objective.

The main pattern for the objectives of the modern audit was established in the Companies Act 1948, which made radical changes to the accounting and auditing provisions of company law. The audit was extended to include the profit and loss account as well as the balance sheet. The auditor's resposibilities were more clearly defined to cover the maintenance by the company of adequate accounting books and records, the agreement between these records and the financial statements and whether these statements gave a true and fair view of the company's performance and financial position. These responsibilities recognise the giving of an opinion on the quality of the financial statements as the primary audit objective followed by the reliability of the underlying records, but detection of fraud and error only arises to the extent that it affects those objectives. The Act also introduced for the first time a requirement for the auditor to be a suitably qualified professional accountant, reflecting the expertise felt necessary to meet the changing objectives and the way audit practice had developed in the preceding twenty years.

Subsequent legislation has changed some aspects of the audit requirement but the main pattern of objectives established in the 1948 Act has remained the same. The Companies Act 1967 made certain changes to the requirements for the audit report. In 1976, the Companies Act of that year provided greater definition of the reporting periods for financial statements and the accounting records which should support the accounts, and also strengthened the provisions dealing with the appointment, removal and qualifications of the auditor. The Companies Act 1980 introduced a requirement for auditors to report whether or not the permissability of a proposed distribution of profits is materially affected by the subject matter of a qualified audit opinion on the financial statements. In 1981 the auditor's responsibilities were extended to include a review to ensure consistency between the information contained in the financial statements and that in the directors' report and to report when there is an inconsistency, and the auditor was also given certain reporting roles where a company is purchasing its own shares.

Audit responsibilities have been affected by the various changes in accounting requirements introduced in successive statutes. For example the 1967 Act greatly increased the level of disclosure required in accounts and the 1981 Act introduced a limited number of set formats for the balance sheet and profit and loss account and auditors must confirm these accounting rules have been complied with. The 1981 Act also gave the auditor additional reporting responsibilities where a smaller company decides to take advantage of the option to report abridged financial statements.

Most recently, the changes in the law introduced in the 1989 Companies Act are, with reference to auditing, mainly concerned with the supervision and organisation of auditing services in general rather than the objectives and responsibilities which apply to an individual assignment. These changes were outlined in a previous section. The Act does permit listed public companies to send summarised financial statements to their shareholders and where this option is exercised there is a requirement for the auditor to report on the consistency of the summarised statements with the full annual accounts.

The requirement for an audit has also been expanded beyond limited companies to other types of organisation, from friendly societies, charities and pension funds to governmental bodies. There are now over thirty Acts of Parliament, covering a wide range of activities, which require the appointment of auditors. In some cases the auditor's responsibilities have been extended to include matters outside the financial statements. For example, under the Banking Act 1987 and the Building Societies Act 1986 auditors must report on the internal control structure of the organisation, a requirement which is mirrored for the financial services industry more generally under the Financial Services Act 1986.

While this brief review of the history of the development of the statutory audit omits much of the detail of individual statutes, it does provide evidence of a number of significant general points. Most importantly it demonstrates that the nature of the audit requirement has rarely stood still for long and that it has continually changed to reflect a changing business environment and changing societal expectations. This response of the statutory audit to its environment can be seen in the pattern of objectives recognised for the audit, moving from concern with solvency to fraud and error to the quality of reported information; in the provisions relating to auditor independence, that is who should audit and how they should be appointed or removed from office; and in the recognition of the need for auditors to be suitably qualified, reflecting a societal concern to ensure the quality of auditing. It is also interesting to note that developments in practice have often led the way for subsequent changes in the legal requirements.

2.5.3 The Auditor's Responsibility for Fraud

The extent to which the auditor is or should be responsible for the prevention and detection of fraud is a contentious issue. In the last section it was argued that while at one time fraud detection would have been the primary objective of the audit this has been replaced by other objectives concerned with the credibility and accuracy of reported information. However, it is undoubtedly true that many people still believe that auditing is about fraud and this is a potential source of conflict between public expectations and the standards to which auditors are working.

The position adopted by the accounting profession over the last thirty or forty years has been that fraud prevention and detection is not the primary objective of the audit and that it is either impractical or too costly to impose such a responsibilty on auditors. This position can be summarised as follow:

● The primary responsibility for prevention and detection of fraud rests with the management of an organisation through the operation of an appropriate system of controls. Auditors will often ̄refer explictly to this responsibility in the audit engagement letter.

● The auditor's responsibility is limited to detecting fraud to the extent that it impairs the truth and fairness of the financial statements. In other words the auditor should be expected to look for material fraud to the same extent as material error from any source, but is not concerned with fraud per se.

● If, however, the auditor's suspicions are aroused that fraud has occurred then he or she should be expected to follow it up either to establish its extent or to ensure that management are made aware of the situation and are taking appropriate action. This position becomes more difficult if the auditor feels that management may be implicated in the fraud.

The acceptability of this approach to the auditor's responsibilities with respect to fraud has been questioned in recent years, notably as a result of changes in the framework for investors' protection. The critical issue, however, has not been so much whether the auditor should be looking for all frauds, but what action or reporting should follow when fraud, or indeed some other form of irregularity is discovered. While simply reporting the matter to management may be sufficient in many circumstances, other situations raise questions about reporting externally to third parties, including regulatory agencies. The accounting profession has argued that normally the auditor's duty of confidentiality prevents reporting to third parties without the client's permission, and that to do so would undermine the auditor-client relationship, unless there is a 'public duty' to disclose. This emphasis on confidentiality can conflict with other views on the social value of auditing which would place greater emphasis on external reporting. At present the situation remains unresolved as the accounting profession seeks to introduce new guidance for practitioners which is considered acceptable by the government and regulatory bodies.

2.6 SUMMARY

This chapter has explored the various demand and supply factors which interact in the auditing environment to produce the level and nature of auditing services provided to companies. The demand for an audit can be explained with reference to the need to ensure accountability or to the economic motivations of the parties to the audit. The manner and extent to which auditing services are supplied by audit firms are influenced by the law, by government mandated regulatory agencies, including the professional accountancy bodies who have attempted to provide rules relating to audit practice and ethical behaviour and whose status as regulatory bodies has changed following the Companies Act 1989, and by the decisions of the courts in interpreting audit responsibilities.

The legal requirements associated with the statutory audit of a limited company can be seen to have changed repeatedly and significantly in the past. Audit objectives have developed over time and are now concerned primarily with the quality, measured as the truth and fairness, of the financial statements. The requirements relating to the qualifications of auditors have also changed, most recently in the Companies Act 1989. As the legal provisions for the statutory audit have changed and developed in the past it is reasonable to expect that they will continue to do so in the future.

CHAPTER 3   AUDITOR BEHAVIOUR — INDEPENDENCE AND ETHICS

3.1   INTRODUCTION

The need for auditing is to some extent based on assumptions about the behaviour of individuals, for example that managers will act and report in their own self-interest rather than the interests of the owners of an enterprise. By the same token, the value of auditing rests on certain assumptions about the behaviour of auditors. In Chapter 1 it was argued that one of the key components in defining auditing concerns the qualities that those undertaking audits should possess. It was noted that alongside the obvious quality of technical competence, are other behavioural qualities or ethical standards such as independence and due care. These aspects of auditing are discussed in this chapter and Chapter 4.

The basic notion of professional ethics is that a member of a profession, such as an auditor, has certain duties which should be observed even though they may conflict with the individual's immediate self-interest, for example the duty to act with integrity and objectivity and to observe the appropriate technical and professional standards in carrying out work. The accounting profession recognises the need for ethical behaviour in the Ethical Guides of the various professional bodies. Although these guides cover a range of matters, greatest attention is given to the area of independence.

3.2   THE IMPORTANCE OF INDEPENDENCE

The concept of independence has long been seen as something which is implicit in the very nature of external auditing. As with the audit itself, the need for independence arises because of the potential conflict of interest between the producers and users of information. If the audit is intended to add credibility to statements which would otherwise be interpreted as subjective management representations, it is implicit that the auditor's opinion should be independent from management influence.

> 'The autonomy of auditors in the performance of their professional duties has always been considered a cornerstone of the profession.' *(Goldman and Barlev* 1974).

> 'There is general recognition that the authority and value of the investigation which is described as audit and of the report which results from that examination are products of and dependent on the degree of independence with which the investigation and report are made.' *(Flint* ,1988, p 54).

While auditing is about the reliability of financial statements, independence is about the reliability of the audit.

The quality of independence should influence all aspects of the auditor's work, from accepting a client through to reporting an opinion. Specifically it has been described as comprising the following components:

- Technical Independence — that the auditor is free from pressure in determining the programme of work and choosing the techniques to be applied.

- Investigative Independence — that the auditor can collect whatever evidence is desired and is free from any personal bias which might restrict the extent of investigation undertaken.

- Reporting Independence — that the auditor is free to express an opinion in whatever way is appropriate in the light of the results of the investigations carried out.

3.3 WHAT IS AUDITOR INDEPENDENCE?

The concept of independence is not a simple one. It involves the individual auditor and the auditing profession as a whole, as it is important that the auditor not only is independent but is also believed to be so. In Statement 1 of ICAEW Ethical Guide independence is described as:

> '. . . an attitude of mind characterised by integrity and an objective approach to professional work.'

Similarly, the Canadian Institute of Chartered Accountants describe it as:

> 'A quality which permits an individual to apply unbiased judgement and objective consideratioin to established facts in arriving at an opinion or decision.'

These definitions emphasise what might be called 'real' independence, that is the position and approach of the individual auditor on each specific assignment. The personal nature of this quality makes it extremely difficult to either measure or regulate. While it is likely to be in an auditor's long term economic interest to behave in an independent manner, because discovery of unindependent behaviour will affect his or her reputation and future business, the remoteness of such consequences may mean that short-term pressures can still threaten individual independence.

To focus on the actual independent state of mind of the individual ignores the perhaps more important aspect of what users believe about the auditor, or 'perceived' independence. As users cannot observe an individual's state of mind, their perceptions of independence will be influenced by more general beliefs about the structure of auditing as an industry, controls that are placed on auditor-client relationships, the reputation of a firm and the independence of the profession as a whole. These beliefs will determine the extent to which the work of auditors will be valued and relied upon.

3.4 FACTORS STRENGTHENING INDEPENDENCE

The way in which auditing is structured and regulated reflects the importance of independence. Attempts have been made through company law, professional guidelines and the rules of individual audit firms to regulate at least the appearance of independence and to isolate the auditor from situations in which threats to independence can arise.

3.4.1 *Company Law*

A number of provisions in Company Law can be seen as having a role in protecting the auditor's independence and giving information on the auditor-client relationship.

(i) Appointment, dismissal and remuneration

Under the Companies Act 1985, the formal 'contractual' aspects of the auditor's relationship with a client, in terms of appointment, removal from office and remuneration, must be approved by the shareholders of a company. The fact that the law considers the shareholders rather than the management as the appropriate group to deal with such matters gives formal recognition to the need for independence from management pressure.

(ii)   Rights to communicate with shareholders and the general public

Additionally, the Companies Acts give the auditor certain rights to make written representations to shareholders and to address the company in general meeting, either about the audit report or should he or she resign from office, and certain matters are required to be put on public record. The ability to communicate directly with shareholders is intended to strengthen independence by protecting the auditor from management pressure, and ultimately from dismissal without recourse.

(iii)   Rights of access

The need for independence in the conduct of the audit work as well as in matters of appointment and reporting can also be seen in the legal provision that the auditor has a right of access to all company records, explanations and other information which are necessary to form an audit opinion. The auditor must report any restrictions on access and there are sanctions against company officials who provide false or misleading information. These provisions are intended to ensure that it is the auditor and not the management who determines the scope of audit work to be carried out.

(iv)   Holding Office in a Client

The 1985 Act prohibited the auditor from being an officer, director or servant of a client company. This prohibition is necessary because the auditor is expected to take a position which is independent from the management view of an enterprise. The Companies Act 1989 has extended this prohibition to involvement with other companies in the same group as an audit client. Additional regulations regarding circumstances in which someone would be ineligible for appointment as auditor may be introduced as a result of the Act.

(v)   Disclosure of Information

Since 1967 there has been a legal requirement for a company's accounts to disclose the amount of the auditor's remuneration, but this did not extend to fees received for services other than audit. It has been argued that disclosure of non-audit fees, while not removing the threat to independence from multiple services, would at least allow financial statement users to make a more complete assessment of the nature of the auditor-client relationship. The 1989 Companies Act introduced a requirement for the disclosure of non-audit fees.

3.4.2   Professional Recommendations

Independence is implicit in the concept of 'professional' behaviour and the accounting profession is therefore concerned to ensure that its members' behaviour reflects this quality. To some extent this is controlled through the entry and training requirements where the ethic of independence can be learned.

In addition, the professional accountancy bodies have also tried to influence the appearance of independence by providing guidelines for the sort of relationships and activities which can be considered consistent with desired standards of professional behaviour. From the starting point that the need to 'present or report on information objectively' is 'the essence of professionalism' the Ethical Guide of the ICAEW goes on to made recommendations about a number of factors which could jeopardise independence.

It is likely that both the status and the content of the guidelines will change as a result of the introduction, through the 1989 Companies Act of a new regulatory regime for auditing. These recommendations have in the past reflected the views of accountants on independence and have been largely internal rules for the profession.

In the future, the ethical guidelines will become more a matter of public law, in that approval of supervisory bodies will be dependant on having adequate rules, and as a result it is likely that the content will also be tightened and made more mandatory. Some research has suggested that groups other than auditors, such as bankers and investment analysts, do have a somewhat more restrictive view of the situations which can threaten the auditor's independence than those which have been permitted in the Ethical Guide (*Firth*, 1980).

The explanatory notes accompanying the statement on independence in the Ethical Guide covers the following areas:

(i)   Fees

It is suggested that the recurring fees from any one client or group of connected clients should not exceed 15% of the gross fees of an audit practice.

(ii)   Personal relationships

The Guide recommends that no one should accept an appointment as auditor if they have been an officer, employee or partner in a client during the preceding two years or if a member of his or her close family has any connection with a client which could raise doubts about independence.

(iii)   Financial involvement with a client.

A wide variety of financial relationships between auditor and client which might threaten independence are referred to in the Guide, including trustee and nominee arrangements. Perhaps the main points to note are: beneficial shareholdings in a client company are not allowed; loans to a client and loans from a client, other than arm's length transactions negotiated in the normal course of the client's business are prohibited; and the threats which result from acceptance of goods or services on favourable terms and from commission which might arise through advising a client are recognised, although little explicit guidance is provided on controlling these threats.

(iv)   Conflicts of Interest

The Guide also recognises the possible conflicts of interest which result from the business relationship between auditors and clients. These conflicts arise due to the dangers of acting in more than one capacity, for example if offering advisory services the auditor could become involved in executive decisions, or if providing accounting assistance the auditing approach to the information for audit may by impaired. While the Guide highlights these risks, it makes little attempt to introduce rigid controls to eliminate or limit them.

3.4.3   *Individual Firms' Rules*

In addition to the formal legal regulations and professional recommendations on independence, individual audit firms may also have their own rules which all partners and staff are required to comply with. These rules may in some cases be more detailed, and more restrictive than those of the professional bodies. Audit firms have an interest in promoting such rules because the appearance of independence, and evidence of instances of apparent non-independent behaviour, will affect the firm's reputation, and this reputation is of economic importance to the long term business of the firm.

3.5 FACTORS THREATENING INDEPENDENCE

It is also possible to identify in the way the provision of auditing services is structured and regulated currently a number of factors which may threaten auditor independence. The principal factor underlying these threats is the nature of economic relationship between auditor and client and the effect this has on their power relative to each other.

3.5.1 *Fees*

Although it is the shareholders who approve the auditor's remuneration, in practice it is management who negotiate the fees the auditor receives. The auditor may feel under pressure to justify to management what they perceive as the 'cost' of having an audit. If fees are squeezed, there is the possibility that this will affect the amount and nature of audit work undertaken. Additionally, if the fee from a particular client is significant to the audit firm's income, or even to the business of an individual partner within a firm, or if the client is prestigious, this will increase the potential for management to influence the auditor.

3.5.2 *Services*

The threat associated with the economic importance to the auditor of fees from a client will be further increased if other services, such as consultancy, are provided in addition to the audit. The reason is that this increases the economic importance of a client to the auditor's business, although it can be argued that in some circumstances providing additional services will actually increase the auditor's power vis-a-vis the client rather than vice versa. It is also possible that undertaking certain services, such as bookkeeping or accounting functions and systems design may affect the objectivity with which the auditor then views organisational information and processes.

3.5.3 *Appointment*

As was noted earlier the legal position is that the auditor of a limited company is appointed by the shareholders. In most practical situations, however, the real power of appointment rests with company management. It is management who will make recommendations on the continued appointment of an auditor and who decide whether to seek alternative tenders from other firms. The potential threat of dismissal which this power confers on management may jeopardise independence if the auditor is concerned to maintain the business generated by a client in the future. The practical position regarding appointment, fees and additional services all act in a way which encourages auditors to see management as the group they are working for and to be sensitive to the kind of audit management values.

3.5.4 *Competition Between Audit Firms*

All of the above points involve the relation between auditor and client. An additional factor which it is sometimes argued can threaten independence is the behaviour of firms in competition with one another. If vigorous competition results in price cutting or 'low-balling' in order to obtain an audit, this may in turn have an impact on the work done. The willingness of audit firms to compete on price terms or to accept particular accounting treatments in return for obtaining an audit will reinforce the potential power of management vis-a-vis the auditor arising from the factors described above.

3.5.5 *Incorporation*

A recent area of discussion in the accounting profession arising out of the European Community Eighth Directive on Company Law, which deals with the regulation of auditors, has been whether accounting firms should be allowed to have incorporated status. Previously, this was not possible under UK Company Law, in contrast to some other European Countries, but the 1989 Companies Act has introduced this option. Professional opinions on the merits of incorporation are divided.

The particular concern in relation to independence is whether the possibility of shareholders from outside an audit firm could result in influence being exerted on the way the firm conducted and reported on an audit. The profession has published a consultative document on this subject (*Independence and Incorporation,* ICAEW, October 1988), in an attempt to define the limits of outside involvement in an audit firm which can be tolerated without independence being threatened, and to determine whether the professional bodies should impose tighter constraints than those introduced in the 1989 Act.

3.6 FURTHER SUGGESTIONS FOR STRENGTHENING INDEPENDENCE

A number of additional suggestions have been made of ways in which auditor independence could be further enhanced and protected. These suggestions involve two principal approaches to the problem:

- Monitoring — Some ideas involve greater monitoring and control of auditor-client relationships but within the same structure as applies at present.

- Structural — Other proposals would change the basic structure of the way in which auditing services are organised and provided.

The sort of suggestions which have been made include the examples described below.

3.7 MONITORING PROPOSALS

3.7.1 *Professional Rules*

While the Ethical Guide does go some way in asserting the importance of independence and in attempting to regulate certain auditor-client relationships, it has also sometimes been criticised as not going far enough. Specifically, it has been argued that it could be structured as a mandatory code rather than as a guide, be more restrictive in certain areas, for example the proportion of total fees which can be accounted for by one client, and provide greater guidance in areas where it does little more than recognise the existence of a threat, for example multiple services.

3.7.2 *Legal Regulations*

An alternative to relying upon a professional code would be to make the same aspects of the auditor-client relationship the subject of legal rules, and hence the subject of legal enforcement. The case for this approach relies principally on the level of compliance with professional recommendations.

3.7.3 *Disclosure of Information*

It has already been noted that the Companies Act 1989 has extended the information disclosed within a company's annual report and accounts in the accounts to include fees received by auditors for non-audit services, in order to assist outsiders to judge the auditor-client relationship.

Another area where greater disclosure has been suggested is where there is a change in auditor. In the United States, for example, auditor changes give rise to a responsibility to report to the Securities and Exchange Commission regarding the reasons and circumstances of the change.

3.7.4 *Audit Committees*

An alternative to simply introducing new or more restrictive rules about auditor-client relationships is to try to increase the auditor's ability to resist management influence. One possible protection in this regard is to introduce and give greater responsibilities to audit committees, for example in approving audit plans and receiving reports from the auditor on the financial statements and other matters such as internal control. The rationale of this suggestion is to enlist additional support for the auditor against executive management pressure. However, fundamental to this rationale is the implicit independence of the audit committee itself, which cannot always be guaranteed. At present, audit committees are not general practice in the United Kingdom although they are increasing in number.

3.8 STRUCTURAL PROPOSALS

3.8.1 *Changing the Tenure of Audit Appointments*

Two ideas concerning the structure of appointment for auditors are, first, that the appointment should be for a longer term, for example five years, in order that the auditor can conduct the required work and report on it without having to be concerned about any immediate threat of removal from office, and, second, that there should be a compulsory change in auditor at a certain minimum frequency, in order to avoid the danger of over familiarity with a client. In the latter case, this could involve a mandatory change in the audit firm appointed or simply in the personnel assigned to the audit.

3.8.2 *Separation of Auditing from Other Services*

The possibility of legal requirements being introduced to prevent auditors offering other services to audit clients, achieved considerable prominence recently when implementation of the EC Eighth Directive was being discussed. This situation applies in some European countries, but the proposal to make this a general requirement was omitted from the final version of the Directive. The rationale for separation of services is that the conflict of interest and additional fee pressure from multiple services would be avoided. The converse argument is that the present situation allows auditors to exploit their expertise and the knowledge gained during an audit to the benefit of clients, and recognises the efficiencies which can arise from the natural overlap of certain services with auditing.

3.8.3 *A Regulatory Agency*

A final, and perhaps the most radical, suggestion which has been advanced in the debate on auditor independence is that a government-backed agency should be established to regulate auditing activity, such as the Securities and Investments Board for investment business or the Audit Commission for auditing in some areas of the public sector. Such a body could have powers to license, appoint or employ auditors or to determine levels of fees for example. The idea of a state-sponsored monitoring agency for auditing would change significantly the balance between state and professional regulation of auditing, but whether it is the best means for directly enhancing auditor independence is debatable.

In implementing the EC Eighth Directive in the Companies Act 1989, the government has preferred the option of allowing the existing professional bodies to become recognised supervisory bodies and qualifying bodies to that of setting up an additional monitoring agency, although there is a provision for the Secretary of State to create such a body if he or she thinks it necessary.

3.9 OTHER ETHICAL CONSIDERATIONS

Alongside the statement on professional independence, fifteen other statements on ethical matters are included in the Ethical Guide, concerning, for example, dealing with clients' monies and the idea of contingent fees. Some of the more important areas, from the point of view of an auditor, are as follows:

3.9.1 *Confidentiality (Statement 2)*

Auditors may obtain information in the course of an audit which, if disclosed, could be damaging or embarrassing for those involved in the organisation being audited, or which the auditor could use to his or her personal advantage. The need to treat such information as confidential unless there is public or legal duty to disclose it, and not to use it for personal advantage is recognised in the Ethical Guide.

Behaving in this way is an important factor in establishing that auditors are capable of trust, which is an essential part of fulfilling audit responsibilities. Recently imposed regulations concerning auditing in the financial services sector have highlighted the possible conflict between confidentiality and a duty to report information to other regulatory authorities ('whistle blowing').

3.9.2 *Obtaining Work. (Statement 5). Publicity and Advertising (Statement 3)*

The Ethical Guide also attempts to place some restrictions on the manner in which auditors can obtain work and advertise their services. These restrictions have been considerably relaxed in recent years such that auditors can advertise much more freely now than just a few years ago. The concern in this area is that if individuals or firms advertise their services in an aggressive commercial manner which attempts to claim superior skills or service in comparison with others, this may compromise independence or the way the profession is perceived by the public.

Activities such as 'cold calling', that is making an unsolicited approach to a non-client in the hope of obtaining work, and charging uneconomic fees just to obtain a client are prohibited and advertising is required to be in 'good taste'. There are, however considerable difficulties in policing these aspects of behaviour particularly in the context of the relaxation of rules and the more commercial attitude of firms in recent years.

3.9.3 *Changes in Appointment (Statement 6)*

In the situation where a company is changing its auditors, the Guide makes recommendations concerning communication between the new and old auditors before an appointment is accepted. This communication is necessary in order that all relevant information is available to the incoming auditor and is intended to encourage firms, in the way they compete with each other, to continue to have reference to wider professional reponsibilities.

3.10 SUMMARY

The main subject of this chapter has been auditor independence. We have attempted to establish the implicit importance of independence to auditing, to describe its nature, show how it is regulated, identify the main sources of threat to independence and introduce some suggestions that have been forwarded for its improvement. Independence is one aspect of a broader requirement for auditors to behave in an ethical manner.

Independent and ethical behaviour is important because public confidence in the auditing profession and the functions satisfied through auditing depends critically upon beliefs about the quality of service being provided. The importance of independence to the professional reputations on which auditors trade may ensure that it is in auditors' best interests to behave independently. However, in order to ensure that the appearance of independence is maintained, the profession has applied some controls to behaviour rather than simply allow the degree of independence to be determined through the market place. Moreover, the existence of adequate ethical rules has become an important condition for the recognition of professional bodies as supervisory bodies for auditing services.

Because of its centrality and importance to the rationale of auditing, independence is always likely to be a controversial subject. Recently considerable attention has been focused on the issues of the compatibility of auditing and other services and the possibility of incorporation of audit firms. These debates have been stimulated by the EC Eighth Directive and the 1989 Companies Act. For the future, it is possible that another EC directive on the specific subject of independence may be introduced.

CHAPTER 4   LIABILITY AND THE DUTY OF CARE

4.1   INTRODUCTION

An audit is required in order to assess the manner in which management have carried out their responsibility to prepare a set of financial statements, and thus improves accountability. It is obviously important that the auditor too should be accountable for his or her actions in conducting and reporting on the results of an audit. The provision of any form of professional service, including auditing, carries with it a duty that the service will be performed with a reasonable level of care. This duty is an implied part of the contract between the person providing the service and the client. If it is not fulfilled, then, on the grounds of negligent behaviour it may be possible to hold the auditor liable for losses sustained as a result.

Liability arises partly from the auditor's responsibility under statute law, for example, the auditor would be criminally liable for knowingly publishing statements which are misleading, false or deceptive (Theft Act, 1968), and partly from the application of the principles of common law, to establish the standards of work and reporting which should be expected from the auditor. In this chapter, the discussion is restricted to what is perhaps the most uncertain area of liability, namely the extent of the auditor's liability for negligence in the execution of audit responsibilities — in what circumstances negligence arises and to whom the auditor can be held liable for negligence. There is only space here to introduce the broad principles of this topic and those wishing to know the detail of the legal liability of auditors should refer to some of the further reading suggested at the end of Part 1.

4.2   CONDITIONS FOR LIABILITY

In order for an auditor to be held liable for negligence, three conditions must be satisfied:

- It must be demonstrated that the auditor's behaviour has fallen short of the standard of care required, for example that he or she has obtained insufficient evidence to support an opinion or has unjustifiably ignored or misinterpreted evidence in arriving at that opinion.

- There must be a legal duty to take care which is owed to those seeking to hold the auditor liable.

- It must be shown that some damage or loss has resulted from the auditor's failure to meet the required standard of care.

While the last of these points is most often a question of the facts and circumstances of the individual case, the other two involve general principles that the courts have recognised regarding what an auditor should do and to whom a duty of care is owed. These two aspects are discussed in the rest of this chapter.

4.3   WHAT STANDARD OF CARE?

It is not possible to be precise about what the auditor's duty of care implies in terms of specific actions or conduct. As a guiding principle, there is a general responsibility to perform an audit in a manner which would be considered appropriate in the circumstances involved. As stated by Lopes LJ in re *Kingston Cotton Mill Co (No 2)* [1896] 2 Ch 279):

'It is the duty of an auditor to bring to bear on the work he has to perform that skill, care and caution which a reasonably competent, careful and cautious auditor would use. What is reasonable skill, care and caution must depend on the particular circumstances of each case.'

The standard of care expected thus rests on notions of 'reasonable' conduct and behaviour which is generally accepted as appropriate by the auditing community.

4.3.1 *Guidance from Cases*

While the precise interpretation of the auditor's duty of care remains flexible to the individual situation, a number of general aspects of the standard of behaviour that is expected can be identified from the judgements in decided cases:

(i) The auditor is expected to know the law as it relates to his or her statutory duties, rights and powers and the current professional standards and recommendations contained in Statements of Standard Accounting Practice and Auditing Standards and Guidelines. The auditor is not obliged to ensure that a client has observed the law except in so far as it relates to audit duties (*Leeds Estate, Building and Investment Co v Shepherd* [1887] 36 Ch D 787).

(ii) The auditor's opinion should be based on appropriate evidence and investigation (*re Westminster Road Construction and Engineering Co Ltd* (1932) 86 Acct LR 38). The evidence collected must be sufficient to allow a proper judgement of the quality of the financial statements. For example, simply confirming the arithmetical accuracy of figures is not sufficient evidence for an audit opinion (*London Oil Storage Co Ltd v Seear, Hasluck & Co* (1904) 31 Acct LR 1). If there are circumstances which seem to call for enquiry, it is the author's duty to follow them up and obtain appropriate evidence (*Arthur E Green & Co v Central Advance and Discount Corpn Ltd* (1920) 63 Acct LR 1).

(iii) The kind of methods used in obtaining evidence should be up to date and utilise procedures and techniques which are generally regarded as good practice (*re Thomas Gerrard & Son Ltd* [1968] Ch 455; [1967] 2 All ER 525).

(iv) The auditor might also be expected to maintain proper audit programmes and evidence of the work undertaken, and to ensure that there is adequate supervision of audit staff so that the intended procedures are properly executed (*Irish Woollen Co Ltd v Tyson* (1900) 26 Acct LR 13).

(v) The auditor is obliged to report the result of the audit to the shareholders (or more generally to the specified report users) in a proper manner and report the facts fully (*re London & General Bank (No 2)* [1895] 2 Ch 673). This report will comprise an opinion on the quality of the information in the financial statements. There is no requirement to advise the report readers on matters concerning, for example, internal control or organisational efficiency unless they directly affect the audit.

(vi) The auditor does have a responsibility for detecting fraud, but only when put on enquiry. The circumstances should be such as to arouse suspicion of fraud before the auditor should be expected to discover it (*Henry Squire (Cash Chemist) Ltd v Ball Baker & Co* (1911) 44 Acct LR 25). However, audit work should be adequate to detect material fraud and error. The auditor could be held negligent if, in circumstances where suspicions should have been aroused through appropriate audit procedures, the actual audit methods failed to do so (*re Thomas Gerrard & Son Ltd* [1968] Ch 455; [1967] 2 All ER 525). The courts have also recognised that it is management who have primary responsibility for preventing and detecting fraud (*re SP Catterson & Sons Ltd* (1937) 81 Acct LR 62).

In summary, the auditor is expected to plan and execute audit work in a manner capable of permitting a proper judgement to be made of the quality of the financial statements and report a proper opinion on that quality, and the way his or her work, judgement and reporting is conducted should be consistent with accepted practice. The standard of care required is a changing concept in that the specific standards that the court will apply at any time will reflect changes in societal expectations and in professional accounting and auditing regulations.

4.3.2 *Audit Risk, Audit Failure and Business Failure*

It is sometimes argued that criticisms directed at auditors for failure to apply an appropriate standard of care often arise because of a lack of understanding of the distinction between audit risk, audit failure and business failure.

Audit risk is the risk that, despite having performed an audit with the appropriate level of care and in accordance with good practice, the results of the audit will fail to detect the presence of significant error. If they are to report within a reasonable timescale at an acceptable cost, auditors cannot generally test financial statements to one hundred per cent accuracy, and there is always a possibility, or risk, that the evidence collected will not be representative of the full picture and that material misstatement will be missed. The risk is implicit in the nature of most audit methods. In contrast, audit failure is where an error in the financial statement is not uncovered because the auditor has not used appropriate methods and exercised the appropriate level of care. It is where the auditor reaches an erroneous conclusion because of the inadequacy of the work done. Business failure arises as a result of the business risk associated with economic activity, and is where, as a result of economic or trading conditions or poor management, an enterprise is no longer in a position to continue trading or repay its providers of capital. It is possible to have audit failure without business failure and business failure without audit failure but in practice the two events are sometimes confused.

When a business fails there is a tendency to ask why problems were not uncovered by the auditor and to infer that there has been some form of audit failure. But, as noted above, the two situations are distinct and the former need not imply the latter, as business failure may result from many circumstances which are outside the scope of the auditor's investigation and objectives. Additionally, where it can be shown that the auditor has not uncovered something which does fall within the scope of his or her investigation and objectives, it may be assumed that this is due to audit failure when it could in fact simply be the result of audit risk.

The standard of care which should apply is one which holds the auditor liable only for audit failure. The auditor should be considered negligent if an inappropriate audit opinion has been issued and this has happened because the conduct of the underlying audit work or the reporting can be shown to be of inadequate quality.

4.4 TO WHOM IS THE AUDITOR LIABLE?

Perhaps the issue of greatest uncertainty concerning the auditor's duty of care is the extent to which he or she should be liable to third parties. Clearly the auditor has got responsibilities and obligations to those who are party to the audit contract. The auditor's contract is with the company, but it is recognised that a duty of care is owed to the company's members, who appoint the auditor and to whom the auditor reports, even though they are legally distinct from the company. The more uncertain point is in what circumstances this duty of care could extend to other third parties.

4.4.1 *Privity*

The traditional approach to the question of liability is based on the doctrine of privity of contract, that is that liability could normally only exist where the parties concerned had a contractual relationship. The auditor has a contractual relationship with the client and therefore has a duty of care as a result but this was not thought to extend to others who may have relied on the financial statements but have no such relationship. The reason for requiring privity was that it was felt that otherwise liability would be unlimited. To quote a much cited American case on this point, auditors could be exposed 'to a liability in indeterminate amount for an indeterminate time to an indeterminate class.' (*Ultramares Corpn v Touche & Co* (1931) 255 NY 170).

More recently the concept of privity has not been used to exclude liability to individuals other than those party to the audit contract as the balance of opinion has shifted to accept that the auditor may have a duty of care to certain third parties.

4.4.2 Proximity

In place of privity the concept of proximity might be applied to determine the boundaries of liability, that is that a duty of care is owed to those who are so closely or directly affected by the audit that the auditor could reasonably be expected to have them in mind when conducting his or her work and reporting on it. The application of proximity may include a 'foreseeability' test—that liability should not be held if the auditor could not be expected to have foreseen the third party's use of and reliance on the audit.

4.5 CASES ON THIRD PARTY LIABILITY

Developments in the area of auditor's third party liability in recent years have centred on the question of how narrow or broad the definition of proximity and foreseeability should be, for example whether the auditor should have foresight of a specific third party and their specific use or a general class of third parties and uses. The trend in these developments can best be seen by reviewing briefly the judgements in a number of significant cases. Some of the cases quoted here have not been formally reported as yet, limiting the case references it is possible to provide.

4.5.1 *Candler v Crane Christmas & Co [1951] 2 KB 164*; [1951]1 All ER 1

To begin with a case which demonstrated the then established position that a duty of care was not owed to parties outside a contract, the action in this case was dismissed even though the defendant, a firm of chartered accountants, was aware of the plaintiff and his intended use of the financial statements being prepared. Candler had invested money in some companies owned by a Mr Ogilvie, having been shown financial statements for the companies which had been prepared by the defendants for Ogilvie. Following liquidation and the loss of the investment Candler sued the defendants claiming negligence in the preparation of the financial statements.

The Court of Appeal dismissed the action on the grounds that no duty of care was owed to the plaintiff in the absence of a contractual or fiduciary relationship. While this judgement appeared to secure auditors from potential actions from third parties, the dissenting view of Lord Justice Denning was to prove influential in subsequent cases. Denning argued that a duty of care was owed to the client and to a third party to whom the auditors show the accounts or are aware the client will show the accounts to induce some action, but that this duty did not extend to include strangers.

4.5.2 *Hedley Byrne & Co Ltd v Heller and Partners Ltd [1964] AC 465;* [1963] 2 All ER 575

The defendant in this case was a merchant bank which had issued a reference on a client which subsequently went into liquidation, knowing that the reference would be shown to the plaintiff. Liability was avoided because of the fact that the bank had inserted a disclaimer in the reference, but the House of Lords supported the dissenting view of Denning in the Candler case and held that a duty of care existed despite the absence of privity of contract. However this duty was limited to those third parties with whom a 'special relationship' existed.

As a result of this case, the ICAEW took Counsel's opinion on the accountant's liability to third parties. The opinion suggested, reassuringly for the profession, that liability was limited to those circumstances where the accountant knew or ought to have known that the accounts would be relied on by third parties in connection with the *specific* purpose or transaction which had given rise to loss. However, this narrow view has not been applied in subsequent cases.

4.5.3   *Scott Group Ltd v McFarlane [1978] 1 NZLR 553*

This New Zealand case involved a takeover by Scott of Duthie Holdings, the consolidated accounts of which had been audited by the defendant. The action was based on the subsequent discovery of a double counting error which had resulted in Duthie's assets being overvalued. The defendants accepted negligence but denied a duty of care. On appeal it was held that a duty of care did exist but damages were not awarded on the grounds that no measurable damage had resulted from the negligence.

In arriving at this decision, it was argued that although McFarlane had no knowledge of the specific interest of the plaintiff at the time of the audit, the possibility of takeover interest in Duthie should have been apparent. A further argument advanced, although not part of the decided judgement, was that the auditor is aware that his or her report is filed as a matter of public record and, while this in itself does not create a duty of care, should foresee that third parties will make use of the accounts and audit report.

4.5.4   *JEB Fasteners Ltd v Marks, Bloom & Co [1981] 3 All ER 289; [1983] 1 All ER 583*

In a similar situation, JEB took over BG Fasteners Ltd in 1975 and subsequently brought an action against BG's auditors for negligence in respect of the 1974 accounts which included an overstatement of stock. This error had the effect that a profit rather than a loss was reported in that year. The defendants were found to be negligent and to have a duty of care to JEB. However the defendant again avoided damages on the grounds that JEB would have proceeded with the purchase even had the error been corrected and thus the loss had not resulted from the negligence.

This judgement was greeted as a significant relaxation in the standard of proximity required for negligence in that the defendants were held to have a duty of care to a third party whose specific existence was unknown to them at the time of the audit, and in respect of a specific transaction about which they had no knowledge. However, the fact that the auditors were aware of the condition of the company and its desire to obtain financial assistance meant they should have foreseen the possibility of this general class of transaction which included the subsequent takeover. This approach is considerably less stringent than the requirement for a 'special relationship' suggested in the *Hedley Byrne* case.

4.5.5   *Twomax Ltd v Dickson, McFarlane & Robinson [1983] SLT 98*

A similar judgement was made in Twomax, another case involving investment in a company, Kintyre Knitwear, which subsequently went into liquidation, the investment being lost. Twomax, and two other small shareholders claimed that the accounts to March 1973, seven months prior to the purchase, had been audited negligently. These accounts showed a profit of £20,000 in comparison to a £12,000 loss in 1972. The plaintiffs argued that had the accounts showed the true position they would not have undertaken the investment.

It was held that the defendants had been negligent in their audit and that a duty of care was owed to the plaintiffs. Although the defendants had no specific knowledge of the plaintiffs or their interest at the time of the audit, the fact that they knew the financial condition of the company, that a director wished to sell his shareholding, and that the accounts were being shown to lenders was taken as sufficient evidence that they should have foreseen that the accounts could be relied upon by a potential investor. Substantial damages were awarded against the defendants.

4.5.6 *Lloyd Cheyham v Littlejohn [1985] BCLC*

A duty of care was also held in this case where the plaintiffs brought an action on the grounds that, in investing substantial sums of money in Trec Rentals Ltd, they had relied on accounts delivered to them by the defendants, the auditors of the company. Within three months of the investment the company had gone into liquidation and the investment was lost. The plaintiffs claimed the accounts on which they had relied had been audited negligently. The circumstances of this case were narrower than those in *JEB* and *Twomax* as the defendant had specific knowledge of the plaintiff and their use of the accounts. Although a duty of care was recognised the action was unsuccessful as it was concluded that the auditor's work had not been negligent. It was also noted that the auditor's duty of care did not mean that the plaintiffs need not take any action to protect themselves.

4.5.7 *Caparo Industries plc v Dickman [1989] 2 WLR 316*

A recent case which has provided a comprehensive examination of the role of foreseeability in relation to the auditor's duty of care is that in which Caparo Industries plc brought an action against Touche Ross, alleging negligence in their audit of Fidelity plc, a company taken over by Caparo in 1984. Caparo had begun buying Fidelity shares on the open market in early June 1984. Following the publication of the accounts to 31 March 1984, Caparo made further purchases, increasing its holding to 29.9% of Fidelity by the end of July. A full take-over bid was launched in September, and, after a slight increase in the terms, was successfully concluded in October. In April 1985 Caparo commenced the action against the auditors claiming that they had been negligent in failing to detect and report certain allegedly fraudulent misrepresentations by the Fidelity directors.

The issue of negligence in this case has not been resolved because the main question addressed in the court hearings so far has been simply whether or not the auditor had a duty of care to the plaintiff, that is, whether there is a case to answer. This question has been considered by the High Court and the Court of Appeal and referred to the House of Lords.

In the High Court, Sir Neil Lawson decided that a duty of care did not exist, principally on the grounds of the relationship between the parties. The judgement was based on evaluation of three criteria: the foreseeability of economic loss as a result of a lack of care; the proximity of the parties, that is whether the auditor should have anticipated the plaintiff's reliance; and whether the imposition of liability would be fair, reasonable and just. Caparo's position as both a shareholder at the time of the audit report and as a potential investor was considered. While it could be foreseen that negligent action by the auditor would result in economic loss, Sir Neil Lawson held that no duty of care to potential investors existed because the relationship between the parties was not sufficiently proximate. Fidelity was a public company and Caparo did not come from a limited class whose reliance on the audit report the auditor could have anticipated. Further, it would not be fair, reasonable or just to recognise a duty of care, as this 'would create a liability for an indefinite period to any member of the public who chose to rely on the auditors' report to invest in the company, or to lend money to the company, or to give credit to the company.' Turning to the question of a duty to Caparo as shareholder the judge concluded that if a duty existed it was to shareholders as a class not as individuals, and that if Parliament had intended auditors to be liable to shareholders, this duty would have been recognised in statute. Again the judge added that to impose a duty of care to shareholders, individually or collectively, would not be fair, reasonable or just as it would mean a liability which was 'indeterminate, unlimited as to quantum, as to time and as to the identity of its beneficiaries.' The remedy available to shareholders was to remove the auditor from office.

In the Court of Appeal this judgement was partially overturned. It was held that there existed a duty of care to Caparo as an existing shareholder but not as a potential investor. This judgement was based on different conclusions concerning the same criteria of foreseeability, proximity and reasonableness. The foreseeability of loss as a consequence of the audit was accepted by the parties. On the question of proximity, Lord Justice Bingham argued that the auditors knew the outcome of the audit would be a report to shareholders, that while the auditor's contract is with the company this is on behalf of the shareholders, and that shareholders as a group can be identified at any point in time. The relationship was sufficiently proximate to support a duty of care. Further, the judge held that it was just and reasonable to recognise such a duty because otherwise no adequate redress was available to shareholders and because the circumstances in which it could give rise to an actual liability would require the plaintiff's claims to satisfy a number of stringent requirements.

Following the ruling, Touche Ross appealed to the House of Lords. At the time of writing, the outcome of this appeal is not known, but a judgment is expected by the end of 1989.

4.5.8 Al Saudi Banque v Clark Pixley

The reasoning in the *Caparo* case was applied to the position of creditors in the action brought by Al Saudi Banque against Clark Pixley. This case arose out of the failure of Gallic Credit Ltd, a company which was compulsory wound up in 1983 leaving an estimated deficiency to unsecured creditors of £8.6 million. The company had secured advances from a number of banks on the basis of bills of exchange. These bills, which represented virtually all the company's balance sheet assets, were worthless, leaving no assets for distribution amongst the creditors.

Ten banks took action against the auditors on the grounds that reliance had been placed on the 1981 and 1982 accounts and audit reports in renewing and extending credit facilities to Gallic Credit. The plaintiffs argued that the auditors were aware that the nature of the company's business required borrowing from the lending institutions and must have foreseen that copies of the accounts and audit reports would be provided to these lenders and relied upon by them in making credit decisions. The lenders' reliance was foreseeable and the probability of reliance sufficiently high to constitute a condition of proximity.

Seven of the banks were existing creditors when the auditors made their reports, three were not. The position of the latter was taken as directly comparable to that of the potential investors in *Caparo*. It was held that they had no close or direct relationship with the auditor, and that proximity was therefore lacking and no duty of care existed.

As regards the seven banks who were existing creditors, they constituted a limited class, whose identity and amount of credit exposure was known to the auditors. However, Mr Justice Millett held that their position was not comparable to that of shareholders. They were not involved in the appointment of the auditors and the auditors did not make their reports to the banks, or to anyone else with the knowledge or intention that they would be supplied to the banks. While it could be foreseeable that any bank would ask for and rely on the accounts, there was no relationship between the banks and the auditors and therefore, despite foreseeabiliy, there was no proximity. The auditors had no duty of care to the lending banks and the case was therefore dismissed.

4.6 SUMMARY

Until recently, the trend in decided cases appeared to be that, having rejected the limitation on third party liability imposed by privity of contract, the courts were successively relaxing the definition of proximity, extending the circumstances in which a duty of care applies and thus reducing the auditor's protection from action. Application of a criterion of reasonable foresight suggested that the auditor could be liable to some classes of third parties whose reliance on the accounts, and potential loss from negligent auditing, could be foreseen. This included those users of accounts that the auditor has specific knowledge of at the time of the audit, but following the *JEB* and *Twomax* cases, also appeared to include third parties whose specific existence is not known to the auditor but who fall within a general class of users whose use could be foreseen.

If confirmed by the House of Lords, the decision in *Caparo,* followed also in *Al Saudi Banque,* establishes that foreseeability is a necessary but not a sufficient condition for liability. In addition, there must be a relationship between the parties sufficient to create a duty of care. There is no simple test to determine what is sufficient and the specific relationship in each case must be analysed. The necessary relationship is present between the auditor and the members of a company because the auditor reports to them and knows they will receive the audit report. It might also exist where the auditor intended or knew that the accounts and audit report would be supplied to the plaintiff or to a class which includes the plaintiff. Knowledge of a specific transaction is not required, rather it is the relationship between the parties that matters. If there is a sufficiently close relationship, liability could arise if the recipients' reliance on the accounts could be foreseen, whether the auditor had it in mind or not. The necessary relationship does not exist between the auditor and potential shareholders and creditors.

Where the boundaries lie to the auditor's duty of care is, therefore, uncertain, and where they will be recognised in future cases is difficult to predict. Perhaps the best and most appropriate guide lies in the words of Lord Pearce in the *Hedley Byrne* case:

> 'How wide the sphere of the duty of care in negligence is to be laid depends ultimately on the court's assessment of the demands of society for protection from the carelessness of others.'

The cases discussed above also demonstrate that even where a duty of care is held to exist it will not always be easy for the plaintiff to gain damages from a defendant auditor. A useful summary of the position was stated in the *Lloyd Cheyham* case where Mr Justice Woolf held that a successful action depends on four 'issues':

   (i) the duty of care issue — that a duty of care was owed by the auditors, because they ought to have realised that the accounts could be used and relied upon the circumstances alleged;

  (ii) the negligence issue — that the audit work was conducted in a negligent manner;

 (iii) the causation issue — that the loss suffered by the plaintiffs is consequent on the auditor's negligence;

 (iv) the quantum issue — the amount of the plaintiff's loss.

In addition, it is possible that the courts will take into account any possible contributory negligence on the part of the plaintiff, for example in placing undue reliance on the accounts alone without pursuing supporting enquiries, before awarding damages against a negligent auditor.

CHAPTER 5   COLLECTING AUDIT EVIDENCE

5.1   THE NEED FOR EVIDENCE

The centrality of evidence to the audit is recognised in both the theoretical foundations of auditing and in the practice rules which govern the way audits are carried out. One of the necessary conditions, or theoretical assumptions, of auditing is that there is available sufficient reliable evidence to allow the auditor to form an opinion within reasonable limits of time and cost. Similarly, on the practical side, the Auditor's Operational Standard states:

> 'The auditor should obtain relevant and reliable audit evidence sufficient to enable him to draw reasonable conclusions therefrom.' (APC, 1980a)

These ideas suggest a number of desirable characteristics for audit evidence but the central point is that auditing depends upon evidence. If the audit opinion is intended to enhance the credibility of financial statements, then it is implicit that this opinion should have some basis in the investigation, verification and corroboration of the financial quantities undertaken by the auditor. That is, the opinion must have an evidential base. As stated by *Mautz and Sharaf* (1961, p 68):

> 'To the extent that he (the auditor) makes judgements and forms his "opinion" on the basis of adequate evidence, he acts rationally by following a systematic or methodical procedure; to the extent that he fails to gather "sufficient competent evidential matter" and fails to evaluate it effectively, he acts irrationally and his judgements can have little standing.

Evidence then is critical to the rationality and purpose of auditing. It is therefore important that the auditor properly considers what evidence can be collected and the appropriate methods for its accumulation on each audit engagement. This chapter introduces in turn the nature of audit evidence, with reference to features such as the sources, types, qualities and problems of evidence, the specification of the objectives that should influence the design of an audit evidence process, and the structure and stages which that process involves — planning, evidence collection and forming an opinion.

5.2   SOURCES OF EVIDENCE

There are three basic sources of audit evidence:

5.2.1   *Internal Evidence*

This is evidence which is created and processed by the client, for example stock records. The value of internally produced evidence is limited by the fact that it is under the control of, and therefore susceptible to manipulation by, the client's staff and management. Internal evidence may therefore be less objective than that obtained from an external source.

The risk associated with internal evidence is to a large extent a function of the control system operated by the client and whether it is likely to ensure the quality of the information available as evidence.

5.2.2 *External Evidence*

Information which is generated by and obtained from third parties to the organisation being audited is external evidence. While this source of evidence is potentially of great value to the auditor because of its independence, the quality of externally generated evidence is sometimes difficult to evaluate and there may be significant problems in obtaining it.

5.2.3 *Auditor – Generated Evidence*

Finally by source, there is evidence which is produced by the auditor him or herself. Such evidence is obviously easier for the auditor to evaluate in terms of quality and less subject to manipulation than either of the other sources already mentioned. The principal difficulty with auditor-generated evidence is that it may be very expensive to produce and major reliance on this source has a significant impact on audit costs.

Each of the above sources of evidence is described independently, but in practice there may be considerable overlap between internal and external information. For example, an invoice from a supplier has an external source, but if it is processed and maintained within the organisation then some of the problems associated with internal evidence may arise, such as duplication, manipulation and processing error. Similarly some evidence may be generated internally but subsequently be subject to external check or processing, for example delivery notes. In looking at the source of available evidence, therefore, what the auditor is concerned with is not only the creation of the information, but also how it has been processed and who has had access to it.

Clearly the relative advantages and disadvantages of evidence from different sources vary, as can be seen in Table 5.1 which categorises the quality of evidence with reference to a number of factors.

Table 5.1 Relative quality of different sources of audit evidence*

	Internal (management)	External (third party)	Auditor-generated
Susceptibility to management manipulation	HIGH	MEDIUM	LOW
Susceptibility to quality assessment by auditor	MEDIUM	LOW	HIGH
Cost to obtain	LOW	MEDIUM	HIGH
*Developed from *Hatherly* (1980) p 16.			

5.3 TYPES OF EVIDENCE

An additional way of classifying evidence to that of its source is by the type of activity undertaken by the auditor in collecting the evidence. Various approaches to obtaining evidence to support the financial statements are available to the auditor.

5.3.1 *Observation and Physical Examination*

The auditor has many opportunities during an audit to observe what is happening in a client's activities, for example the operation of control systems, the nature of the business and the condition of its assets. These observations can provide valuable, if somewhat informal and unsystematic, evidence. Although it is rarely sufficient by itself, observation can provide evidence of matters worth additional audit investigation.

Of more direct importance in testing specific financial quantities, the auditor may confirm the existence of an asset by physical inspection. Examples of this type of confirmation include counting stock, examining fixed assets and counting cash. Physical examination is an extremely useful means of verifying an asset's existence, but it does not necessarily provide evidence on other attributes such as ownership and valuation.

5.3.2 Documentary Testing

A considerable proportion of the evidence process in most audits involves substantiating information contained in the financial statements with reference to other documentary evidence and records. The amounts in the financial statements will be confirmed to the underlying accounting records and the validity of those records will be tested with reference to source documents. For example, in confirming the figure shown for turnover, the auditor will check its agreement with the sales records and these records will in turn be confirmed against invoices, delivery notes and orders. Other records such as fixed asset registers or documents such as suppliers' price lists may also be used for particular tests. The records and documents used may also extend beyond the period covered by the audit. For example, documentary evidence of payment by a customer after the end of the accounting period may be used as evidence of the validity of an amount included in the balance sheet total for debtors.

5.3.3 Reperformance

A particular type of test which the auditor may apply to documentary evidence is the reperformance of some part of the processing relating to a transaction or account balance. For example, the auditor might reperform the pricing and check the mathematical accuracy of a sales invoice or recompute the depreciation calculations on fixed assets. This type of evidence is very objective but is also very narrow in scope as it relies on the validity of the source data used in the reperformance.

All of the above steps rely primarily on evidence which is available within the organisation itself prior to the auditor's investigation. In contrast, certain evidence steps involve the auditor in the creation of new material for use in the evidence process.

5.3.4 Enquiry and Confirmation

At various stages of the audit the auditor will make requests for information which is not already available in documentary form. At one level the auditor may make enquiries of the management and staff of the client, for example concerning the structure and operation of internal controls or seeking explanations for particular matters arising from the audit work. Much of this information will be provided orally rather than in documentary form but the auditor may wish to formalise the evidence, for example through completing a questionnaire concerning internal control and by requesting that management representations should be provided in written form.

Evidence in the form of written confirmations may also be requested from parties external to the organisation being audited. The most common example of this is where the auditor circularises a sample of the client's customers to confirm the amount of the recorded outstanding debt at the end of the accounting period. The procedures followed in obtaining such evidence must be controlled; for example the auditor should mail the requests to third parties and ensure that responses are received directly rather than via the client if the reliability of this evidence is to be protected.

5.3.5 Analytical Procedures

A final, and increasingly important, form of evidence is the use of analytical techniques as a means of confirming the validity of information in the financial statements. This type of evidence procedure depends on the investigation of the relationships between different components of the financial statements, or between the financial statements and other external variables. At its simplest and most informal this process might involve reviewing the accounts for whether the figures seem reasonable given the auditor's knowledge of the client's activities; at its most sophisticated it involves modelling the factors underlying the financial statements in order to obtain predictions which can be compared to the actual reported figures. Normally, analytical procedures are limited to comparisons of ratios and other relationships, for example the gross margin in the current year with that in previous years, but even this analysis involves an assumption that past figures are a good model or predictor for current relationships. As a form of evidence, analytical procedures rely on inference, that 'reasonable' relationships indicate the absence of error, rather than direct substantiation. A difficulty with analytical procedures is determining how far relationships can fluctuate before that inference is questioned, in other words defining what constitutes an 'error'.

Analytical procedures have been used by auditors for many years, but mainly in the context of an overall review of financial statements. Recently there has been a growing emphasis on their use as a direct evidence source. They may be relied upon exclusively in some relatively immaterial areas of the accounts but the main growth in their use is as a means of reducing the extent of other detailed testing.

5.4 DESIRED QUALITIES OF AUDIT EVIDENCE

The overriding general qualities for audit evidence which can be identified in the Auditor's Operational Standard quoted earlier are the relevance and reliability, which together may be thought of as the competence, of evidence and its sufficiency. The notion of competence concerns the degree to which evidence can be considered worthy of trust for a particular purpose. It combines the characteristics of relevance, reliability and objectivity which are described below. The sufficiency of evidence relates to the amount of evidence collected by the auditor and involves considerations of the comprehensiveness and conclusiveness of evidence. The sufficiency of audit evidence is one of the most difficult issues facing the auditor and is fundamental to the planning and execution of the entire audit.

5.4.1 Relevance

Evidence must be pertinent to, or relevant to, the objective the auditor is pursuing. It is important that evidence not only relates to the subject of a particular test but is also directly useful for the conclusions the auditor intends to draw. For example, checking from a sample of suppliers' invoices to goods received notes will be relevant to an assessment of the validity of the liabilities being tested, but will not allow any conclusions about their completeness.

5.4.2 Reliability

The reliability of evidence will be dependent on the particular circumstance of the audit. Some general guidelines on the factors which will influence reliability are:

- Oral vs documentary evidence
  Documentary evidence usually is more reliable than oral evidence. For example, written confirmation of a debt, obtained from a customer, is, in general, more reliable evidence than simply talking to the customer by telephone, and a signed contract is more reliable evidence than an oral representation as to the terms of the agreement.

  Oral evidence is often useful as a supplement to documentary evidence. In some areas, such as bad debt reserves and inventory obsolescence, little or no documentary evidence may be available. In those cases, the auditor must find other sources of evidence such as preparing his or her own analysis supplemented by discussion of relevant factors with the client, comparison of results to the client's figures and consideration of the reasons for any differences.

● *Direct personal knowledge*
Evidence of which the auditor has direct personal knowledge through examination, observation, computation, and inspection generally is more reliable than evidence obtained from others, because the conditions under which it is produced are under the auditor's control. For example, observing a stock count is more reliable than receiving a report from a public warehouse.

● *Independence of source*
In general, evidence obtained from independent sources outside an entity provides greater assurance of reliability than evidence obtained solely from within the entity. For example, a confirmation from a customer provides more reliable evidence of the amount due from the customer than the amount shown on an internally-generated invoice. In addition, management representations are not, by their nature, independent and therefore should not be relied on as a substitute for other available forms of evidence.

● *Qualifications of source*
The auditor should always consider whether the source of the information is someone qualified to be providing it. For example, answers to questions about a change in pension expense from the personnel and benefits department are usually more reliable than answers to similar questions from persons not working in that department. Whether the auditor's own expertise is sufficient to generate reliable evidence in particular situations must also be considered.

5.4.3 *Objectivity*

Evidence which relies on a significant degree of subjective judgement for its interpretation and evaluation is less reliable than that which is capable of replication and confirmation by others.

5.4.4 *Conclusiveness*

The auditor must evaluate whether evidence which has been obtained is conclusive enough on its own to warrant the conclusion the auditor is trying to establish or whether additional evidence is required to support it. The interrelationships between evidence collected at different points should be recognised to ensure that more evidence than is necessary is not collected, incurring unwarranted costs, but equally care must be taken to avoid placing too much reliance on a single piece of evidence.

In most cases, the auditor must rely on evidence that is persuasive rather than conclusive. For example, economic constraints mean that not every transaction can be verified and there is therefore a risk that some errors will be undetected. Even if it were cost-effective to test every transaction recorded by a client, there would still be some audit risk because there might be concealed transactions, audit procedures might be incorrectly applied or their results misinterpreted, and documents might be altered or forged.

5.4.5 *Comprehensiveness*

As far as possible the evidence collected in an audit should provide comprehensive coverage of all significant aspects of the financial statements. This will mean that all areas subject to the possibility of material error will have to be supported by appropriate evidence and also, in terms of income statement quantities, that evidence in one form or another is available for as much of the period concerned as possible.

The auditor is concerned with both the competence and the sufficiency of evidence. Together these qualities represent the overall persuasiveness of evidence. The need for competence will influence the type of approach and procedures chosen while the need for sufficiency will affect the extent or quality of work planned.

5.4.6 *Efficiency*

A further quality which will be relevant to the collection of evidence in practice is the relative efficiency, or cost effectiveness, of different alternative procedures and types of evidence. The auditor will therefore have to consider such questions as:

- Is the least time-consuming source being used where alternative sources of evidence are available? Generally, the most efficient test should be chosen, all other factors being equal. However, a satisfactory blend of evidence from various sources is sometimes needed even if gathering the additional evidence requires additional time. For example, even after testing the build-up of stock costs through detailed records the auditor might compare significant unit costs to those of previous years and obtain explanations for unexpected variances.

- Will the greatest possible use be made of the evidence collected? A single test may be used to support conclusions in more than one area. For example, checking income from investments not only provides evidence that income is properly stated, but also provides some supporting evidence of the existence and title to the asset.

- Will the evidence be too detailed? For example, an analysis may be sufficient for audit purposes if amounts were calculated to the nearest thousand units of currency, rather than to exact sum.

5.5   PROBLEMS IN USING AUDIT EVIDENCE

A number of problems can arise in practice in satisfying the desired qualities which have just been described for audit evidence.

5.5.1 *Availability*

One of the most obvious problems is simply the availability of evidence. This includes the difficulties which arise if the records of a business are incomplete, but also refers to the constraints of time and cost within which the auditor works. The need to obtain evidence within a reasonable time and at reasonable cost may mean that certain possible approaches to collecting evidence may have to be omitted or that the comprehensiveness of the evidence that is collected is limited.

5.5.2 *Quantity v Quality*

As has already been pointed out, the evidence which is most easily available, internally produced information, is not that of the highest possible quality, as it is subject to the possibility of management manipulation. The auditor must ensure that the appropriate balance of evidence is collected for the objectives being followed.

5.5.3 *Inappropriate Reliance*

A number of problems can arise with the ways in which audit evidence is used, or the reliance that is placed upon it. First there is the possibility that the auditor may simply misinterpret the evidence, possibly because of limitations in expertise or possibly because of prior held beliefs about the organisation which influence the way the auditor reads the evidence collected. Second, as noted earlier, there is a problem that very little audit evidence is conclusive in an absolute sense of proving or disproving something. Rather, most information collected through the audit process is persuasive. There is a danger of evidence being treated as more conclusive than it actually is. In addition there is the possibility that the auditor may draw unwarranted inferences from available information, for example about some parameter of a financial quantity to which the information does not directly relate.

5.5.4 *Aggregation*

Much of the audit evidence process involves disaggregation of the financial statements and audit objectives and tasks into successively lower levels of detail. When the resulting audit programme has been carried out there may be a problem in trying to aggregate the evidence collected from different procedures and in testing different financial statement quantities into conclusions about particular objectives and ultimately into an overall audit opinion.

5.6 AUDIT OBJECTIVES

Having looked at the general sources, types and qualitative characteristics of evidence, it is also important to be aware of the particular objectives which the auditor must apply in designing his or her evidence procedures on a particular assignment.

While the overall audit objective is to form an opinion on the truth and fairness of the financial statements, this must be translated into more operational objectives to determine actual audit work. Most of the work done in forming an opinion on the financial statements consists of obtaining and evaluating evidence concerning *assertions* in the financial statements.

Assertions may be thought of as the management representations that are embodied in the financial statement components or as assumptions or expectations about the quality of financial information. They can be either explicit or implicit, and can be classified according to the following broad categories:

● existence or occurrence

● completeness

● rights and obligations

● valuation and allocation

● presentation and disclosure.

5.6.1 *Existence or occurrence*

The recorded assets and liabilities should actually exist at the date of the financial statements and recorded transactions should have actually occurred during the period covered. For example stocks of finished goods in the balance sheet should be available for sale, and turnover in the profit and loss account should represent the exchange of goods or services with customers for cash or other consideration.

5.6.2 *Completeness*

Completeness implies that all transactions and accounts that should be presented in the financial statements are so included. For example accrued liabilities in the balance sheet include all such obligations of the entity and all incurred expenses should be recorded and included in the financial statements.

5.6.3 *Rights and obligations*

The recorded assets represent the rights of the entity and recorded liabilities are the obligations of the entity at the date of the financial statements. For example, it is implied that amounts capitalised for leases in the balance sheet represent the cost of the entity's rights to leased property and that the corresponding lease liability represents an obligation of the entity.

5.6.4 *Valuation and allocation*

It is expected that all items are presented in the financial statements at appropriate amounts, for example that plant and machinery are recorded at historical cost and that such cost is systematically allocated by means of depreciation charges over appropriate accounting periods, and that debtors included in the balance sheet are stated at net realisable value.

5.6.5 *Presentation and disclosure*

All financial statement items should be properly classified, described, and disclosed. For example, it is implied that obligations classified as long-term liabilities in the balance sheet will not mature within one year and that amounts presented as extraordinary items in the profit and loss account are properly classified and described.

Audit procedures and tests are designed to meet the audit objectives. However, there is not a one-to-one relationship between audit objectives and audit tests. Certain audit tests may achieve more than one audit objective and, conversely, a combination of audit tests may be needed to achieve another objective. The design of audit tests should take account of the likelihood, or risk, of material error relating to each of the audit objectives, the nature of the account balance or class of transactions being tested, the competence of available evidence and the expected effectiveness and efficiency of intended procedures.

5.7 THE AUDIT PROCESS

Figure 5.1 shows how the various aspects of evidence which have been discussed so far in this chapter relate to the individual audit. A variety of types of evidence generated from a number of different sources are available. The auditor has certain objectives for the audit and in order to determine how to satisfy these will evaluate the evidence possibilities with reference to certain characteristics or desired qualities.

Figure 5.1 Evidence in the Audit Process

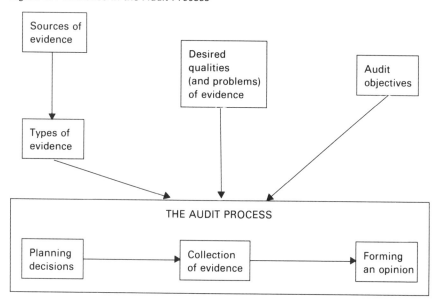

In order to meet the objectives of the audit and determine whether the assertions in the financial statements are valid, the auditor must undertake a process of collecting and evaluating evidence. This process should follow a defined methodology which will ensure that the evidence collected meets the criteria of competence and sufficiency described earlier, and that the process is efficient. It involves three main activities or stages, which are shown in Figure 5.1 — planning, collecting evidence and forming an audit opinion. These three stages are described briefly in the remainder of this chapter and are discussed in more detail in Part 2 of this book.

5.8 PLANNING

An audit can be carried out in a variety of ways and there are therefore a number of decisions, judgements and choices which must be made before embarking on the process of collecting evidence. The main elements in audit planning are outlined below:

5.8.1 *Understanding the Business*

In order to both plan the audit in an adequate way and interpret evidence collected through audit procedures, the auditor must have an understanding of the nature of the client's business and its industrial context. For example the approach required for a manufacturing company will differ from that which is appropriate in a financial services organisation and interpretation of the factors which are significant for a company which is a major importer and exporter will differ from those relevant to a company with a largely domestic market.

Understanding of the business will also be relevant to the evaluation of inherent risk and the identification of high risk areas which require particular attention in the evidence process. It is therefore critical to the planning of an effective and efficient audit.

5.8.2 *Assessing Risk and Materiality*

The twin concepts of audit risk and materiality provide the parameters for audit evidence collection and ultimately for the audit report. Materiality refers to the notion that the auditor is not attempting to confirm the precise accuracy of the financial statements but rather that they are free from material error, that is error which would affect the picture gained by a user and which could potentially affect decisions taken on the basis of the financial statements.

The related concept of risk derives from the fact that the auditor cannot guarantee with certainty the absence of material error. For example, much audit evidence is based on tests of samples of items only. There is therefore a possibility, or risk, that material error is present even when it has not been revealed by audit procedures.

Overall audit risk can be defined as the product of three separate risks:

Inherent Risk (IR)   — the probability of material error in the financial statements before the operation of internal control procedures;

Control Risk (CR)   — the probability that material error in the financial statements will not be prevented or detected by the internal control system;

Detection Risk (DR)   — the probability that audit procedures will fail to detect material error in the financial statements;

Overall Audit Risk (AR) — the probability that the financial statements contain material error although the audit has been completed and an unqualified opinion issued.

$$AR = IR \times CR \times DR$$

Each of these components of risk should be considered, although in practice the distinction between the assessment of inherent and control risk may often be blurred.

The auditor should determine both the level of error which can be tolerated without undermining the financial statements, or materiality, and the level of risk that he or she is prepared to accept that undetected material error is present. These parameters are critical influences on the amount and nature of evidence that will have to be collected to support the audit opinion. Because of their impact on the amount of evidence required, risk and materiality interact with a further parameter, that of audit cost. For a given amount of evidence, the auditor can reduce audit risk by increasing the amount of error which can be tolerated before being considered material, or reduce the definition of what is material and accept a greater audit risk. The only way of both reducing risk and specifying a lower materiality is by collecting more evidence and thus incurring additional audit costs.

5.8.3 *Understanding and Evaluating Internal Control*

The system of internal controls and accounting processing will influence the type of evidence available to the auditor and the reliability of information before it has been audited. This system provides the basis for the auditor's evaluation of control risk. In addition to the existence of specific detailed controls which apply to individual transactions, the auditor will also be concerned with assessing the general control environment within which accounting recording and financial reporting occurs. This involves the overall approach to control established by management, for example their operating style, attitude to financial reporting, monitoring of business risks and ability to supervise overall company activities.

The Auditing Guideline 'Internal Controls' (APC, 1980b) adopts a broad definition covering all forms of controls, although normally the audit will be most concerned with the accounting functions:

> 'The whole system of controls financial and otherwise, established by the management in order to carry on the business of the enterprise in an orderly and efficient manner, ensure adherence to management policies, safeguard the assets and secure as far as possible the completeness and accuracy of the records.'

In order to plan the audit properly, the auditor must understand how transactions and information are processed and controlled within the organisation. The necessity of this understanding is recognised in the Auditor's Operational Standard, which states:

> 'The auditor should ascertain the enterprise's system of recording and processing transactions and assess its adequacy as a basis for the preparation of financial statements.' (APC, 1980a)

Ascertaining the system may involve discussions with client personnel, flowcharting document flows, observation of activities, inspection of manuals and completion of control questionnaires. With this information the auditor can then assess the strength of internal controls to prevent or detect error, that is determine the control risks referred to earlier. A strong control system will mean a low level of control risk and reduce the amount of audit evidence to be collected subsequently.

5.8.4 *Determining Audit Approach and Procedures*

The next planning decision which must be addressed is the choice of audit approach to be followed in the evidence collection process, that is where the assurance required for the audit opinion is to be drawn from. The main strategic choice concerns whether to place reliance on the operation of the internal control system as evidence of the validity of the resultant information or whether to rely solely on direct substantiation of the quantities in the financial statements. Reliance on internal control will reduce but not entirely remove the need for substantive evidence.

At a more detailed level, the audit approach adopted must be developed into a programme of audit tests and other procedures, both compliance and substantive, which will be undertaken. The audit programme is the final product of the planning process.

5.8.5 *Segmenting the Audit Process*

In order to develop a strategy to meet the audit objectives, assess risks and create a detailed audit programme, it will be necessary to divide the financial statements into smaller segments. In this sense the audit involves a process of disaggregation in order to determine the appropriate evidence which should be collected and specify the tests to be carried out.

One approach to segmentation is to approach each balance in the financial statement independently. To do so, however, ignores the obvious interdependencies which exist between different balances. It is therefore more common to structure the audit around certain transaction cycles through which related transactions and account balances can be audited. For example, sales, debtors and receipts form one cycle and it may be efficient to devise tests which recognise the relationships between these items.

The appropriate cycles may vary from client to client, but normally the principal cycles around which audit programmes will be developed will be:

- Sales, debtors and receipts
- Purchases, creditors and payments
- Stock and production
- Payroll
- Financing

5.9 COLLECTION OF EVIDENCE

The second major stage in the audit evidence process is the execution of the programmes resulting from audit planning. Two main components can be identified within his collection of evidence.

5.9.1 *Tests of Controls*

Where, following the assessment of the internal control system and control risk, a decision has been taken to rely on internal controls, then evidence must be collected that the controls have in fact operated in a manner which warrants the intended reliance. These tests are normally referred to as 'compliance tests' because the object of the audit procedure is to establish that internal control procedures valued by the auditor are being applied as prescribed.

5.9.2 *Substantive Testing*

In contrast, substantive evidence is collected through direct testing of the completeness, quantitative accuracy and validity of transactions or balances recorded in the accounting records and financial statements. The object of substantive tests is to provide direct evidence relating to particular assertions about balances in the financial statements or classes of transactions. They may include tests of details, for example third party confirmation, physical observation, documentary confirmation and recomputation, and analytical procedures where evidence is drawn from the relationships between account balances. Substantive testing may be applied to individual account balances or to transactions streams.

As noted earlier, tests of controls may give the auditor confidence which allows a reduction in the amount of substantive testing considered necessary but some of the latter will always be required on each audit engagement. After compliance testing has been completed, the results should be reviewed and if necessary the amount of substantive testing adjusted to reflect the confidence which can be taken from these results in comparison to that intended or anticipated when the audit programmes were originally planned.

5.10 FORMING AN OPINION

The final stage of an audit involves forming and reporting an opinion on the overall financial statements.

5.10.1 *Aggregating Evidence*

Evidence collection involves a process of disaggregation whereby the overall audit objective is split into separate objectives and assertions and the financial statements divided into smaller segments for testing. In order to complete the process, the auditor must therefore aggregate the results of different procedures and the individual pieces of evidence obtained into an overall conclusion. In practice this combination of evidence goes on throughout the audit. One aspect is the maintenance of a record of all errors discovered during the audit in order that their aggregate effect on the acceptability of the financial statements can be evaluated. Evidence aggregation is often a very subjective and judgemental process as it involves relating to each other the results of different procedures, possibly carried out at different times, in different areas of the accounts.

5.10.2 *Overall Review of the Financial Statements*

One specific procedure which will be carried out before an audit opinion is finalised is an overall review of the picture presented in the financial statements of the enterprise's activities and state of affairs. This review may involve similar procedures to those employed when using analytical tests as evidence to support individual balances but the objectives at this stage of the audit are different. They are to ensure that the financial statements meet the relevant standards for presentation and disclosure of information and that they are compatible with the auditor's knowledge of the client's business.

5.10.3 *Deciding an Opinion*

When all completion procedures have been carried out the auditor must decide an opinion to express his or her subjective judgement of the truth and fairness of the information in the financial statements. This opinion is communicated in the audit report issued with the company's annual report and accounts. The requirements for and influences on audit reports are discussed in more detail in the following chapter.

5.11 SUMMARY

Auditing relies upon evidence. In this chapter the nature of audit evidence has been discussed by looking at the various sources of evidence, the types of activity through which the auditor generates evidence, the kind of qualities that evidence should possess to satisfy audit purposes and problems that arise in making use of evidence.

For the collection of evidence to be properly structured and effective it is also important to specify clearly the objectives being pursued and in particular the assertions present in the financial information which the audit is trying to validate. The audit evidence process itself consists of three main stages: planning, the actual collection of audit evidence and the forming of an opinion. Each of these stages has been introduced only briefly in this chapter but the various steps, procedures and components they involve are described in more detail in Part 2.

CHAPTER 6   REPORTING AN AUDIT OPINION

6.1   INTRODUCTION

In order to fulfil the responsibilities recognised in company law, the auditor must make a report to shareholders to accompany the published financial statements. This report communicates the auditor's opinion on the quality of the information in the financial statements. It expresses his or her expert judgement on the basis of the results of the work undertaken in the audit.

At present in the United Kingdom, the structure and content of audit reports are governed by certain standards and conventions. In the latter part of this chapter the way in which these rules apply to the development of an audit report on a limited company is described. Before looking at this aspect of current practice, however, some more general considerations are examined which are relevant to interpreting and understanding the nature of the auditor's reporting function.

6.2   OBJECTIVES OF AUDIT REPORTING

The overall objective of an audit report is to communicate in a meaningful way with those with a legitimate interest in the results of the audit. Its intention is to indicate the type of assurance concerning the financial statements the auditor feels is warranted based on the evidence obtained. If an audit report communicates something which is not warranted this could have serious consequences for those who place reliance on the audit opinion when making decisions. It is therefore desirable that audit reports should be:

- complete and explicit, that is they should not omit or simply imply something the auditor should be communicating; and

- clear, understandable and unambiguous, that is they should be capable of interpretation by the reader if the intended communication is to be achieved.

Achieving meaningful communication in practice is complicated by a number of major problems:

- The audit itself is a complex process, involving the collection of large quantities of evidence and information, some of which may be conflicting. The audit report can communicate only a simplified and limited amount of the understanding of the organisation that the auditor obtains.

- It is often unclear exactly who the readers and users of the financial statements and audit report will be, and what level of technical understanding they will have. While the audit report is addressed to shareholders, it is clear that it also acquires the status of public information. There is therefore a problem in deciding how technically complex or simple audit reports should be.

- The audit report expresses the professional judgement of the auditor on the quality of the financial statements. For this judgement to be properly interpreted, it is important that the criteria against which it has been formed are properly understood and accepted by those reading the audit report.

The way in which audit reports are worded attempts to meet these problems of what level of detail to communicate, who it is assumed the report is communicating with and how the information can be made understandable and capable of interpretation by those readers.

6.3 A JUDGEMENTAL OPINION

It is important to recognise that what the audit report contains is the auditor's *opinion* on the quality of the financial statements. This opinion, which is required by the Companies Act 1985, is the result of auditor's judgement of the evidence and information collected to support the examination of the accounts.

As we have seen in the last chapter, dealing with audit evidence, the audit is carried out within certain limits of risk and materiality, or the probability that the financial statements could contain significant error even after completion of the audit. Thus the audit report should not be interpreted as a guarantee of the accuracy of the financial statements nor as a statement of fact. As an opinion, it is a statement of personal belief about the financial statements, made within certain boundaries of possible inaccuracy or error, although these boundaries are not themselves recognised explicitly in the audit report. The fact that the auditor is reponsible for an opinion, based on judgements about available evidence, should influence the circumstances in which an audit could be considered negligent in fulfilling this responsibility.

6.4 READERSHIP OF AUDIT REPORTS

Studies of the readership of company annual reports and accounts have tended to find that the audit report is regarded as the least important of the various documents, such as chairman's statement, directors' report and the financial statements, included in the annual report, and that those who do read it tend to do so 'briefly for interest' or simply check that it is there. This finding does not mean that the audit itself is not valued or the audit report is not relied upon by users of accounts. Rather, it reflects the fact that the normal form of audit report contains little new information and simply confirms what has already been anticipated by users. A reaction to an audit report might only be expected where it contains some new unanticipated information, and there is some evidence to suggest that the presence of an audit qualification can influence the decisions of some users, although obviously it is difficult to test in actual situations how decisions would have differed if a qualified report had not been given.

It is possible that audit reports are read as standardised signals. If users do react to audit reports in this way then they will equate a report with whatever level of assurance they perceive that particular signal to mean, whether or not it is explicitly stated in the report or even intended by the auditor. To return to an earlier point, it is therefore important that audit reports are constructed in a manner which attempts to ensure that the signals taken from a report are those intended, in other words that the report is complete, unambiguous and understandable.

6.5 STANDARDISED REPORTS

For the company auditor, the basic requirement to report is found in the Companies Act 1985 which specifies that the auditor must state whether, in his or her opinion, the balance sheet and profit and loss account have been prepared in accordance with the provisions of the Act, and whether they present a true and fair view of the state of affairs of the company at the balance sheet date and its profit or loss for the period up to that date.

The accounting profession has developed a set of standardised audit reports for use in meeting this requirement. Audit reports therefore follow a very codified framework which is intended to ensure that similar circumstances are reported in a uniform way. This framework is described in more detail below.

Some have argued that the use of standardised wording conditions users to treat audit reports as codified symbols and is the reason that they are regarded as uninformative. This view suggests that free form non-standardised wording would promote readership and enhance the value of reports. However, while a 'unique' report for each audit client might be read with more interest and thus avoid the problem of reports being treated as codified symbols, this does not mean that it would be more effective as a means of communication. It is possible that the difficulty of understanding and the danger of misinterpretation would be greater with a free form report than with consistent standardised messages.

Thus the problem may not be the use of codified reports but rather whether the particular codes employed are well understood by report readers. The degree of consistency between the auditor's intended message and the user's interpretation of the report will depend on the user's knowledge of the coding system used. At present, for example, the nature and purpose of qualified audit reports and the technical distinction between different types of qualifications and between a qualification and an 'emphasis of matter' may not be appreciated by users of accounts. Indeed auditors have been criticised for the technicality and understandability of the language used. The Department of Trade Inspectors in the investigation of Peachey Properties expressed the view the the audit report used 'hieratic' language, which they defined as 'language which is neither comprehensible as ordinary speech nor adequately defined to a specialist.'

6.6 THE ELEMENTS OF THE AUDIT REPORT

Having discussed some of the general objectives and considerations which are relevant to the use of the audit report as the main vehicle for the auditor to communicate the results of the audit to groups external to the management, the remainder of this chapter is devoted to outlining the form and content of audit reports in accordance with professional recommendations in the United Kingdom. An audit report should contain a number of basic components, which may be considered under four headings:

6.6.1 *The formal lines of communication*

The report should identify the name of the person or people to whom it is addressed, which in the case of a limited company will be the shareholders, or 'members'. The fact that shareholders are the stated recipients, in line with the auditor's legal responsibility, does not, however, preclude the possibility of other users. The report should be titled, it should give the name of the auditor, and if appropriate the location of the office within the audit firm, and it should indicate the date it is signed. Once the regulatory structure introduced by the Companies Act 1989 is in place, those signing audit reports are likely to be required to use the designation 'registered auditor.'

6.6.2 *The scope of the report*

The financial statements which are the subject matter of the audit should be clearly identified. This will normally be done by referring simply to the pages of the annual report which contain the financial statements. They will include the balance sheet, profit and loss account, funds statement, statement of accounting policies and the notes to the accounts.

6.6.3 *The basis of the auditor's opinion*

The report should refer to the basis on which the opinion has been formed. At present this is limited simply to a statement that an audit has been carried out in accordance with the relevant auditing standards. This statement does not give any clue as to what these standards require and therefore what the audit has involved, but it is intended to give a signal that the audit methods which have been used are consistent with what the accounting profession currently recognises as good practice.

6.6.4 *The content of the opinion*

The final, and most important, component of the audit report is the opinion itself. This should be expressed in terms of established criteria. The criteria which are relevant for an opinion in the context of a statutory audit of a limited company are compliance with statute and truth and fairness:

(i) Compliance with statute.
The audit report must indicate an opinion on whether the accounts have been prepared in accordance with the requirements of the Companies Act 1985. The Act specifies the formats for the balance sheet and profit and loss account which are permissible, detailed requirements for the disclosure of specific information and certain rules on the accounting principles which can be applied in measurements and valuation.

(ii) A true and fair view.
The main criterion which the auditor must apply in forming an audit opinion is the notion of a 'true and fair view.' A company's financial statements must satisfy this standard of truth and fairness. The concept is not defined in the Companies Act, however, and so forming an opinion on a true and fair view is one of the most difficult and judgemental aspects of the auditor's responsibilities.

(iii) Other reporting responsibilities
Compliance with the Companies Act 1985 and the concept of truth and fairness are the main criteria that the auditor makes positive reference to in the audit report. Other less dominant criteria also apply as a result of additional responsibilities placed on the auditor to report negatively if these other criteria are not met. These relate to the general context within which the financial statements are prepared and reported—whether proper books of account and other records have been maintained, ie the basis for reporting; whether the financial statements are in agreement with those books and records; and whether there is any inconsistency between the financial statements and information in the directors' report. Additionally, the auditor has a professional responsibility to report any instances of non-compliance of the financial statements with the accouting standards developed by the accounting profession.

An example of an unqualified audit report incorporating the features described above is shown in Table 6.1

Table 6.1 Unqualified Audit Report Example

AUDITOR'S REPORT TO THE MEMBERS OF XYZ PLC
We have audited the financial statements on pages ... to ... in accordance with Auditing Standards.
In our opinion, the financial statements give a true and fair view of the state of the company's affairs at 31 December 19XY and of its profit and source and application of funds for the year then ended, and have been properly prepared in accordance with the Companies Acts.
ABC
Chartered Accountants and Registered Auditors*
London
31 March 19XZ
* The use of this designation is likely to be required when the 1989 Companies Act becomes effective.

6.7 TRUTH AND FAIRNESS

Given the importance of the true and fair concept to the auditor, it may be helpful to consider its application to company financial reporting in more detail.

6.7.1 *The Meaning of True and Fair*

Ultimately whether a particular set of financial statements provides the required truth and fairness will depend on the circumstances of the particular situation. While the concept is now deeply ingrained in the training and approach of the UK accounting profession, it is debatable whether having such in ill-defined and flexible concept as the main standard of corporate reporting is a good thing or a bad thing. Certainly, if there is to be consistency in audit reporting, auditors must apply some common understanding of what is necessary for a true and fair view, even in the absence of a universally accepted definition. *Lee* (1986) attempts to explain and define true and fair as separate qualities in terms of, respectively, the correspondance of information to the underlying activities or position being represented and its objectivity:

> '*True* means that the accounting information contained in the financial statements has been quantified and communicated in such a way as to correspond to the economic events, activities and transactions it is intended to describe.'

> '*Fair* means that the accounting information has been measured and disclosed in a manner which is objective and without prejudice to any particular sectional interests in the company.' (page 50)

Others prefer to regard true and fair as a single overall quality perhaps related to notions of 'not materially mistated' or 'not misleading', which is more difficult to define. Ultimately as the true and fair view is a legal requirement, its meaning is a question of law. However, it has never been authoritatively decided in a judgement in the courts. Indeed, in a legal opinion on true and fair obtained by the Accounting Standards Committee in 1983, it was argued that while the *meaning* of the legal concept is unchanging its *content*, ie what is required to show a true and fair view, will change over time, and that:

> 'Accounts will not be true and fair unless the information they contain is sufficient in quantity and quality to satisfy the reasonable expectation of the readers to whom they are addressed.' *(Hoffman and Arden*, 1983).

One implication of the idea of truth and fairness is that absolute accuracy is not taken as the objective for reporting. Consequent on this, the auditor's judgement on the financial statements will be influenced by the concept of materiality.

6.7.2 *An Overriding Requirement*

The legal requirement for accounts to show a true and fair view overrides the individual detailed accounting provisions contained in company law. Under the Companies Act 1985, this flexibility was available only where the conflict with the detailed provisions could not be resolved by additional disclosure. The 1989 Companies Act has relaxed this limitation on the true and fair override to permit departure from detailed requirements 'to the extent necessary' to give a true and fair view.

6.7.3 *Establishing Truth and Fairness*

In order to establish whether a set of financial statements gives a true and fair view, the auditor must rely on a mixture of factual support for the accounting data and subjective judgment of the suitability of the reporting policies applied by the company. The auditor must:

- collect evidence about the business and its transactions both to support the values contained in individual account balances and to evaluate overall truth and fairness;

- make a judgment regarding the degree of potential error which can be tolerated without prejudicing the true and fair view, that is decide on a level of materiality;

- establish that the accounting policies used in the preparation of the accounts are in agreement with generally accepted accounting principles, do not contravene basic accounting concepts and have been properly and consistently applied;

- confirm that the financial statements disclose all information which is necessary to represent a true and fair view.

6.7.4   *The Influence of Accounting Standards*

The difficult judgements in forming an audit opinion often relate not so much to the facts of underlying transactions and events as to the more subjective choice of policies which govern the way these phenomena are represented. Statements of Standard Accounting Practice (SSAPs) provide assistance to the auditor to determine whether such policies are acceptable, and also try and persuade management to adopt particular accounting treatments.

When SSAPs were first introduced the intention was to provide 'a definitive approach . . . to a true and fair view' and the Accounting Standards Committee's policy is to develop standards for application to all accounts intended to show a true and fair view. Members of the accounting profession have an obligation to ensure that SSAPs are followed and, when acting as auditors, are required to report any situations where an accounting standard has been departed from without their agreement and to quantify the effect of the departure.

Prior to the Companies Act 1989, accounting standards did not have any formal legal status with respect to true and fair. However, a judical view had been expressed (in the case of *Lloyd Cheyham v Littlejohn* [1985] BCLC) that the court would regard them as very strong evidence as to the proper standards that should be adopted in accounts, such that an unjustified departure would be regarded as a breach of duty. The 1989 Act introduced a requirement for accounts to include a statement on compliance with applicable standards, giving particulars, with reasons, for any material departures.

6.8   TYPES OF OPINION

The wording of audit reports is governed by a limited number of standard types of opinion. There are four categories of audit report that may be issued — an unqualified opinion; a qualified opinion; an adverse opinion; and a disclaimer, where no opinion is expressed.

6.8.1   *Unqualified opinions*

An unqualified opinion, which is also sometimes described as a 'clean' report, will be issued by the auditor in those cases where he or she is satisfied that in all material respects:

- the financial statements have been prepared using acceptable accounting policies, consistently applied;

- the financial information complies with relevant regulations and statutory requirements;

- the view presented by the financial statements is consistent with the knowledge of the business acquired during the audit;

- there is adequate disclosure of all material matters relevant to the proper presentation of the financial statements.

There may in certain circumstances be a need to draw attention to items or policies within the financial statements where the accounting or reporting treatment is, although not in dispute, of significant importance in understanding the financial statements as a whole. Such emphasis of matter does not constitute a qualification of the auditor's opinion.

6.8.2 *Reports giving other than an unqualified opinion*

The circumstances that may lead to a report containing other than an unqualified opinion being issued include:

- limitations on scope — where due to a limitation of the scope of the audit the auditor is unable to gather sufficient evidence to support an item in the financial statements (for instance, where the appointment as auditor has been accepted after the date of the physical stock count).

- uncertainties — where the auditor is unable to satisfy him or herself as to the correctness of an element or elements of the financial statements (for example situations where the presentation of an item in the financial statements depends on the outcome of some future event, such as pending litigation).

- disagreements — where the auditor's conclusion, based on the audit work performed, is that the financial statements contain a material misstatement that the client does not agree to correct.

Disagreement with elements of the financial statements can refer to the appropriateness of accounting policies, the method of their application, or the adequacy of disclosure. In practical terms, disagreement over policies or their application will equate to disagreement that the results and state of affairs — as determined by management's policies — do not, in the auditor's view, present a true and fair view of the choice of enterprise's position.

6.8.3 *Material v Fundamental*

The effects of limitation on scope, uncertainties or disagreements will normally need to be material for the auditor to issue a report that is other than unqualified. However a distinction can be made between matters which, although material, are not pervasive or fundamental, and fundamental matters.

Fundamental matters are those of such significance that the auditor would not feel that a simple qualification is sufficient to indicate to the users of the financial statements the extent to which in his or her judgment those statements may be or are misleading. Table 6.2 shows the type of report that would normally be issued in the various circumstances when an unqualified report is not appropriate.

Table 6.2 Types of Audit Report

Nature of circumstances	Material but not fundamental	Fundamental
Uncertainty or scope limitation	Qualified opinion - 'subject to'	Disclaimer of opinion
Disagreement	Qualified opinion - 'except for'	Adverse opinion

- In a 'subject to' qualification, the auditor is effectively disclaiming an opinion on a part of the financial statements that is material but not fundamental.

- In an 'except for' opinion an adverse opinion is expressed on a particular item within the financial statements.

- In a disclaimer of opinion, the auditor states that he or she is unable to form an opinion on the financial statements as a whole.

- In an adverse opinion, the auditor is stating that the financial statements do not present a true and fair view of the results and state of affairs of the client.

In all circumstances the audit report should be unequivocal in making clear which type of opinion (or disclaimer) is being issued.

The decision to issue a qualified audit report is a critical one as it can affect the client's business and the auditor-client relationship. Likewise a decision not to qualify in circumstances which might be described as 'borderline' requires extreme care. Accordingly, it is common within audit firms to find procedures for consultation with a second partner or with the firm's technical department in all circumstances where a report expressing anything other than an unqualified opinion is being considered.

6.9   OTHER REPORTS

It is possible that, in addition to the main audit report, the auditor may make other reports. For example, there may be special industry or statutory requirements to report on compliance with specific regulations. The most common additional report is the 'management letter' which is produced voluntarily or by agreement between the auditor and the management rather than because of a statutory obligation.

The management letter is a means whereby the auditor can communicate observations on the business and its systems and management as well as on the financial statements at a more detailed level than the overall audit opinion. For example the auditor may comment on particular areas of internal control which could be strengthened or systems which are not working as they should and which may have caused difficulty in the conduct of the audit. The main purpose of a management letter is to provide constructive advice which will be of assistance to the client.

It is possible that in some cases management will regard this report as a more valuable output of the audit than the formal audit opinion. However, it is important to remember that a management letter is only a by-product of the audit and is not mandatory, and that the main purpose of the audit is to report to groups other than the management. A chapter giving some guidance on the structure and content of a management letter is included in Part 2.

6.10   SUMMARY

The audit report is the main, and in many cases the only opportunity that the auditor has for communicating with those outside the management of the company being audited. In that report the auditor attempts to indicate, in the form of an audit opinion, the assurance that he or she considers appropriate regarding the credibility of the information in the financial statements. Audit reports are governed by standards set by the accounting profession which codify audit opinions into a limited number of possibilities which are reported using standardised wording. These opinions express the auditor's judgement on the quality of the financial statements as measured by established criteria of compliance with legal requirements and truth and fairness.

The overall objective of an audit report is to communicate the auditor's opinion in a complete, unambiguous and understandable way. The main problems in reporting an opinion are that the readers may in fact misinterpret or misunderstand the signals which are intended in the codified framework within which auditors currently frame their opinions.

References and Further Reading

Listed below are a number of other publications on auditing. Many of these have been referred to specifically in Chapters 1 to 6. Several, however, are provided as general references which those with an interest in the issues discussed in these chapters, and in auditing theory more generally, can pursue.

Accounting Standards Steering Committee (ASSC) 1975, *The Corporate Report.*

Allan, R and W Fforde 1986, *The Auditor and Fraud,* Auditing Practices Committee.

Auditing Practices Committee (APC) 1989, 'Explanatory foreword to Auditing Standards and Guidelines (revised)', reproduced in *Auditing and Reporting*, published annually by the Insitute of Chartered Accountants in England and Wales.

APC 1980a, 'The auditor's operational standard', *Auditing and Reporting,* op cit.

APC 1980b, 'Internal controls', Auditing Guideline, *Auditing and Reporting,* op cit.

APC 1986, *APC – The first ten years.*

Buckley, R 1980, *What is an Audit?,* Auditing Practices Committee.

Carmichael, D R and J J Willingham (eds) 1986, *Perspective in Auditing,* Fourth Edition, McGraw-Hill Book Company.

Firth, M 1980, 'Perceptions of auditor independence and official ethical guidelines', *Accounting Review,* Vol. 55.

Flint, D 1988, *Philosophy and Principles of Auditing*, Macmillan.

Goldman, A and B Barlev 1974, 'The auditor-firm conflict of interests', *Accounting Review,* Vol 49.

Gwilliam, D 1987, 'The auditor, third parties and contributary negligence', *Accounting and Business Research*, Vol 18.

Gwilliam, D 1987, *A Survey of Auditing Research*, Prentice Hall/The Institute of Chartered Accountants in England and Wales.

Hatherly, DJ 1980, *The Audit Evidence Process*, Anderson Keenan Publishing.

Hoffman, L and M H Arden 1983, 'Legal opinion on true and fair', *Accountancy,* November.

Institute of Chartered Accountants in England and Wales (ICAEW) 1979, *Guide to Professional Ethics*, (and revisions).

ICAEW 1988, *Independence and Incorporation — a discussion document.*

Kent, D, M Sherer and S Turley (eds) 1985, *Current Issues in Auditing*, Harper and Row.

Lee, T A 1984, *Materiality — A review and analysis of its reporting significance and auditing implications*, Auditing Practices Committee.

Lee T A 1986, *Company Auditing*, Third Edition, Van Nostrand Reinholt.

Mautz, R K and H A Sharaf 1961, *The Philosophy of Auditing*, American Accounting Association.

Sherer, M and D Kent 1988, *Auditing and Accountability*, Paul Chapman Publishing.

Woolf, E 1984, *Legal Liabilities of Practising Accountants*, Butterworths.

Part Two
A Practical Approach to An Audit

INTRODUCTION TO PART 2

As introduced in Part 1, the auditor's main objective in the audit of financial statements is to express an opinion on the truth and fairness of those statements. In Part 2, an audit approach and framework of audit procedures are described which will allow this objective to be satisfied in an effective and efficient manner. An audit must be carried out in accordance with accepted auditing standards. The approach set out in this part is consistent with such standards, although it does not attempt to deal with all matters addressed in profesional standards covering audit engagements, and these should also be referred to in practice.

An important feature of the methodology suggested in Part 2 is that while it involves a common general approach to each audit, this approach relies upon a series of specific judgements to be made on each assignment with the aim of ensuring that the actual strategy and procedures to be performed are tailored to the particular circumstances of the audit.

In Chapter 5 the audit process was described as involving three principal stages: planning, collecting audit evidence and forming an audit opinion. Each of these stages is addressed in turn in this part. Chapters 7 to 13 give guidance on the various phases of audit planning. These chapters deal primarily with the process of obtaining an understanding of the client's business, its organisation, activities and systems, and developing first an audit strategy and, then, detailed audit plans suited to the particular circumstances of that engagement. They include guidance on establishing the terms of engagement, what an auditor needs to know about his client, evaluating audit risk and materiality, assessing the internal control structure, formulating audit strategies and documenting audit plans and programmes.

The audit plan and programmes, which are the products of the planning stage, provide a road map for use in conducting the audit. Chapters 14 to 19 focus on various aspects of the way in which audit evidence is collected and documented. In particular, these chapters deal with different types of evidence procedures (eg tests of controls and substantive tests), different types of substantive evidence (eg test of details and analytical procedures), specific areas such as auditing accounting estimates and computer-assisted audit techniques, and aspects of control of the process of collecting evidence.

The third stage of the audit involves aggregating evidence and forming an audit opinion. This is where the auditor must stand back and look at the engagement as a whole and draw together the findings of the audit to arrive at an opinion. The nature of the audit report has already been described in Chapter 6, and in this part the discussion is confined mainly to completing the evidence collection process after the main testing and detailed examination of the accounts. Chapter 20 looks at the review procedures involving post balance sheet date events and the overall review of the financial statements. Final clearance procedures, whereby the auditor confirms that all audit procedures have been completed and that there is sufficient evidence to support an audit opinion, are described in Chapter 21 and the reporting considerations associated with management letters in Chapter 22.

The remaining chapters in this part provide guidance on a number of special areas: going concern, which might have an impact on procedures at all stages of the audit, the audit of consolidated financial statements and the new audit engagement.

CHAPTER 7   PLANNING AND AUDIT OBJECTIVES

7.1   WHY THE AUDITOR MUST PLAN THE AUDIT

Planning has long been recognised in professional standards to be one of the most important aspects of the audit. It is generally accepted that the auditor should plan his work to enable him to conduct an effective audit in an efficient and timely manner and that planning should be based on a knowledge of the client's business and internal control structure. The planning should cover among other things assessing audit risk and materiality, developing an audit strategy and determining the nature, timing, and extent of the audit procedures.

Proper audit planning ensures that appropriate attention is devoted to areas of audit significance, that potential problems and sensitive areas are identified promptly, that scheduling of work at interim dates and at the year end is given appropriate consideration and that personnel are utilised properly.

The audit strategy should be tailored to the facts and circumstances of the client situation. Accordingly, factors such as the size and complexity of the client entity and the nature of its business and internal control structure will cause our audit strategy to vary from client to client. For example, the existence of an effective internal audit function coupled with oversight provided by an audit committee of a board of directors is common in large, publicly-held entities but rare indeed in small, owner-managed businesses. These factors lead to very different decisions in terms of the nature, timing and extent of the audit procedures for each type of client.

Similarly, audit planning also provides the opportunity to identify areas, outside the audit, where the client can benefit from an auditor's assistance. The knowledge obtained about the client in planning the audit will often reveal existing needs that can be addressed effectively by other professional services offered by the auditor. Some audit clients may need accounting assistance, others may need tax advice or assistance in formulating tax planning strategies, and still others may need management consulting services of one type or another.

7.2   WHO SHOULD PERFORM THE PLANNING

The primary responsibility for planning rests with the audit partner and manager. Wherever possible, depending upon the circumstances of the client and the engagement, much of the detailed work in planning should be delegated to the staff. However, the partner and manager should actively participate in the appropriate stages of planning.

7.3   SCOPE AND NATURE OF AUDIT PLANNING

The extent of planning and the degree of detail in which the plan is to be thought out and documented are matters requiring the exercise of judgement.

Audit planning should be tailored to the size, complexity, and nature of the business of the client, the audit risk, and the engagement team's experience with the client and its industry. Special circumstances (eg the client being part of a group) and business considerations (eg the client's need for non-audit services) also affect the scope and nature of planning.

Other matters which will influence planning include changes in the client's business or in the way it is conducted and the reliability and the nature of sources of information available to the auditor. A new client normally requires a more extensive planning effort than an existing client.

7.4   PHASES OF PLANNING

Audit planning is a continuous process and takes place in one form or another throughout the audit. A significant amount of planning is performed before fieldwork commences. However, new or changing circumstances, unforeseen at the initial planning stage, may cause an auditor to alter his plans.

In planning, the auditor will need to gather and analyse sufficient information about the client to enable him to develop an audit strategy, determine the detailed audit procedures, and identify and design any other services that may be rendered in addition to the audit engagement.

The planning process can be considered in terms of a number of phases.

The first phase of the process must be to determine the objectives of the engagement (this is discussed more fully below).

Subsequent planning phases typically involve:

- obtaining or updating the auditor's knowledge of the client's business and industry

- assessing audit risk and materiality

- obtaining or updating the auditor's understanding of the client's internal control structure

- carrying out preliminary analytical procedures

- considering other planning matters, such as the use of specialists

- developing an audit strategy

- scheduling the work

- communicating and documenting planning decisions

- preparing or updating audit programmes.

Each of these phases is discussed in the chapters that follow.

7.5   DETERMINING THE OBJECTIVES OF THE ENGAGEMENT

The auditor's basic audit objective is to perform sufficient audit work to enable him to express an opinion on the financial statements. He needs to obtain evidence to enable him to draw reasonable conclusions concerning the assertions in the financial statements. The concepts of detailed audit objectives and financial statement assertions have been explained in Chapter 5.

Audits are required by law for many undertakings. Apart from the audit of the limited company required by the Companies Acts, other undertakings such as building societies, charities and housing associations may require statutory audits. In such cases, the main audit objectives will be determined by the form of the audit report which the auditor will be required to issue under the relevant legislation.

Other engagement objectives may originate from requests by the client, and from obligations that the client may have to provide audited information to third parties. Such other engagement objectives might include

- reporting on the client's internal control structure or some aspect of it

- reporting to regulatory authorities

- issuing special reports, such as reports on compliance with covenants of a loan agreement, or letters to a partnership concerning the balances of and changes in partners' capital accounts

- investigating certain matters or testing certain account balances for reasons other than the audit of the client's financial statements

- providing management consulting, accounting or tax assistance, or other specific services requested by the client.

An auditor should be responsive to a client's request to increase the scope of his work to meet these other objectives. For example, if an auditor were requested to pay particular attention to executives' travel and entertainment expenses, he might need to extend his procedures in this area beyond those otherwise necessary to form his opinion on the client's financial statements. However, an auditor should never assent to a client's request that would result in doing less work than is necessary to express an audit opinion on the client's financial statements.

It is particularly important to identify all of the engagement objectives during the planning phase of the audit. The clearer an auditor's understanding is of the specific objectives, the easier it will be to design those procedures that will best achieve the objectives. For example, if an auditor is to report on the client's compliance with the specific terms of a loan agreement, he might need to extend his procedures regarding compliance with specific covenants in that loan agreement which may otherwise not have been necessary for audit purposes. No matter how important these other objectives may be, however, an auditor should never lose sight of the primary objective of any audit engagement which is to express an opinion on the client's financial statements.

7.6 ENGAGEMENT LETTERS

An engagement letter to a client documents and confirms the objective and scope of the auditor's work and the extent of the responsibilities of both the auditor and client management in connection with the audit. It is in both the auditor's interest and that of the client to have an engagement letter, as this helps in avoiding misunderstandings with respect to the engagement.

The terms of an auditor's engagement with each client should be clearly set out in an engagement letter. The form and content of the letter should be determined by the circumstances of each engagement. It could, for example, consist of a memorandum of the terms of engagement together with a covering letter. A specimen is shown in Appendix 7.1 to this chapter

On recurring audits, the auditor should consider the need to revise the engagement letter each year, particularly when there are

- revisions to the terms of the engagement

- significant changes of management

- significant changes in the nature or size of the client's business

- significant changes in the regulatory structure affecting the audit.

APPENDIX 7.1

SPECIMEN MEMORANDUM OF TERMS OF ENGAGEMENT FOR A COMPANY CLIENT

Notes

The specimen memorandum below is designed to be tailored to the circumstances of the particular engagement. Items in the memorandum which are particularly likely to require amendment or omission are italicised.

The covering letter to which the memorandum is attached should contain a paragraph requesting the client to approve the terms set out in the memorandum and to evidence this by signing a duplicate copy of the memorandum on behalf of the board.

In the case of an appointment to a group of companies where the terms of engagement are common to all, a single letter could be sent, the auditor should list all the relevant companies on the letter and memorandum. He should further request that copies of the memorandum are forwarded to the directors of all the companies concerned. Where a new subsidiary is formed or acquired, and the auditor agrees to act for the new company, he should refer to the existing group memorandum of terms of engagement in his letter accepting appointment as auditor.

MEMORANDUM OF TERMS OF ENGAGEMENT BETWEEN [AUDIT FIRM] AND [ ] LIMITED *(AND ITS UNDERMENTIONED SUBSIDIARIES)* AS REFERRED TO IN OUR LETTER OF [DATE]

The purpose of this memorandum is to set out the basis on which we act for the company *(and its subsidiaries)* and the respective areas of responsibility of the board*(s)* of *the/each* company and of ourselves.

1   AUDIT

Our responsibilities

Our responsibilities as auditors under the Companies Acts are to examine the annual financial statements of *the/each* company and to report to the members whether, in our professional opinion, the financial statements give a true and fair view of the state of the company's financial affairs as shown by the balance sheet, and of the profit or loss for the period under review as shown by the profit and loss account. We are also required to state whether the financial statements have been properly prepared in accordance with the Companies Acts.

In arriving at our opinion, we are required by the Companies Acts to consider the following matters and report on any in respect of which we are not satisfied:

(i) whether proper accounting records have been kept by the company and proper returns adequate for our audit have been received from branches not visited by us;

(ii) whether the company's balance sheet and profit and loss account are in agreement with the accounting records and returns;

(iii) whether we have obtained all the information and explanations which we consider necessary for the purposes of our audit; and

(iv) whether the information in the directors' report is consistent with that in the audited financial statements.

In addition, there are certain other matters which, according to the circumstances, may need to be dealt with in our report. For example, where the financial statements do not give full details of directors' remuneration or transactions with the company, the Companies Acts require us to disclose such matters in our report.

We also have a professional responsibility to report if the financial statements do not comply in any material respect with relevant Statements of Standard Accounting Practice, unless in our opinion non-compliance is justified in the circumstances.

Conduct of the audit

Our audit will be conducted in accordance with the Auditing Standards issued by the accountancy bodies and will have regard to relevant Auditing Guidelines. Furthermore, it will be conducted in such a manner as we consider necessary to fulfil our responsibilities and will include such tests of transactions and of the existence, ownership and valuation of assets and liabilities as we consider necessary. We shall obtain an understanding of the accounting system in order to assess its adequacy as a basis for the preparation of the financial statements and to satisfy ourselves that proper accounting records have been maintained. We shall expect to obtain such relevant and reliable evidence as we consider sufficient to enable us to draw reasonable conclusions therefrom. The nature and extent of our tests will vary according to our assessment of the company's accounting system, and where we wish to place reliance on it, the system of internal control, and may cover any aspect of the business operations. We shall report to you any significant weaknesses in, or observations on, the company's systems which come to our notice and which we think should be brought to your attention. As our audit work is designed primarily to enable us to form an opinion on the financial statements taken as a whole, our report cannot be expected to include all possible comments and recommendations that a more extensive special examination might indicate.

The Companies Act gives/You have agreed to give us a right of access to the accounting and other records of the/each company and to require from the officers of the/each company such information and explanations as we think necessary for the performance of our duties.

As part of our normal audit procedures, we may request you to provide written confirmation of certain information and explanations we receive during the course of the audit.

We shall plan our audit so that we have a reasonable expectation of detecting material misstatements in the financial statements or accounting records resulting from irregularities and fraud, but our examination should not be relied upon to disclose irregularities and fraud which may exist. If you so require, we can of course carry out specific investigations into suspected improprieties.

Responsibilities of directors

As directors, you are responsible for ensuring compliance with the requirements of the Companies Act relating to the maintenance of adequate accounting records and the production of financial statements that give a true and fair view and have been properly prepared in accordance with the Acts. *Any accounting services we provide are to assist you in discharging your responsibilities under the Companies Acts.*

The responsibility for establishing and maintaining the system of internal accounting control and for the prevention and detection of errors, irregularities and fraud rests with yourselves. In fulfilling this responsibility, management must make estimates and judgements to assess the expected benefits and related costs of control procedures. *It needs to be borne in mind that the objectives of a system and the related procedures are to provide management with reasonable, but not absolute, assurance that assets for which the/each company has responsibility are safeguarded against loss from misappropriation, unauthorised use or removal; and similarly that transactions are executed in accordance with established authorisation arrangements and are recorded properly and comprehensively to permit the preparation of financial statements in accordance with the statutory requirements.*

We appreciate that, in common with many businesses of a similar size and organisation, the/each company's system of control over transactions is at present dependent on the close involvement of the directors/managing director (who are major shareholders). In planning and performing our audit work we shall take account of this supervision; we may ask additionally for written confirmation that all the transactions of the/each company have been reflected in the books and records (and our audit report may refer to this confirmation).

To assist us in our examination of your financial statements and to maintain our knowledge of your business we should be grateful if you would supply us with copies of all communications between your company and its shareholders, for example interim statements.

2 GROUP ACCOUNTS

As auditors of the holding company we are required to report, in similar terms to those outlined above, on the group accounts, which comprise the financial statements of the holding company and its subsidiary and associated companies of which we are not auditors, it may be necessary for us to communicate directly with the other auditors concerned in order to satisfy ourselves that:

(i) so far as is practicable, there is uniformity within the group in the application of accounting policies;

(ii) the group accounts give the information required by the Companies Acts and any other legislation or extra-statutory regulations affecting the production of financial statements; and

(iii) all material aspects of the group accounts have been subjected to an audit examination, the nature and extent of which is adequate and reasonable, in our view, for the purposes of forming an opinion on the group accounts.

3 BOOK-KEEPING AND OTHER ACCOUNTING SERVICES

(N.B. With reference to the CCAB's Statement 1 on Independence the auditor may not participate in the preparation of the accounting records of a listed company audit client save in exceptional circumstances.

We shall:

(i) complete the postings to the nominal ledger from accounting records maintained by your staff;

(ii) extract a trial balance; and

(iii) prepare draft accounts for your approval at *quarterly/half-yearly/yearly* intervals. Except for the annual financial statements, these will be unaudited.

We shall carry out these accounting services as your agent and on the basis that you will make full disclosure to us of all relevant information. We must emphasise that we will not be carrying out these services in our capacity as auditors and that in law you will retain the ultimate responsibility for maintaining the accounting records and preparing the financial statements.

4 SECRETARIAL ASSISTANCE

You wish us to assist the company's secretary to comply with the legal requirements and maintain the statutory books. In particular we are required to prepare notices for general meetings, draft minutes for board and general meetings, and prepare and submit to the Registrar of Companies the annual return and accounts.

5 TAXATION

Commencing with the period ended .... we shall be responsible for the preparation and submission of the (UK) tax computations of *the/each* company based on the annual accounts and the agreement of such computations with the Inland Revenue, as your agent. We shall also keep you informed of any major questions raised by the Inland Revenue in the course of agreeing the computations. *Before submitting any computations to the Inland Revenue, we shall submit the drafts to you.*

We shall be responsible for reviewing copies of all notices of assessment sent to us. Where appropriate, we shall arrange for all incorrect assessments to be appealed, and for applications to be made to postpone the payment of all or part of the tax demanded, where relevant. Based on these assessments, we shall also recommend to you suitable payments on account.

We will be pleased to advise on the taxation implications of particular business transactions or a particular aspect of the company's affairs and on other taxation matters which are specifically referred to us, such as employee taxes, employee benefits, value added tax, capital gains tax and inheritance tax.

6 GENERAL FINANCIAL ADVICE

(The rules of the accountancy bodies require that terms of engagement are agreed with all clients for whom investment services are provided. The content of the agreements and the methods for bringing them into effect vary according to the client involved.)

7 FEES

(This section of the letter should be tailored to fit the auditor's practice and the particular circumstances of each client. It could also be extended to set out a billing timetable with specific dates for issuing fee notes.)

Our fees are computed on the basis of the time spent on, and expertise applied to, your affairs by partners and staff. Unless otherwise agreed, our fees will be charged separately for each class of work mentioned above. We would normally expect to discuss with you the likely amount of our fees before carrying out the relevant work. Disbursements and other out of pocket expenses incurred by us on your behalf will be shown separately on our fee notes.

Our normal practice will be to issue our fee notes at monthly intervals (at quarterly intervals/on completion) for all significant assignments and payment is due within 14 days of the date of presentation of each fee note.

Please confirm by countersigning, dating and returning the enclosed copy of this memorandum that we have understood your requirements and you agree to the terms of the memorandum.

....
[Audit Firm]   Date

FOR AND ON BEHALF OF

....LIMITED AND SUBSIDIARIES

....
Director   Date

....
Director   Date

CHAPTER 8   UNDERSTANDING THE CLIENT'S BUSINESS

8.1   WHY AN AUDITOR NEEDS TO UNDERSTAND THE CLIENT'S BUSINESS

Obtaining an understanding of the client's business is the key to an effective and efficient audit. It enables an auditor not only to tailor his work to meet the individual facts and circumstances of each client, but also to carry out that work and to evaluate his findings in an informed manner. The auditor's knowledge of the client's business also helps him to develop and maintain a positive professional relationship with the client.

This chapter provides guidance on what an auditor needs to know and how he should develop that knowledge. It does not deal in any detail with his understanding of the client's internal control structure; that matter is covered in chapter 10.

To plan his work adequately, the auditor needs to understand the nature of the client's business, its organisation, its method of operation and the industry in which it is involved. This understanding enables him to appreciate which events and transactions are likely to have a significant effect on the financial statements.

The understanding of the client's business helps for example, to:

- identify the areas of high risk where the audit effort should be concentrated
- assess the potential for use of analytical procedures, by enabling the auditor to identify the information which he can use to make predictions and comparisons
- obtain an understanding of the internal control structure and assess the inherent and control risks in the key areas of audit significance
- develop an audit strategy enabling an auditor to obtain the necessary audit evidence in the most effective and efficient manner possible.

Knowing the client's business helps the auditor in a number of ways both during the conduct of the audit, and when he comes to complete the audit.

This includes, for example, helping him in:

- asking the right questions and evaluating the reasonableness of the answers he receives
- making judgments about the appropriateness of the client's accounting principles, policies and procedures
- identifying unusual or unexpected transactions and related party transactions
- interpreting the results of audit tests and evaluating their effect
- carrying out an overall review of the financial statements in an informed manner.

Knowledge of the client's business and the industry in which it operates is essential also to the development of a positive professional relationship.

It helps, for example, in:

- understanding the management's philosophy and its aspirations for the business
- understanding the business strategy and plans

● providing relevant and practical business advice to the client.

8.2 WHAT AN AUDITOR NEEDS TO KNOW

8.2.1 *Introduction*

What an auditor needs to know, and the extent of that knowledge, should be firmly based on his need to attain the objectives of the engagement. He should not simply gather information haphazardly or for its own sake.

He should consider:

● the nature of the business - the type of entity, the key business activities, the products or services and customers, the industry, competitors, and so on

● the organisation and operating characteristics of the business — the structure of the business, how it is run, the methods of production, distribution and compensation, and the management information system

● the business strategy — management's overall goals and policies for achieving those goals and the internal and external constraints on the development of the business.

The paragraphs that follow provide further explanation of each of the above aspects.

8.2.2 *The nature of the business*

The type of the entity affects the way an auditor plans and conducts the audit, because each type has its own special characteristics. For example, a client might be a business enterprise or a not-for-profit organisation, a corporation or a partnership, publicly-held or closely-held.

It might be helpful to think of the client's business in terms of its key activities. For example the key activity of a merchant is buying and selling goods at a mark-up. Ancillary functions may include a transport fleet, a warehousing operation and miscellaneous administrative functions.

Businesses often have more than one key activity. For example, producing goods and selling them are the major function for a manufacturing company, and may therefore be regarded as key. But if it also retails, then there are two functions which are key business activities.

Each key business activity has its own characteristics. For example, an investment bank takes quite a high, though calculated, risk in providing equity finance or venture capital and is normally concerned with the capital growth of its investment. A bank that provides financial advisory and consulting services, however, normally takes a different type of risk.

The following examples illustrate other characteristics of key business activities:

● a mass-production car manufacturer's objective may be to have a range of cars which would fulfil the basic needs of average drivers at a reasonable price. There is competition and the business is 'price' sensitive and relies on a large customer base. An exclusive sports car manufacturer, on the other hand, is more concerned with cars which have 'special' features (eg performance, design, quality, antique value, exclusivity) because it caters to a smaller, targeted market. In this case, the business is far less 'price' sensitive and is more sensitive to the acceptance of its special features by its narrow customer base

- a commodity merchant's primary business objective is to sell a large quantity of goods at relatively low margins. There is usually a known market price for the commodity and the business is 'price' sensitive. Therefore, successful buying will allow a better margin on each deal, as will hedging when appropriate and the successful timing of sales and purchases

- a business providing financial consulting services may have, as its primary objectives, the quality, responsiveness, and range of its services. In normal circumstances, the clients choose an advisor for these qualities and, therefore, the business is not 'price' sensitive because comparison is difficult

- in a venture capital business, the primary objective is choosing the right investment for growth in line with a specific portfolio policy.

It is important that the auditor identifies all of the client's key business activities, and understands the characteristics of each activity. He needs to consider the client's products or services, the characteristics of the industry, competitors, customers, suppliers and so on. Appendix 8.1 gives a checklist of items that an auditor may consider in this respect. The auditor should not attempt to plan or carry out an audit without a basic understanding of the nature of the client's business.

8.2.3 *Organisation and operating characteristics*

The auditor should develop a thorough understanding of the way the business operates and the way it is controlled, performance is monitored and responsibility is delegated. Appendix 8.1 gives a checklist of items that he may consider in this respect.

Knowledge of how management controls the business principally affects the auditor's assessment of the internal control structure as the examples below show. This matter is dealt with in greater detail in Chapter 10. Also, the auditor's assessment of management affects the degree of reliance he can place on their explanations and representations.

Examples:
  (i) a business may have an entrepreneurial style due to the personality of the chief executive, owner or manager. In these circumstances, the auditor should be alert to the fact that power and influence may be concentrated or entirely invested in one person who may, for example, override internal controls. This individual's attitudes to risk and achieving performance are also relevant as they may indicate, for example, a desire to manipulate certain information in a particular way

  (ii) similarly, key personnel may have an incentive artificially to improve results if this would affect their compensation (eg profit sharing)

  (iii) if key executives lack sufficient experience, errors become more likely, and the internal control structure will be weakened.

Another important consideration is the data used by the management to control and run the business. These include budgets, variance reports, statistics regarding sales, margins and employees, externally produced data in trade and industry journals and non-financial data such as volume and tonnage statistics.

Examples:
  (i) A commodity merchant needs to know the margin on each deal and also that goods bought have been sold or are in inventory at a specific value. Profitability by 'deal' is a useful piece of information. Also, the latest information on market price for buying and selling (external data) is crucial to the business.

  (ii) A production based company, with a complex production process (say a mass-production car manufacturer) may rely on a sophisticated computerised costing system. Variance analysis is a powerful tool to control the business.

79

(iii) A business involved in long-term contracts with items being built to specific orders would normally have sufficient data to enable the management to monitor the progress of each contract and assess its profitability.

The auditor's knowledge of the management information system affects his audit strategy, for example, in identifying:

- areas where use of analytical procedures are likely to be efficient and effective (in example (i) above, he might audit sales by applying audited margins to an audited purchases figure)

- areas where he can use computer-assisted audit techniques, (example (ii) above)

- how best to select items for testing — for example (iii) above, he might choose to audit on a contract by contract basis, rather than on separate samples for sales, purchases and work in progress.

8.2.4   *The business strategy*

There are two main reasons why the auditor needs to know the goals that management has for developing the business, the potential for this development and any limiting factors. First, and primarily, it helps him to assess the risk of material misstatement in the financial statements.

Examples:
(i) artificial manipulation of results — A public company is subject to stringent reporting requirements and scrutiny by analysts and a wide range of third parties. Management may well feel under pressure to produce results with a steady upward trend. Such a company may also be involved in take-overs. A private company (family owned or controlled by a few individuals) is subject to a lesser degree of external scrutiny and matters such as minimising tax liabilities may be more relevant than a good trend of results.

(ii) preoccupation with a public offering of its shares — When a company is considering a public offering, a major preoccupation of management is to accomplish the offering successfully. This preoccupation which may last two or three years, and the inevitable demand on the time of senior management and the business' resources generally may affect the performance of the business and, in extreme cases, impair the judgment of management.

Secondly, it also demonstrates an overall concern and appreciation of the business extending beyond the audit itself. This meets the expectation of clients who increasingly assume that the auditor's professional knowledge and experience is being brought to bear on their businesses.

Examples where the auditor's understanding of management's goals and potential may help are:

- identifying the client's future needs (eg human resources) and responding accordingly

- recognising danger signs (eg the business may be expanding too rapidly) and providing relevant and timely advice.

Points to consider under the heading of 'Business strategy' include those shown in Section 5 of Appendix 8.1.

8.3   LEARNING ABOUT THE CLIENT'S BUSINESS

8.3.1   *Planning the information gathering exercise*

The extent of work involved in obtaining an understanding of the client's business varies from client to client and depends upon the complexity of the business, the nature, quality and reliability of information already available from the client, the auditor's experience with the industry and whether the client is a new or existing one.

It is important for auditors to be realistic in their aims — they should recognise that they can seldom, if ever, obtain the same level of understanding of the business as management.

At the preliminary stage of audit planning, the engagement partner and manager should let the other members of the engagement team know the extent of information required and the methods to be used to collect and assimilate the information. It is important to avoid the inefficiencies that result from accumulating and documenting excessive detail.

The information gathering exercise should be scheduled to provide sufficient time to allow the audit team to plan the audit properly. In the case of a new client, this exercise should be carried out at a very early stage of the audit. For existing clients, the information accumulated in previous years should be revised and updated as one of the first stages of planning. In either case, auditors should always be alert to any new information concerning the client's operations.

8.3.2 *Sources of information*

The auditor can obtain much of his knowledge of the client through experience from previous audits of the client (or similar businesses in the same industry) and through discussion with client personnel during the normal course of fieldwork. The value of direct and detailed knowledge of the client's business developed through a sustained relationship over a period of time cannot be overemphasised. Every effort should be made to build and consolidate such a relationship.

Audit files. All the members of an audit team should be familiar with the information on the nature of the client's business contained in the auditor's permanent or standing files. The following documents held in the previous year's audit file should also be reviewed:

- financial statements
- planning documents, including audit strategy documentation
- points recorded for the partner's attention and points forward
- management letters
- schedules showing the composition of the amounts in the financial statements (eg lead schedules).

This will help the audit team:

- to anticipate potential problem areas in the coming audit
- to improve the audit strategy when a previous strategy is deemed inefficient or difficult to implement in practice
- to avoid 'reinventing' the approach when there have been no significant changes in the client's operations, and the approach in prior years has proved effective and efficient.

Correspondence. An auditor should aim to keep himself informed of developments in the client's business and industry by regular contact with the client. Important aspects of telephone conversations and meetings with the client should be documented so that the information is available to other members of the audit team. Each client should be encouraged to inform the auditor of any significant business changes; it is particularly helpful for the auditor to be aware of important developments at the audit planning stage.

Information that may be useful to the auditor includes:

- changes in accounting procedures

- changes in management structure or key personnel

- significant changes in the business (eg product range, volume of turnover, marketing strategy, major customers, suppliers or markets)

- any other matters likely to cause an audit problem

- acquisitions and disposals of businesses and significant fixed assets.

Client staff. The audit manager or senior audit staff member will normally talk first to the senior financial officer and senior members of the accounting department. To build up a rounded picture of the business as a whole, the audit manager or senior audit staff member should also talk to key personnel outside the client's accounting function about the business and their particular roles in it. Such contacts, once made, should be maintained and developed as part of the continuing process of knowing and understanding the client's business.

Industry-specific guidance. Information on an industry may be obtainable from government agencies, trade associations or independent information agencies. If a client is unable to help an auditor obtain this kind of information, libraries may be able to provide assistance in finding out what information is available. Training courses may also be available for certain industries.

Further useful background information can often be gained by reading available published material, such as financial statements of other companies in the industry, trade journals, magazines and textbooks. Other sources might include industry audit and accounting guidance issued by professional accountancy bodies, articles in the national or local press and economic reports, government or trade association statistics, and stockbrokers' reports.

Observation of operations. The auditor should observe the business operations and processes in the client's offices and factories. If the client has significant operations abroad, a visit may be particularly helpful in gaining a first-hand appreciation of the local business environment. Viewing the premises and the operations being carried out helps the auditor to interpret accounting data by providing a visual frame of reference within which such assets as work-in-progress and factory equipment can be evaluated. He can actually see the physical safeguards over assets.

Information produced by the client. Useful information can often be obtained from the following material produced by the client:

- brochures explaining the products or services

- booklets concerning employee benefits and policies

- organisation/responsibility charts

- business plans and budgets

- promotional and marketing literature

- minutes of operational committee meetings

- internal management reports.

In the case of the larger client, its own public relations department or advisors may be willing to supply the auditor with press-cuttings relating to the client on a regular basis.

Previous auditors. For new/initial audits, the working papers of previous auditors may contain much useful information (eg on the history and nature of the client's business, the accounting system, the internal control structure).

8.3.3 *Recording and assimilating the information*

The extent to which the auditor will document his understanding of the client's business depends on the circumstances. Information and documents of ongoing value, to which he will need to refer in the future, should be filed on a permanent file.

APPENDIX 8.1

UNDERSTANDING THE CLIENT'S BUSINESS — CHECKLIST

This appendix lists many matters that the auditor might consider in developing his knowledge and understanding of the client's business. It is fairly extensive and not every point listed will have to be considered on every audit.

WHAT AN AUDITOR NEEDS TO KNOW

1. **Nature of business, brief history**

   - principal activities, products, services

   - articles of incorporation, by-laws

   - commercial development, eg
     — change in activities
     — product history
     — history of ownership/control other significant events (eg major acquisitions and disposals, public offerings of shares, major industrial disputes)

   - financial development — key balance sheet ratios

   - declining profitability, deteriorating financial or income statement ratios, analysed where position appropriate, for recent years

   - extent of doing business with affiliated companies or related parties.

2. **Features of the client's industry**

   - nature of the industry (eg clothing industry) and the particular sector (eg retail shops sector) in which the business operates

   - economic factors affecting the industry or sector (eg consumer disposable income, competing products, cyclical/seasonal demand)

   - long-term trends and prospects, economic conditions

   - position of the company in the industry (eg market share, number of domestic/ foreign competitors, names of major competitors, growth potential, quality level)

   - degree of regulation from government or trade associations (special operating, accounting or financial requirements)

   - glossary of specialised terms

   - external constraints on the business (eg government price controls, parent company policies)

   - whether the business is capital or labour intensive

   - major dependencies (eg on a particular supplier or customer, or on the availability of a commodity, manpower or finances)

   - factors which may affect the industry significantly (eg foreign exchange movements, product substitution, taxation structures, price of oil)

   - whether the business is seasonal

   - accounting practices common to the industry.

3. **Organisation and locations**

   ● chart or description of organisational structure (eg subsidiaries, divisions, branches)

   ● list of companies/divisions/branches with locations and activities

   ● operating locations

   ● description of properties occupied.

4. **How management controls the business**

   ● chart of senior management, showing their responsibilities (and the key audit contacts)

   ● the degree of autonomy given to individual executives by the chief executive officer

   ● the management style of the chief executive officer and other senior executives

   ● the manner by which delegation of major responsibilities is effected throughout the organisation

   ● management's attitude towards setting and meeting budgets, profit targets, etc

   ● nature and degree of supervision by parent company management

   ● the quality of the key executives and their assistants (eg length of service, experience)

   ● methods used to compensate key personnel

   ● overview of other general control features (eg segregation of duties, authorisation and supervision procedures)

   ● nature, quality and type of operating information relied upon by senior management and the Board of Directors (including detailed operating information about specific areas such as sales and purchases)

   ● nature of information systems (eg manual, computerised, integrated)

   ● details of timing, relevance and reliability of reports produced for management and management's methods of response and follow-up

   ● areas of management priority

   ● employee rights and representation within management.

5. **Business strategy**

   ● the business' strengths and weaknesses and opportunities and threats in the market in which it operates

   ● management's overall goals for the business

   ● management's policies for achieving those goals

   ● whether the business has sufficient resources (eg human, financial) to carry out the strategy

   ● industry and market trends

   ● technological advances affecting the future of the business

   ● current or potential problem areas

   ● limiting factors which may affect the business adversely

   ● limitations caused by parent company policies (eg on choice of suppliers or customers, on capital expenditure)

6. **Products and services**

- description of principal products and services, number and range of products and services

- relative volumes

- relative profitability of different products and services

- description of major manufacturing or processing operations

- research and development – nature, locations, resources

- production information
  — volume of production per product
  — nature of production planning and control, production budgets, cost centre analysis
  — product planning, analysis of product contribution, constraints on volume/ mix of products
  — raw material usage, wastage factors, machine downtime
  — variances (eg production capacity, efficiency, downtime).

7. **Selling**

- customers (eg numbers and size, domestic or foreign, retail, wholesale, inter-company, repeat sales and terms of trade)

- pricing policy (eg price lists, mark-ups, government or trade regulation, customer-dictated, quantity/loyalty incentives, forward sales)

- selling methods (eg advertising, promotions, representatives, agents, commission arrangements, consignments, sale or return, tendering or competitive proposals, sales by telephone/data link, mail order)

- distribution (eg warehouse, road, rail, sea, sub-contracted transport, use of returnable containers or pallets, freight recharges)

- credit control (eg trade references, credit ratings, normal/extended terms, early settlement discounts, policies on bad debts, collection agencies, receivables factoring, credit insurance, arrangements for foreign customers such as letters of credit)

- after sales service (eg warranties, unconditional replacement, free service periods, spares, product liability customer claims)

- operating information
  — gross margin report by product or service
  — sales and order analysis by area, product or service, salesman, outlet, etc
  — selling and distribution costs by area, product or service, salesman, outlet, etc
  — ratios of sales to staff, sales staff, sales area, etc
  — sales order processing indicators eg outstanding orders, delivery times
  — customer reports, slow payers, bad debts, age analyses, collections, customer queries
  — analyses of after sales costs, customer claims and goods returns.

8. **Purchasing**

- nature of purchases (eg raw materials, purchased parts, services) and dependence on basic commodities (eg oil or timber)

- suppliers (usual suppliers, alternative sources, imports, inter-company purchases) and terms of trade (eg price determinants such as market and availability, exchange rates, price regulation, competitive bids, forward contracts, quantity and loyalty incentives)

- trade creditors (credit allowed, early settlement discounts, sale or return)
  - unauthorised price changes
  - competitive bids not obtained
  - abnormally high freight costs

- operating information
  - purchase budgets and targets
  - purchase analyses by product or service, cost-centre, outlet
  - purchases by supplier and average prices and past price movements
  - raw material usage and reorder cycle
  - standard, price and usage variance analyses
  - analyses of payments and outstanding trade creditors

9. Stocks

- nature of stocks (raw materials, purchased parts, work in progress, finished goods, consignment inventories)

- quantities held and values by category

- stock locations

- risk factors (obsolescence, deterioration, price volatility, fashion changes, "shrinkage")

- operating information
  - physical stock counts
  - budgeted stock levels/usage projections
  - analyses of reorder points and lead times
  - reorder levels and economic order quantities
  - slow moving item reports

10.   Plant and equipment

- nature and amount of plant and equipment (for example, warehousing, manufacturing, offices), locations of plant and equipment

- plant capacity, technology utilisation, age and replacement cycle

- owned or leased

- operating information
  - reports on age, condition, life expectancy, usage, current values
  - forecasts of replacement needs
  - acquisition and disposal budgets

11.   Other sources of income

- investment income

- patents, royalties, agency fees and commissions

- scrap sales.

12.   Investments

- types of major investments, reasons for investment, investment strategy and attitude towards risk.

13.   Financing

- capital
  - classes of capital
  - history of authorised and allotted capital from incorporation

  — voting rights, other rights, (eg convertibility, redemption, options) dividend provisions

- long-term debt
  - — financial terms (eg interest, repayment dates, conversion or redemption rights, sinking fund requirements, collateral)
  - — loan covenants (eg restrictions on other borrowings, working capital requirements)
  - — collateral
  - — lines of credit

- bank borrowings, treasury management

- other forms (eg off balance sheet, government grants).

14. Personnel

- employee numbers and locations

- categories (eg full or part-time, permanent or seasonal, analysis by departments or business activity)

- methods of compensation (eg salaried, weekly/hourly paid, piece-work, overtime, holidays, bonuses, commission, profit-sharing)

- benefits (eg pension plan, company cars, medical insurances and stock options)

- operating information
  - — forecasts of staff requirements
  - — staff turnover statistics
  - — time recording (analysis of productive and lost time, absenteeism figures)
  - — analysis of labour variances.

15. Professional advisors (with addresses)

- bankers

- legal advisers

- tax advisers

- others, such as appraisers/valuers, investment bankers, stockbrokers, etc.

CHAPTER 9   AUDIT RISK AND MATERIALITY

9.1   INTRODUCTION

Materiality and audit risk are concepts that are integral to an effective and efficient audit. Materiality relates to how precise an auditor wants to be in auditing the financial statements. Audit risk relates to how confident an auditor wants to be that the financial statements are free of material misstatements.

Financial statements are materially misstated when they contain errors whose effect, individually or in the aggregate, causes them not to give a true and fair view. (For the purposes of this chapter, the term 'error' encompasses irregularities (ie intentional misstatements or omissions in the financial statements) as well as unintentional errors.)

Auditors need to assess the risk that errors may cause the financial statements to contain a material misstatement. Based on that assessment, an auditor will plan his audit and design his audit procedures to provide him with reasonable assurance of detecting errors that are material to the financial statements.

An auditor must also consider audit risk and materiality when evaluating, on the basis of his audit findings, whether the financial statements taken as a whole give a true and fair view.

This chapter focuses on audit risk and materiality considerations in planning the audit and designing audit procedures. In summary, it explains

- the concepts of audit risk and materiality and their interrelationship
- expressions such as inherent and control risk, detection risk and planning materiality
- the need to form a preliminary assessment of overall risk on each audit
- that an auditor should assess the inherent and control risks of material misstatement at the individual account balance or class-of-transactions level — this in turn determines the acceptable level of detection risk upon which he can plan the nature, timing and extent of his tests
- how and why a level of planning materiality should be set for each audit
- that an auditor should consider setting a monetary level above which he will keep track of errors.

The final section of the chapter addresses materiality considerations in forming an audit opinion.

9.2   NATURE OF AUDIT RISK

Audit risk is the risk that the auditor may unknowingly fail to qualify his opinion on financial statements that are materially misstated.

Auditors can reduce the level of risk associated with an audit engagement but cannot eliminate it altogether. In other words, practice recognises that it is impossible for auditors to be certain that the financial statements under audit are free of material misstatement. Even if it were cost-effective to test every transaction recorded by a client, there would still be some audit risk because there might be concealed transactions, an auditor might incorrectly apply his audit procedures or misinterpret their results, or documents might be altered or forged.

As a result, an auditor must accept some audit risk on each audit. The key is to plan the audit so that this risk will be limited to what is, in his professional judgment, an appropriately low level. This level of overall audit risk need not be measured in quantitative terms; it is doubtful whether it is possible to do so.

In addition to audit risk, auditors are also exposed to practice risk in every audit engagement. Practice risk is the risk that a professional practice will suffer loss, injury, or client dissatisfaction from litigation, adverse publicity, or other events perceived as connected with a particular audit. Practice risk exists even though the auditor has conducted his audit in accordance with professional standards.

Clearly, an auditor needs to be aware of practice risk in planning his audit. Because of such a risk, he may perform more extensive procedures than would otherwise be necessary under professional standards. However, the converse is not true; he should never perform less extensive procedures than would otherwise be necessary under professional standards because he believes that an engagement poses a low risk to his practice or reputation.

9.3 NATURE OF MATERIALITY

Materiality is the magnitude or nature of an omission or misstatement of accounting information that, in the light of surrounding circumstances, makes it probable that the judgment of a reasonable person relying on the information would have been changed or influenced by the omission or misstatement.

An auditor should plan his audits to detect errors that could be large enough, individually or in the aggregate, to be quantitatively material to the financial statements.

It should be recognised that errors of relatively small amounts could have a qualitatively material effect on the financial statements. For example, a small reclassification between current and long-term liabilities may be immaterial by itself but it may cause a sufficient change in the current ratio to cause the client to be in violation of a debt covenant, which in turn may require long-term debt to be reflected as a current liability or a contingent liability to be recognised. Although the auditor should be alert for errors that could be qualitatively material, it is normally impractical to design procedures to detect them.

In planning the audit, materiality serves as a guide in determining the level of the testing it is planned to do. It also assists in identifying the accounts or classes of transactions included in the financial statements on which the audit effort should be focused.

Holding everything else constant, the lower the level of materiality, the higher the risk becomes that an undetected error would be material. As materiality decreases, the extent of audit testing would need to increase if the auditor is to be assured that the risk of material misstatement of the financial statements remains acceptably low.

Determination of what constitutes a material misstatement is fundamental to every aspect of the audit. If a value that is too low is chosen the auditor is likely to over audit — to be *inefficient* — and if a value that is too high is chosen the auditor is likely to under audit — to be *ineffective* — and run the risk that material misstatements will go undetected.

9.4 ASSESSMENT OF AUDIT RISK

9.4.1 *Overall assessment at the financial statement level*

In planning the audit, a preliminary assessment should be made of the overall level of risk of misstatement in the financial statements to be audited. The assessment of this risk as either high, medium or low should be included in the audit planning documentation.

The assessment is primarily one of *audit* risk. However, in arriving at this assessment, the auditor should also consider whether there are any particular *practice* risks present (see 9.2 above) that might require him to raise his assessment of the overall level of risk.

This overall risk assessment is made in addition to assessing audit risk at the account balance or class-of-transactions level. It is based on the existing facts and circumstances regarding the engagement that have an impact on the risk of material misstatement. Such facts and circumstances relate to, among other things, the entity, its industry, its financial and operating characteristics, its management characteristics and the auditor's experience in auditing the client in previous years. Many considerations are involved. These are dealt with in the checklist in Appendix 10.1.

The overall risk assessment is a key factor in planning the audit. It guides the auditor in maintaining an appropriate level of professional scepticism, in determining staffing requirements (both number of people and experience levels needed) and in planning the nature, timing and extent of the procedures to be performed.

All other things being equal, a higher overall audit risk assessment would cause the auditor, for example, to:

- assign more experienced staff to the engagement

- increase the supervision of staff

- apply the audit procedures closer to year-end

- insist on more persuasive evidence to support material balances or transactions

- apply additional quality control procedures such as the appointment of an additional reviewer to the audit team.

9.4.2 *Assessment at the account balance or class-of-transactions level*

Audit risk, as it directly affects the specific audit procedures on an engagement, is generally considered at the account balance or class-of-transactions level. At this level, audit risk consists of:

- the risk (consisting of *inherent and control risk*) that the account balance or class-of-transactions contains misstatements that could be material to the financial statements, either individually or when aggregated with misstatements in other balances or classes

- the risk (*detection risk*) that the auditor will not detect such misstatements.

Each of these component risks is discussed below.

Inherent risk is the susceptibility of an account balance or class of transactions to material misstatement assuming that there were no related internal controls. The inherent risk of misstatement is greater for some types of transactions or accounts than for others. For example:

- account balances and transactions subject to complex calculations are more susceptible to error than those based on simple calculations

- assets such as cash are more susceptible to theft than assets such as fixed assets

- account balances subject to judgment and estimation are more likely to be misstated than account balances based on historical, factual data.

Control risk is the risk that misstatements that occur in an account balance or class of transactions, when aggregated with misstatements in other balances or classes, would be material and would not be prevented or detected on a timely basis by the internal control structure. Control risk will vary inversely with the level of effectiveness of the internal control structure. However, because of the inherent limitations of any internal control structure (e.g., those due to human error), there will always be some level of control risk for any internal control structure.

In practice, it is often difficult for the auditor to distinguish between inherent and control risk because of the close relationship between the two. It may be hard for the auditor to judge whether a low risk situation is due to a good internal control structure or low inherent risk, or, in a high risk situation, whether it is the poor internal control structure that engenders the risk of error or the nature of the business. In any event, it is the combined effect of inherent and control risk that influences the acceptable level of detection risk for the auditor (see below) and hence his audit procedures. As a result, one practical approach is for the auditor to consider them together and make a combined assessment of *inherent and control risk*.

The assessment of inherent and control risk is dealt with in greater detail in Chapter 10.

Detection risk is the risk that the audit procedures used will lead the auditor to conclude that there is no misstatement in the account balance or class of transactions that could be material, when aggregated with misstatement in other account balances or classes of transactions, when in fact such material misstatement does exist.

Detection risk is a function of the effectiveness of the audit procedures used and how well they are applied. Such risk exists partly because auditors typically examine less than 100% of an entity's transactions (sampling risk) and partly because they may select inappropriate audit procedures, apply audit procedures improperly, or interpret the results of the procedures incorrectly.

Detection risk is the only one of the three components of audit risk over which auditors have complete control. Inherent risk and control risk exist independently of an audit and, for that reason, the level of detection risk that an auditor is willing to accept is usually determined based on the assessed level of inherent and control risk. It is the level of detection risk that determines the nature, timing and extent of the substantive audit procedures.

The level of detection risk that can be accepted varies inversely with the level of inherent and control risk. The higher the inherent and control risk, the less detection risk that the auditor can accept if he is to keep the risk of material misstatement at an acceptably low level. The less detection risk that the auditor can accept, the more reliable the substantive procedures must be. The reverse is also true. The lower the level of inherent and control risk, the more detection risk can be accepted and, thus, the less persuasive the substantive evidence need be.

9.5 CONSIDERATION OF MATERIALITY

9.5.1 *Planning materiality*

The materiality amount that is used in planning the nature, timing and extent of the audit procedures is referred to as 'planning materiality'. There are several considerations affecting the quantification of the amount to use as planning materiality. These considerations are discussed below.

Materiality is a relative concept. What is material to one client may not be material to another. For this reason, determining the amount that is material to a client requires consideration of the particular circumstances of the client's financial and operating situation.

As indicated previously, an auditor needs to consider materiality both in planning the audit and in evaluating whether the financial statements taken as a whole are fairly stated. The primary difference is that, in setting planning materiality, an auditor will often use preliminary (often estimated) numbers, while at the evaluation or review stage he is evaluating specific issues in the context of known numbers. For this reason, setting an amount for planning materiality does not commit an auditor to any particular measure of materiality in deciding whether or not a particular error needs to be corrected and whether or not the report needs to be qualified.

It is important to exercise care and prudence in setting a level of planning materiality appropriate to the client's business because, in practical terms, it is not a decision that can be lightly revised. If an auditor was to conclude that he had not performed sufficient testing (because too high a level of planning materiality was used to determine the extent of testing), he might have to go back and perform additional substantive tests to obtain the appropriate level of audit evidence. Such tests could consist of additional tests of details where he had applied sampling procedures, carrying out analytical procedures or applying them at a more detailed level, or performing additional substantive tests. In some audit tests it is not easy to rectify the error of having tested too few items (eg physical stock counts and securities counts).

Setting a level of materiality at the planning stage should not stop the auditor from revising that level as the audit progresses. He should reassess the materiality level used in planning the nature and scope of his audit procedures to ensure that he has performed sufficient work to render an audit opinion. The point at which he decides that he needs to go back and do some more work is a matter of professional judgment in the circumstances.

The basic steps for estimating planning materiality include the following:

- obtain a copy of the latest trial balance or interim financial statements, previous years' financial statements, and budgets or forecasts, if available

- use "rules of thumb", as appropriate

- consider the results produced by using the "rules of thumb" and apply professional judgment in choosing an appropriate level

- document the decision made, and rationale therefor, in the audit planning memorandum.

The following paragraphs discuss each of the above steps and the major factors that should be considered.

Obtain the latest financial information from the client. It is important that the auditor has as clear a picture as possible of the client's likely financial position at the balance sheet date and its likely operating results for the period then ended. The normal sources of information to give him this picture include the latest trial balance or interim financial statements, the most recent budgets or forecasts, and discussions with the client. In addition, the auditor should ascertain from the client whether there have been any significant events during the year that might have a bearing on the determination of materiality. See Chapter 11, for a more comprehensive discussion of planning procedures with respect to the client's latest financial information.

Use 'rules of thumb', as appropriate The starting point in the estimation of planning materiality is usually the application of a percentage to an appropriate financial statement base. A number of rules of thumb or guidelines have evolved in practice to assist an auditor in this regard. These rules of thumb are usually expressed as ranges

- between 5% and 10% of profit before tax

- between 1/2% and 2% of turnover

- between 1/2% and 2% of total assets

- between 2% and 5% of net assets (shareholders' funds).

The first two rules of thumb are based on the profit and loss account and the last two rules of thumb are based on the balance sheet. The client's industry and the nature of its business are factors in determining which rule of thumb should be used in estimating planning materiality. In most cases, companies are judged primarily on operating results. Accordingly, in these cases, planning materiality might be based primarily on the profit and loss account — usually, profit before tax. For some industries, such as financial institutions, the balance sheet tends to become more important and planning materiality might be based primarily on the balance sheet. However, there are no hard and fast rules for purposes of determining planning materiality. In considering the various rules of thumb, an auditor should be influenced primarily by the one he believes provides the best measure of the client's financial activities.

The above rules of thumb are the ones most widely used by auditors as aids in estimating planning materiality but are not necessarily the only ones that may be used. Others may be appropriate for entities in specialised industries or other particular situations. For example, fluctuations in the securities markets and surges or declines in trading activity can cause the above rules of thumb to lose relevance for the purpose of estimating planning materiality for a stock brokerage firm. Overhead expenses of such a firm, particularly the fixed component of overhead, may be an appropriate alternative base to use.

Another consideration in choosing a rule of thumb is the likelihood of audit adjustments. On clients that typically have a lot of adjustments, it also may be advisable to choose the base least affected by those adjustments. An auditor might, however, elect to apply a different factor to the base to avoid using too high or too low a measure of materiality.

Income variability is another consideration in estimating planning materiality. While profit before tax may be the most preferable or attractive base, it may be the most susceptible to fluctuation. Other bases may be less preferable but they provide more stability. Accordingly, turnover, total assets and net assets are often used where profit before tax is subject to significant fluctuation or is too small to be useful. Another technique that is frequently used where profit before tax in a particular year is not representative of the profitability of the entity is to calculate a three year average and use that amount as a base.

The following situation illustrates these concepts. Profit before tax for 19X1 and 19X2 is £800,000 and £900,000, respectively. Estimated profit before tax for the current year, 19X3, is only £400,000, primarily due to a temporary downturn in the market. To use £400,000 as a base for determining planning materiality might not be appropriate in this situation and could result in unnecessary over-auditing. A better approach might be to use either a more stable base such as turnover, total assets or net assets or to use the three year average of profit before tax (£700,000). The key is that the base to be used in estimating planning materiality depends on the auditor's judgment in the particular circumstances.

In exercising judgment an auditor can use a sliding scale concept. This approach uses a relatively lower percentage to be applied as the absolute monetary value of the selected base increases. The reason for this is that elements of the financial statements of larger businesses are usually measurable to a greater relative precision (i.e., finer percentage accuracy) than those of smaller businesses. Thus, the costs of refining the precision of an audit opinion on smaller organisations to the same level as for larger organisations would normally be disproportionate to the benefits gained.

The sliding scale concept is illustrated in Table 9.1 below:

Table 9.1 Sliding scale rule of thumb for planning materiality

Range of turnover £			Planning materiality £ + % excess over lower limit of range		
0	to	75,000	0	+	4.0%
75,000	to	150,000	3,000	+	2.0%
150,000	to	750,000	4,500	+	1.25%
750,000	to	3,000,000	12,000	+	0.8%
3,000,000	to	7,500,000	30,000	+	0.5%
7,500,000	to	37,500,000	52,500	+	0.35%
37,500,000	to	75,000,000	157,500	+	0.3%
75,000,000	to	375,000,000	270,000	+	0.15%
375,000,000	to	750,000,000	720,000	+	0.12%
750,000,000	to	3,750,000,000	1,170,000	+	0.07%

Taking a turnover of £3,500,000 as an illustration of use of the table.

Planning materiality 'rule of thumb' is

£25,000 + 0.5% (3,500,000 – £2,5000,000) = £30,000.

Decide upon an appropriate amount. It is emphasised that the decision as to the level of planning materiality rests ultimately on professional judgement, combined with a sound knowledge of the client's affairs. Once the estimates of planning materiality using one or more of the alternative bases have been made and all other factors relevant to the determination of materiality have been assimilated, professional judgment needs to be exercised to choose an appropriate level.

Document the decision. The amount selected for planning materiality and the process used in making the selection should be included in the audit planning documentation.

9.5.2 Keeping track of errors

The concepts and methods of keeping track of errors discovered during an audit, so as to be able to judge their cumulative effect, are discussed in Chapter 15. At the planning stage, the auditor should determine an amount below which proposed adjusting journal entries will not be tracked. Professional judgment is required in determining this amount. The figure selected, with a brief rationale therefor, should be included in the audit planning documentation.

The amount below which proposed adjusting entries will not be tracked should be set at a sufficiently low level so that, were such proposed adjusting journal entries to be aggregated, the total would not be material. The minimum level for tracking errors therefore will depend not only on the level of planning materiality but also on the expected volume of errors (based on the experience of previous audits); a figure of 5% of planning materiality is suggested as a general guideline.

On some audits, the auditor may wish additionally to set an amount below which proposed reclassification entries will not be tracked. Since materiality for entries that merely reclassify recorded amounts is generally considered to be greater than for entries that affect income or recognise unrecorded transactions, the effect would be to require the audit team to keep track of fewer errors.

The auditor should consider informing the client about his decision only to keep track of errors above a particular amount. It may be that the client will wish to be informed about all errors, or about all errors above a different amount.

9.5.3 *Materiality at the account balance or class-of-transactions level*

Planning materiality is important at the account balance, or class-of-transactions, level in determining the areas of audit importance that should be focused on during the audit. Without being able to identify those areas, the auditor runs the risk of focusing his audit effort on areas in which the risk of material misstatement is low. This is not only inefficient but also may result in giving too little attention to the areas in which the risk of material misstatement is high.

Planning materiality helps an auditor to decide what to test exhaustively, what to sample, and what merely to review for reasonableness. In using audit sampling to test individual account balances or classes of transactions, the determination of sample sizes is directly affected by the amount of misstatement that can be accepted in the sampling application. This is commonly referred to as tolerable error and is discussed in more detail in Chapter 16.

Planning materiality serves as a guide in determining the nature, timing and extent of auditing procedures to apply to a particular account balance or class of transactions. An auditor should design procedures to detect misstatements that he believes, based on his estimate of planning materiality, could be material, when aggregated with misstatements in other balances or classes, to the financial statements as a whole.

9.6 FORMING AN AUDIT OPINION

In the closing stages of the audit the auditor needs to assess the impact of known errors and uncertainties in the financial statements and to determine whether they are sufficiently significant, if uncorrected or unresolved, to affect his audit opinion on the financial statements.

Materiality needs to be considered when determining whether:

- a known error requires correction
- an item should be separately disclosed
- an uncertainty should be referred to
- a contingent gain or loss should be disclosed
- an accounting policy should be stated
- the effect of a change in an accounting policy should be disclosed
- the departure from an accounting standard or fundamental accounting concept should be disclosed.

The materiality of a specific item must be judged in its context in the financial statements. In most instances there will be a 'base figure' against which the item in question can be measured, for example an item affecting pre-tax profits can be measured against net profits before tax, the misclassification of a balance sheet item can be measured against net assets, net current assets or the appropriate balance sheet heading. As *initial* guidance in deciding upon the materiality or otherwise of an item, the auditor may presume an amount of 10% or more of the appropriate base figure to be material, while an amount of 5% or less of the appropriate base figure may be presumed to be immaterial.

Where an item is assessed for its effect upon profits, it is usually sensible to use the 'normal' or 'expected' level of profit, adjusting for non-recurring or unusual items; in addition, items such as directors' remuneration, bonuses and management charges should be added back where these are in effect distributions of profit rather than operating costs.

These guidelines should be applied only in conjunction with the factors set out below: they should never be relied upon as the sole measure of materiality.

9.6.1 *Degree of estimation*

A greater degree of latitude is normally permissible in determining the materiality of an uncertainty relating to an item that is by its nature imprecise or based on estimates or assumptions (such as the net realisable value of a stock item, depreciation or a bad debt provision) than when considering an item capable of precise determination (such as a bank balance).

9.6.2 *Critical points*

The materiality of an error needs particularly careful assessment when it bears upon a critical point in the financial statements: for example, where its correction would:

- change a marginally upward trend into a marginally downward one

- turn a small profit into a small loss

- leave the dividends for the year uncovered

- change a marginally solvent balance sheet into a marginally insolvent one

- materially affect a key ratio (such as the ratio of current assets to current liabilities).

Whilst the level of materiality may be lower in such cases, it is important not to lose sight of the true dimensions of the business. Although the emotional impact of a small loss is very different from that of a small profit, it is important to bear in mind that the *rational* reader of the financial statements should be more concerned with the shortfall below an adequate return on capital employed: the fate of a company on the verge of insolvency will often be determined well before the appearance of audited financial statements. Thus the small error should not have a material impact on the user.

Particular difficulties arise if the company is close to the limit of its borrowing powers and an error is discovered that would not otherwise be considered material, but which if adjusted would cause the limit to be exceeded. The consequences of exceeding the limit will depend, *inter alia*, on the nature and source of the restrictions. For example, long term liabilities may have to be reclassified as current liabilities, if loans would then become repayable immediately, and doubt may be cast on the appropriateness of the "going concern" assumption.

9.6.3 *Accounting policies*

The Companies Acts require disclosure of the accounting policies adopted; SSAP 2 specifically states that policies judged to be material or critical in determining the results and financial position must be disclosed. It is usual to continue to disclose a policy even though the effect may not be material every year. For example, the difference between the closing rate method and the temporal method of translating foreign currency items may only be material in years when the exchange rate has moved sharply, but it would be normal practice to retain the accounting policy note on foreign currency in other years.

Where a change of accounting policy occurs and this materially affects the financial statements, it will be disclosed as a prior year adjustment. There may be instances, however, when the effect of the change is small in the actual year of change, but has been or is expected to be material in past or future years — for instance, a change from the temporal to closing rate method of foreign currency translation in a year of unusually stable exchange rates. It will still be necessary to disclose the change in policy and its effect because of the effect on the business trend over a number of years.

9.6.4 *Separate disclosures*

For items required by the Companies Acts to be disclosed separately, such as directors' emoluments and loans to directors, auditors' remuneration, interest payable, etc., the relative size of the figure is irrelevant. An error in such an item must be judged by comparing it with the size of the item itself rather than with amounts in the balance sheet or profit and loss account. Items for which the auditor has a specific reporting obligation, such as directors' emoluments and loans to directors, are particularly sensitive; almost any error might be considered important enough to require correction.

The Companies Acts, as amplified by SSAP 6, require the separate disclosure of exceptional items, extraordinary items and prior year adjustments, where these are material. The precise nature of such items, as well as their relative size, will have a bearing on whether or not separate disclosure, or restatement of the previous year's figures in the case of prior year adjustments, is in fact required.

CHAPTER 10 INHERENT AND INTERNAL CONTROL RISK

10.1 INTRODUCTION

10.1.1 *What this chapter is about*

The auditor uses his understanding of the client's business and internal control structure to assess the inherent and control risk relating to assertions for the material components of the financial statements. This enables him to determine the nature, timing, and extent of his substantive tests to gather evidence regarding management's financial statement assertions.

This chapter explains the process of obtaining an understanding of the internal control structure and of assessing inherent and control risk. It addresses the following questions

- **What does the internal control structure consist of?**
  An entity's internal control structure consists of three elements: the *control environment* within which financial reporting occurs, the *accounting system* and the *control procedures* and policies put in place by the entity's management (each of these expressions is explained below). A diagrammatic explanation of the internal control structure is given in Table 10.1.

- **Why does an auditor need to understand the internal control structure?**
  An auditor needs this understanding to enable him to plan the audit — to identify potential misstatements, to assess the risk of such misstatements and to design his substantive audit tests. It will also help him to identify weaknesses in the structure and to suggest improvements to the client.

- **How does an auditor go about the task of gaining this understanding?**
  For continuing clients, the auditor updates his understanding by observation and enquiry. For new clients, or those with major changes in systems, he may use checklists and questionnaires to aid the task.

- **How does an auditor document this exercise?**
  There are various ways of doing this, from preparing narrative descriptions to completing standard questionnaires, checklists or matrices. Key features of the control environment that affect the audit as a whole should be documented in the audit planning memorandum. Key features of the control environment that affect only individual areas of the audit may be documented in the systems notes for those areas. The accounting system and control procedures may be documented in flowcharts and supporting notes.

- **What is the minimum level of understanding required?**
  The minimum level of understanding required, sufficient for audit planning, is a matter of professional judgement. The audit working papers should normally at least
  (a) document evaluation of the control environment;
  (b) document the flows of accounting information in respect of all the major classes of transaction;
  (c) identify the main control procedures by which management ensure the completeness of those information streams and the auditor should check, through walk-through tests and observation and enquiry, that the documentation reflects actual practice.

- **In what circumstances would an auditor seek a deeper level of understanding of the internal control structure?**
  There are broadly three sets of circumstances in which an auditor would seek to deepen his understanding of the internal control structure through both a more detailed identification of controls and an assessment of how effectively they operate in practice:
  — where it is probable that this additional work will lead to a lower assessment of inherent and control risk and a cost beneficial reduction in the level of substantive testing
  — where the auditor is required to do so by the terms of his engagement, as may be the case in certain regulated industries, or at the specific request of the client
  — where there are likely to be genuine benefits in terms of generating advice for the client.

10.1.2 *Requirement to understand the internal control structure*

The auditor should obtain a sufficient understanding of his client's internal control structure to enable him to plan the audit. This is essential for all audits, whatever the audit strategy or the degree of audit assurance he intends to seek from the internal control structure. The auditor uses this understanding to:

- identify potential misstatements

- consider factors that affect the risk of material misstatement

- design his substantive audit tests

The amount of work the auditor needs to do to gain that understanding is a matter of professional judgement and is influenced by a number of factors including:

- his knowledge from previous audits

- his understanding of the client's business and the industry in which it operates

- the complexity and sophistication of the client's operations and systems

- his assessment of inherent risk

- his judgement regarding materiality.

10.1.3 *Computerised and Manual Systems*

By and large the assumption in this chapter is that the recording and processing of information is computerised. However, the general principles are equally applicable to manual systems and the two types of system are therefore not given separate consideration.

10.2 THE CONTROL ENVIRONMENT

10.2.1 *Importance of the Control Environment*

The control environment within which financial reporting occurs is often the most important factor contributing to the integrity of the financial reporting process. It reflects

Table 10.1 Internal control structure

Control environment
- management philosophy/operating style
- client's organisational structure
- board of directors
- assignment of authority and responsibility
- management control methods
- personnel policies and procedures
- external influences

Accounting systems

Control procedures
General controls
- segregation of duties
- supervision
- systems development/maintenance controls

Application controls
- data capture controls
- data processing controls

Controls over assets
- custody controls
- accountability controls

Security of data

the overall attitude of management to the importance of control and the emphasis it should be given throughout the entity. Therefore, it has a pervasive effect on the entity, significantly influencing the risk of material misstatements in the financial statements.

Control environment factors include:

- management's philosophy and operating style
- the client's organisational structure
- the board of directors and its committees
- the methods used to assign authority and responsibility

- management control methods

- personnel policies and procedures

- external influences on the entity.

Examples of factors to be considered under each of the above headings are given below:

Management's philosophy and operating style

- management's approach to taking and monitoring business risks

- management's attitudes, awareness and actions toward financial reporting (eg whether financial reporting is considered to be important in communicating information to users or a requirement to be complied with at minimum cost and levels of disclosure; whether management is aggressive or conservative in reporting the results of operations; and how it has discharged its stewardship responsibility)

- likelihood of management override

- management's emphasis on meeting budget, profit, and other financial and operating goals

- management's emphasis on safeguarding of assets (eg security of physical assets)

- management's involvement in systems development and attitude towards data security.

The client's organisational structure

- form and nature of the client's organisation units and related management functions and reporting relationships.

The board of directors and its committees

- the role the board of directors and, if appropriate, the audit committee (or other equivalent body) takes in overseeing financial reporting

- how the board fulfils its fiduciary and accountability responsibilities.

The methods used to assign authority and responsibility

- whether the client has policies regarding appropriate business relationships, conflicts of interest, and codes of conduct

- the assignment of responsibilities and delegation of authority to deal with both financial reporting and operating matters

- the use of employee job descriptions

- computer systems documentation indicating the procedures for authorising transactions and approving systems changes.

Management control methods

- management's ability to supervise effectively overall company activities

- the methods used in exercising direct control over company activities and over those given authority to carry out those activities

- management's use of budgetary and similar forecasting control methods that set out management's plans, monitor how those plans are implemented and follow up on variations from those plans

- management's use of appropriate internal and external data to control and run the business (eg budgets, variance reports, operating statistics regarding sales, margins and employee numbers, production data such as volume or tonnage statistics and data from trade and industry journals)

- extent to which management use the information provided by the accounting system to control the entity and for other aspects of decision-making, planning and evaluating performance

- policies for developing and modifying accounting systems and control procedures, including the development, modification, and use of any related computer programs and data files

- existence, independence and effective use of an internal audit function.

Personnel policies and procedures

- policies and procedures for hiring, training, evaluating, promoting and remunerating employees and providing them with the necessary resources to discharge their assigned responsibilities.

External influences on the entity

- external influences which, while outside management's control, might heighten management's consciousness of and attitude toward the conduct and reporting of the entity's operations and might prompt management to establish specific internal control policies and procedures

- monitoring and compliance requirements imposed by legislative and regulatory bodies, such as examinations by bank regulatory agencies and reporting systems requirements imposed by broker/dealer regulations.

Appendix 10.1 contains a checklist which addresses control environment factors to be considered when evaluating inherent and control risk.

10.2.2 *Effect of dominant individual*

Where management is dominated by one individual, as is often the case in small owner-managed businesses, the attitude of the dominant individual becomes very important in enhancing or, conversely, undermining the internal control structure. If, for example, the dominant individual is controls-conscious, the overall impact on the internal control structure might be favourable. But, if the dominant individual does not place great emphasis on controls and, in fact, is known to override existing controls, the overall impact on the internal control structure is adverse. In a larger business, other controls such as those of an oversight or monitoring nature (eg an independent audit committee) might counterbalance the effect of a dominant member of management. In the absence of any such controls, as will usually be the case in a smaller business, the auditor's assessment of the impact of the dominant individual will often be crucial in his assessment of the control environment.

10.3 ACCOUNTING SYSTEM

10.3.1 *Importance of the Accounting System*

The accounting system consists of the methods and records established to identify, assemble, analyse, classify, record, and report the client's transactions and to maintain accountability for its assets and liabilities.

An effective accounting system will

- identify and record all valid transactions

- describe the transactions in sufficient detail to enable them to be correctly classified in the financial statements

- measure the value of transactions on an acceptable basis

- determine the time period in which transactions occurred

- present properly the transactions and related disclosures in the financial statements.

The accounting system has a significant effect on the potential for material misstatements and on the design of substantive tests. A well designed accounting system can provide reliable accounting data and prevent or detect misstatements that could otherwise occur.

On the other hand, a poorly designed accounting system may significantly increase the risk of misstatement, and the auditor should consider this risk in the design of his substantive tests. Furthermore, the auditor cannot design tests of documents and records unless he knows what documents and records are available and how they relate to the amounts in the financial statements.

The auditor should identify the major classes of transactions (eg sales, commission income, interest, debtors, stocks) and, for each, ascertain

- what and who initiates the transactions

- what accounting records, supporting documents and financial statement accounts are involved

- how transactions, including computer generated amounts, flow through the accounting records and into the financial statements.

The auditor should become familiar with the nature and complexity of these transactions and other factors that affect the potential for material misstatements. However, he will not normally need to know about all of the supporting documents, processing steps and accounting records for a class of transactions. Many documents, records, and reports that are useful for managing a client's business may not be relevant to the audit of its financial statements. For example, the same system that produces sales invoices and a sales journal may also produce a report of sales by salespersons. An understanding of this aspect of the system may not be necessary to plan the audit. Neither is it necessary to understand how each copy of every accounting document is used by the client. For example, where a purchase order is prepared in triplicate, the auditor may need to know only that two copies are used effectively. The use of the third copy may be irrelevant.

Instead, the auditor should concentrate on those accounting records which are relevant to the flow of information into the financial statements, the processing steps which produce the accounting records and the supporting documents which are used in those processing steps. In many cases an effective method is to begin with the significant financial statement amounts and trace the flow of accounting data backwards to the original source. However, the auditor should also be alert to the danger that this approach may overlook a separate sub-system (eg sales of scrap), which may have failed to flow through to the financial statements.

The effort required to understand an accounting system will depend upon its nature. The accounting systems the auditor will encounter range from straightforward manual systems to complex computer systems allowing users on-line, real-time access to data. Characteristics that matter include:

- **the extent to which computers are used in each significant accounting application.** Computers might be used simply to prepare detailed listings of transactions and to accumulate totals (eg cash receipts or disbursements journal) or they might be used to process files of transactions, perform significant logic checks, match the transactions against other files, and produce a report in detailed or summary form (eg pricing inventories from a physical inventory of quantities).

- **the complexity of the entity's computer operations.** The computer might use batch processing in which all input during a period (eg daily) is accumulated in a batch and the entire batch is processed together. In more advanced on-line and real-time computer systems, transactions are input and processed by the computer immediately as they are entered.

- **the organisational structure of the data processing activities.** This can range from a centralised data processing department with segregation of functions within that department to a structure in which there is little, if any, segregation of functions related to data processing (often found in smaller businesses or where data processing is highly decentralised).

- **the availability of data.** Source documents used to enter information into the computer for processing, certain computer files (eg daily transaction files), and other accounting records (eg tables or factors used in calculations) that the auditor might need to examine might exist only for a short period or only in computer-readable form. In some computer systems, input documents might not exist at all because information is directly entered into the system.

10.3.2 *Legal Requirements*

Auditors are required by the Companies Acts to carry out such investigations as will enable them to form an opinion as to whether proper accounting records have been kept by the company.

The question of what accounting records need to be kept by a company is also dealt with in statute. Records must be sufficient not only to show and explain the company's transactions but also to disclose with reasonable accuracy at any time the financial position of the company at that time. To this end, they must contain detailed information (as specified in the legislation) relating to receipts and payments, assets and liabilities and, where appropriate, sales and purchases, stocktaking statements and statements of year-end stocks. These records must be kept for three years in the case of a private company and six years in other cases.

At both the planning and completion stages of the audit, therefore, the auditor should review the standard of the client's accounting records in the context of the statutory requirements. The review should answer the following questions:

- do the records contain all the information which the law specifically requires?

- are they sufficient to show and explain the company's transactions?

- are they sufficiently up-to-date to 'disclose with reasonable accuracy, at any time, the financial position of the company at that time'? It is not clear precisely how up-to-date the accounting records should be to comply with this requirement and to some extent this will depend upon the materiality of the sums involved and on the nature of the company's affairs. In the case of receipts and payments, the legislation requires entries to be made from day to day but it would seem reasonable to assume that this means the entries themselves should be on a daily basis and not that the cash book must be written to daily: in many cases this will not be practicable. As a general rule, unless records are brought up-to-date on at least a monthly basis (quarterly in the case of the nominal ledger), the company concerned would probably not have complied with this requirement. However, the availability of the information necessary to update the records, if required, at short notice, will be the essential feature

- are they adequate to enable the directors to prepare accounts which show a true and fair view?

The records should probably include as a minimum:

- cash book, containing entries on a day-to-day basis

- purchases/sales journals or some similar type of record supported by invoices; detailed records are not required, however, for goods sold by way of ordinary retail trade

- year-end stock summaries (prepared from stock records or physical counts) together with statements of any stocktakings on which those summaries are based. Statements of stock counted on a cyclical basis during the year should be retained

- nominal ledger

- some form of record of fixed assets

10.4 CONTROL PROCEDURES

10.4.1 *Types of control procedure*

The third element of the internal control structure comprises control procedures. Control procedures are policies and procedures (other than the control environment and accounting system) that management has established to provide reasonable assurance that specific entity objectives will be achieved.

Control procedures may be categorised as follows:

- general controls
- application controls
- controls over assets
- security of data.

A checklist of common control procedures is given in Appendix 10.2

10.4.2 *General controls*

General controls comprise:

- segregation of duties
- supervision
- controls over systems development, implementation and maintenance.

Unless general controls are working effectively, there is no assurance that application controls and controls over assets and the security of data are working properly.

Segregation of duties. If different people handle different parts of the same transaction they act as a control on each other, picking up mistakes and reducing the chance that an individual can perpetrate and then conceal an irregularity. If one of them wishes to act fraudulently, he or she will have to arrange for the collusion of one or more of the other people involved, which is likely to be a significant deterrent.

The client may have segregation of duties at a number of stages to ensure that errors and irregularities are detected as quickly as possible, thus minimising the damage they can do. Segregation of duties may occur between:

- the person authorising a transaction (eg a purchase or a sale)
- the person with control over the assets involved (eg cashiers and storekeepers)
- the person who enters the transaction in the accounting records (eg purchases or sales ledger clerk)
- the person who performs integrity checks on the accounting records (eg suppliers' statement reconciliations, aged list of debtors) and initiates correcting action
- the person who maintains the accounting system (eg programmers, systems analysts).

However, from an audit point of view, an auditor is principally concerned that detection occurs at some stage before the financial statements are prepared. He is therefore unlikely to need to appraise segregation of duties at every point, so long as he is satisfied that duties are adequately segregated to ensure that each key audit objective is achieved.

It is important to look at the whole extent of a person's duties, as proper segregation of duties over one type of transaction may be compromised by tasks performed by the same individual in another area.

In an owner-managed business, good owner-manager control may significantly mitigate the lack of segregation of duties. If, for example, the owner-manager carefully reviews and approves disbursements and monthly operating reports (and it becomes evident through discussion, for example when carrying out detailed analytical procedures, that the owner-manager's review is indeed thorough) the auditor may well conclude that the control risk of an undetected misstatement of operating expenditure is low.

Supervision. Supervision should exist throughout the client's organisation to make sure that:

- procedures are properly carried out

- errors are promptly corrected

- systems are promptly changed when weaknesses become apparent

- changes happen as envisaged and are effective

- systems are developed to meet the demands of new transactions or business developments within the organisation.

Without adequate supervision, there is no guarantee that the client's accounting procedures and controls are working properly.

From an audit point of view, supervision should preferably be carried out by specific observable routines and be evidenced by:

- initialling of reconciliations, vouchers, exception reports, log books of routines

- completed checklists

- written reports.

Supervisors should be competent to perform their duties and should not be overburdened with detail or be carrying out the basic accounting procedures and routines themselves — these should be carried out by an adequate number of competent staff. Signs of inadequate supervision include:

- late production of financial statements, reports, etc

- an excessive number of errors and exceptions

- an air of chaos or permanent crisis in a department.

Systems development, implementation and maintenance controls. Systems development and maintenance controls are needed to ensure that effective application controls are included in all new systems and the integrity of those application controls is preserved after the system has been implemented. A weakness in, or lack of, controls over applications systems development and maintenance, particularly updating and changing programs, may affect the integrity of a system and, accordingly, the reliability of the results produced by data processing.

Such controls include:

- involvement of accounting personnel, internal auditors, if any, and other users in the design of systems and in selecting software purchased from software vendors

- review and approval of written specifications by appropriate level of management and by users

- testing of new applications by both information technology specialists and users, including the manual phases of the system

- obtaining final approval for implementation from appropriate level of management.

Implementation controls are required to ensure that a system has been tested and authorised before implementation, that staff are conversant with the accounting system and control procedures and that the typically high volumes of data transferred or created on implementation are correct and authorised.

10.4.3 *Application controls*

General controls provide the necessary conditions for the application controls which should be operating within each accounting area. Application controls are controls over the capture and processing of accounting information as discussed below.

Data capture controls. Data capture controls ensure the completeness, validity and correctness of data captured by the accounting system when assets enter or leave the company and when accounting information is created.

They include, for example:

- the authorisation and approval of transactions and amendments, particularly to standing data, at appropriate levels and at the appropriate time to ensure unauthorised data cannot be entered for processing

- the use of pre-numbered documents, sequence checks and logs

- comparisons or matching with independently produced transaction documents

- procedures for investigating and correcting or resolving errors, rejections, etc

- edit checks — checks of format, screen, existence, check digits

- reasonableness checks — credit checks, volume checks.

Data processing controls. Data processing controls maintain the integrity and correctness of the items as they are processed through the accounting system. They ensure that data is not lost or corrupted at any of the points at which it is created, processed or transferred.

They include, for example:

- the agreement of control accounts with detailed accounts and investigation and correction or resolution of any differences

- the preparation of trial balance and periodic management accounts.

10.4.4 *Controls over assets*

In order to safeguard its assets, a business employs **custody controls** to control assets in its possession and when they enter and leave the business's premises.

They include, for example:

- restricting access to authorised personnel (see segregation of duties above). This includes restricting indirect access to assets (eg access to requisitions)

- authorisation for movements and transfers of assets

- counts and inspections when assets enter and leave the client

- periodic or continuous counts or checks of quantities or items.

Accountability controls over assets are to ensure that the financial statements of an enterprise accurately reflect its actual assets.

They include, for example:

- periodic or continuous counts or checks of quantities or items

- independent reconciliation of book records with physical amounts and investigation and correction/resolution of any differences.

In the absence of adequate controls over assets, the auditor may well find it necessary to perform an extensive count or check of assets at the balance sheet date.

10.4.5 Security of data

Once created, processed and recorded, data should remain correct until deleted or amended by authorised processing. Particular consideration should be given to permanent data. Unauthorised changes to such data (such as a pricing master file) would be of particular significance as they would affect all subsequent transactions which extract data from that file until the change is corrected.

10.4.6 Identifying and assessing controls

An auditor's understanding of control procedures need not extend to every assertion relevant to a particular account balance or class of transactions. Nor need he obtain any understanding of control procedures for other than significant account balances or classes of transactions. The key is to obtain sufficient understanding of key control procedures related to relevant assertions for significant account balances and classes of transactions for him to be able to:

- identify the types of potential misstatements that could occur
- consider factors that affect the risk of material misstatements occurring, and
- design substantive tests.

The auditor needs to exercise judgement in determining those control procedures about which he needs to develop knowledge. Various factors to be addressed in making such judgements include

- his knowledge of the client's business
- the nature of its industry
- key controls identified in previous years.

To identify the relevant controls the auditor should:

- identify the significant control objectives of management in relation to the various assertions in the financial statements which must be met if substantive testing is to be reduced
- determine what could go wrong in achieving those objectives.

For example, one of the control objectives management might need to achieve to ensure the completeness of recorded sales revenues could be that 'all shipments are invoiced'. The auditor should determine what could happen to keep all shipments from being invoiced. It might be that not all shipping documents are forwarded to the sales department with the result that some shipments are not invoiced.

Once the auditor has determined what could happen to keep an objective from being achieved, he determines whether there are any controls in place to prevent the condition or detect it on a timely basis once it has occurred.

In the situation described immediately above, the client might perform a reconciliation of all shipping documents maintained by the shipping department and investigate any differences. If the auditor could determine that this reconciliation would be effective in detecting uninvoiced shipments if applied consistently and appropriately, he might conclude that, in relation to the completeness assertion regarding sales, he should obtain an understanding of its design and operation.

10.4.7 Detect v prevent controls

The auditor usually focuses on periodic detect controls that are performed for significant or high-risk accounts. *Detect controls* are

- designed to detect errors or misstatements that have occurred during processing

- normally performed on groups of transactions

- usually applied outside the normal processing of data.

Examples include bank reconciliations, reconciliations between control and subsidiary accounts, physical stock counts, budget to actual comparisons, variance analysis and comparisons of shipping logs and sales records.

Prevent controls are controls designed to prevent errors or misstatements during processing of data. These are generally applied to each transaction and these controls are usually built into the system.

Examples of prevent controls include controls such as the checking of the account coding of disbursements and the mathematical accuracy of invoices.

The auditor normally places more emphasis on detect controls than on prevent controls because they usually:

- are more efficient from an audit point of view than prevent controls because they are applied to entire groups of transactions rather than to one transaction at a time

- are usually operated by management rather than more junior levels of personnel

- provide more persuasive evidence than prevent controls because they usually require the physical preparation of a schedule, a reconciliation, a follow-up of an edit listing, or some other kind of documentation. Prevent controls, by their nature, often do not provide such persuasive evidence that a procedure was actually performed. For example, the initials of a clerk on an invoice do not necessarily mean that the clerk actually checked its arithmetical accuracy; the clerk may have simply initialled the invoice without executing the control of checking the mathematical accuracy

- involve fewer applications than prevent controls and provide greater coverage. For example, a detect control such as a monthly bank reconciliation may involve only twelve applications. Prevent controls may involve thousands of applications.

10.4.8 *Focus on completeness*

The auditor's understanding of control procedures should also focus on controls that address the **completeness** assertion for significant classes of transactions, such as the use of pre-numbered documents and application of cut-off procedures. The absence or ineffectiveness of these key control procedures could be important to his assessment of the risk of material misstatement. In particular, the stage at which transactions are captured always merits separate consideration. It is relatively easy to obtain assurance that all transactions, once recorded, are accurately processed through to the accounting records, but much more difficult to be confident that all the transactions have been recorded in the first place.

10.4.9 *Outside service centre*

For a client that uses an outside service centre or clearing house for processing significant accounting data, the auditor should understand the processing of accounting information at the service centre as well as at the client's organisation. He might be able to obtain an understanding of the control environment and transaction flow by reviewing client procedures and output records, reviewing system documentation provided to the client by the service centre and having discussions with knowledgeable personnel in the client's organisation. If the auditor is unable to obtain a sufficient understanding by performing procedures at the client's organisation or if he plans to base his assessment of risk on controls located at the service centre, he might need to visit the service centre to complete these procedures. Alternatively, the service centre might have engaged an independent auditor to prepare a report on the accounting applications processed by the service centre.

10.5   DOCUMENTING THE INTERNAL CONTROL STRUCTURE

The form in which an auditor will document his understanding of the internal control structure is influenced by the size and complexity of the client and the nature of its internal control structure. He should be flexible in his approach and avoid excessive detail. Detailed documentation will be justified where:

- the auditor is likely to obtain a cost beneficial reduction in the level of substantive testing based on an assessment of a lower level of inherent and control risk

- an auditor is required by the terms of his engagement to report on specific aspects of the internal control structure, as may be the case in certain regulated industries, or is specifically requested by the client to do so

- an auditor believes that there are likely to be genuine benefits in terms of generating systems advice for his client.

As a minimum, an auditor should normally

- document his evaluation of the control environment

- document the flows of accounting information in respect of all major classes of transaction

- identify and document the principal control procedures by which management assures the completeness of those information streams.

The auditor's evaluation of the control environment may be documented either by completing a checklist or by preparing a narrative that identifies and describes the significant control environment considerations applicable to the entity. The checklist in Appendix 10.1, which deals with the control environment together with considerations of inherent risk, may help in the preparation of such a narrative.

For the purpose of documenting the client's accounting system and control procedures, the auditor can normally divide it into sub-systems reflecting the major categories of transactions. For example, for a typical manufacturing or commercial client, these will comprise principally

- the sales or revenue cycle

- the purchases or expenditure cycle

- wages and salaries

- stocks (and work in progress).

In addition to the routine flows of information, the auditor should document the client's year-end accounting procedures to assure the completeness, accuracy and validity of the records as of that date. For example, at any accounting date partially processed transactions will exist which will need to be allocated to the correct accounting period.

One or more of the following formats are used to document the auditor's understanding of the accounting system and the key control procedures

- **narrative descriptions** of the accounting system and related control procedures for the significant areas

- **flow charts** depicting the flow of accounting transactions between origination and the general ledger as well as certain key control procedures

111

- **internal control questionnaires (ICQs)** listing the most common accounting and internal control procedures for specific applications (eg cash, debtors) as well as general control procedures

- **control matrices** identifying, in a matrix form, significant transactions or files and the controls over completeness, accuracy and validity of data capture, processing and recording, and the controls over maintenance and security of both transaction and permanent data once recorded in the files.

10.6 WALK-THROUGHS

The auditor will normally confirm his understanding of the accounting system and control procedures by performing a walk-through of one or more transactions. A walk-through consists of following the selected transactions through the accounting system and related control procedures from start to finish to confirm that the understanding he has obtained of the processing of the transactions is accurate. The number of items that he walks through should be limited to as few as are necessary for him to confirm his understanding.

The walk-through is carried out on a new audit after the documentation has been drafted for the first time and, on a continuing audit, after it has been reviewed and amended as necessary. The extent to which a walk-through is performed on a continuing audit depends on

- whether there have been any changes to the system since the previous audit

- the extent of the staff member's familiarity with the system.

A disproportionate amount of time should not be spent in this area; the subsequent audit work will, indirectly, provide additional confirmation of the accuracy of the documentation. Because of the limited number of items that are typically walked through, the auditor normally does not gain much audit evidence regarding the effectiveness of control procedures in performing walk-throughs.

There may be procedures which cannot be confirmed in the manner described above because there is no visible evidence of their operation (eg computer program procedures). In these circumstances the auditor is left to rely solely on the client's documentation to represent the system in operation. If these procedures are considered significant to the audit, the auditor may need to employ computer-assisted techniques (eg test packs or interrogations) in order to confirm their existence and operation. However these techniques would not be used merely to carry out the walk-through of the system; they would usually also form part of the main programme of compliance or substantive tests.

An auditor should document the detailed results of his walk-through. This may be done by preparing a working paper memorandum identifying the item(s) walked-through and the results. Alternatively, where he has flowcharted the system, he could indicate on a copy of the flowchart itself the items tested and the processing steps confirmed by the walk-through.

10.7 ASSESSING INHERENT AND CONTROL RISK

10.7.1 *General principles*

As explained in Chapter 9, it is often difficult (and would serve little practical purpose) to assess separately inherent risk (the susceptibility of an account balance or class of transactions to material misstatement assuming that there were no related internal controls) and control risk (the risk that such material misstatements would not be prevented or detected on a timely basis by the internal control structure). The two elements of risk are so closely interrelated that it is often difficult to decide whether particular factors contribute to one element or the other. The auditor may therefore well choose to consider them together and to make a combined assessment of inherent and control risk.

On all audits there will be at least some inherent and control risk. An entity's internal control structure, no matter how well designed, is subject to inevitable limitations. Mistakes might occur in the application of policies and procedures because of misunderstandings, human error, carelessness, fatigue, and the like. In addition, control policies and procedures might be circumvented by collusion and by management override. For these reasons, among others, the auditor cannot obtain all his audit evidence through reliance on the internal control structure. He should, in all audits, perform some substantive tests (in the form of tests of details, analytical procedures, or a combination of both) on all account balances and classes of transactions that are susceptible to material error.

On the other hand, nearly every system, however rudimentary, provides the auditor with some confidence that material errors will be prevented or detected. The problem lies in assessing the level of this assurance and in obtaining suitable evidence in support of the assessment by tests of controls. The auditor needs to

- identify specific policies and procedures relevant to particular assertions that are likely to prevent or detect material misstatements in those assertions

- perform tests of controls (also known as compliance tests) to evaluate the effectiveness of such policies and procedures (as explained in Chapter 14).

In determining his audit strategy, the auditor should compare the time and effort to be spent in assessing inherent and control risk at a particular level for particular assertions, including the required evaluation and testing of controls, with the time and effort that may be saved on substantive tests. Generally speaking, the lower the assessed level of inherent and control risk, the stronger the evidence the auditor will require to support the assessment, and therefore the greater the time and effort involved in making the assessment. The auditor is therefore unlikely to seek to assess inherent and control risk at a low level if an account comprises relatively few large items (eg long-term borrowings) or if it may be audited relatively easily by performing analytical procedures as a substantive test (eg rental expense or income).

Staffing pressures or tight client deadlines (rather than cost-benefit considerations) might cause an auditor to plan to obtain some assurance from the internal control structure rather than relying solely on his substantive tests. For example, on audits where there is a tight reporting deadline he may assess inherent and control risk below the maximum level and perform tests to obtain assurance about the entity's internal control policies and procedures at the interim stage even though this approach may not be the most cost-effective. It should then be possible for him to reduce or modify his substantive tests performed at the year-end, even though he may not anticipate any total time or cost savings as a result of this approach.

10.7.2 *Preliminary assessment of inherent and control risk*

In planning the audit, the auditor should make a preliminary assessment, based on his understanding of the client's business and the internal control structure, of the inherent and control risk relating to assertions for each material component of the financial statements. He should consider:

- management's philosophy and operating style
- the operating structure and methods of control
- the accounting environment
- the business environment

- specific factors that make individual assertions particularly susceptible to material error

- the accounting system and control procedures in the individual areas.

The checklist in Appendix 10.1 deals with these considerations in more detail and may be helpful in carrying out a preliminary assessment of inherent and control risk.

This preliminary assessment of inherent and control risk is not necessarily a comprehensive evaluation. As explained earlier in this chapter, there will be circumstances where the auditor would not seek a detailed understanding of the internal control structure.

On the other hand, the auditor should not at this stage assess the level of inherent and control risk at lower than the level supported by the evidence (of the effectiveness of control policies and procedures) obtained during the process of developing an understanding of the internal control structure, for example when documenting the system and carrying out walk-through procedures. To assess risk at a lower level he would have to perform additional work as explained below.

10.7.3 *Further reduction in assessed level of inherent and control risk*

The auditor should consider performing additional work by way of a more comprehensive identification and testing of controls, if it is likely to lead to a lower assessment of inherent and control risk and a cost beneficial reduction in the level of substantive testing.

The greater the auditor's assurance that the internal control policies and procedures relevant to an assertion are designed and operating effectively, the lower he can assess inherent and control risk. However, as already stated he should, in all audits, perform some substantive tests on all account balances or classes of transaction that are susceptible to material error.

Chapter 14 discusses the testing of controls.

APPENDIX   10.1

CHECKLIST OF ENVIRONMENTAL INHERENT AND CONTROL RISK FACTORS

A   MANAGEMENT PHILOSOPHY AND OPERATING STYLE

- management and operating decisions dominated by one or few individuals

- attitude of management to internal control structure

- likelihood of management override.

- management emphasis on meeting budget, profit and other financial and operating goals

- management emphasis on safeguarding of assets (eg security of physical assets)

- management involvement in systems development and attitude towards data security

- management experience and knowledge needed to operate business

- rate of management turnover

- management's approach [aggressive/conservative attitude] to taking and monitoring business risks

- management's financial reporting philosophy (may be characterised for example as maximising reported profits, maintaining earnings level, maintaining net asset value, maintaining share price, minimising taxable income or accurately reflecting financial results)

- quality of accounting policies selected

- management willingness to adjust financial statements for misstatements

- management attitude towards regulatory compliance

- incidence of transactions entered into for no apparent business purpose

- extent of ongoing consultation with auditors on accounting issues

- management relationship with auditors, eg responsiveness to previous recommendations by auditors, absence of restrictions on audit procedures or of abnormal fee pressures

- management relationship with other advisers (rate of turnover)

- extent and nature of transactions or arrangements with related parties.

B   OPERATING STRUCTURE AND METHODS OF CONTROL

- clearly defined organisation, lines of authority, responsibility and reporting

- frequency of changes in organisational structure

- policies for authorisation of transactions defined at adequately senior levels

- mechanisms for monitoring adherence to/reporting departures from company policies

- adequacy of control over decentralised operations

- degree of management involvement in day-to-day operations

- past experience with operation of controls

- effectiveness of the board of directors and, if appropriate, the audit committee (or other equivalent body) in overseeing financial reporting

- how the board fulfills its fiduciary and accountability responsibilities

- whether the client has policies regarding appropriate business relationships, conflicts of interest, and codes of conduct

- management objectives (financial and operating goals) clearly defined, communicated, and monitored

- management's ability to supervise effectively overall company activities

- the methods used in exercising direct control over company activities and those given authority to carry out those activities

- management's use of appropriate internal and external data to control and run the business and for other aspects of decision-making, planning and evaluating performance (eg budgets, variance reports, operating statistics regarding sales, margins and employee numbers, production data such as volume or tonnage statistics and data from specially commissioned market research and trade and industry journals)

- adequacy of mechanisms for identifying, reporting and investigating variances from planned performance

- quality of operating information systems

- the organisational structure of data processing activities

- policies for developing and modifying accounting systems and control procedures, including the development, modification, and use of any related computer programs and data files

- existence, independence and effective use of an internal audit function

- policies and procedures for hiring, training, evaluating, promoting and compensating employees and providing them with the necessary resources to discharge their assigned responsibilities

- appropriate policies and procedures for developing new uses, and modifying existing uses, of information technology.

C THE ACCOUNTING ENVIRONMENT

- competence (background, training, and experience) of accounting personnel

- attitude and morale of accounting personnel

- rate of turnover of accounting personnel

- adequacy of both human resources and data processing resources in relation to the workload

- previous audit experience with accounting personnel

- previous audit experience with late accounting adjustments and reasons therefor

- time pressure imposed by financial reporting timetable

- likelihood of material transactions or adjustments near the financial year-end

- frequency of contentious accounting issues in the past and new problems expected in the current year

- overall degree-of-day to day supervision of accounting personnel

- extent of judgment and estimation involved in accounting routines
- adequacy of policies and procedures for developing accounting estimates
- likelihood of biases in accounting estimates
- adequacy of procedures for developing and modifying accounting systems
- rate of change in accounting systems and procedures
- in a computerised system
  - degree of integration of systems
  - use of package (standard, purchased) systems or in-house developed systems
  - reputation of package or external data-processing bureau.

D EXTERNAL INFLUENCES

- monitoring or compliance requirements imposed by external regulatory bodies
- active monitoring or review by regulators, insurers, lenders, customers, suppliers or other third parties
- requirements and needs of investors in the company
- spread of holdings of equity interests beyond those of management and employees
- likelihood of sale of equity interests by significant existing holders
- likelihood of public offering of shares
- industry in which client operates (profitability, maturity, growth, competition, degree of specification, stability, influence of technology and other factors)
- history of litigation against client or management, including disputes with, or special investigation by, the tax authorities, and any current or expected litigation
- liquidity and profitability of client relative to industry norms
- liquidity and profitability of client relative to previous years
- relationship with bankers and needs for additional funds.

E ADDITIONAL CONSIDERATIONS BY SPECIFIC AREA

- past audit experience with the area
- extent of use of accounting estimates/judgment in the area
- adequacy of policies and procedures for developing accounting estimates in the area
- complexity of accounting issues in the area
- size and volume of transactions in the area
- complexity of accounting calculations involved
- frequency or significance of difficult-to-audit transactions in the area
- susceptibility of related assets to misappropriation
- quality of specific accounting policies

CHECKLIST OF COMMON CONTROL PROCEDURES

1 INTRODUCTION

This checklist sets out common controls procedures. It is divided into the following sections:

- general controls
  - segregation of duties
  - supervision
  - systems development, maintenance and implementation

- application controls
  - data capture
  - data processing

- controls over assets
  - custody controls
  - accountability controls

- security of data

It is important that the auditor's review of controls considers not just the capture and processing of data but its maintenance in a correct form until reported. Particular consideration should be given to permanent data (such as a pricing master file), because an error introduced into such data would affect all subsequent transactions which use that data until the error is corrected. The significance of unauthorised changes to transaction data will depend upon the nature of the accounting system. For example, in a system which generates debit and credit records in respect of a transaction, the unauthorised amendment of one record, at a transaction or balance level, will lead to an imbalance in the trial balance. In a sophisticated database system where a transaction gives rise to a single record which is interpreted as a debit or credit for the purpose of generating accounting reports, an unauthorised change may be self-balancing and not highlighted by a trial balance.

2 GENERAL CONTROLS

2.1 *Segregation of duties*

There should be segregation of duties between:

- the person authorising a transaction (eg a purchase or a sale)

- the person with control over the assets involved (eg stocks)

- the person who enters the transaction in the accounting records (eg creditors or debtors ledger)

- the person who performs integrity checks on the accounting records (eg suppliers' statement reconciliations, aged list of debtors) and initiates correcting action

- the person who maintains the accounting system software (eg programmers, systems analysts).

In the data processing department there should be:

- segregation of function between data processing departments and users

- segregation of function within the data processing department (eg systems analysis, programmers, operators)

- division of duties between preparation, authorisation and input of source documents.

- general authorisation by management and users over execution of transactions

- authorisation by users of source documents

- independent 'control' function responsible for receiving all data, ensuring it is recorded, following up on errors discovered during processing and distributing output

- maintenance of operating instructions (eg a written manual of systems and procedures)

- restriction of physical and logical access to computer hardware (eg physical security, control logs)

- restriction of physical and logical access to computer files (files on the computer and files removed on tapes, disks etc)
    - attempted breaches reported by the system
    - controls over availability and knowledge of passwords
    - passwords changed frequently

- access restriction at a functional level (eg different access capabilities for programmers and operators)

- both physical and logical access to hardware, software and data may be restricted to specified personnel by the use of a personal identifier together with one or more of the following
    - passwords (changed frequently to maintain confidentiality)
    - personal characteristics (eg palm print, retina scan)
    - physical devices (eg keys, magnetic strip cards)
    - time constraints (eg time locks, programmed procedures that allow software to be run only on certain dates or days or a restricted number of times in a particular period).

- there should be means of
    - identifying and controlling individuals rather than groups
    - reporting and investigating attempted breaches of security
    - controlling availability of physical devices
    - controlling availability and knowledge of passwords
    - disabling terminals etc if an excessive number of security breaches take place in a particular time span.

2.2 Systems development, implementation and maintenance

Relevant controls include:

- the involvement of accounting personnel, internal auditors, if any, and other users in the design of systems and in selecting software purchased from software vendors

- review and approval of written specifications by appropriate level of management and by users

- testing of new applications by both information technology specialists and users, including the manual phases of the system

- obtaining final approval for implementation from appropriate level of management

- control of all master file and transaction file conversions to prevent unauthorised changes and to provide accurate and complete conversion results

- after new systems have been installed, control of updates and changes to programs to determine they are authorised, tested and documented

- standards for systems documentation.

3 APPLICATION CONTROLS

3.1 *Data capture*

Controls over the capture of data (including transaction entry, file maintenance transactions, inquiry transactions and error correction transactions) may involve:

- the authorisation and approval of transactions and amendments, particularly to standing data, at appropriate levels at the appropriate time to ensure unauthorised data cannot be entered for processing
  — authorisation on each source document
  — user approval on a batch of documents

- use of prenumbered source documents, sequence checks and logs — programmed or manual sequence checks, with investigation into missing items

- checks and reviews of authorisations, calculations

- the reproduction or repetition of data or procedures

- comparisons or matching with independently produced transaction documents

- procedures for investigating and correcting or resolving errors, rejections, etc

- edit checks
  — limit tests
  — range tests
  — field tests
  — validity tests (eg check digits for customer account numbers)
  — format checks

- reasonableness checks — credit checks, volume checks

- computer matching of input with details already on file to identify missing input (eg shipping records for which no invoice has been input)

- review of computer-generated data (eg overall totals and large, or otherwise exceptional, items)

- program checks for duplication of input.

3.2 *Processing*

Controls over processing include the following:

- certain data capture checks may be performed/reperformed at this stage (eg edit checks, sequence checks, duplication checks, computer matching)

- accounting data can be changed only by appropriate programs

- verification that entries in financial records, including journals, are correct as to amount, account and date

- matching with existing data (eg credit notes and payments to invoices)

- use of test/batch procedures (transactions logging or other form of "batch generation" for on line computer systems)
  — batch approval by user
  — mismatches investigated and errors/queried items returned to user for correction (where applicable)

- the agreement of control accounts with detail accounts and investigation and correction or resolution of any differences

- the agreements of control totals and account balances

- the preparation of trial balance and periodic management accounts

- output reviewed for unusual items

- output distributed to authorised users only

- monitoring actual and expected cumulative balances.

4. CONTROL OVER ASSETS

4.1 *Custody controls*

Custody controls include:

- restricting access to authorised personnel (see segregation of duties above). This includes restricting indirect access to assets (eg. access to requisitions)

- adequate protection from and insurance against accidental destruction, deterioration, being mislaid, pilferage

- authorisation of movements and transfers of assets

- counts and inspection when assets leave the client

- clear allocations of responsibility

- segregation of duties between those holding assets and those preparing financial records

- periodic or continuous counts or checks of quantities or items.

4.2 *Accountability controls*

Accountability controls include:

- periodic or continuous counts or checks of quantities or items

- independent reconciliation of book records with physical amounts and investigation and correction/resolution of any differences.

5 SECURITY OF DATA

Controls should address the security of both permanent and transaction data and data-bearing media. They include:

- restriction of physical and logical access to hardware, software and media to authorised personnel and/or software

- adequate protection from (and insurance against) accidental destruction, deterioration, being mislaid, pilferage

- back-up provisions
  - off premises back-up of data, programs and documentation
  - formal disaster recovery plan

- hardware and systems software control
  - checks to ensure that the correct data is being processed
  - detection and reporting of hardware malfunction
  - systems software subjected to strict development controls

— checks to ensure that only authorised software can access data and then only in an authorised manner

● the agreement of control totals to underlying records
    — hash totals
    — record counts
    — value totals
    — reconciliation of brought forward and carried forward balances.

Such checks may take place each time the data is processed and, dependent on the frequency of processing, at intervals in between. In addition to these 'internal' checks other periodic reconciliations will take place, for example to bank statements, suppliers' statements and physical assets and inventory.

CHAPTER 11   OTHER INFLUENCES ON AUDIT PLANNING

11.1   PRELIMINARY ANALYTICAL PROCEDURES

11.1.1   *Nature of Analytical Procedures*

Analytical procedures are used to evaluate financial information by studying plausible and predictable relationships among both financial and non-financial data. They involve comparisons between recorded amounts, or ratios developed from recorded amounts, and expected amounts or ratios that the auditor develops. The procedures range from simple comparisons of data (eg current period to prior period comparisons) to the use of complex models involving many relationships and elements of data.

Analytical procedures are applied

- to assist in planning the nature, timing, and extent of other auditing procedures (the focus of this chapter)

- as a substantive test to obtain evidential matter about particular assertions related to account balances or classes of transactions (covered in chapter 15)

- in an overall review of the financial statements in the final review stage of the audit (covered in chapter 20).

A basic premise underlying the application of analytical procedures is that plausible and predictable relationships among data may reasonably be expected to exist and continue to exist in the absence of known conditions to the contrary. Variations in these relationships can be caused by particular conditions, which may include, for example, specific unusual transactions or events, accounting changes, business changes, random fluctuations, and misstatements. It is because of this last condition, namely that variations between recorded amounts or derived ratios and expected amounts or ratios may be indicative of misstatements in the financial statements, that an auditor identifies and investigates such variations.

Usually the most effective and efficient use of analytical procedures involves ratios and other relationships that management uses itself as part of its day-to-day management of financial and operating activities. If management uses a ratio or relationship in managing the business:

- it is undoubtedly relevant and important for the auditor's own understanding of the client's business

- the necessary data is readily available.

In applying analytical procedures, the auditor needs to understand

- the reasons that make particular financial relationships plausible and predictable

- the client and the industry or industries in which it operates

- the purposes of the procedures and their limitations.

During the planning stage, analytical procedures help to determine the audit strategy by identifying, among other things, significant matters that require consideration during the audit, such as material accounts, increases or decreases in account balances, and changes in relationships among accounts. In effect, applying analytical procedures at this stage of the audit helps to direct attention toward accounts with potentially high inherent risk. An unexpected increase in sales, for example, should alert the auditor to consider carefully the extent of cut-off tests that should be performed.

123

Examples of sources of information an auditor might use in developing expectations include:

- financial information for comparable prior periods, giving consideration to known changes

- anticipated results (eg budgets and forecasts, including extrapolations from interim or annual data)

- relationships among elements of financial information within a period (eg month-to-month comparisons)

- information as to the client's industry (eg industry gross margin ratios)

- relationships of financial information with relevant non-financial information (eg sales in a retail store with square footage of selling space).

11.1.2 *Analytical Procedures in Audit Planning*

Preliminary analytical procedures used in planning the audit should focus on

- enhancing understanding of the client's business and of the transactions and other events that have occurred since the last audit

- identifying areas that may represent specific risks relevant to the audit.

The extent of the preliminary analytical procedures will of course depend on the quality of draft financial information available at the planning stage.

The preliminary analytical procedures commonly applied to the client's most recent financial statements include

- computation of ratios and percentage relationships for comparison with prior years, budgets, and industry averages

- comparison of current balances in the financial statements with balances of prior periods and budgeted amounts

- scanning the financial statements for unusual or significant transactions or balances.

To be most effective, preliminary analytical procedures should cover as long a period as practical. Generally they should cover a three-year period (current and two prior periods) to minimise the appearance of fluctuations in the current period that are, in fact, caused by unusual relationships in the immediate prior period. Using a three-year period also enhances the auditor's ability to discern trends in data or relationships.

Preliminary analytical procedures generally involve the use of data aggregated at a high level. The auditor would normally use financial data at the level of a line item or major component of the financial statements (eg accounts receivable, costs of goods sold). As noted above, the auditor tries to focus on the data and relationships used by management themselves in running the business.

The sophistication and extent of the procedures to be applied are matters of professional judgment and vary widely, depending on the client's size and complexity, and the availability of information. For some entities, the procedures may consist of reviewing changes in account balances from the prior year to the current year. In contrast, for other entities, the procedures might involve an extensive analysis of monthly or quarterly financial statements. In either case, the analytical procedures, combined with the auditor's knowledge of the business, serve as a basis for additional inquiries and effective planning.

On audits in which an auditor performs interim work, he will ordinarily perform preliminary analytical procedures based on the latest available interim information. He may want to update his analytical procedures using preliminary year-end balances after considering such factors as:

- the inherent stability of the client's business

- the length of the intervening period

- changes to the client's operations during this period.

Although preliminary analytical procedures often involve financial data only, key relevant non-financial information is also considered, particularly where this represents performance measures used by management. For example, an auditor may be able to establish relationships such as the following between non-financial information and financial statement items:

Number of employees	Payroll cost
Square footage of space occupied	Rent expense
Volume of goods produced	Cost of goods sold.

Similarly, where industry financial or non-financial statistics are available, a comparison with industry-wide trends may also be helpful.

In using preliminary analytical procedures, an auditor needs to remember that the information he is working with is typically unaudited. He often uses a preliminary trial balance or other interim information to which he will have applied no auditing procedures. For this reason, preliminary analytical procedures are used primarily to highlight areas that need to be focused on during the audit rather than to provide specific audit evidence.

It should be recognised that certain activities — for example, market-making in the brokerage industry — are such that financial information is not readily comparable from one point in time to another. The value of carrying out preliminary analytical procedures may be diminished in such circumstances.

11.1.3 Examples of Financial Information and Ratios

The following are examples of financial information and ratios that might be particularly relevant when compared to information and ratios for prior periods (preferably two prior periods):

- **sales**
  - sales
  - sales compared to budgets or forecasts
  - sales by major division of product line
  - sales divided by some measure of capacity (eg number of employees)
  - average sales price per 'unit' sold
  - sales discounts/allowances to total sales

- **cost of sales**
  - gross margin percentage
  - gross margin percentage by major division or product line
  - average cost per 'unit' sold

- **trade debtors**
  - trade debtors and related bad debts
  - trade debtors 'turnover' ratio
  - ageing of trade debtors

- **stock**
  - stock 'turnover' ratio

   — components of closing stock (eg raw materials, work-in-process, finished goods) as percent of total

   — average "unit" costs of finished goods

   — stock and related provisions

- **operating expenses**
  - operating expenses (eg selling costs, freight out, bad debts) which are variable in nature as a percentage of sales
  - total salaries divided by average number of employees
  - payroll tax expense as a percentage of total salaries
  - maintenance and repairs expense as a percentage of fixed assets, at cost
  - depreciation expense as a percentage of fixed assets, at cost
  - interest expense as a percentage of fixed assets, at cost
  - interest expense as a percentage of total debt subject to interest

- **liquidity**
  - current ratio (current assets divided by current liabilities)
  - quick ratio (cash, marketable securities, and current receivables divided by current liabilities)

- **other indicators**
  - debt to equity ratio
  - net sales to tangible operating assets
  - operating income to tangible operating assets

11.1.4 *Documenting Preliminary Analytical Procedures*

In documenting preliminary analytical procedures an auditor should include the following information in his audit planning working papers:

- key financial information or ratios, with comparative data for periods (preferably two prior periods)

- explanations of any unusual or unexpected relationships

- effect on audit plan.

The audit planning memorandum should be used to document highlights from the preliminary analytical procedures, particularly the relationships that are unusual or otherwise considered to be key to the planning decisions.

The historical financial and non-financial data used for the analytical procedures may be filed in permanent file working papers to facilitate their use in subsequent years.

11.2 INVOLVEMENT OF OTHER AUDITORS

Other auditors may be involved in the audit either as principal auditors, or supporting auditors, and the effects of their involvement need to be addressed in planning the audit.

The principal auditor, the auditor with the responsibility for the audit opinion given on the financial statements, should communicate with supporting auditors during the planning stage to make them aware of his requirements and to give them the opportunity to discuss any potential problems. Before significant work begins, supporting auditors will need to know:

- the scope of their work

- due dates for completing their part of the audit

- reporting requirements

- other planning information, such as materiality and known related parties.

To the extent that a principal auditor plans to rely on the work of supporting auditors, he will need to obtain reasonable assurance that their work is adequate and that they are independent. Naturally, if the business segment to be audited by other auditors is not material to the financial statements as a whole, planning requirements may be reduced. Dealing with the audit of groups of companies is dealt with in more detail in Chapter 24 of this book.

The supporting auditor, the auditor with reporting responsibilities for a segment of the auditee enterprise or a group of assets or liabilities, will need to communicate with the principal auditors during the planning stage regarding the matters mentioned above and other instructions and guidance that might be needed.

11.3 USE OF INTERNAL AUDITORS

Management may establish an internal audit function to assist it in fulfilling certain of its responsibilities. Specific responsibilities of the internal auditors depend on the entity's size and structure and management's requirements. Generally, internal audit departments are responsible for

- reviewing and testing internal accounting controls and monitoring the functioning of the accounting system
- examining financial and operating information
- reviewing operations and related operating controls to promote increased efficiency and economy
- making special studies at management's discretion.

Internal auditors play a different role in an internal control structure from employees who execute specific controls; instead, they act as a separate, higher level of control to determine that the internal control structure is functioning effectively. Accordingly, when a client has internal auditors, the external auditor should obtain an understanding of their role in relation to the internal control structure to determine if their work should affect the planning of the nature, timing, and extent of his audit procedures.

The auditor should consider their competence and objectivity. Specifically, he should

- enquire about their technical qualifications and the relative depth of their technical training and proficiency. (This might involve reviewing the client's hiring and training policies for internal auditors, and their experience and professional qualifications)
- consider the organisational level to which internal auditors report the results of their work and the organisational level to which they report administratively. This could affect their ability to act independently of the individuals responsible for the function being audited. Internal auditors should have no operating responsibility and no constraints or restrictions on their work should be imposed by management or by those directly responsible for the operations being audited.

If he is satisfied with the objectivity and competence of the internal auditors, the auditor needs to further evaluate internal audit work if he is to place reliance upon it. He should review the working papers supporting selected audits performed during the year and consider such factors as whether:

- the scope of work is appropriate
- audit programmes are adequate
- working papers adequately document the work performed
- conclusions reached are appropriate in the circumstances
- reports issued are consistent with the results of the work performed.

The auditor should also perform tests of some of the work of the internal auditors. The extent of his tests will vary depending on the particular circumstances, including the type of transactions and their materiality. The tests may be of two types; the auditor can either re-examine some of the very transactions or balances that the internal auditors examined or examine similar transactions or balances but not those actually examined by the internal auditors. Whether or not his tests support those performed by the internal auditors will enable an auditor to conclude the extent to which, if at all, he can rely on internal audit work.

An auditor should consult with the internal auditors concerning work that they have in progress or plan to initiate, relating to the year end under audit, since the work they have not yet completed may also have a bearing on audit.

Further guidance on the procedures to be followed when placing reliance on the work of internal auditors is contained in Auditing Guideline 3.408 'Reliance on Internal Audit'.

In addition to using the work performed by the internal auditors in determining the nature, timing, and extent of his procedures, the auditor also might obtain direct assistance from internal auditors during the course of the audit. They may assist him in many ways, including the performance of both substantive tests and tests of controls. Whether he relies on the work of internal auditors or obtains direct assistance from them, judgements as to the effectiveness of internal controls, sufficiency of tests performed, materiality of transactions, and other matters affecting his audit report must be his own.

If an auditor plans to use the direct assistance of internal auditors, he should inform management as soon as possible and arrange to meet with the internal auditors to discuss their involvement in the audit and to establish tentative time schedules and deadlines. When using their direct assistance and supervision, he should also consider their competence and objectivity, and test their work to the extent appropriate in the circumstances.

11.4   USE OF THE WORK OF SPECIALISTS

Though retaining full responsibility for the audit, an auditor occasionally uses the work of specialists in forming his audit opinion. Specialists are individuals or firms with skills or expertise in a particular profession or field other than accounting or auditing, such as actuaries, valuers, engineers, geologists and lawyers.

Situations that might require the special knowledge of a specialist include the following:

- legal opinions and interpretations of statutes, regulations and agreements

- valuation of specific assets (eg property held for sale, works of art, precious stones, restricted securities) or liabilities (eg accrued pension benefits, court settlements, damages)

- determination of amounts using specialised techniques or methods (eg actuarial calculations)

- determination of the quality or condition of assets (eg mineral reserves).

In planning the audit, an auditor relies on his knowledge of the client's business and industry to identify situations that might require the services of a specialist. When use of a specialist's work is anticipated, the audit plan should be modified to recognise the work to be carried out by the specialist and the degree of assurance expected from those procedures.

As soon as he considers the work of a specialist to be necessary, the auditor should request the client to engage a specialist. Alternatively, with the approval of the client, he may engage the specialist himself. However, if the client is unwilling to engage a specialist, the auditor should consider the effect of such a scope limitation on his audit report.

The specialist's professional qualifications and reputation will be important factors in an auditor's consideration of the level of reliance he can place on his work. Competence usually will be indicated by technical qualifications, experience, and membership of an appropriate professional body.

The specialist preferably should be independent of the client, because the work of an independent specialist is presumed to be more objective, and thus provides evidence of a higher quality than the work of a specialist who is not independent.

If an independent specialist is engaged by the client, rather than by the auditor himself, he might wish to ascertain the overall volume of services that the specialist provides to the client and the extent of any unbilled or uncollected fees outstanding from the client, because these factors could influence the specialist's objectivity.

If the specialist is not independent of the client, an auditor should consider whether he needs to and can perform procedures to compensate for this lack of independence. Alternatively, another specialist may need to be engaged to review the work of the non-independent specialist.

The auditor should have an understanding with the client and the specialist as to the nature of the work to be performed by the specialist. Preferably, the understanding should be documented and should cover

- the objectives and scope of the specialist's work
- the specialist's representations as to his relationship, if any, to the client
- the methods or assumptions to be used
- a comparison of the methods or assumptions to be used with those used in the preceding period
- the specialist's understanding of the auditor's use of the specialist's findings in relation to the assertions in the financial statements
- the form and content of the specialist's report.

The auditor should plan to review the work of specialists. His objective is to assess the basis for reliance on their findings. This review might include consideration of the source data, assumptions, and methods on which those findings are based.

The auditor should normally ascertain the completeness and validity of accounting-based source data provided by the client (for example, data provided to actuaries for pension scheme actuarial report purposes) by conducting appropriate tests or, less frequently, by assessing the procedures used by the specialist to accomplish the same objective.

The appropriateness and reasonableness of the assumptions and methods used and their application are the responsibility of the specialist. An auditor should, however, obtain a sufficient understanding of them to enable him to determine whether they are reasonable for evaluating the financial statement assertions and are consistent with prior periods. Normally, he accepts the specialist's judgment and work as being reasonable in the absence of evidence to the contrary. If the assumptions or methods have been changed from prior periods, the auditor should consider the effect, if any, on the financial statement presentation.

CHAPTER 12   DEVELOPING AN AUDIT STRATEGY AND AUDIT PROGRAMME

12.1   STRATEGY AND DETAILED PLANNING

The earlier chapters of this book have dealt with the process of the auditor familiarising himself with the particular audit and of analysing the risks he faces in seeking to meet the engagement objectives. This chapter gives guidance on developing a strategy for the audit and preparing a detailed programme of work.

The audit strategy is the 'master plan' for how the auditor is going to approach the audit engagement. It guides the detailed decisions about the nature, timing and extent of his audit procedures.

The sort of decisions that need to be taken — the sort of questions needing to be answered — in developing the audit strategy are:

- How best can this engagement be broken down into more manageable, but identifiable, areas?

- What, for each area, are the major components?

- For each major component, what are the audit objectives, what is the assessment of inherent and control risks involved, and what should the principal audit procedures be?

These decisions need to be taken in a 'top-down', ordered way. The auditor needs to stand back and look at the nature of the engagement as a whole, and methodically work his way down to a reasonably precise assessment of how he is going to approach each area. Only then, with the strategy in place, can he proceed to set out in his audit programmes the detailed steps that need to be carried out in the field.

The extent of work involved in developing an audit strategy depends upon whether the client is a new or an existing one. In the case of existing clients, the auditor would normally review and update the audit strategy used in the previous year in the light of his experience with that strategy and any changes in the client's business, operations or internal control structure.

In the case of a new client, the audit strategy would be based on a more extensive process of familiarisation with the client's business and on experience with similar businesses and the relevant industry.

12.2   DECISION LEVELS IN AN AUDIT STRATEGY

The decisions in developing an audit strategy can be seen as coming at a number of strategic levels:

- at the top level, decisions relate to the financial statements as a whole, such as the determination of overall audit risk and materiality

- at intermediate levels, the decisions relate to how the engagement should be broken down into more manageable areas (which may be, for example, into areas of business activity, into geographical areas, or into transaction cycles) and what are the major components in each area

- at the basic detailed level, decisions relate to identifying the audit objectives for each major component, establishing an appropriate balance between detection risk and inherent and control risk, and determining the principal audit procedures.

The number of strategic levels will vary from client to client. In many cases, with smaller clients, there may be no need to analyse the engagement into "manageable areas"; developing the audit strategy, once overall audit risk and materiality have been decided, may simply be a matter of:

- identifying the key financial statement items

- assessing inherent and control risk for those key items and thereby determining the amount of evidence to be obtained from substantive audit testing

- determining the principal substantive procedures.

In contrast, more complex assignments can often be approached in a number of different ways. For example, consider a company that domestically retails its products through its own distribution division, but for foreign sales deals with wholesale importers in the respective foreign countries. Thus at the year end trade debtors are made up of amounts due from domestic retail consumers and amounts due from foreign wholesale distributors. The audit strategy might either:

- elect not to distinguish the two types of business (domestic and foreign), having assessed inherent and control risk for both as high, and treat the whole trade debtors balance (for audit purposes) in a uniform way

- recognise the different risks associated with domestic and foreign business by splitting the audit of trade debtors into two.

In the above example, if the product range is different for domestic and foreign sales, it may be worthwhile to separate completely the two businesses; for instance, it may be possible to use analytical procedures in respect of gross margins to prove stock or cost of sales figures only if the two sides of the business are separated.

The larger and more complicated the client, the greater the number of strategic alternatives there tend to be. In developing the audit strategy an auditor seeks to choose the alternatives that will provide the most efficient, effective audit.

However complex the client, the auditor needs to develop his strategy in sufficient detail to enable him to select specific audit procedures for each major component at the basic detailed level.

Thus in the example given above, the decisions in developing the strategy that determine the auditor's approach to trade debtors in respect of foreign sales, are:

- at the intermediate strategic level, to audit foreign debtors separately from domestic debtors

- at the basic detailed level
  - to assess inherent and control risk in respect of foreign debtors as (for instance) high
  - to obtain direct confirmation of balances from foreign customers on a sample basis as at the year end date.

12.3 DEVELOPING AN AUDIT STRATEGY

The auditor should keep the following criteria firmly in mind while developing the audit strategy (if not, he will probably waste time revising it later).

Completeness and balance. Does the strategy cover everything it should, and is audit effort being targeted appropriately? In particular, the auditor needs to be satisfied that he is focusing his audit effort on the areas in which audit risk is greatest.

Efficiency and practicality. Is the strategy cost-effective and feasible? In particular the auditor needs to be satisfied that:

- effective use will be made of management information in his analytical procedures

- the audit work planned responds to the way in which management runs and controls the business

- he has taken into account the results of performing other non-audit services (eg accounting and taxation work) for the client

- the work planned is capable of being performed by the audit personnel available and in the required timeframe

- he has considered suggestions based on experience from previous audits (points forward, etc) for enhancing efficiency and practicality.

Business relationships. Have all business relationships between account balances been considered in determining the audit approach? In every type of business, there are basic relationships between different elements of the financial statements. The more use is made of these relationships, the more efficient the audit is likely to be. These, for a company that simply buys and sells goods, include the relationships shown in the diagram below:

Relationship III can be used to provide assurance on sales from tests of cost of sales and gross margin. Alternatively, the same relationship can provide assurance on cost of sales from tests of sales and gross margin. This can be a powerful tool where the gross margin can be easily verified, for example in a company with a small number of products, each with a fixed mark-up.

In addition to the basic relationships, other relationships (often involving non-financial data) may be used. For example:

● for a manufacturer of plastic bottles, raw material consumption can be used to determine the number of bottles produced. This in turn may be used to verify both sales and closing stock

● for a school, tuition income has a direct correlation with the number of students enrolled, which should normally be easily verifiable

● for a newspaper publisher, revenue from sale of newspapers (excluding advertising) may be ascertained by verifying usage of newsprint in producing the newspaper

● the year-end trade debtors and creditors normally have a direct correlation with the last few months sales/receipts and purchases/payments, respectively.

12.4 EXAMPLES OF STRATEGIES

Example 1 — *Travel Agents*

A common feature of all agency business (and the brokerage industry is a prime example of this) is the juxtaposition of very large balance sheet risk with relatively low income per transaction. In this example the client is a travel agency operating a number of branches, with a central computerised accounting function. Features of the business may be:

● the customer base includes companies (with which it trades on credit terms) and private individuals (with which it trades on a cash basis)

● there are strict internal control procedures designed to ensure, for individual customers, that no liability will be incurred to suppliers that will not be covered by cash recovered from customers

● there are industry regulations governing procedures for handling customer cash received in advance of bookings being made

● commission rates are fixed and (depending on the quality of the accounting system) might allow very powerful analytical procedures to be applied on a branch-by-branch basis

Risks associated with a business of this type are usually greater in respect of individual customer business than in respect of the corporate business. These include:

● the risks of misappropriation of customer monies at the branches

● the risks of incurring liabilities to carriers which are not subsequently recoverable from customers

There may be a number of strategic questions an auditor might consider at the intermediate level:

● are the accounting system and the internal control procedures strong enough to make a transaction-based audit preferable to a balance sheet approach?

● could he benefit by approaching the audit on a branch-by-branch basis, or is it more efficient to examine the business as a whole?

● is there a case for separating the company's corporate-based business from its individual customer business?

- if he does separate the two sides of the business, can he exploit the one-to-one nature of assets and liabilities in an agency balance sheet — ie for every liability to suppliers he should be able to trace a debt from customers, and vice-versa?

For a business like this, with the high level of balance sheet risk, the auditor would normally expect to concentrate his efforts on the balance sheet, relying on tests of controls coupled with analytical review procedures on a branch-by-branch basis for satisfaction as to the profit and loss account. Within the balance sheet, he would also expect to approach corporate customer and individual customer debtors differently.

Having decided this approach, the auditor would then develop the detailed strategy for each of the major areas — corporate debtors, individual debtors, creditors and cash. For example, for individual debtors, he would consider

- the inherent and control risks involved

- the extent of evidence he needed from subsequent cash receipts testing

- the extent to which he obtains his evidence from the reconciliation with corresponding liabilities to carriers.

Example 2 — *Small 'cash and carry' retail shops*

Typical features of this type of business might be:

- sales made for cash

- a high volume of low value transactions in both sales and purchases cycles

- predictable gross margins by product type

- a goal of minimising taxes.

The key area of high risk will probably be sales and cash — there will be a higher than normal risk that sales may be made but not recorded (either deliberately or unintentionally) and cash may be 'pocketed' by employees and management or spent on unrecorded purchases.

In such a case, the auditor will clearly have to focus at an early stage on the controls over cash receipts and to assess the viability of a detailed analytical review of gross margins.

An alternative and more time-consuming way to address these risks may be by:

- auditing the purchases cycle (purchases, creditors and inputs to stock records) using detailed transaction tests and confirmation of creditor balances

- auditing the gross margin by considering internal and external factors affecting the pricing policy

- proof of the sales figure by considering purchases and margins audited as above.

However, the client may not maintain the records to enable the auditor to do this — for example, the sales or purchases accounts may not be analysed (even broadly) by category of item sold or purchased. In the absence of such analyses, he would be forced either to perform detailed transactions tests on both purchases and sales, or to consider qualifying his audit opinion because of this inability to verify the completeness of sales.

Example 3 — *A large processing company*

The client is a large producer of basic foodstuffs. The features of this type of industry are likely to be:

- a high volume of low-value sales

- the existence of a strong relationship between quantities input into a process and quantities output from that process, and a strong management information system that fully exploits this relationship

- a relatively low number of major suppliers for the key raw materials

- an integrated standard costing system, with sophisticated stock records.

In the absence of factors such as pressure to show a steady upward trend of profits, or a domineering chief executive, such a client may well not have any high risk audit areas related to the key business activity.

Given the level of inherent and control risk and the availability of detailed and reliable management information, the auditor may again decide to concentrate on the balance sheet, and use mainly analytical procedures in respect of the profit and loss account.

Example 4 — *An engineering company*

The client is a manufacturer of large, expensive machines to specification under long-term contracts. Thus:

- the entire business cycle will be 'driven' by customer orders rather than being production based

- there will be a low volume of high value items sold

- each machine is budgeted, quoted for and contracted individually

- margins are likely to be unpredictable, since each contract is negotiated individually.

The valuation of long-term contract work-in-progress (and consequently, the recognition of turnover and profit in the financial statements) is likely to be the key area of high risk for this client.

The most efficient way to approach this audit is likely to be to:

- test the sales cycle on a job-by-job basis, selecting orders received and following through to either sales, cost of sales and debtors/amounts receivable on contracts or to work-in-progress, via job records

- test the costs accumulated in job records for validity.

Any attempt to audit margins on an overall basis (as was suggested in Example 1 above) is likely to prove ineffective.

In such businesses, management will typically use the budgets prepared for individual machines to monitor and control costs on jobs, rather than simply for initially quoting for the job. Most of the assurance required as to validity of costs could be derived by testing the client's control over costs (eg by selecting a sample of jobs with cost variances, and ensuring there is evidence that management has acted on them).

In addressing the high risk identified the auditor would:

- arrange for a senior member of the audit team to perform the work involved

- focus the selection of jobs for testing on high risk contracts (for example those showing large differences between recorded amounts and internal or external valuations, those running significantly behind schedule, and so on) based on a review of progress monitoring reports and discussions with operational management

- pay particular attention to the competence (and perhaps past track record) of client's staff involved in the valuation of work in progress.

Example 5 — *Alloy manufacturer*

The company makes precision alloys which it sells to manufacturers of electrical equipment. The manufacturing process involves purchasing base metals (such as copper, nickel, iron) and melting them together in a range of formulae to make alloys with varying specifications and electrical characteristics. The level of precision required in the alloy mix makes for a complicated and expensive manufacturing process and the raw material costs only account on average for about a third of total manufacturing costs. This, taken together with the fluctuations in metal and foreign exchange markets, means that gross margins are highly erratic. The company produces four or five main types of alloy, each of which it sells at a number of stages of purity.

Features of the business are:

- despite sophisticated costing systems, difficulty in allocating overheads in the process which has to be repeated a number of times before the product reaches a satisfactory condition

- the need to maintain high levels of stocks in the forms of raw materials and alloys constantly being recycled through the process, in order to generate sufficient output

- management's need to make very difficult estimates both in pricing their products and valuing stocks

- a weak relationship between turnover and cost of sales, due both to the nature of the process and fluctuations in raw material costs

- stock quantities are very difficult to audit because the auditor cannot easily check quality — in that he can identify how *much* weight there is at the year end, but not how near to being in saleable form it is.

The key area of risk will be stock valuation, this risk being compounded by the extensive use of estimates.

Alternative strategies in this area might be:

- to carry out extensive analysis of standard costing procedures, reconciling opening stock, closing stock, purchases and cost of sales both for raw material and overheads, taking into account different processing characteristics of the main alloy types in production

- to concentrate on a very detailed year end stock count, with extensive testing (by assaying) of the quality of the stock control, and then assess the reasonableness of overhead absorption on a less detailed basis.

The other areas of the balance sheet in such a company with a small number of suppliers and a relatively modest number of customers would be unlikely to cause difficulty. The auditor would probably opt for a 'balance sheet' approach, using standard audit techniques to confirm balances at the year end, rather than looking to carry out detailed audit testing on transactions in the year or seeking to exploit business relationships.

12.5 COMMUNICATING THE AUDIT PLAN

No matter how well the auditor has planned the audit, if planning decisions are not promptly and properly communicated to all relevant parties, it will be difficult to perform an effective and efficient audit, and to complete it on a timely basis.

Moreover if the auditor does not properly document his planning decisions he may not be able subsequently to demonstrate that the audit was properly planned.

The method used to communicate and document the audit plan should take into account the needs of the various parties who have an interest in the plan.

The members of the *audit team* will have different interests in the audit plan depending upon their level of seniority and their role on the audit. All members of the audit team should be informed of:

- their responsibilities
- the objectives of the procedures that they are to perform
- matters that may affect the nature, timing and extent of these procedures such as the nature of the client's business and possible accounting and auditing problems.

Planning decisions that are important to the *client* include:

- timing and duration of the audit visits and the likely completion date
- confirmation of the audit timetable and dates of scheduled meetings
- the identities of the person in charge of the audit team, other general audit staff and any involvement of specialist audit staff
- the detailed nature, timing and extent of assistance which the client will be relied upon to provide
- areas which are to be covered at interim and final visits
- fee arrangements

The method of communication with the client, the type of information which should be communicated and the level of client personnel involved are matters which need to be tailored to the particular characteristics of and relationships with the client. For example, the chief executive may only wish to know about the audit fee, overall timing and timetable. The chief financial officer, however, may need to know all of the matters referred to above in order to make the necessary arrangements. Whatever the initial methods of communication, these matters should preferably be confirmed in writing with the client.

In practice, communication of certain planning decisions occurs throughout the various planning phases. For example, communication is maintained between the audit partner, manager and the staff members carrying out the detailed planning in determining the objective of the engagement, the key areas of high risk and matters related to work scheduling and staffing.

While it is usually desirable for an audit planning meeting to be held to discuss the proposed audit approach and other planning considerations, this may not always be practical or necessary although some matters, such as setting materiality levels, will usually require joint consideration by the audit partner and senior members of the audit team.

Additionally, before fieldwork commences but after the audit planning meeting there should be a team briefing, whereby all audit staff involved on the engagement are briefed on the audit plan and their particular role or allocation in it.

In every case all parties need to be aware of the relevant audit planning decisions once they are finalised. The most efficient way to do this is to prepare one set of consistent audit planning documents structured to permit the different parties to access information relevant to their needs.

The audit manager and partner should decide the format, content and level of detail of planning documentation most appropriate to the circumstances of a particular engagement and should make clear their decisions to other members of the team before planning commences.

In general terms, the documentation used should deal with:

- objectives of the engagement

- understanding of the client's business

- audit risk and materiality decisions

- understanding of the internal control structure

- preliminary assessments of inherent and control risk

- preliminary analytical procedures

- other planning matters (eg the involvement of specialists)

- audit strategy (overall, and for key areas of high risk)

- work scheduling and staffing.

The planning documentation used should not reproduce information contained elsewhere in the auditor's current or permanent working papers, unless repetition clearly enhances the clarity and usefulness of the documentation. Cross-referencing or photocopies should be used wherever practicable.

Standard forms or checklists help to facilitate the preparation and documentation of an audit plan that is complete, balanced, efficient and practical.

Planning documentation should be structured to facilitate subsequent review. For example, it is normally most efficient if the documentation highlights matters to which the audit partner should pay particular attention.

The diagram set out below illustrates a modular format of documentation.

In the diagram, the **Audit Planning Memorandum** provides an overview of the audit plan, in particular highlighting for the audit partner's special attention recent developments in the client's business or industry, an overall risk assessment and the planned approach to areas of audit significance or high risk. Appendix 12.1 provides a checklist of matters to be included in such an overview memorandum. The **Section Plan** in the diagram is prepared for an area of work and its principal purpose is to help audit assistants and those reviewing the work to understand the rationale behind the detailed steps in the audit programme for that section of work. The Section Plan might contain:

- an analysis (with comparative amounts) of the financial statement components subject to audit in the relevant section of work

- an assessment of risk relating to those amounts

- an explanation of the rationale behind the audit work in the section

The **Audit Programme**, the third element in the diagram, is discussed in section 12.6 below.

The audit partner should actively participate in the planning process, and should decide how much of the detailed planning documentation he himself needs to review and how much he can delegate to the audit manager.

During the audit, the audit team should remain alert for new or changed circumstances indicating a need to modify the audit plan. For example, unexpected errors in tests of controls may result in a reassessment of inherent and control risk.

If the audit is structured into interim and final phases, the partner and manager should reconsider the audit plan and modify it as necessary in the light of findings from the interim phase.

As with the original audit plan itself, any changes made should be communicated, documented and reviewed.

12.6 DEVELOPING AUDIT PROGRAMMES

The main purpose of an audit programme is to enable effective delegation of the actual detailed audit work needed to implement the audit strategy. Proper audit programmes also:

- facilitate the prior approval of the detailed audit work planned
- allow continuous control by means of comparison of actual to planned work
- facilitate review of the work done
- provide evidence that the work has been done in accordance with generally accepted auditing standards
- provide a basis for planning the following year's audit.

To serve these intended purposes, audit programmes should be prepared with the needs in mind both of those members of the audit team who are to perform the work and those who are responsible for supervision and review of that work. Thus the programme should:

- be consistent with, and firmly based on, the audit strategy
- be individually tailored to meet the needs of each particular audit
- clearly indicate what detailed procedures are to be carried out.

The programme should preferably:

- clearly state the audit objectives
- describe the procedures designed to attain each objective in turn
- indicate the timing of the procedures (interim or final visits) and (where relevant) the steps to be taken to extend interim audit conclusions to the balance-sheet date
- state the extent of each test
- describe the method of selection relevant to each test (eg what client records are needed, period covered, whether random, systematic or haphazard selection)
- describe step by step the work which is to be performed (the description should be sufficiently clear and comprehensive to enable an audit assistant to complete each step without further instruction)
- specify any relevant client personnel (eg personnel with whom to discuss queries)
- refer, where appropriate, to audit work performed in other areas
- refer, where appropriate, to particular relevant documents or background material in the auditor's permanent file.

The programme must complement, and be consistent with, the relevant audit section plan. The latter will give the rationale behind the detailed sequence of steps set out in the programme. Duplication of information in the audit programme and section plan should be avoided.

The audit programme also serves to document which members of the audit team actually performed the procedures listed in the programme. This may be accomplished by the individual who performs a particular procedure placing his initials and the date (day and month) next to the listing of the procedure on the audit programme. The individual should also cross-reference the procedures to the appropriate workpapers (if any) supporting the work done in the particular area.

In certain unusual cases, it may be inefficient to try to prepare or update audit programmes before detailed work commences because it has not been possible to collect the detailed information needed. For example:

- the client is new

- there have been major changes in the client's business or systems but adequate assessment has not been possible (eg because the changes were poorly documented).

In such cases, the auditor may prepare an outline audit programme, and complete it as the audit work is being performed. Alternatively, he might prepare a summary of work done for the current audit and a detailed audit programme for the following year's audit. In either event, if detailed programmes are not prepared in advance the auditor will need to ensure that less experienced staff are supervised especially carefully.

APPENDIX 12.1

AUDIT PLANNING MEMORANDUM — CHECKLIST

The tables below provide a checklist of matters that might be included in an overview planning memorandum described in section 12.5 of Chapter 12.

MATTERS FOR PARTNER'S PARTICULAR ATTENTION

Major changes
- Industry/market as a whole
- Client's business, organisation, systems etc.

Previous audit problems
- Should already be listed on last year's audit file as "Points forward" — photocopy and indicate proposed action against each point

Highlights from preliminary analytical procedures

Risk and materiality overview
- Overall risk assessment with brief rationale (consider both audit and business risk, and use Appendix 10.1)
- Planning materiality level, with rationale
- Tolerable error for audit sampling purposes

- Errors and omissions — minimum level(s) for tracking errors
- Parameters for group accounts work

Overall audit plan
- Summarise overall audit plan. Concentrate on explaining how it responds to the client's particular circumstances (business cycles, inherent risks etc)
- Individual areas of high risk
  - list areas/give reasons why high risk
  - (very broadly) nature of audit testing response
  - suitability of audit staff proposed for high risk work

OTHER KEY MATTERS

Reporting framework (if non-standard)
- Legal requirements
- Professional requirements
- Special requests from client or holding company auditors

Other major constraints/requirements
- Related organisations and related audits
- Involvement of other professional firms or offices — confirm that work to be done/timing/costs agreed with them

- Third party specialists eg valuers — confirm that work to be done/timing/costs agreed with them
- Other internal specialists (eg tax, computer audit) — confirm that work to be done/timing/costs agreed with them
- Critical dates (eg deadline for figures for holding company group accounts)
- Audit fee constraints if stricter than usual

CHAPTER 13 WORK SCHEDULING AND STAFFING THE AUDIT

13.1 INTRODUCTION

For the audit strategy to be implemented effectively, efficiently and on a timely basis, decisions in two broad areas are needed:

- work scheduling (deciding *when* to carry out the work)
- staffing (deciding *who* will carry out the work).

These matters are amplified below.

The end product of the work scheduling and staffing decisions is an audit time budget — discussed further below.

13.2 WORK SCHEDULING

The first step in scheduling the audit work is to determine, in conjunction with the client, critical deadlines such as those relating to

- announcements of the results to the public
- consolidated group reporting timetable
- approval by management of the financial statements
- issuance of the audit report
- issuance of reports to regulatory or other bodies (eg to lenders)
- issuance of accounts to regulatory or other bodies (eg to the Inland Revenue with tax computations, or to the Registrar of Companies).

The auditor should also ascertain the client's timetable for completing accounting procedures that are important to the scheduling of his audit work. These may include

- bank reconciliations
- reconciliation of control accounts to subsidiary ledgers
- stock counts
- completion of stock valuation
- third party confirmations
- trial balance and supporting schedules
- first draft of the financial statements
- final draft of the financial statements
- the earliest date that the audit may commence.

The auditor should confirm these dates with the client, preferably in writing, to avoid possible subsequent misunderstandings or disputes.

The timetable should be realistic, with sufficient latitude for any unexpected events or delays.

A timetable for an audit typically includes:

- an interim visit, usually at least half-way through the financial year
- the final visit, shortly after the financial year end.

In the case of new clients, an initial visit shortly after appointment will be necessary, for example, to obtain information and document the internal control structure. In certain regulated industries, an interim visit to review the internal control structure is mandatory.

Interim visits help to:

- identify possible audit problems at an early stage
- meet client deadlines
- smooth the workload in the auditor's office
- keep the audit team to a manageable size.

The actual work to be completed during an interim visit will vary from client to client, depending upon the particular circumstances. Typically it will include the completion of the more detailed aspects of audit planning, such as the updating of the auditor's knowledge of the client's business and the assessment of inherent and control risks in the various areas of audit significance. Two other examples are given below.

First, the outcome of certain tests and inquiries may have a significant bearing on the audit strategy; such tests should be carried out as early as possible — either at the interim stage or, if there is no interim visit, early on at the final visit. For example, errors found during tests of controls may cause a major revision of the audit strategy, since it may require a reassessment of inherent and control risks; thus, for example, larger samples for substantive tests or possibly additional tests that had not originally been considered necessary may be required.

Second, if client deadlines are very tight, it may be possible to obtain assurance on certain year-end amounts from substantive tests carried out at an earlier date. Examples of this include third party confirmations and observing physical counts of stocks carried out before the year end. Although the additional work needed to cover movements between the balances tested and the year end may add to overall audit hours, this method may be the only practical way of meeting very tight deadlines.

13.3 STAFFING

13.3.1 *The main influences on staff allocation*

The main factors to consider when allocating the work to individual members of the auditor's staff are

- the scope and complexity of the engagement and the levels of risk
- timing factors
- the degree of client assistance available
- the need for specialist skills (eg tax, computer audit)

These matters are amplified below. The composition of a typical audit team and the respective responsibilities of each member are set out in Appendix 13.1.

13.3.2 *Scope, complexity and risks*

It is the scope and complexity of the engagement and the associated levels of audit risk that primarily determine the required calibre and experience of the staff to be assigned.

In assigning individuals to particular engagements the auditor should take into account the expertise and experience of each individual and the skills required for the particular engagement concerned. Generally, the higher the risk relating to the audit as a whole or to a particular audit area, the more experienced the personnel should be and the more expertise they should have. The audit team preferably should include some members who have visited the client previously, not only to maintain good client relationships, but also because they will already have gained detailed knowledge of the client and its industry.

In certain specialised industries, it is highly desirable (and in some cases essential) that some members of the audit team have previous audit experience in that industry. Examples might be the audits of banks, broker-dealers, and clients in the insurance industry.

In addition to the knowledge and engagement handling skills that the audit partner and audit manager bring to the engagement, the staff member in day-to-day charge of the engagement should have the necessary technical knowledge, experience and managerial and personal skills to be able to deal with the complexities of the assignment, organise and supervise staff and develop a good relationship with the client.

13.3.3 *Timing factors*

The auditor's own resources and timing constraints (who is available to do the work and when) will need to be efficiently matched to the particular client circumstances. The following steps will need to be carried out:

● arrange for the audit manager and partner to be available for critical stages of the assignment

● ascertain the availability of key client personnel who will be involved in the preparation of financial statements and dealing with audit enquiries

● the availability of selected audit staff, including any specialists (eg tax, computer audit)

13.3.4 *Client's assistance*

Client personnel should be used to the extent possible and practical. Not only does client assistance help keep fees to a manageable level but it also serves to free up the audit team members to devote their efforts to gathering evidence to support the audit opinion. Areas in which client personnel can assist include:

● preparing the supporting schedules in a useful format

● preparing analyses and other workpapers specifically required for the audit

● assisting in the preparation of confirmation requests (eg debtor and creditor circularisations)

● reconciling confirmation replies

● obtaining and assembling requested invoices and other documents.

These possibilities should be discussed with the client at the planning stage.

The auditor should agree the relevant job scheduling matters with the client, preferably in writing. If he is working to a tight timetable, it is particularly useful to have an agreed record of the dates by which the client undertakes to complete essential schedules and, subsequently, the dates on which the schedules were actually completed. If the audit time and, consequently, audit costs, are increased because of delays for which the client is responsible, such a record will be helpful in substantiating any request the auditor might make for an increased fee.

13.4 PREPARING AUDIT TIME BUDGETS

Audit time budgets put the work scheduling and staffing matters decided upon above into time and cost terms. This enables the audit manager and partner, when reviewing the audit plan, to assess whether an appropriate proportion of effort will be devoted to each area of the audit, and also to check whether audit cost recovery will be satisfactory.

Budgets also help:

- the audit senior in charge of the field work in monitoring subsequent progress of the audit (by allowing the senior to compare the actual time spent with the budgeted amount) and taking any necessary corrective action, having first consulted the manager where necessary

- the staff to monitor their own progress and performance in the areas of work allocated to them.

The level of detail necessary in budgets and actual time records will depend upon the size and complexity of the audit.

Normally, the budget can only be prepared accurately once detailed planning is completed. This may result, for example, in revisions being necessary after the interim visit.

After the budget has been completed it should be reviewed by the audit partner and manager to determine whether time appears to have been allocated appropriately between the sections, bearing in mind their complexity and relative materiality. The totals budgeted for each level of staff should be compared with staff availability and adjustments made where necessary. Every effort should be made to reduce the time required to a minimum compatible with the objectives of the engagement.

In particular, the previous year's working papers should be reviewed to determine whether more use can be made of client's staff to prepare analyses, reconciliations and other schedules. If the budget differs materially from the previous year's 'actual' figure, then a note of the main reason for differences should be prepared for the audit partner and manager to consider.

The total budgeted hours should be evaluated in monetary terms to give a budgeted cost, broken down by levels of staff, other specialists, other offices as appropriate to facilitate control.

In controlling the engagement, it is normally helpful periodically to compare the time actually spent with the budgeted time. This process will be useful in identifying areas in which budgeted hours have been exceeded and facilitates timely action on the part of the audit team to address the causes and consequences of budget overruns.

At the end of the interim visit, the actual time spent must be summarised and compared with the budget. Any significant variation should be noted for the attention of the audit manager and partner together with the reasons. The overruns and their recoverability should be considered as the audit plan and budget is finalised prior to the final audit.

APPENDIX 13.1

THE AUDIT TEAM

On each engagement, all the members of the audit team should understand clearly their responsibilities and the objectives of the procedures which they are expected to perform. This section gives a general indication of the respective responsibilities of partners and audit staff. The degree of supervision required and the extent to which responsibilities may be delegated will depend on the size and complexity of the assignment and on the experience and proficiency of the audit staff.

Engagement partner

The engagement partner (or client service partner) has overall responsibility for all services provided to the client. He has a general duty to keep up to date with audit, accounting, tax and similar professional matters and to maintain a knowledge of the client's business and future strategy and of the particular industry in which the client operates. This enables him to assess the practical effect of new developments on the individual client.

The engagement partner is also responsible for monitoring changes in the client's circumstances (eg in ownership, management, directors, financial position, nature of operations) to ensure that no conditions have arisen which would have caused him to refuse appointment as auditor (or, indeed, in any other capacity), had such conditions existed at the time of initial acceptance.

It is for the engagement partner to establish the scope and objectives of the firm's engagement (in a letter of engagement), to review these regularly and to discuss additional services with the client. He approves all budgets and fees, arranges regular meetings of the client service team, and reviews the membership of that team.

In most audit-based practices the engagement partner will also be the audit engagement partner and the expressions are used synonymously in this book. The audit partner is responsible to his fellow partners for the audit report on the financial statements. He needs to be satisfied that the work on each audit is being performed to an acceptable standard. He will approve the planning of the audit and review the audit files and financial statements to ensure that the audit evidence obtained is sufficient to enable him to express an audit opinion on his own behalf and that of his partners.

His responsibilities include the following:

- to maintain regular contact with the client and to ensure client satisfaction with the audit service provided

- to approve the general and detailed audit strategy

- to approve the audit budget and the assignment of appropriate staff to the audit team

- to review the work of the audit manager and to assess his performance

- to ensure that objectivity is maintained unimpaired

- to discuss and resolve points of contention, seeking appropriate specialist advice where necessary

- to approve management letters sent to the client

- to approve the audit fee.

146

Audit manager

The audit manager is responsible to the audit partner for the satisfactory completion of the audit work. This requires that the work be carried out to acceptable standards in accordance with any laid-down procedures by the audit practice and within budgeted cost and time limits.

In order to achieve this overall objective the audit manager will normally be responsible for:

- understanding the client's business, supporting systems and operating procedures

- supervising and advising the senior in deciding on the nature and scope of the work to be carried out and preparing an audit planning memorandum and budget, to be approved by the audit partner.

- ensuring that the senior has agreed the audit timetable with the client and made arrangements for travel, hotels and accommodation at the client's offices

- selecting audit staff who have appropriate training, experience and proficiency

- ensuring that staff are adequately briefed about the client's affairs, the nature of the business and the audit strategy

- supervising the programme of work by paying regular visits and providing audit staff with technical advice and any on-the-job training required

- generally reviewing the work of the audit senior, assessing and reporting on his performance, and identifying any training needs or other remedial action. The audit manager should monitor the supervision of audit assistants' work by senior staff and ensure that senior staff have in turn reported on audit assistants' work and identified any training needs or other remedial action

- liaising with tax and other specialists involved in the audit

- keeping the audit partner informed of all significant developments during the course of the audit

- ensuring that appropriate consultation procedures (eg on difficult technical issues) are followed, where applicable

- ensuring that audits are finalised efficiently

- ensuring that adequate debriefing takes place.

In addition to his responsibilities with regard to each annual audit, the audit manager is responsible for maintaining the continuity of relationship with the client from year to year. In particular, he should:

- keep up to date with the major developments in the client's industry

- anticipate the effects of new legislation and other technical developments, and discuss these with the client where appropriate

- respond promptly to any communication from the client

- report to the engagement partner any important developments, correspondence or discussion with the client.

Audit senior

The audit senior is appointed by the audit manager to plan and control the day-to-day running of the audit. He is responsible, inter alia, for:

- liaising with the audit partner and manager in planning the audit

- preparing an audit plan budget and audit programme for approval by the audit manager and partner

147

- ensuring that the audit work is carried out as planned

- specifying the work to be carried out by staff reporting to him and ensuring that they understand and are capable of carrying out the work

- providing audit staff with adequate technical support and on-the-job training

- keeping the audit manager informed of any technical or administrative difficulty arising during the course of the audit, and of the progress of the audit compared with the planned timetable and budgeted costs

- making appropriate note of matters which should be brought to the partner's attention. Major audit points should be discussed in good time with the client and audit manager and partner

- keeping the audit staff informed of the overall progress of the audit

- reviewing the work of staff reporting to him, assessing their performance in formal reports, and identifying any training needs or other remedial action

- ensuring that all audit work is completed in good time and that the results of the work adequately support the conclusions drawn

- organising the working papers in a form that facilitates review and answering and following up partner or manager review points

- preparing and finalising the financial statements, the management letter and letter of representation and points for partner attention

- debriefing audit staff and preparing points forward for the following year's audit.

As the member in charge of the audit team at the client's premises, the senior is responsible for maintaining a good working relationship with the client's employees.

Audit assistant

An audit assistant is responsible for carrying out the work given to him by the senior. In order to do so he must ensure that he understands clearly the objectives of the work he is expected to perform and the degree of detail and level of materiality to which he should work.

In particular he should:

- ensure by discussion with the senior that he has all the necessary background information concerning the assignment

- review the relevant sections of the permanent audit file and the previous year's audit files

- be aware of the time budgeted for the task given to him and record the actual time taken

- keep the audit senior informed of his progress with the task given to him

- record and bring promptly to the senior's attention any significant discrepancy he might find

- prepare clear working papers, which carry conclusions and proper cross-references

- ensure that review points are adequately answered.

CHAPTER 14   TESTS OF CONTROLS

14.1   INTRODUCTION

As discussed in Chapter 10, on each audit engagement an auditor obtains an understanding of each of the three elements of the internal control structure (control environment, accounting system and control procedures). This understanding is used:

- to identify potential misstatements
- to consider the factors that affect the risk of material misstatement
- to design substantive audit tests.

Based on his understanding the auditor assesses the level of inherent and control risk for the significant assertions applicable to the material components of the financial statements. As explained in Chapter 10, this assessment usually involves

- identifying specific internal control policies and procedures relevant to those assertions that are likely to prevent or detect material misstatements in those assertions
- performing tests of controls to evaluate the effectiveness of such policies and procedures.

The first aspect of this assessment, the identification of specific policies and procedures, is dealt with in Chapter 10. This chapter deals with the second aspect, the performing of tests of controls.

For reasons of efficiency, an auditor sometimes performs tests of controls at the same time that he obtains his understanding of the internal control structure (eg inspecting bank reconciliations throughout the period). In other words, some procedures that he performs for the purpose of obtaining his understanding may provide evidence regarding the design and operating effectiveness of controls.

14.2   OBJECTIVE OF TESTS OF CONTROLS

An auditor performs tests of controls to enable him to evaluate

- **effectiveness** regarding the design of the control procedure or policy
- **effectiveness** regarding the operation of the control procedure or policy.

The types of procedure adopted to evaluate both design and operating effectiveness include:

- observation
- inquiries
- inspection of documents and records
- reperformance of the specific control procedures (although this is principally relevant to evaluating operating effectiveness).

These are discussed in more detail in Section 14.3 below.

In evaluating effectiveness regarding **design** an auditor considers whether controls are suitably designed to prevent or detect material misstatements in financial statement assertions. In many situations, he may not need to go much beyond the procedures he performed in obtaining an understanding of design. However, there may be circumstances in which he may need to expand upon the procedures performed in gaining an understanding of design. For example, he may make additional inquiries to corroborate the findings and to assess the effectiveness of the controls in preventing and detecting misstatements. Similarly, he may make additional observations of the controls being applied.

In evaluating **operating** effectiveness, an auditor considers how the control was applied, the consistency of its application and by whom it was performed.

14.3   TYPES OF TESTS OF CONTROLS

14.3.1 *Observation*

Observation of control procedures actually being performed may provide information as to:

- how the procedures operate in practice
- whether client personnel are competent and conscientious in performing those procedures
- the extent of supervision and review provided
- how exceptions and errors are handled and resolved
- whether established procedures are closely or only vaguely followed
- whether the position of departments within a building is conducive to segregation of duties
- whether access to valuable assets, important documents and accounting records and processing equipment is properly restricted.

While observation can be a strong procedure in determining whether a control procedure is operating, it should be borne in mind that there is a natural tendency on the part of the individual being observed to make sure that he or she is performing his or her duties appropriately while being observed. Accordingly, the observation may not provide an accurate reflection of how the procedure is applied in the absence of the observer. It is normally necessary to combine observation with one or more other procedures in gathering evidence regarding operating effectiveness.

14.3.2 *Enquiry*

Inquiries of the people who perform the control procedure may be used to supplement our observations as to:

- the specific tasks performed
- the extent of supervision
- the nature of exceptions or errors encountered and how these are dealt with.

In assessing effectiveness, an auditor normally extends his enquiries beyond those directly involved with performing the procedure to personnel responsible for supervision and review and others who may be indirectly involved. Frequently explanations received from one member of staff may be corroborated by inquiry of another, while conflicting accounts of procedures will indicate that procedures are not properly understood or supervised. The auditor may also gain a fuller understanding of the strengths and weaknesses of a system by asking whether errors have occurred and, if so, why these have occurred and how they are detected.

It should be recognised that the audit evidence obtained by enquiry is, by its nature, not as persuasive as that obtained directly through observation, inspection or reperformance. Accordingly, an auditor normally combines enquiry with other tests of controls to obtain evidence regarding effectiveness. For example, he may enquire as to the procedures performed in following up on exceptions identified in an edit procedure. To corroborate the response to his enquiry, he might observe the procedures being performed and/or inspect documentation evidencing the follow-up procedures.

14.3.3   *Inspection*

Inspection of documents and records entails selecting documents or records and examining the visible evidence that the control procedure was applied. For example, an auditor may examine purchase vouchers to determine whether they contain the appropriate forms of approval (eg initials, signatures).

14.3.4   *Reperformance*

Reperformance of control procedures involves repeating the specific control procedures that the auditor is testing. For example, in testing controls over purchases, he may compare information on goods received documents to related information on the vendor's invoice. Reperformance can be accomplished manually or by using computer-assisted auditing techniques (see Chapter 18).

14.4   EXTENT OF TESTS OF CONTROLS

As explained in Chapter 10, the lower the assessment of inherent and control risk, the more assurance is needed regarding the effectiveness of the design and operation of control procedures. An auditor can perform more extensive tests of controls in a number of ways, including observation at more than one date, inquiring of more than one person regarding the same information and selecting a larger sample size for tests of inspection and reperformance.

14.4.1   *Assurance provided by evidence*

In any evaluation of controls, the degree of assurance an auditor obtains from evidence is a matter of professional judgement in the particular circumstances. These considerations are discussed below.

For some controls, there may be documentary evidence of design and/or operating effectiveness; in these circumstances an auditor may inspect the visible documentation. For example, management's authorisation for an expenditure may be indicated on an invoice. He can, therefore, inspect the invoice for evidence of authorisation. In another example, a computer-produced error listing might be compared to listings of the data contained in the transaction files used by the same application computer program before processing (these would include the errors) and after processing (these would exclude the errors).

For other controls, documentary evidence may not be available or relevant (eg segregation of duties, or a control procedure performed by a computer); in these circumstances an auditor may observe the functioning of the control or may use computer-assisted audit techniques to reperform the computer controls. While substantive tests may verify the accuracy of the underlying records, they frequently cannot provide affirmative evidence of the operation of the controls, because the records may well be accurate even if the controls were absent.

In evaluating evidence an auditor should consider whether the evidence pertains to the entire period under audit or only to one point in time. For example, evidence obtained from observation only pertains to the particular point in time that the observation was made. He may need to supplement his observation with other evidence regarding the effectiveness of operation of the controls throughout the period.

Tests designed to verify the operation of control procedures applied to a class of transactions (eg sales or wages and salaries) are effective only if reasonable assurance is obtained that these controls were functioning throughout the period under examination. For example, an auditor may obtain reasonable assurance that a computer program performs a control effectively by testing the operation of the control at a particular occasion. But he will need evidence of systems maintenance and development controls over that computer program during the period covered by his audit if he wishes to obtain evidence about whether the programmed control procedure operated throughout the period.

On the other hand, if he is only obtaining assurance from procedures at a specific date (eg logic checks in the year-end stock file), he may not need to be concerned with the operation of these controls throughout the period.

14.4.2 *Evidence from prior audits*

In assessing inherent and control risk, an auditor should consider evidence regarding effectiveness of controls that was obtained in prior audits. He should make sure that the conclusions drawn from such evidence relate to the controls which were in existence during the period covered by the audit. It is therefore essential that he should note the nature, timing and extent of any changes in the internal control structure during the current period.

To evaluate the use of such evidence in assessing risk for a current audit an auditor should consider:

- the significance of the assertions involved
- the specific control procedures that were tested in the prior audits
- the extent of that testing
- the results of the tests
- the length of time elapsed since the performance of the tests
- the continuity of client's staff
- the evidence about design or operation that he may obtain from performing substantive tests in the current period.

The auditor should not rely solely on evidence obtained in prior audits to the exclusion of performing tests of controls in the current period. The results of prior year audits may, nevertheless, permit him to decrease (or, on the contrary, may cause him to increase) the amount of evidence that he needs to obtain in the current year.

14.4.3 *Evidence obtained at an interim visit*

Having obtained evidence about the design or operation of control procedures during an interim period, an auditor must decide the extent of the evidence he needs to cover the remaining period. In making that decision he should consider

- the significance of the assertion involved
- the specific control procedures that were evaluated during the interim period
- the extent and results of his evaluation of the effectiveness of the design and operation of those controls
- the length of the remaining period between interim and year-end

- whether the control environment and disciplinary controls overall are of sufficiently high standard to assure consistent performance of procedures

- the nature and extent of evidence related to the controls that is obtained from substantive tests performed during the remaining period

- the nature, timing and extent of any changes in the internal control structure between the interim audit visit and the period end.

14.4.4 Consistency of evidence

In evaluating evidence obtained from more than one source, an auditor should consider whether the evidence is consistent. Generally, when the various types of evidence support the same conclusion about the design or operation of a control procedure, the degree of assurance provided by the evidence increases. Conversely, if various types of evidence are inconsistent and lead to different conclusions about the design or operation of a control procedure, the assurance provided decreases.

Similarly, the auditor should consider whether evidence obtained that relates to one element of the internal control structure affects another element of the internal control structure. An otherwise effective control procedure might be adversely affected by an ineffective control environment. For example, a control environment that is likely to permit unauthorised changes in a computer program may reduce the assurance provided by evidence obtained from evaluating the effectiveness of the program at a particular point in time. In such circumstances, an auditor may decide to obtain additional evidence about the design and operation of that program during the audit period. He might obtain and control a copy of the program and use computer assisted audit techniques to compare that copy with the program that the entity uses to process data.

14.4.5 Sufficiency of evidence

The amount of evidence needed that particular controls are operating varies depending on the nature of the control.

Detect controls — those used by management to detect errors — are such that their 'population size' tends to be small. For example, for the control procedure whereby each month the debtors listing total is reconciled to the debtors control account, the 'population size' is twelve — corresponding to the twelve months of the financial year.

On the other hand, prevent controls — those designed to prevent errors — are often applied at a particular point in a transaction stream to all transactions flowing through that stream, and the 'population size' is often large. For example, where all invoices must be approved by the financial controller before payment and this evidenced by his signing the invoice, the population includes all invoices received.

As explained in chapter 10, for reasons of efficiency an auditor prefers to focus on detect controls. In looking at a particular control of this sort where the population is small (such as in the case of weekly or monthly accounting routines) no detailed guidance can usefully be given on the sample size. In general terms, however, the number of times that he examines the operation of the control and the depth in which he examines its operation will depend on the importance he attaches to the operating effectiveness of the control. Taking the example of the debtors ledger reconciliations given above, the auditor may choose (depending on the circumstances) to scrutinize briefly all to ensure that they have been carried out and that there are no unusual reconciling items. Alternatively he may examine a number in detail, vouching balances to the appropriate ledger and verifying that the reconciling items have been promptly and properly dealt with, and to scrutinize briefly the others for unusual reconciling items. The scope of his work is essentially a matter of judgement.

For the larger populations normally encountered when looking at prevent controls, it will normally be necessary to take a sample. Guidance in this area is dealt with in chapter 16, Audit Sampling.

It should be remembered that there can be detect controls with large 'populations' and equally there can be prevent controls with small 'populations'. Irrespective of the type of control, in determining how much evidence is needed as to its proper operation, an auditor needs to have a good understanding of the frequency of operation so that he can select levels of testing that are appropriate.

14.5 DOCUMENTATION

An auditor's workpapers should be sufficient to document:

- the nature of the tests of controls (ie observation, inquiry, inspection, reperformance)
- the extent of his tests
- for inquiry and observation, the applicable client personnel involved in the inquiry and/or observation process
- the period during which the tests of controls were performed
- the results of the tests and the auditor's conclusions.

CHAPTER 15   SUBSTANTIVE TESTS

15.1   TYPES OF TESTING

An auditor carries out two broad categories of substantive tests that directly substantiate assertions in a set of financial statements:

- **tests of details** — tests of details of transactions and account balances, such as direct verification of items by vouching to invoices, third party confirmations, recalculations of amounts, and the like

- **analytical procedures** — comparisons of recorded amounts, or ratios developed from recorded amounts, to expectations the auditor develops; these can be applied to individual account balances or relationships between account balances and to other financial or non-financial data.

Both categories of substantive tests have the same objective: to provide audit evidence as to particular assertions related to account balances or classes of transactions, as discussed in Chapter 5.

15.2   TESTS OF DETAILS

Tests of details generally fall into four broad categories:

- inspection of documents (vouching and tracing)

- inspection of assets

- direct confirmation with third parties, and

- reperformance of computations and reconciliations.

15.2.1   *Inspection of documents*

The most common method of obtaining evidence regarding a transaction or an item in an account balance is to inspect relevant documents and records. Inspection of documents and records provides evidence of varying degrees of reliability depending on the nature and source of these documents and records. In particular, items originating from outside the client are generally more persuasive than those generated internally.

In testing a transaction or item in this way, an auditor should check not only that the monetary amounts involved agree but also that all relevant details, such as dates, descriptions of goods or services and prices, appear correct and do not appear to have been altered.

The auditor should also consider whether the document inspected provides adequate supporting evidence (eg a journal voucher is normally insufficient evidence of the validity of the entry) and whether all the documents that would normally be expected to exist are available (eg an expense report would be expected to accompany a request to reimburse an employee for business expenses).

Documents that clients provide might not always be originals. For example, some documentation might be in the form of photocopies, facsimiles or microfilm. While the auditor may accept such forms of documentation in some cases, he should recognize that relying on them poses greater risks because of the added difficulty of identifying any alterations or falsifications.

The inspection of documents can be performed in two ways: vouching and tracing. The distinction between vouching and tracing lies in the direction of the test. When vouching, an auditor first considers a recorded transaction or amount and then inspects source documents that support it; when tracing, he first inspects source documents and then determines whether the transaction or amount has been recorded.

Vouching is generally used to test the existence or occurrence assertion; tracing is generally used to test the completeness assertion.

15.2.2 *Inspection of assets*

Physical inspection is principally a means of testing the existence assertion; it is sometimes necessary to obtain other evidence such as title documents before concluding as to the ownership of the asset. For example, physical inspection of a factory or plant and machinery will verify that they exist, but the factory may be mortgaged and the machinery may be leased. Nevertheless in many instances (eg stock) possession may be taken as prima facie evidence of ownership. However, evidence of ownership should be obtained if the item inspected is in the possession of a third party (eg stocks held at an independent warehouse).

Physical inspection of assets provides evidence as to quantities but little else unless an auditor is able to identify the quality of the assets (ie it tells little of the valuation assertion). For example, an auditor could physically inspect jewels but might not know whether they were authentic or artificial. In these instances, he should apply alternative procedures or seek the help of a specialist.

15.2.3 *Direct confirmation*

Written confirmation with third parties independent of the client can provide strong evidence relating to balances or transactions. Moreover, such evidence can generally be obtained at relatively low cost.

The reliability placed on third party evidence should be based in part on:

- the knowledge of the individuals giving the confirmations

- the evidence likely to be available to them

- the likely motivation of those individuals.

For example, a bank loan officer is more likely to know about more unusual matters such as oral guarantees made by the client whereas a clerk who fills out a standard bank confirmation reply may only have access to more straightforward information such as cash balances and direct loans; a purchase ledger clerk will be able to confirm that a client's sales invoices have been recorded in the customer's purchase ledger but may not be aware of any outstanding disputes.

In assessing the independence of a third party, an auditor should consider the substance of the third party's relationship with the client and not simply the legal form. In practice, the managements of two companies may be closely linked through economic interdependence without there being any common legal ownership or control.

15.2.4 *Reperformance of computations and reconciliations*

Testing an account balance or transaction often involves checking the accuracy of computations. These computations vary in complexity from totalling lists of trade debtors to lengthy computations to calculate the profit on a leasing contract. In addition to testing the arithmetical accuracy of the computations, an auditor should satisfy himself as to the reasonableness of the principles and assumptions underlying the computations.

Although computational errors by computers are rare, computers could be programmed (unintentionally or intentionally) to print out, for example, amounts that do not represent the total of the items purported to be added. Accordingly, an auditor should exercise judgment in determining the extent of checking of the mathematical accuracy of computer generated reports. He should consider whether the report is generated from purchased software, internally developed software, or from spreadsheet programs and, if applicable, the related controls over the application.

Before performing lengthy computations on a computer-based accounting system, the auditor should consider the possibility of using computer-assisted audit techniques (see chapter 18).

To test an item, an auditor will often need to prepare or reperform a reconciliation, for example:

- between recorded amounts and third party statements (eg from banks or suppliers)

- between different parts of the accounting system (eg between the purchase ledger and the purchase ledger control account in the general ledger).

If client-prepared reconciliations are used, these usually will need to be tested. One method of testing a bank reconciliation, for example, involves checking items from the cash book to the bank statement, and vice versa, to verify the reconciling items, and explaining and following up those reconciling items.

15.2.5 *Other procedures*

An auditor normally performs other procedures which are more concerned with directing his attention to items which need to be tested than with actually testing them. The procedures nevertheless contribute towards his audit assurance and can be very cost-effective. They include:

- **scanning** — scanning or scrutiny of accounting records is aimed at identifying for further investigation any unusual or suspicious items likely to contain material error (eg unusual amounts, unauthorised items or items authorised by an unusual authority, altered, defaced or misfiled items, and any items that do not follow the normal business pattern).

  Scanning tests involve considerable experience and judgment and it is not always possible to pre-define what is unusual or what precisely to look for. Examples include
  — reviewing files of copy sales invoices for unusual discounts or inappropriate VAT amounts
  — reviewing suspense accounts for unusual items, and making sure that these accounts are cleared on a timely basis
  — reviewing cash receipts and payments

  In computer-based systems, advantage may be taken of computer audit software to interrogate (edit) the computer files, but whether these techniques can be used depends on, among other things, the auditor's ability to specify selection criteria and the retention of sufficient data in an appropriate form

- **analysis** — analysis of an account balance into its components is a common audit step preliminary to verifying particular components (eg the larger items). It should be distinguished from analytical procedures (see below) where such analysis (together with further inquiry and corroboration as appropriate) is itself sufficient to provide reasonable assurance that the balance is not materially misstated

- **enquiry** — asking the client's staff and management for information or explanation is by far the most widely used audit technique. However, since all responses of material consequence require corroboration, it can only be regarded as a preliminary step to a test of details.

15.3 SELECTIVE TESTS OF DETAILS

Frequently, an auditor will decide to carry out tests of details on a selective basis rather than examine 100 per cent of the population, due to cost-benefit considerations and on the fundamental premise that an auditor seeks to obtain reasonable but not absolute assurance.

By adopting a selective approach, an auditor accepts a risk that his conclusion on the population as a whole may be wrong. He should therefore select the items for his tests of details in such a way as to be reasonably sure that the conclusions he draws from his selective tests would not be altered if he were to examine the whole population.

There are three principal methods of selection; an auditor might select:

- **high-value items**, where all the items that are in excess of a certain monetary amount are selected;

- **error-prone items**, where only those items that he believes have a high risk of misstatement are selected (eg items with a history of errors in previous audits, unusual or suspicious items identified by scanning or analytical procedures);

- **a sample** of items from the population, where he makes an unbiased selection of a number of items designed to be representative of the population as a whole. (Audit sampling is the subject of Chapter 16).

An auditor would normally use a combination of two or all three of these methods.

In some cases it may be sufficient to identify the high-value items that go to make up an accounts balance and verify these; if the remaining items are immaterial no further testing may then be necessary. For example, in performing a search for unrecorded liabilities, an auditor may determine some monetary amount (based on planning materiality and other considerations) and examine all disbursements after the year end that equal or exceed that threshold amount. In doing so, he decides that the items below the threshold amount need not be considered due to the low risk of material misstatement.

Where the auditor adopts high-value or error-prone item selection, he should document in his working papers how he intends to address the remaining portion of the population. For example, he may be able to state that further work is waived due to the collective immateriality of the remaining portion and the low risk of material error. Alternatively, he may sample the remaining items or perform analytical procedures. The point is that he must address these remaining items and document his consideration of them.

15.4 TIMING OF TESTS OF DETAILS

An auditor usually performs his substantive tests of details of account balances as at the date at the financial statements. However, because of the desire to identify potential problem areas early in the audit as well as considerations of job scheduling and completing the audit within prescribed deadlines, there are often circumstances in which he would want to perform certain substantive tests of details as of an interim date and then apply 'roll-forward' procedures to the remaining period. For example, he may want to confirm trade debtors one or more months prior to the year end.

This section provides guidance on:

- factors which influence his ability to perform substantive tests at an interim date

- roll-forward procedures the auditor should apply to the remaining period.

15.4.1 *Factors to consider*

Applying substantive tests of details to selected balance sheet accounts as of an interim date potentially increases the risk of not detecting a material misstatement in those accounts at year end. Thus, an auditor should consider the difficulty of controlling this increased risk.

Firstly, he should normally extend his tests of controls to cover the roll-forward period since it is during this period that the internal control procedures are particularly important. If controls are weak and the inherent and control risk is high the auditor should *not* use the technique of performing substantive tests at a date prior to the year end.

Secondly, he should consider whether:

- there are rapidly changing business conditions or other circumstances which may indicate a management predisposition to distort financial statements in the roll-forward period

- the year end balances of the asset and liability accounts tested at the interim date are reasonably predictable with respect to amount, relative significance and composition

- the client has adequate controls over establishing accounting cut-off at the year end

- the accounting system will provide sufficient information (as of the year end as well as in relation to the roll-forward period) to permit him, as auditor, to investigate
  - significant unusual transactions (including those at or near the year end)
  - other causes of significant fluctuations, or expected fluctuations that did not occur, and
  - changes in the composition of the accounts.

15.4.2 *Extending audit conclusions to the year end*

When adopting a roll-forward approach the auditor's conclusion with respect to amounts included in the financial statements is based on:

- substantive tests of details applied to accounts as of an interim date

- assurance provided based on his assessment and tests of the internal control structure (if applicable), and

- substantive tests to cover the remaining period (roll-forward procedures).

Substantive tests to cover the roll-forward period should normally include

- comparison of information regarding balances at year end with the comparable information at the interim date, to identify and investigate amounts and/or relationships that appear unusual

- analytical procedures and/or substantive tests of details applied to the remaining period.

In addition, the auditor would normally pay particular attention to the client's accounting cut-off procedures.

The nature and extent of these substantive procedures are a matter of audit judgment. Two examples of tests sometimes carried out at an interim date are:

- **confirmation of trade debtors**. Where trade debtors are circularised as of a date before the year end, the roll-forward procedures often include
  - analysing activity in the sales ledger control account (eg sales, cash collections, adjustments), along with supporting details for the intervening period
  - performing substantive tests of transactions during the intervening period (eg by performing more extensive tests of the accounting cut-off at the year end)

— analysing any unusual changes in the accounts.

- **attendance of stocktaking**. Most clients normally take a stock count at or very near the year end. If the physical stock count is not performed at the year end, an auditor should perform roll-forward procedures for the intervening period. The nature and extent of these roll-forward procedures will depend on whether or not stock is determined from perpetual stock records and on the length of the roll-forward period. The nature and extent of his roll-forward procedures will also depend on his assessed level of inherent and control risk and the results of his tests of controls. They might include test checks of individual movements of stock in the roll-forward period or reconciliations of movements in entire lines of stock.

15.5 ANALYTICAL PROCEDURES AS SUBSTANTIVE TESTS

An auditor's use of analytical procedures as substantive tests involves comparisons of recorded amounts, or ratios developed from recorded amounts, with expectations developed by him from other financial and non-financial data.

Analytical procedures vary from a relatively simple comparison or ratio (eg a comparison of depreciation expense for the current year with that of the prior year or a comparison of the ratio which depreciation expense bears to the carrying amount of a category of fixed assets with the client's rate of depreciation for that category) to the use of complex models and time series analyses. They can be applied on an overall client basis or broken down, for example, by branch, product or geographical area.

Other common applications of analytical procedures as substantive tests include trend analyses and comparisons of actual results with budgets or standards.

All these various examples of analytical procedures follow a four-stage pattern of work

- assessing the likely effectiveness of the test

- designing the test — choosing the bases of comparison and defining the precision required

- performing the test — gathering the data, making the calculations, and summarising or organising the results

- interpreting the results — considering whether the results conform to expectations, so that valid audit conclusions can be drawn.

The effective design of an analytical procedure and the interpretation of its results requires experience, judgement and thorough knowledge of the business and of the factors that might affect it. It is important therefore that:

- the design stage should receive appropriate attention from the audit manager

- the task of identifying and investigating significant differences should be performed by senior members of the audit team who are sufficiently familiar with the client's operations, accounting system, personnel, and changes in the economic and competitive environment affecting the client, to interpret the results knowledgeably.

15.6 WHEN TO USE ANALYTICAL PROCEDURES

Analytical procedures are more likely to be efficient where it is possible to use the client's own analysis. Provided the information is reliable, this will save preparation time. Analytical procedures should thus be given particular consideration where the client produces reliable management information which is used in running the business.

An auditor should not consider an analytical procedure which would require him to generate a lot of data, unless it is clear that the analysis would be cost effective. The more complex the analysis, the more time consuming it is to prepare, and the greater the risk that there will be difficulty in interpreting its results.

In assessing the likely effectiveness of an analytical procedure as a substantive test, an auditor should consider:

● the financial statement item or assertion under test

● the plausibility and predictability of the relationship between the data

● the availability and reliability of the data used to develop his expectations

● the precision of his expectations.

15.6.1   *The financial statement item or assertion*

Analytical tests are more effective in providing audit assurance for certain financial statement items or assertions than for others.

Examples of analytical tests that can provide a high level of assurance and can be more cost effective than tests of details include:

Financial statement item	Analytical Procedure
Depreciation expense	Overall depreciation rates applied to asset costs (straight line) or net book values (reducing balance) allowing for cost of additions, disposals, and fully depreciated assets.
Property rental income	Number of units let multiplied by average rental income per unit.
Loan interest expense	Comparison of loan rate of interest with the ratio of interest expense to the loan balance.
Fixed overhead expenses	Comparison with previous years' levels of expenditure and the budgeted levels for the current period, adjusted for known changes in circumstances.
Direct labour cost	Comparison with numbers of employees, hourly wage rates and hours worked.
Sales commission expense	Average commission rates applied to sales volume.

Analytical tests that provide limited assurance can, nevertheless, be used to reduce the required level of tests of details. Examples are:

Financial statement item	Analytical procedure
Sales	Review of ● gross margins ● stock shortages ● average monthly selling price (by product).
Debtors	Monthly analysis, expressed in days, of credit given to customers. Review of sales and credit notes trends for unusual movements around year-end.

Trade creditors	Monthly analysis of credit taken from suppliers, expressed in days.
Purchases/expenses	Comparison of actual and budgeted purchases and expenses.
Payroll costs	Review of average or weekly earnings per employee. Comparison of budgeted and actual payrolls.

Analytical procedures are often an effective means of testing the completeness assertion.

15.6.2 *Plausibility and predictability of the relationship*

The effectiveness of analytical procedures depends on the plausibility and predictability of the relationships identified for comparison and evaluation. Some relationships are stronger than others. For example, certain selling expenses may bear a strong relationship to sales in a merchandising business in which the sales force is paid by commissions. Likewise, total sales may be expected to vary directly with the quantities of units sold, the sales mix and the average unit prices. The relationship between a client's sales volume and the expansion or contraction of the market for its products as a whole would not normally be a strong relationship.

The greater the level of assurance sought from analytical procedures, the more predictable the relationships need to be. In assessing the predictability of a relationship, an auditor should bear in mind that:

- relationships are normally more predictable in a stable environment than in a dynamic or unstable environment

- relationships that involve components of the profit and loss account tend to be more predictable than those that involve only balance sheet accounts since the former represent transactions over a period of time, whereas balance sheet accounts represent amounts as of a point in time (eg the level of trading activity of a brokerage house tends to be more closely related to commission expense than it does to debtors at a point in time)

- relationships that involve transactions subject to management discretion tend to be less predictable than those not as subject to management influence (eg management may opt for maintenance instead of replacing plant and equipment, or may delay incurring advertising expenditure).

The risk that an auditor might draw the wrong conclusion by misinterpreting the results of an analytical test is greater than for other forms of substantive test. There will be circumstances where he should expect inconsistencies and fluctuations; in such cases apparent consistencies may be misleading. The auditor should understand the reasons that make relationships plausible because data sometimes appear to be related when they are not. Without such an understanding, it is only too easy to come to a false conclusion.

15.6.3 *Availability and reliability of data*

The data necessary to develop expectations as a basis for analytical procedures has to be both available and reliable. The information may be drawn from a variety of sources, both within and outside the business, including:

- comparative figures for prior periods adjusted for changes in circumstances

- budgeted figures for the current period

- other information contained in the financial statements or accounting records (eg using turnover and commission rates to predict sales commissions or selling expenses)

- other records maintained by the business which do not form part of the primary accounting records (eg using occupancy statistics and room rates to predict room revenue in an hotel)

- external information, such as price indices and industry statistics.

A key determinant in an auditor's decision to test an assertion by means of an analytical procedure is the availability of the data needed to develop an expectation for that assertion. For example, he may be able to test the completeness assertion for some clients by developing an expectation for sales from readily available production statistics or, in a retail business, from square footage of retail selling space. For other clients, however, the data needed to develop such an expectation may not be readily available.

The reliability of the data available is also an important factor. The reliability of the data should be commensurate with the level of assurance sought from the analytical test. For example, in auditing the tuition revenue of a college or university, the bulk of the audit evidence may come from simply multiplying the number of students enrolled by the standard tuition rate. An important part of applying this procedure is determining the reliability of the enrolment figures and the tuition rate. Without this, the value of the procedure would be limited.

An auditor should consider the following factors in assessing the reliability of data to be used in analytical procedures.

The source of the data. Data that comes from independent sources outside the client (such as published information on interest rates) is generally more reliable than internally produced data. Likewise, data obtained from a variety of sources tends to be more reliable than data obtained from a single source (provided of course, that the information is all consistent). The reliability of data is also enhanced if it is developed independently by client employees that are not responsible for the amounts being tested (eg data from records maintained by a personnel department, such as numbers of employees and rates of pay, that are produced independently of the accounting function).

Every analytical test involves comparison of at least one item with another. If the items being compared are generated from the same source, the validity of the comparison would be questionable unless the other item is verified by means of another audit test.

The conditions under which the data was developed. Data developed by a good accounting system with adequate control policies and procedures and within a favourable control environment is generally more reliable than other internally generated data.

Other knowledge the auditor may have about the data. Data that has been successfully tested during the audit, or during the prior year's audit, can obviously be considered more reliable than untested data. The reliability of data also tends to be enhanced if it has a strong interrelationship with other data that has been tested.

Also, the auditor's knowledge of the client and its internal control structure and the results of his other audit procedures may enable him to assess certain data as being more reliable than other data. For example, he might consider data extracted from a factory's production records to be more reliable than comparable data generated by its standard cost records, or vice-versa.

15.6.4 *Precision of the expectation*

An auditor's ability to use analytical procedures as substantive tests is based largely on the expectations he develops about the relationships in question. Without the capability of developing sufficiently precise expectations among identified relationships, the evidence ultimately obtained from these procedures may be limited. The expectations developed from available data should be precise enough to enable the identification for further investigation of inconsistencies that may be indicative of possible misstatements. The more precise the auditor's expectations, the narrower is the range of expected differences between his expectation and the recorded amount and the greater the potential for detecting material misstatement.

In assessing the precision of his expectations, an auditor should bear in mind that:

- many factors can influence financial relationships (eg sales are affected by volume, price, and product mix and each of these themselves are affected by several factors) and, therefore, offsetting factors could obscure a material misstatement

- expectations developed at a detailed level are preferable to those developed at a broader level (eg using monthly rather than year-to-date sales statistics and product-line information or sales by location rather than overall, company-wide sales statistics). A certain amount of disaggregation of information may be necessary. For example, where there is a wide variety of sales mix, analytical test of gross margin will not be effective unless the analysis is carried out by product or appropriate groups of products

- the frequency with which a particular relationship can be measured is particularly important. The more frequently he can observe a particular relationship in operation, the better an auditor's chances of developing more precise expectations

- in a time series analysis, the period should be sufficiently long to compensate for short term fluctuations. An auditor should always be conscious of seasonal variations in preparing time series analyses and build them into his calculation of the expected figure.

It may contribute towards an objective approach if, when designing an analytical procedure, the auditor designates an amount of difference from the expectation to be developed that can be accepted without further investigation. For example, he may have found in the past that distribution costs have approximated 10% of sales. He might then design a test to compare actual recorded distribution costs by month with 10% of the comparable monthly sales figures, and designate as significant a difference of, say 10% or more (ie 1% of sales) from the expected distribution cost figures.

15.7 IDENTIFYING AND INVESTIGATING SIGNIFICANT DIFFERENCES

An auditor should obtain an understanding of any significant difference revealed by the analytical procedure. Whether a difference between the expected and actual relationship is significant depends on how close the relationship under review was originally expected to be (ie how much of a difference could be accepted without further investigation).

His investigation will normally involve:

- reconsidering the methods and factors used in developing the expectation

- enquiry of management and corroboration of responses.

Differences could be caused by more than one factor. For example, differences between an actual and expected relationship between distribution costs and sales may be explained by the following factors, among others

- distribution costs may contain a substantial element of fixed cost (e.g. depreciation and insurance of the distribution trucks) that will cause costs to be out of proportion when sales are unusually high or low

- higher input costs may not be passed on immediately through higher sales prices (a temporary change in the relationship)

- market pressures may prevent a corresponding increase in sales prices (a permanent change in the relationship).

Differences caused by abnormal factors should be isolated. Abnormal factors include unusual or non-recurring transactions or other events for which there is an acceptable business explanation. Such an explanation should be corroborated with substantive audit evidence and may, depending on significance, require separate disclosure in the financial statements.

Explanations should be evaluated not only in relation to the difference which they purport to explain, but also in terms of their impact on other elements of the financial statements. For example, if a significant increase in a particular month's sales amount was attributed to a one-time special order, an auditor could substantiate the order by reference to the appropriate documentation. He should also consider the implication of this special sale on other relationships under review, such as cost of sales for that month if the order is particularly profitable and cash collections if the order is on special credit terms.

In deciding whether he can accept the explanation of management to resolve a difference, the auditor should consider:

- the responsibilities of the individual replying to his questions. The individual should preferably have responsibility over the subject matter of the inquiry and be someone to whom the answers are also of concern

- the knowledge or attitude of the individual. Preferably, the individual should be in a position to consider the matter properly. Casual responses should be viewed with scepticism

- the objectivity of the individual

- other known facts. The more convincing the explanation in the light of other known facts, the less additional confirmation is needed.

An auditor should follow up any differences not explained to his satisfaction. An inability to obtain a satisfactory explanation from the client may be indicative of a material error. Accordingly, in such a situation, he would have to perform other procedures to obtain sufficient evidence about the assertion under test. In designing such other procedures, he should note that unexplained differences may be indicative of an increased risk of material misstatement.

15.8 DOCUMENTATION OF ANALYTICAL PROCEDURES

Various methods of documentation may be used to facilitate the comparison and evaluation of the information under analysis. In most cases the simplest presentation will be a tabulation in columnar form showing the amounts or relationships under review, together with comparative figures, budgeted figures, variances from budget and so on. In certain circumstances, graphs may provide a clearer presentation, for instance, where there is a seasonal trend in the data under review, or where there is a predictable time lag in the information being compared (eg sales and levels of trade debtors).

The audit programme should define the objective of the analytical procedure and specify in comprehensive detail the steps to be followed. The working papers should identify any differences investigated, together with the explanations provided by the client and conclusions drawn from the audit work done to corroborate those explanations. It is important to note the names of the officials supplying answers or information and the dates of the interviews.

15.9 DEALING WITH ERRORS

15.9.1 *Nature of errors*

Errors are misstatements or omissions of amounts or disclosures in financial statements. Errors might involve:

- mistakes in gathering or processing accounting data

- incorrect accounting estimates resulting from misinterpreting the specific facts or from oversight

- mistakes in the application of accounting principles relating to amount, classification, or manner of presentation or disclosure.

Irregularities are intentional misstatements or omissions of amounts or disclosures. Irregularities include both fraudulent financial reporting (ie management fraud) and misappropriation of assets (ie defalcations).

In the remainder of this chapter, the term "errors" is used to encompass irregularities and to be synonymous with misstatements in the financial statements.

15.9.2 *Kinds of error*

Errors may be categorised as follows:

- known errors

- errors in accounting estimates

- projected errors

Known errors are errors that an auditor specifically identifies by means of his audit procedures. Known errors include, for example, failure to recognise expenses incurred, cut-off errors, and errors resulting from arithmetic inaccuracies.

Errors in accounting estimates (eg provision for stock obsolescence) are differences between a client's estimate and the closest estimate that the auditor believes to be reasonable.

Projected errors, as discussed in Chapter 16, result from audit sampling applications in which an auditor substantively tests less than 100% of the items in an account balance or class of transactions in order to evaluate some characteristic of the entire population. When he uses audit sampling in substantive tests, he projects the known errors identified in the sample he examined to the total population from which he selected the sample.

15.9.3 *Other discrepancies*

In addition to errors that affect the financial statements, two other types of discrepancies might be found during substantive testing:

- deviations in control procedures

- mistakes that do not affect the financial statements.

In performing a substantive test, an auditor may detect a deviation from a control procedure. If so, he should consider the implications of this deviation on his assessment of inherent and control risk applicable to the related assertion. If he has assessed inherent and control risk for the assertion to be high, this control deviation would probably have no effect on his audit approach.

However, if he has assessed inherent and control risk at a lower level and has performed tests of controls to support that reduced assessment, he should reconsider his assessment. Depending on the nature and extent of the deviations, explanations for those deviations, and the original level of inherent and control risk assessed, he might revise his assessment of inherent and control risk.

Some mistakes do not affect the financial statements, for example the misposting of an invoice between two sales ledger accounts. These mistakes should be recorded in the working papers and reported to the client, unless they are trivial or have already been identified and corrected by the client's staff. Any indication of a deliberate manipulation of accounts or other suspicious discrepancy needs to be brought to the attention of the manager and the partner for more experienced consideration.

15.9.4 *Dealing with individual errors*

When an error is detected the auditor should:

- consider what caused the error, if readily determinable
- consider the likely effect of the error on other areas of the audit
- assess whether the error is unintentional or intentional (an irregularity)
- document the error in the working papers
- encourage the client to adjust the financial statements for all known errors and errors in accounting estimates that are other than trivial and to consider adjusting the financial statements for projected errors
- aggregate all the uncorrected errors large enough to be tracked (see below) and evaluate their effect on the financial statements.

Each of these steps is discussed below.

An error might be one of principle or of misapplication.

The effect of an error of principle usually is easier to determine than one of application. For example, an inexperienced clerk might have posted all sales credits as if they were sales invoices, while an experienced bookkeeper might have incorrectly posted one sales credit because of carelessness. By establishing that the clerk had made an error of principle, an auditor probably would be able to determine the total effect of the error because all sales credits would probably be misposted. Establishing the likely effect of the bookkeeper's error would be more difficult because there would be no easy way of finding out how often the bookkeeper was careless.

The auditor should promptly discuss with appropriate client personnel errors detected (other than those that are trivial or inconsequential), because

- the mistake might be the auditor's, resulting from his misinterpretation or misunderstanding, and might not be an error in the financial statements at all
- the client's knowledge of the business might be helpful in assessing the full effect of the error and the possibility of similar errors existing
- the client might wish to take immediate action to prevent the recurrence of similar errors
- some errors, such as the failure to invoice goods shipped or the double payment of purchase invoices, might result in financial loss to the client if not rectified promptly
- there might be practical difficulties in getting the client to consider correcting the error at a later stage of the audit.

Having investigated the cause of an error, an auditor should consider its likely effect on other account balances or classes of transactions. For example, he may find errors in purchases which may also affect his audit approach and conclusions relating to stock and trade creditors.

Special considerations arise if an error indicates an irregularity (ie is intentional).

If he concludes that an error is or may be an intentional error, an auditor should take the following additional action:

- refer the matter to an appropriate level of management that is at least one level above those individuals who are involved or suspected to be involved in the irregularity, and discuss the approach to further investigation

- consider the implications, if any, for other aspects of the audit in view of the organisational position of those individuals involved and the amount of the irregularity

- if appropriate, suggest that the client obtain legal advice

- if appropriate, consider the need to communicate with the client's audit committee or board of directors.

None of the above steps should be taken without consultation with the manager and partner.

A petty cash misappropriation, for instance, normally would have little significance on other aspects of the audit because of the small balance and relatively small volume of transactions and because of the relatively low organisational level of the petty cash custodian.

On the other hand, a major embezzlement by a senior official or an instance of fraudulent financial reporting would probably have significant implications for other aspects of the audit.

15.9.5 *Keeping track of errors*   .

For each error detected, an auditor should document in his working papers covering the area in which he detected the error:

- the amount of the error

- the nature of the error (identifying any irregularities)

- the cause of the error, if known.

He should maintain on a separate summary the amount of each known, estimated, or projected error that exceeds his predetermined level for keeping track of errors. Guidance on setting this minimum level for keeping track of errors is given in paragraphs 9.5.2 of chapter 9.

Care should be taken not to include the same error on the summary twice. For example, an error detected from sales cut-off work might also be detected in tests of debtors.

The summary of errors should be updated to reflect those errors which have been corrected by adjustments to the financial statements.

Running totals should be maintained on the summary to monitor the cumulative effect of the uncorrected errors on the financial statements.

The auditor should encourage the client to correct all known errors and errors in accounting estimates that are other than trivial and to consider adjusting the financial statements for projected errors.

15.9.6 *Prior period errors*

The effect of uncorrected errors in the preceding financial year should also be considered.

In the prior period, errors may have not been corrected because their effect on the preceding financial statements was not material. It is therefore unlikely that they will need to be corrected in the current year as "prior-year adjustments" under SSAP 6. However, many prior year errors reverse in the current period and thus affect a current period item. For example, a prior period unrecorded accrual for interest paid in the current year would increase the amount of the current year interest expense if the appropriate liability for the current year was recorded at the end of the current period. The Companies Act requires the effect to be stated where any amount relating to a preceding financial year is included in the profit and loss account. As with many other disclosure requirements, this is subject to considerations of materiality.

Further, there could be other uncorrected prior period errors that do not reverse in the current period but may nevertheless have a continuing effect on the financial statements. For example, a client may have made an inadequate provision for warranty costs at both the end of the prior period and at the end of the current period.

Accordingly, an auditor should consider the effect on the current period of those prior period errors which were not corrected, and include them in his aggregation of errors if he believes that there is an unacceptably high risk that the financial statements could be materially misstated when those prior period errors are considered along with errors arising in the current period.

15.9.7 *Aspects of materiality judgements*

The auditor should recognise that errors might be immaterial to financial statement totals (eg profit before tax or total assets) but might nevertheless so affect the fair presentation of an individual line item (eg trade debtors or creditors), subtotals (eg current assets or current liabilities) or relationships (eg working capital or debt to equity ratio) as to cause the financial statements, taken as a whole, to be materially misstated. For example, an amount that is not otherwise material to the financial statements of a client with a major liquidity problem might affect adversely a ratio required by a debt covenant and cause the related debt to become payable in the short term.

The auditor will need to consider the aggregate effect of uncorrected errors on individual line items, subtotals, and relationships in the financial statements as well as their overall effect. Thus a classification error which has no effect on total assets may nevertheless materially distort the way the financial statements present the client's liquidity. This consideration, however, is not intended to imply any focus other than whether the financial statements, taken as a whole, give a true and fair view and are prepared in accordance with the relevant requirements.

Professional judgment should be exercised in considering the qualitative aspects of errors and their effects on the financial statements. Such qualitative factors may include:

- type of error (ie known error, error in accounting estimate or projected error) and its inherent precision or subjectivity

- cause of error (eg error of principle or application)

- sensitivity of the error (eg illegal transactions)

- possible bias on the part of management (eg to inflate earnings or minimise taxable income)

- special user needs (eg closely held business)

- trends in financial statement components (eg effect on trend of earnings)

- client's financial condition (ie strong or deteriorating financial condition)
- effect on future financial statements (eg a continuing build-up of underprovisions or overprovisions)

Materiality is discussed in Chapter 9

15.9.8 *Risk of further undetected error*

Even if the auditor concludes that any uncorrected errors would not cause the financial statements to be materially misstated, he still needs to recognise that there might be further undetected errors that could cause the statements to be materially misstated. The risk that the statements might be materially misstated increases as total uncorrected error increases and approaches materiality. If he believes that such risk of material misstatement is unacceptably high, he should reduce it to an acceptable level by:

- performing additional audit procedures or
- satisfying himself that the client has adjusted the financial statements sufficiently to reduce the risk of further undetected error to an acceptable level.

15.9.9 *Resolving material differences*

If the auditor concludes that the total of all uncorrected errors causes the financial statements to be materially misstated, he should request management to eliminate the misstatement. If the misstatement is not eliminated, he should consider qualifying his report.

CHAPTER 16   AUDIT SAMPLING

16.1   INTRODUCTION

Due to cost benefit considerations and the fundamental premise that an auditor seeks to obtain reasonable but not absolute assurance, audits are normally based on the concept of selective testing. This usually involves sampling. Efficient use of audit sampling can help prevent over-auditing by ensuring that the minimum sample size necessary to obtain the level of assurance needed is used.

A substantive sampling application generally includes the following steps:

- determine the objective of the sampling application

- define the population to be tested

- define the sampling unit

- consider the completeness of the population

- determine the sample size

- determine the method of selecting the sample

- perform the sampling application

- evaluate the sample results

This chapter looks at the basic background to audit sampling, identifies when there is a need to sample, and then goes through each of the steps above in relation to a substantive sampling application. It then deals with sampling in tests of controls.

16.2   BACKGROUND TO AUDIT SAMPLING

16.2.1   *Meaning of sampling*

Audit sampling is defined as 'the application of an audit procedure to less than 100% of the items within an account balance or class of transactions for the purpose of evaluating some characteristic of the balance or class'.

An auditor is therefore sampling when his objective is to infer something about a population based on the results of testing less than all of the items in the population.

He is not sampling when he examines less than 100% of the items in a population to:

- obtain an understanding of an entity's operations

- confirm his understanding of the design of the accounting system and whether the controls over the system are in operation

- draw a conclusion with respect to only the particular items examined (eg items over a specific monetary value or error-prone items)

- compare, in certain situations, selected information from one listing of client-produced data to another source of client data to make sure that the second source contains the same information as the first

- review and test reconciliations (eg bank reconciliations, reconciliations of subledgers to general ledgers)

- perform analytical procedures.

As a more detailed illustration, in designing his approach to selecting trade debtors for confirmation, an auditor may determine for a particular client that by confirming all customer account balances equal to or in excess of £25,000, he can obtain sufficient coverage of the recorded account balance so that consideration of customer account balances less than £25,000 is not necessary because of the low risk of material error. If this approach were adopted it would not involve sampling; although he would be examining all the significant items within the population, the results of his confirmations would relate solely to those items and could not be projected to the remainder of the population.

16.2.2 *Sampling risk*

By adopting a sampling approach an auditor accepts some level of risk that the results of the sample do not reflect the true characteristics of the population as a whole. This risk is referred to as sampling risk. Since the level of sampling risk varies inversely with the size of the sample, an auditor determines the level of sampling risk that he is willing to accept by varying the size of his samples. The less risk that he can accept, the larger his sample size must be and vice versa.

16.2.3 *Non-sampling risk*

Sampling risk should not be confused with 'non-sampling risk'. Non-sampling risk relates to the way audit procedures are conducted and it exists regardless of whether or not an auditor is sampling. For example, he may apply an audit procedure incorrectly, not recognise an error when his tests uncover one, select an inappropriate audit procedure in the circumstances, and so on. Whereas sampling risk is controlled by the size of the sample, non-sampling risk is controlled by adequate planning and supervision and by the functioning of quality control procedures, such as those relating to recruitment, training and the assignment of appropriate staff to the audit.

16.2.4 *Substantive tests and tests of controls*

In performing substantive tests, an auditor is concerned with detecting monetary errors and assessing the effect of those errors on the financial statements. Where he performs tests of controls, his objective is to determine the effectiveness of a specific control procedure. Audit sampling may be employed in both substantive tests and tests of controls. The guidance in this chapter deals first with substantive sampling applications. Guidance on sample tests of controls is given in the final section of this chapter.

16.3 WHEN TO SAMPLE

While sampling may be the most practical means of auditing many populations, there may be situations in which sampling is not appropriate. For example:

- an auditor may determine that sampling risk in a particular sampling application would be too great and he may instead elect to perform a 100% test

- where the number of items in the population is not large, he may determine that it is cost beneficial to examine 100% of the items rather than sample them, because of the additional time involved in designing the sample and selecting items for test

- he may decide that it is more efficient to examine all items of a population that are in excess of a certain monetary amount and to ignore the remaining items because they are collectively immaterial

● for some populations (eg certain overhead expenses) he may believe that performing analytical procedures is more appropriate than sampling

Whether audit sampling is appropriate in the circumstances is a matter of judgment.

16.4 HOW TO DESIGN A SUBSTANTIVE SAMPLE TEST

When an auditor designs a sample, he should:

● determine the objective of the test and define an 'error'

● define the population and the sampling unit

● check that the population is complete

● consider certain factors in determining the size of the sample

● choose an appropriate selection method.

16.4.1 *Objective of the test and error definition*

In designing a sample an auditor should consider the specific audit objective to be achieved and:

● make sure that the procedures to be applied are appropriate to that objective

● define in advance what will constitute an error.

The pre-definition of an error is important because the auditor will need to project errors found in drawing conclusions about the population from the sample. He might, for example, decide in certain tests to exclude from his definition of an error:

● mispostings (eg sales postings made to the wrong sales ledger account which do not affect total trade debtors)

● errors already independently detected and corrected by the client on a timely basis

● errors of a particular type (eg cut-off errors) which will be more fully evaluated by some other substantive test.

16.4.2 *Defining the population and the sampling unit*

The results of a sample test can only be projected to the population from which the sample was selected. An important consideration, therefore, in designing a sample is defining the population to be sampled. For example, an auditor should normally exclude from the population to be sampled

● items to be substantiated by other audit procedures

● items to be tested 100%, such as items above a certain monetary value, unusual items and other items particularly susceptible to the risk of misstatement

● items not to be tested because, for example, there is an insignificant risk of misstatement in such items.

There will often be a choice of physical units of the population on which to base a sample selection. For example, in a confirmation of trade debtors, the physical unit of selection may be the customer balance, the individual sales invoices constituting the customer balance, or the items constituting the sales invoice. The auditor would select the unit that he believes the customer would be most likely to confirm.

16.4.3 *Completeness of population*

The auditor should check that the source from which he is selecting his sample represents the complete population. For example, if he is confirming trade debtors and using the sales ledger to select the items to confirm, he should make sure that all trade debtors are included in the sales ledger. One way to do this might be to check that the balances in the sales ledger add up and agree to the general ledger.

Any items of the population that are not present when he selects a sample must be separately addressed (eg a separate sample might be taken covering the excluded items or alternative analytical procedures might be performed).

16.4.4 *Determining sample size*

In determining the size of a substantive sample, the following factors should be considered:

- risk of incorrect acceptance of the sample results

- tolerable error

- expected error

- variation within the population

- population size and value.

These factors are discused below.

Risk of incorrect acceptance of sample results. As indicated previously, when an auditor samples he is subject to sampling risk. The more sampling risk that he can accept in a sampling application, the smaller the sample size need be. The risk that he is most concerned with is the risk that the monetary error in the population is greater than the error detected by applying his sample.

Generally, the more assurance obtained from other substantive tests (eg analytical procedures, tests of related populations) directed towards the same objective and the lower the assessment of inherent and control risk, the more risk can be accepted regarding the sampling application, and vice versa. Where an auditor is obtaining little assurance from other substantive tests, he must obtain most of the assurance that he believes necessary (based on his assessment of inherent and control risk) from the sampling application.

This relationship between the various sources of evidence can be expressed in the form of an audit risk model. The audit risk model states that the audit risk (AR) of an incorrect conclusion regarding an accounting population is a combination of the following risks

- the inherent risk of material misstatement being present (Inherent Risk — IR)

- the risk that the internal control structure failed to prevent or detect the misstatement (Control Risk — CR)

- the risk that audit procedures would fail to detect the misstatement (Detection Risk — DR).

These risks can be represented in the following formula:

$$AR = IR \times CR \times DR$$

Because of the close relationship between inherent risk (IR) and control risk (CR), a practical approach is to consider them together as one combined risk — the risk of misstatement occurring and not being prevented or detected by the internal control structure (inherent and control risk — ICR).

The risk model now simplifies to:

$$AR = ICR \times DR$$

As indicated above, audit assurance is derived from other substantive tests directed towards the same objective (eg analytical procedures, tests of related populations) as well as from the sampling application. Detection risk is therefore comprised of two elements, the sampling risk (SR) and the risk that the other substantive tests (OST) would fail to detect existing misstatement.

Accordingly, the risk model can alternatively be presented as follows:

$$AR = ICR \times SR \times OST$$

ICR represents the combined inherent and control risks, SR represents the sampling risk in the tests of details and OST represents the risk that other substantive tests would fail to detect misstatement.

The risk factors comprising the formula are multiplicative. In other words, the risk of misstatement occurring and not being detected by the internal control structure and not being detected by the audit procedures is the product of both risks.

For example, if the risk of error occurring and not being detected by the internal control structure is 50% and the risk that the audit procedures would not detect such error is 20%, then the risk of the error occurring and not being detected by either the internal control structure or the audit tests is 50% × 20% or 10%. Stated differently, this means that an auditor can be 90% sure that misstatements will either be prevented or detected by the internal control structure or detected by his audit procedures.

The audit risk model can be used to assist in determining the amount of testing that an auditor needs to perform related to a particular financial statement assertion. Once he has assessed:

● the amount of audit risk that he can accept

● the risk that misstatements will occur and not be prevented or detected by the internal control structure

● the risk that other substantive tests will not detect misstatements

he can determine the level of risk that he can accept that his substantive sample test of details will not detect misstatements. By rearranging the audit risk model slightly he can mathematically determine the acceptable sampling risk:

$$SR = \frac{AR}{ICR \times OST}$$

To illustrate the process, assume the following:

● the amount of audit risk that is acceptable (AR) for the specific audit objective is equal to 10%.

● the combined assessment of inherent and control risk is 75%. This means that there is a 75% chance that a material misstatement might occur and not be prevented or detected by the internal control structure (a relatively poor structure)

● the risk that other substantive tests (OST) will not detect misstatements is 50%.

Solving for SR in the formula:

$$SR = \frac{0.10}{.75 \times .50} = .27 \text{ or } 27\%$$

Thus the auditor in this instance can accept a 27% risk that his sample tests of details would not detect a material misstatement.

Reliability factors. While the foregoing calculation may be relatively straightforward to explain from a theoretical standpoint, it is often difficult to apply in practice, particularly when dealing with risk in terms of percentages. To facilitate this process of quantifying assurance, an auditor can use what are referred to as *reliability factors*, rather than percentages. Reliability factors are merely the natural logarithm of percentages. The table below lists the corresponding reliability factors for the percentages of risk.

Reliability factors

% Risk	Reliability Factor	% Risk	Reliability Factor
100	0	22	1.5
90	0.1	20	1.6
82	0.2	18	1.7
74	0.3	17	1.8
67	0.4	15	1.9
61	0.5	14	2.0
55	0.6	12	2.1
50	0.7	11	2.2
45	0.8	10	2.3
41	0.9	9	2.4
37	1.0	8	2.5
33	1.1	7	2.7
30	1.2	5	3.0
27	1.3	2.5	3.7
25	1.4	1	4.6

The characteristic of reliability factors that makes them easier to use than percentages is that the various risks, when expressed in terms of reliability factors, can be combined by addition. Taking the example described above, where the inherent and control risk is 75% and the risk that other substantive tests will not detect misstatement is 50%, these can be expressed as reliability factors of 0.3 and 0.7, respectively, resulting in a total of 1.0. If the total audit risk acceptable for the particular audit objective were 10%, equivalent to a reliability factor of 2.3, the acceptable sampling risk for the sample test of details would be equivalent to a reliability factor of (2.3 − 1.0) = 1.3, or 27%.

The relationship between the reliability factor for a sample, the assessment of inherent and control risk (also expressed as a reliability factor), the risk that other substantive procedures will not detect material misstatement, and the audit risk for the particular audit objective is illustrated by the examples below.

	Strong internal control structure		Weak internal control structure	
	Case A	Case B	Case C	Case D
Target reliability factor to achieve acceptable *audit risk*	2.3	2.3	2.3	2.3
Reliability factor in respect of *inherent and control risk*	(1.0)	(1.0)	(0.2)	(0.2)
Reliability factor in respect of *detection risk*				

Analytical procedures	(0.4)	(0.0)	(0.7)	(0.0)
Other tests of details	(0.0)	(0.3)	(0.3)	(0.3)
Substantive sample	0.9	1.0	1.1	1.8

The reliability factor attributed to the substantive sample can then be used to calculate a sample size, as shown below.

Tolerable error. Tolerable error is the maximum amount of error that can be accepted in the population to be tested without causing the financial statements to be materially misstated. Sample size varies inversely with the amount of tolerable error. As the amount of tolerable error decreases (ie the amount of error that the auditor can accept decreases) the size of the sample increases to enable him to identify and quantify such error. The reverse is also true. Tolerable error is a function of planning materiality; the latter concept is discussed in Chapter 9. There is no general agreement within the profession as to an appropriate practical basis, other than use of experience and judgment, for deriving tolerable error from planning materiality. A suggested guideline is that tolerable error should be set at 75% of planning materiality.

Expected error. Where an auditor expects to find errors, for example based upon past experience, he should consider whether sampling is an appropriate method to use. Errors increase the imprecision of the conclusions that can be drawn from a sample — larger samples may be required in order to draw conclusions within the limits of tolerable error at an acceptable level of sampling risk. Error-prone term selection and analytical procedures may be more effective in such situations.

Variation within the population. Variation in the characteristics of a population — whether quantitative (as in the case of populations with items of varying size) or qualitative (where individual items are of a different nature) — affects the size of sample needed.

In respect of variations in value, the auditor should aim either to apply a monetary unit sampling approach (MUS) and thereby reduce the number of individual items that need to be examined or to identify an upper stratum of high value items (ie higher than the sampling interval value) to be tested 100%.

For example, consider that the sales ledger balance for a client was £1,000,000, consisting of 10 balances of £50,000 and 1,000 balances of (on average) £500. Suppose also that the formula described below gives a sampling interval of £25,000. This would give a total sample size of 40 items. Were strict MUS procedures applied, the auditor would in fact end up examining less than 40 account balances because the large balances would have been selected 'twice'.

In respect of variations in qualitative characteristics within the population, an auditor would normally stratify the population into its main qualitative subgroups and assess the inherent and control risk for each group separately. For example, where a client has trade debtor balances in respect of both domestic and foreign customers, and the inherent and control risk associated with both types is assessed to be different, then he would separate the two 'strata' in the population and determine sample sizes for each separately. Where the risk is assessed as the same, a sample can be drawn from the combined population, the sample size being calculated in the normal way.

Population size and value. The number of items in a population has virtually no effect on sample sizes unless the number is very small. In the formula for calculating sample size given below, the sample size is influenced by the relationship between tolerable error and the value of the population. The greater the value of the population relative to tolerable error, the larger the sample, and vice versa.

Calculating sample size. The following formula may be used to calculate sample size:

$$\frac{\text{value of adjusted population}}{\text{tolerable error}} \times \text{reliability factor}$$

- the adjusted population is the population to be sampled, after excluding items to be substantiated by other procedures, items to be tested 100%, such as high value items and error-prone items, and items not to be tested

- the reliability factor expresses the amount of tolerable risk of incorrect acceptance of the sample results, which is calculated by expressing the overall audit risk for the particular audit objective as a reliability factor and subtracting from it the inherent and control risk and the detection risk attributed to analytical procedures and other substantive tests, all expressed as reliability factors.

To illustrate the use of the formula, consider the following situation:

Sales ledger balances are to be circularised. A sampling approach will be employed.

The population from which the sample will be selected totals £3,000,000 (ie after excluding high-value items and certain other items for separate testing).

Tolerable error is £100,000.

Previous experience indicates that errors in the population will be few and relatively small; they are not expected to amount to more than £20,000.

Overall audit risk for that audit objective is 10% (ie 90% assurance is needed).

The combined assessment of inherent and control risk is 50% (ie a moderate level of risk).

Other substantive tests (analytical procedures and shipping cut-off) have a high detection risk of 90% (ie they provide little assurance).

The first step is to calculate the reliability factor for the sampling application. Translating the percentages indicated above into reliability factors:

		Reliability factor
Overall audit risk (10%)		2.3
Less:		
Inherent and control risk (50%)	0.7	
Other substantive tests (90%)	0.1	0.8
Reliability factor for sample		1.5

The next step is to insert the information set out above into the formula to calculate the size of the required sample.

$$\text{Sample size} = \frac{£3,000,000}{£100,000} \times 1.5 = 45$$

This gives a sampling interval of £66,667, were monetary unit sampling to be used. Alternatively, customers would be selected as suggested below.

16.4.5 *Sample selection*

A sample can only be taken as representative of the population as a whole if it has been selected in an unbiased way, so that every item in the population has a chance of being included in the sample. This freedom from bias is important whether the sample is one of a large number of customers' balances selected from the sales ledger or of a few fixed asset additions selected for physical inspection.

Bias may enter the selection of a sample in many subconscious ways — for example, a tendency to select items from the more recent months rather than the earlier part of the year for which invoices have been put into storage; or a reluctance to choose items dealt with by a clerk with illegible handwriting — as well as more conscious decisions to overlook items known to be more time-consuming, such as invoices without a cross-reference to a shipping document, or from a supplier with a reputation for inaccuracy.

To make sure that a sample is demonstrably free from bias, the selection can be made using a sampling plan or method. There are many such methods available to cover different situations. In particular, random, systematic and haphazard selection methods will, when designed properly, result in a sample that is representative.

In a **random sample,** each item in the population being sampled has an equal chance of being selected. This selection method, which is usually performed using a random number table or a random number generator in a computer application, will result in a representative sample.

In a **systematic sample,** an auditor selects every nth item based on a selection interval that is determined by dividing the population being sampled by the sample size. A random starting point (or multiple random starting points) is often used to determine the first item to be selected.

For example, a sample of 50 items is to be selected from a population of £100,000. The sampling interval is calculated as:

$$\frac{\text{value of population}}{\text{sample size}}$$

$$\text{or in this case } \frac{£100,000}{50} = £2,000$$

A random number is then chosen between 1 and the sampling interval, say 477. The sample is then chosen as the 477th pound, the 2477th, the 4477th, 6477th etc. The items to be tested will then be the invoices or balances containing the 477th and 2477th pound and so on.

Samples may readily be selected in this manner using a computer-based interrogation package. The method may also be carried out manually, using a calculator. Where the addition of items needs to be checked in any event, selecting a sample in this way involves little extra work. The provision of frequent sub-totals (for example, page totals in a list of trade debtors) may reduce the time required to select the sample.

Where it is impractical to add through the entire population, the following method provides a reasonably unbiased alternative to fixed interval sampling:

- remove (or isolate) high value or error-prone items for separate selection

- divide the remainder of the population into sub-divisions broadly equal in value (eg mark off sales ledger so that each section, after exclusion of high value or error-prone items, is roughly equal in value)

- within each sub-division select the number of items required to achieve the desired sample size (eg if there were 10 sub-divisions one would select a tenth of the total sample from each division)

- in selecting the sample items within each sub-division, choose high and low value items according to their relative proportions within the population (eg if larger items make up more than half of the value of the population more than half the selections should be made from these larger items).

179

Where it is not practicable to divide the population even in this way, it may be possible to stratify the population broadly in terms of value. For example, purchases may be obtained from a few major suppliers of raw materials, a slightly larger group of component suppliers and a large group of other suppliers; while in terms of volume of transactions the last group would dominate the records from which the selection is made, the three categories may each represent a third of total purchases in value. It is on the latter basis that the selection should be made.

When selecting from a non-monetary population (eg shipping documents) the fixed interval method may be adapted by using an interval of a number of items rather than monetary units. Alternatively the random sampling method described above may be used. Neither of these approaches may be wholly satisfactory, as the sample will not be weighted towards the higher-value items. However, no totally satisfactory method of selecting a sample from unpriced items is generally available. A practical solution may be to select, say, a third of the sample by looking through the items and choosing those that appear to be of high value, and then selecting the remainder of the sample by one of the methods discussed above.

The systematic sampling method has the disadvantage that the population may contain a pattern which coincides with the interval at which sample items are selected. Such coincidences are rare but an auditor should nevertheless be alert for them.

For example, in using systematic sampling to select sample items in a payroll test, an auditor may determine that the sample interval is every 20th item in the payroll register. Every 20th item may be from the same department, which would result in a biased sample which would not be representative of the population.

A **haphazard sample** also consists of selecting sample units without any conscious bias, that is, without any particular reason for including or omitting items. It does not mean careless sampling and, when applied properly, will result in a representative sample. As an example of a haphazard sample, assume that an auditor is selecting sample items from a cabinet drawer full of invoices. As long as he does not consciously omit certain items (eg first or last invoices) or consciously select certain items (eg physically small items) his sample should be representative.

One other method that has sometimes been used by auditors is called **block sampling**. In a block sample, all items included in a block are selected for testing. The block may be one day's transactions, those for a week, a month, and so on. Unless the number of blocks is sufficiently large, a block sampling approach will usually not result in a representative sample. Also, even when the number of blocks is sufficiently large to result in a representative sample, the benefits of sampling may be lost because of the large of individual items selected for testing. Therefore, block sampling is rarely used if a representative selection of items is being sought.

16.5   EVALUATION OF SAMPLE RESULTS

Once an auditor has selected his sample and applied his audit procedures to the sample, he should:

● project the results of his sample over the population subjected to sampling

● compare the projected error (together with any error in items examined 100%) with tolerable error and consider his sampling risk

● investigate the cause of the errors and the implications for other phases of the audit and other areas of work.

16.5.1 Projection of errors

Regardless of the size (value) of the errors found in the sample, they should be projected over the rest of the population. This is done in order to obtain a broad view of the scale of possible error for comparison with tolerable error and is not meant to imply that the precise amount of error in the whole population is known. Nevertheless, sample errors cannot be explained away as isolated instances or because they are immaterial. As explained below, however, once an auditor has projected the errors to determine their overall significance, he should gain an understanding of how and why they occurred and what effect they might have on the audit. In doing so, he may be able to isolate the cause of the errors and correct the errors by looking at all items affected. This process is explained more fully below.

The sampling method used will determine how sample errors are projected over the population. For example, in a statistical sampling application, sample errors generally are projected over the population and sampling risk is measured by the sampling application itself. Where an auditor is applying non-statistical sampling, he has two methods of projecting errors:

- calculate an error rate per monetary amount of his sample and extend that rate over the book value of the population (ratio method)

- calculate an error rate per sample item and extend that result over the number of items in the population (difference method).

The choice between these two methods is based on whether errors are more closely related to the value of the items in the population or to the number of items in a population. The use of the ratio method is usually preferable, because most accounting populations have great variability in the values of the individual items. In such cases, errors noted probably relate more to monetary values than to the number of items and therefore the ratio method would be appropriate. It is important that an auditor has a sufficient understanding of the nature of the population to make a choice because the two methods can result in significantly different projections in certain circumstances.

Where the population is stratified, the auditor would normally project error for each stratum individually and sum up the projected error for each of the strata (including the known error in any items examined 100%, such as high value items) to arrive at projected error for the population as a whole.

16.5.2 Comparison of projected error to tolerable error and consideration of sampling risk

An auditor should compare his projected error for the population as a whole with his predetermined tolerable error to see whether the population error is likely to be within the boundary of what he can accept. In doing so, he also should consider the possibility (sampling risk) that the results he obtained in applying the sampling approach actually differ from the true state of the population. As discussed previously, the quantification of sampling risk is judgemental where an auditor has not used a statistical sampling approach. The closer total projected error gets to tolerable error, the more important sampling risk becomes.

To illustrate this process, assume that a non-statistical but stratified sample is selected. The sample consisted of three strata — a high value stratum in which the auditor tested 100% of the items with a value equal to or in excess of £100,000, a second stratum of items of a value between £10,000 and £100,000 and a third stratum of items greater than £0 but less than £10,000. The known errors found in each of the three strata were as follows:

Stratum 1 — £15,000
Stratum 2 — £10,000
Stratum 3 — £ 5,000

Projected error for strata 2 and 3 were £30,000 and £40,000, respectively. Total projected error for the population is therefore £85,000 (£15,000 + £30,000 + £40,000).

Assume tolerable error is £150,000. The auditor compares total projected error to tolerable error and finds that he is under tolerable error by £65,000.

He next considers sampling risk and whether the £65,000 adequately allows for sampling risk. In a non-statistical sampling application this determination requires experience and judgement. When total projected error is very close to tolerable error or very far from it, the decision is relatively easy. Where projected error is close to or exceeds tolerable error he may not be able to accept the sampling results. Where it is well below tolerable error, sampling risk probably is not a concern. One indication of the possible impact of sampling risk is how close projected error is to his original expectation of error. Where the two are relatively close, sampling risk may not be as important as when the two are significantly different.

If the sample results support the recorded amount of the population (ie total projected error plus sampling risk is acceptably below tolerable error), an auditor should, nevertheless, consider the difference between his sample results and the recorded population, along with other actual or potential misstatements in other account balances or classes of transactions, in determining whether the financial statements are materially misstated (see 'Dealing with errors' in chapter 15).

If the auditor is not able to satisfy himself, at an acceptable level of sampling risk, that the actual error in the population is within the limits of tolerable error, he should consider asking the client to investigate the errors, to identify their cause and assess the potential for further similar errors and to correct the account balance.

16.5.3 *Investigation of cause and implications of errors*

An auditor should consider the reasons for the errors noted and the effect of those errors on the rest of the audit. In doing so, he should consider:

- the nature and cause of the deviations, such as whether they are errors or irregularities or are due to misunderstanding of instructions or to carelessness

- the possible relationship of the deviations to other phases of the audit (eg where he has obtained assurance from controls, is such assurance still justified or where he has found more errors than were believed to exist) or to other related areas of work.

In assessing the effect of errors noted, the auditor may be able to isolate the errors that are due to specific circumstances. Where this is possible and all transactions affected by such circumstances are reviewed and corrected, both known and projected error are eliminated. For example, all errors in valuing marketable securities may be isolated to one individual responsible for one particular class of securities. If the client then revalues all such securities and corrects the misstatements, the auditor need not consider any further adjustment based on his sample.

Further guidance on dealing with errors is provided in Chapter 15.

16.6 TESTS OF CONTROLS

As explained in Chapter 14, an auditor may decide to perform a test of controls to determine the extent of compliance with a specific control procedure.

The considerations involved in determining the correct sample size for such a test are complex. They include:

- the nature of the control procedure and the importance of its role within the internal control structure

- the continuity of client personnel and previous audit experience.

One approach is to vary the sample size from test to test according to various factors, including the sampling risk acceptable and the maximum rate of deviation from prescribed procedures that could be tolerated without modifying the assessment of inherent and control risk.

For example, if an auditor wishes to be 95% confident that the rate of deviation from prescribed procedures is 5% or less, he can establish, using statistical tables, that the sample size necessary to support this conclusion (assuming no errors are found) is 60. A sample of 60 would also support other conclusions such as 70% confidence that the deviation rate was less than 2%. In this way it is possible to adjust the sample size to the conclusion he wishes to draw from each test.

Such an approach would be similar to that used for substantive sampling but there are some important differences. The following table compares the concepts involved in substantive sampling with those involved in a sample test of controls.

Substantive test	**Test of controls**
Sample item is an amount expressed in monetary terms.	Sample item is typically a document or part thereof.
An error is a monetary misstatement.	An error is a lapse in the operation of a control procedure, which may not necessarily result in a monetary misstatement.
The amount of acceptable difference is expressed as tolerable error.	The amount of acceptable difference is expressed as tolerable deviation rate.
Amount of expected errors is the expected error in monetary terms.	Amount of expected errors is the expected error rate.
Combined projected error and sampling risk should not exceed tolerable error.	The achieved deviation rate should not exceed the tolerable deviation rate.

An alternative approach is to adopt a fixed sample size for such tests of controls and to adjust the conclusions drawn from the test according to the findings. (Here too statistical tables can help in giving an indication of the range of possible statements about deviation rates and sampling risk that might be made based on the results of the sample). The sample needs however to be large enough to ensure that the range of possible conclusions falls within acceptable norms.

Action plan for sample test of controls

An auditor's approach to a sample test of controls should generally include the following steps:

- determine the objectives of the test

- define what constitutes a deviation

- define the population

- define the period covered by the test

- define the sampling unit

- consider the completeness of the population
- determine the method of selecting the sample
- determine the sample size
- perform the sampling application
- evaluate the sample results

CHAPTER 17   AUDITING ACCOUNTING ESTIMATES

17.1   INTRODUCTION

Accounting estimates are pervasive in financial statements. They are needed becau ʒ the measurement of certain types of amounts depends upon the outcome of future events and because sufficient detailed information about recent past events cannot always be accumulated on a timely, cost-effective basis.

Examples of accounting estimates include:

- provisions for doubtful debts
- writedowns of obsolescent stock to net realisable value
- valuations of unquoted investments
- provisions for contingent losses relating to litigation
- useful lives of plant, property and equipment
- accruals for expenses incurred but unbilled.

By their very nature, accounting estimates are

- subject to a range of possible outcomes
- often based on subjective assumptions about conditions and events that are expected to exist or occur in the future, rather than on existing conditions or known, past events
- often not part of the client's routine information processing system
- generally not subject to the same controls that cover more routine processing of data
- usually made directly by management or indirectly by management through its supervision of those who directly make the estimates.

The last characteristic of accounting estimates is of particular significance because management's direct influence over the development of accounting estimates is double-edged; management involvement helps ensure that the process benefits from its expertise and knowledge, but it renders the process susceptible to manipulation to achieve the results that management desires.

An auditor is responsible for evaluating the reasonableness of accounting estimates made by management. Obtaining evidence to support estimates is more difficult than for objectively determined amounts for completed transactions. The unique characteristics of accounting estimates increase the risk that financial statements could be materially misstated, either intentionally or unintentionally.

This chapter provides guidance on the audit of accounting estimates. Recognising the difficulty and importance of the topic, the auditing profession in the United States has developed an auditing standard on the subject and this chapter draws heavily on the standard.

If the auditor identifies certain accounting estimates as significant risk areas, he should consider the need to extend his auditing procedures in those areas. For example, if he believes that a client's stock accounting system and control procedures have not kept pace with its growth in operations and, as a result, stock obsolescence is a key audit risk, he should consider extending his procedures relating to provisions for stock obsolescence.

17.2   DEVELOPING ACCOUNTING ESTIMATES

It is the task of client management to decide when estimates are needed and to make such accounting estimates.

Although the process of making an estimate is often informal, it typically involves:

- identifying the factors that affect the estimate
- accumulating data on which to base the estimate
- developing assumptions that represent management's judgement of the most likely circumstances and events concerning the relevant factors
- determining the estimated amount based on the assumptions and other relevant factors
- ensuring that the amount is properly presented and adequately disclosed.

The process can range from a simple calculation, based primarily on information and results from prior years, to a complex process requiring the preparation of an accounting model.

The risk of material misstatement will vary depending upon:

- the complexity of the process
- the availability and sufficiency of relevant and reliable data
- the number and significance of assumptions involved
- the degree of uncertainty and subjectivity associated with the assumptions.

For example, an estimate of the value of a security for which no ready market exists may be more susceptible to misstatement than an estimate of provision for product warranty for which there is experience of past claims.

17.3   INTERNAL CONTROL STRUCTURE RELATED TO ACCOUNTING ESTIMATES

The client's internal control structure may reduce the likelihood of material misstatements of accounting estimates. Specific relevant aspects of that structure include these factors:

- communication by management to all concerned of the need for proper accounting estimates
- accumulation of relevant, sufficient, and reliable data on which to base accounting estimates
- preparation of the accounting estimates by qualified personnel
- adequate review and approval of the accounting estimates at appropriate levels of authority, including a review of the reasonableness of the assumptions, the factors that have been taken into account and due consideration of the need to use a specialist
- comparison by management of previous accounting estimates with subsequent results to assess the reliability of the process used to develop them

- consideration by management of whether the resulting accounting estimates are consistent with operational plans.

17.4 EVALUATING ACCOUNTING ESTIMATES

In evaluating the reasonableness of an accounting estimate the auditor should first obtain an understanding of how management developed the estimate. Factors to consider in doing so include:

- the competence of the management personnel who developed the estimate

- the complexity and subjectivity of the process, including any indication of management bias

- any other inherent or control risk considerations that impact the risk of material misstatement

- the availability and reliability of relevant data

- the significance of the assumptions made.

Because management tends to influence the making of accounting estimates, the auditor should understand management's attitudes and motivations in the preparation of the financial statements. Further, because of the high level of judgement that may be involved in evaluating accounting estimates, he should make sure that appropriately experienced audit staff are assigned to this area of the audit.

An auditor normally concentrates on key factors and assumptions that are:

- significant to the estimates

- sensitive to variations

- deviations from historical patterns

- subjective and susceptible to misstatement and bias.

In addition, he should consider the client's experience in making past estimates as well as the auditor's own experience in the industry.

An auditor should use one or more of the following approaches:

- review and test the process used by management to develop the estimate

- develop his own independent expectation of the estimate to corroborate the reasonableness of management's estimates

- review events or transactions occurring after the balance sheet date.

Review and test the process used by management. In following this approach, the auditor normally should:

- identify the controls in effect over the process, the sources of information used to develop assumptions, and the assumptions that form a basis for the estimate

- see that management has considered all the key factors and developed assumptions for each key factor — consider whether there are alternative assumptions

- gather suitable support for each assumption and evaluate the relevance, reliability and sufficiency of such support

- evaluate the completeness of the assumptions and their consistency with each other, the supporting data, relevant historical data, industry data, the client's business plans, and any known changes in the business or industry

- compare prior period estimates with the actual results

- test management's calculations that translate the factors and assumptions into the accounting estimate.

For complex estimating processes involving specialised techniques, the auditor may need to use the work of a specialist.

Develop independent expectations to corroborate management's estimates. An auditor may take this approach by using other key factors or alternative assumptions about those factors based on his understanding of the facts and circumstances. For example, if management used a rule of thumb based on historical experience to estimate its allowance for doubtful debts (such as a percentage of sales), he could develop his own independent expectation based on information as to specific customer accounts (eg ageing, current credit evaluation, collection experience).

Some clients, particularly smaller ones, frequently request that an auditor develops accounting estimates for them. In doing so, he should make sure the client understands and concurs with the results. Before seeking management's concurrence, he should preferably request knowledgeable client personnel to review his work. Because an auditor is likely to be less informed about all of the relevant factors than client personnel involved in the particular subject area, he should attempt to obtain as much input from them as possible. He should also make sufficient audit tests to support his conclusions. To maintain his independence, he needs to be satisfied that the client accepts responsibility for the accounting estimates, irrespective of who develops them and how they are developed.

Review post balance sheet events. This is generally the most effective (and often the most efficient) approach. For example, the allowance provided for doubtful debts can best be audited by reviewing subsequent accounts receivable collections. However, timing considerations often preclude an auditor from using this approach.

Due to the characteristics of estimates, including the inherent subjectivity associated with them, no one accounting estimate can be considered accurate with certainty. Accordingly, a difference between a client's estimate and the auditor's estimate may not necessarily indicate that the client's estimate is unreasonable. Where an auditor does conclude that the client's estimate is unreasonable, the difference between it and the closest estimate that he believes to be reasonable should be proposed as an adjustment to the financial statements and considered in conjunction with all other proposed adjustments in determining whether the financial statements are materially misstated. For example, when management has calculated the reserve for uncollectable receivables to be £100,000 and his audit work indicates that the reserve should be somewhere in the range of £125,000 to £150,000, he should propose an adjustment of £25,000 (the difference between the client's estimate of £100,000 and the closest amount that he considers to be reasonable — ie £125,000).

Where management has made a number of estimates that he determines to be within the range of reasonableness, the auditor should also consider whether those estimates are consistently at one end of that range and, if they are, whether that represents a possible bias on management's part. For example, if each accounting estimate included in the financial statements is determined to be individually reasonable (ie within a range of reasonableness), but the effect of the difference between each estimate and the estimate supported by the evidence available was to increase reported profits, he should consider the estimates taken as a whole in assessing the reasonableness of the financial statements.

CHAPTER 18   COMPUTER-ASSISTED AUDIT TECHNIQUES

18.1   INTRODUCTION

This chapter describes various ways in which computers can be used to assist with the audit process. It is not intended to provide complete guidance on available computer-assisted audit techniques ('CAATs') but only as an overview of those more commonly employed.

Wherever the client's records are partially or wholly computerised, and whether microcomputers, minicomputers or mainframe computers are used, an auditor needs to consider the effect of computer processing on his audit approach. In particular, he may need to use CAATs in his audit. There are four main reasons for this:

● CAATs may be the only way to extract data or create an audit trail in the absence of human-readable records

● allied to the above, CAATs may permit efficient forms of audit testing not possible using clerical procedures. For example, although audit trails permitting detailed substantive tests on purchases, sales, etc may exist, an auditor may be able to use CAATs to audit in terms of total quantities bought/sold and to develop average prices which he can apply to these quantities

● CAATs may be used to perform audit procedures that are lengthy or error-prone (eg complex calculation checks)

● CAATs may permit 100% checks when clerical checks would be limited to samples (eg ageing of the debtors ledger).

The table below lists the CAATs discussed in this chapter and indicates the uses to which each may be put.

Table 18.1 Uses of CAATs

	Test of controls		Substantive tests	
	General controls	Application controls	Tests of details	Analytical procedures
Computer Audit Software				
— Interrogation of data files			●	●
— Simulation of program logic		●	●	
Miscellaneous Techniques				
— Audit Test Data, including the use of an integrated test facility		●		
— Embedded audit facilities		●	●	●
— Utility programs		●	●	●
— Program comparison	●	●		
— Program code analysis	●	●		
— Interrogation of system activity files	●			

18.2 COMPUTER AUDIT SOFTWARE

Computer audit software, sometimes referred to as interrogation software, is the most widely used computer-assisted audit technique. The technique may be defined as 'the processing of a client's data files by the auditor's computer programs'.

In some situations the auditor's computer programs are used to interrogate the client's data on the client's computer. However, it is usually more convenient for an auditor to take copies of the client's files and interrogate them using his own audit computer programs on his own mini or microcomputers.

One of the benefits derived from a client storing data on magnetic media is that data can be accessed and retrieved from the files by audit interrogation programs. Large volumes of data can be read and processed, and information can be extracted in a way which is not possible in a manual system. The use of file interrogation programs offers several advantages over clerical or manual audit methods. In particular:

- the work is carried out faster and more accurately

- greater volumes of data can be reviewed, enabling the scopes of audit testing to be increased significantly without a proportional increase in costs

- clerical or manual audit work can be devoted to an examination of those items selected based on criteria specified in the interrogation program as significant for audit purposes. The audit staff can therefore concentrate on investigation and seeking explanations, rather than on selection.

Computer audit software may be used in either tests of controls or substantive tests. The more common applications of computer audit software are described below.

Data file interrogation. The use of computer audit software to interrogate financial data files is a form of substantive testing, as it involves the direct examination of transactions and balances.

Data file interrogation can be used to carry out a variety of audit procedures including:

- creating for audit purposes an audit trail which, although present in the records on the client's data files, is not produced in printed form by the client's system

- adding, summarising and performing other mathematical operations on the data in the client's files

- extracting data items which meet particular selection criteria (eg balances greater than a specified monetary amount where the customer has exceeded his credit limit)

- surveying or stratifying data items in a file

- selecting a sample of transactions or balances

- analysing, by age, data items in a file

- comparing data items on two or more current files (eg matching account balances on a receivables master file with the individual sales invoices, cash and credit notes on the sales ledger transaction file)

- comparing files created at different times (eg comparison of the current and previous years' inventory master files to identify significant price changes, obsolete inventory, new products)

- preparation of confirmation letters

- reporting duplicates or gaps in sequences of numbers on data items (such as goods received notes).

Program simulation or reperformance. Program simulation, sometimes referred to as reperformance, is a special application of data file interrogation. Computer audit programs can be used to perform the same procedures that are performed by client programs. This technique is normally carried out using the same type of computer audit software as is used in data file interrogation and, in most cases, forms part of the interrogation. Program simulation is commonly used to reperform clients' programmed procedures such as the calculation of bad debt provisions, accrued interest, sales commissions, etc.

Program simulation may also be used to verify that the resulting balances have been derived correctly from the input data. The computer audit program is applied to the client data file(s) and the results obtained are compared with the results of processing the same file by the corresponding client program. In some cases this comparison can be carried out clerically. However, it is usually more efficient to use the computer audit software to compare the results with those produced by the client program and held on the client's files, in order to identify only those items that differ sufficiently to warrant further investigation.

The following example illustrates a more complex use of program simulation. A company whose main business is the rental of office equipment uses a series of computer programs to generate sales invoices and sales and ledger postings by processing a master file of rental contracts. An audit computer program could be developed to simulate this task and then run against a copy of the rental contracts master file previously processed by the client's programs. The sales and ledger analyses thus obtained would be checked against the actual ledger postings.

The basic steps involved in using computer audit software are:

- planning — the identification of audit objectives and requirements

- gaining a sufficiently detailed knowledge of the client's system to identify the files to be interrogated, the data file structures and record layouts

- liaison with the client (eg asking the client to retain copies of files required)

- development of the program(s) — the technical specification and documentation of the audit software, the coding, compilation and test running of program(s)

- running the program(s) — this will either be done at the client's premises, or on one of the auditor's own microcomputers or in-house minicomputer installations

- review of output — a brief examination should be carried out as soon as possible to confirm the completeness and accuracy of any reports produced before the detailed audit tests are carried out

- post-audit review — this should be performed immediately after the completion of the audit to identify and document any improvements that could be made to the existing programs as well as other possible uses of software in subsequent audits.

The initial identification of the need on individual audits for computer software to satisfy audit objectives and the specification of the requirements will usually come from the partner, manager or audit staff on the engagement; the technical design, development and running of the program will normally require computer audit specialists.

If the partner deems it necessary to involve a computer audit specialist, the partner or manager should:

- communicate to the specialist the objectives of the work to be done

- evaluate whether the specified procedures will meet the audit objective

● evaluate the results of the procedures applied as they relate to the nature, timing and extent of other planned audit procedures.

The computer audit specialist requires supervision and review in the same way as any other member of the audit team.

18.3 GENERAL PURPOSE SOFTWARE

There is a variety of general purpose software aids (mainly spreadsheets, database, graphics and word processing packages) that can be used to support the audit process and that run on microcomputers, either in the office or on the client's premises. These packages are relatively easy to use and, in general, do not need the support of a computer audit specialist.

Spreadsheet packages are particularly suitable for administrative tasks such as work scheduling, time recording, and monitoring job progress.

Spreadsheets may also be used to prepare:

● lead schedules and supporting working papers

● consolidations

● statements of cash flow.

Furthermore, spreadsheet worksheets may be adapted to the particular requirements of a single client or an entire category of clients (eg investment partnerships) and are particularly useful for complex accounting calculations that are updated from period to period (eg allocation of income, expenses, gains and losses to partners' capital accounts).

Database packages are generally more effective than spreadsheets at handling large volumes of data. For example, a database package may be used to develop a system which records information about the bank accounts of every client in an auditor's office. This application can generate confirmation letters automatically to be sent out to each bank at the designated time.

Analytical procedures can, where appropriate, be made more effective by the use of spreadsheet or database software.

Graphics facilities, which may be available in the form of a separate package but are more commonly supplied as part of a spreadsheet package, can be used to improve the quality of presentations or reports to clients. For example, they can be used to illustrate trends identified by analytical procedures in the form of a bar chart which may be more readily understood than a column of numbers.

More specialised forms of graphics packages may be used to create flowcharts which form part of the audit working papers. Flowcharts produced in this way use conventional flowcharting symbols but are more presentable and are more easily maintained from year to year than conventional 'pencil and paper' flowcharts.

18.4 SPECIAL AUDIT PACKAGES

These software packages are normally designed to be used by general auditors rather than computer audit specialists to carry out such routine tasks as:

● preparation of financial statements

● tax computations

- analytical procedures.

There are a number of packages available that can assist in both the preparation of financial statements and in performing and documenting audit procedures. They can be distinguished from more traditional accounting packages by the fact that they provide some of the audit working papers as well as the financial statements. Some of these packages commence at the incomplete records stage and proceed towards draft financial statements. Others start with a trial balance and produce some form of lead schedule and an audit trail of audit adjustment journals.

Similarly, there is a variety of PC based packages available that can be used to prepare personal or corporate tax computations.

There are also a number of packages ٖvailable to assist in carrying out analytical procedures using techniques such as trend analysis, ratio analysis etc.

18.5 MISCELLANEOUS COMPUTER AUDIT TECHNIQUES

The computer audit techniques listed in this section are probably less widely used than those covered earlier in this chapter. They are more likely to be used by internal than external auditors, but have been included here in order to provide a reasonabe coverage of the techniques currently in use.

18.5.1 *Audit test data*

The use of audit test data (test packs) may be defined as 'the controlled application of auditor's test data to client application program procedures and an evaluation of the results'. The purpose normally is to perform tests of controls on a client's programmed procedures to ensure that they are achieving their objectives.

An auditor's test data can either be included with the client's data as part of the client's production processing run (in which case it may be referred to as 'live' data testing) or be processed separately by the client's programs (in which case it may be referred to as 'dummy' data testing or dummy processing). When using live test data, it is essential to anticipate all the effects that the test data will have on the client's system, and it will normally be necessary to delete the test transactions from the system after the tests have been performed.

Before using a test pack an auditor should have a detailed understanding of the client's system; particularly where live data is to be used and the risk of disrupting the client's system is not insignificant. Consequently, the use of a test pack is normally reserved for those situations where either conventional tests of controls are not practical or there is a loss of audit trail.

An illustration of typical circumstances in which a test pack may be used might be where a client uses a purchase ledger system which also produces an analysis of invoices, by category of expense. Were this analysis only to give a single total for each code at the end of each month, with no sub-analysis to invoice level, and the volumes of invoices involved were large, then there would be a break in the audit trail.

The basic steps involved in using a test pack are:

- planning — the identification of audit objectives, determination of the method to be used (live or dummy data testing) and liaison with the client

- obtaining a sufficiently detailed understanding of the client's system (including consideration of any unintended effects on the client's records) to facilitate the design and carrying out of the tests

- creating of test data

- predicting the results — this is needed both to enable a comparison with the actual results to be made and to prepare for possible effects on the client's records

- running the test pack — it is essential that the current programs are used, not obsolete or test versions, otherwise the entire exercise becomes pointless. It will be especially difficult to ensure this where a separate audit run is performed, as opposed to the test data being included within one of the client's runs

- comparing actual and predicted output, investigating differences and drawing conclusions on the results.

In the first year that a test pack is run the responsibility for the design and performance of the test packs usually lies with a computer audit specialist. In subsequent audits the major responsibility may be transferred to general audit staff. This will depend on individual circumstances (ie the complexity of the application and the experience of the audit team).

As indicated above, there is a choice between using live or dummy data. This decision will be influenced by such factors as:

- the characteristics of the system

- the need to ensure that the test data is processed by the current programs

- the attitude of the client, particularly with respect to any potential effects upon its records and processing schedules.

These various options should be considered at as early a stage as possible in the development of a test pack.

When using test packs, however, an auditor needs to ensure that it is the operational versions of programs which are tested and that the integrity of programs and data files is maintained throughout the period being audited. In other words, the general controls over the processing system must also be adequate and operating effectively.

It follows therefore that a test pack will not normally be used in a computer installation with weak general controls. Where the installation is well controlled and the auditor wishes to place particular reliance on certain program procedures, a test pack may be used to obtain evidence that the program procedures are operative.

In some cases a test pack represents the best audit approach even though the general controls are weak. In such circumstances a test pack might still be used if it could be run on a number of occasions during the period, preferably on a surprise basis. This approach might be adopted in a complex computer environment if the achievement of a control objective were to be heavily dependent on program procedures; here a test pack may provide the only means of ensuring that the program procedures are operating consistently throughout the period.

The results of running a test pack also help to confirm the auditor's understanding of the system; it is very unlikely, however, that a test pack will be used solely for this purpose because of its cost.

18.5.2 *Test data generator*

Test data generators are software packages which can be used either to construct data to be tested or to create dummy master files. The user describes the characteristics of the data required and the software generates a file of appropriate data and produces a listing of it. This data can then be used as a 'test pack' (see above). Test data generators are only cost effective if either the system is complex and there are many programmed procedures that the auditor needs to test, or large volumes of test data are needed.

18.5.3 Integrated test facility

Integrated test facility (ITF) is a particular form of test pack involving the establishment of a dummy entity through which data may be processed. For instance, a fictitious operating unit might be set up.

Once the dummy entity is established, an auditor can input live hypothetical transactions that affect only the dummy entity and process these 'transactions' using the client's information system alongside the client's live data. It will usually be necessary to delete the test transactions from the system after the test has been performed. As with all test packs, the output produced is compared with predicted results to determine whether the programmed procedures being tested are operating correctly.

An ITF can be particularly useful in more complex environments, for example in an on-line, real time banking system. A single terminal can be set up as an 'audit bank' (a separate branch which is not consolidated into the bank's financial statements) which can then be used to perform any of the banking functions for its own dummy customers. In this way, extensive testing of the entire system may be carried out without the client's staff being aware that it is taking place.

In order for the ITF technique to be effective:

- the auditor should have a detailed knowledge of the complete system, including the possible effects of the ITF data on all related system files

- knowledge amongst the client's staff of the existence of the facility should be limited to those who need that knowledge in order to perform their tasks properly.

18.5.4 Embedded audit facilities

Embedded audit facilities consist of program procedures written by an auditor, which are inserted into the client's application programs and are executed simultaneously with those programs. The main purpose of the technique is to review transactions as they are processed, to select items according to criteria specified in the resident code, and to write details of these items to an output file for subsequent audit testing.

This technique can be used as part of a substantive approach, to test the validity and accuracy of input data processed through a system, and also to test the operation of controls within the system. As with interrogation, much larger volumes of data can be reviewed than by manual methods. Items can be selected over a period of time — possibly the entire accounting period — for subsequent further investigation.

It is fundamental that the embedded audit code is neither altered nor bypassed and that the output file of selected items is maintained intact. Use of this technique should therefore be restricted to well controlled installations. Sophisticated on-line real-time applications (for example, banking), where continuous and timely audit testing is a priority, probably represent the best environment for the technique.

18.5.5 Utility programs

Most hardware manufacturers provide software known as 'utility programs' that are designed to perform common tasks, such as copying or sorting files or printing details of records for visual inspection. A particular type of utility program that can be of audit use is sometimes referred to as a 'report generator' or 'query facility'. These programs may be useful in the performance of tests of controls or substantive tests; for instance, they may be employed to produce copies of data files required for interrogation purposes or to print out internal file labels which can be used to determine whether the correct file has been obtained.

18.5.6 *Program comparison*

Having confirmed the operation of a particular program (for instance by using a test pack), program comparison software may be used to compare a security copy of the program (taken by the auditor) to the program in the client's live program library. In this manner, it is possible to confirm that no changes have been made and that the original audit work confirming the operation of the program procedures is still valid.

Any differences between the two copies will be identified and reported for further investigation. These differences will be reviewed to assess their audit impact (if any). Such differences would be checked against documentation authorising amendments to the relevant program.

18.5.7 *Program code analysis*

Not strictly a computer-assisted audit technique, program code analysis involves looking at the original set of instructions to the computer (the source program listings) to see whether particular program procedures exist; such findings would then be corroborated using test data. The technique is more complex than this brief description suggests and requires a high level of technical skill if it is to be applied effectively.

18.5.8 *System activity file interrogation*

Many modern computer operating systems automatically produce a log of every event occurring in the system, both user- and computer-initiated. This information is usually written to a disc file and may be printed out periodically.

As part of the audit testing of general controls it may be useful to review the computer log for a whole period and, where possible, identify unauthorised or unusual activity for further investigation.

Where a suitable system activity file is retained on magnetic media, it is possible to select and report exceptional items of possible audit interest such as:

- the use of utility programs instead of the relevant application programs to alter data file contents

- apparent attempts to breach password access controls or other security devices

- the running of programs out of the normal schedule or sequence, or simply at unusual times

- amendments to key application programs.

18.5.9 *Flowcharting*

When writing a computer program, the programmer usually constructs a logic chart as a preliminary step in coding, using a conventional set of programming symbols. This logic chart is also useful once the program is written to assist in an appreciation of how the system works. It is also of obvious interest to the auditors since it can help to identify control procedures and system changes.

Rather than relying on the client's own chart (which may or may not be up-to-date), it may be possible to generate a flowchart from the program itself using a flowcharting package. Such packages usually only work for a particular programming language and, sometimes, only on a particular computer. They are designed to identify and report every process and logical path through the client's program, in diagrammatic form.

The usefulness of this technique in practice is limited by:

- its cost in comparison with alternative methods

- the relatively crude level of most flowcharting software

- the quality and complexity of the coding in the program to be flowcharted.

However, in situations where there is a lack of adequate documentation of a sophisticated system and confirmation of what the system actually does cannot be obtained in any other way, this technique should be considered.

CHAPTER 19   EXECUTION AND CONTROL

19.1   EXECUTION

19.1.1   *Introduction*

This chapter provides guidance on the various aspects of execution, communication, and documentation of an auditor's work, including procedures for controlling these areas.

It is important that the audit team should carry out the audit work as planned.

The main tools used to achieve that objective are:

- audit programmes
- supervision
- review.

The audit programme, the ultimate end-product of the planning process, is dealt with in Chapter 12.

19.1.2   *Briefing and supervision*

Continual supervision of staff is central to controlling the quality and efficiency of the audit.

Each member of the audit team should satisfy himself that any staff reporting to him fully understand:

- their responsibilities
- the objectives of the work assigned to them
- matters that affect the nature, timing and extent of assigned procedures.

Junior staff in particular should be briefed on the degree of detail to which they should work. Without clear scopes and materiality guidelines, they might perform unnecessary tasks or go into excessive levels of detail.

Staff should be instructed to discuss promptly with their direct superiors any problems arising in the course of that work; they should not wait until the working papers are formally reviewed.

On-the-job training in the form of supervision and review is important to the individual's professional development. Typically it involves:

- practical advice on carrying out tasks
- timely guidance so as to draw lessons from mistakes
- praise where a task has been performed well.

The extent of supervision required in any given circumstance depends on many factors, such as:

- the complexity of the delegated tasks
- the risk of material misstatement in the area being audited
- the experience of the persons performing those tasks.

19.1.3 *Review of working papers*

The purpose of reviewing working papers is to make sure that:

- the planned work has been completed

- it has been adequately performed and properly documented

- appropriate conclusions have been drawn and documented.

The working papers and the conclusions drawn from the work done should be reviewed by staff member of greater seniority and experience than the individual carrying out the work.

The working papers should be reviewed as soon as possible after they are completed and before the audit team leaves the client's premises at the end of the audit so as to enable review points to be answered by the staff members who did the work.

Raising and clearing long lists of review points is time-consuming and inefficient. Many such points can be avoided through the exercise of appropriate supervision.

The reviewer should determine that:

- all working papers are initialled, dated (day and month), and properly headed and indexed

- all working papers have been cast and/or cross-cast

- all working papers are cross-referenced

- totals on lead schedules agree with the trial balance and, where appropriate, with the financial statements

- audit programmes are initialled and referenced to working papers

- the work done is in accordance with the audit programme and was adapted where necessary to meet unforeseen situations or changed circumstances

- appropriate conclusions have been drawn from the work performed

- material matters are noted for the attention of the audit partner

- errors or omissions found are fully investigated and are properly documented and aggregated

- all points for the representation letter or management letter have been noted appropriately

- the audit time spent has been properly recorded and summarised

- documents of continuing importance are filed in the auditor's permanent file

- working papers contain no gratuitous comments

- documents no longer relevant have been removed from the permanent file.

The normal procedures for writing and clearing review points are as follows:

- review comments should be sequentially numbered, clearly and unambiguously stated, and referenced to the related working papers. Most auditors use special review stationery

- any points relating to non-audit matters should be segregated from the audit working papers

- the reviewer should discuss all the important points with the particular staff member when giving him the detailed list of review points. It can be demoralising for staff members to be given a list of review points without encouragement or discussion, particularly if some points are difficult or critical

- the staff member should initial and date (day and month) each review point as it is answered

- the working papers should be adjusted as necessary to reflect the resolution of review points. Amending the working papers when answering a review point also prevents the same point from being raised by a subsequent reviewer

- the reviewer should review the answer to each point, referring, where appropriate, to the amended working paper.

- all significant points have to be answered to the reviewer's satisfaction before the report is issued.

19.2 COMMUNICATION

Good control depends upon good feedback from members of the audit team. Important findings need to be communicated promptly to those directing the fieldwork.

Audit findings vary widely. Examples include:

- discovery of a minor error on an audit test in which that error is unrelated to the objective of the test and is clearly of little significance (this presumes that the error is not related to a sampling procedure)

- suspicion of defalcation, manipulation of accounts, or other potentially fraudulent activity

- failure of an important control feature noted by audit staff while carrying out a substantive test.

Whether such findings should be communicated and to whom depends on the circumstances. However the following is a useful guide for the individual member of an audit team:

- briefly consider whether the findings might affect the audit approach, the financial statements, or the client

- if the answer to any of the above is 'yes', or if the implications are uncertain, the team member's direct superior should be informed

- only if the person making the findings is satisfied that the error is inconsequential, would it be appropriate not to communicate them

- it is generally appropriate to note findings in the working papers, however inconsequential they may seem. A person reviewing the papers subsequently will normally have a broader understanding of the nature of the findings and may have cause to reassess the original interpretation of the consequences.

An auditor might identify ineffective or missing control procedures, even though this might not directly affect his audit. As with any other findings, these matters should be noted in the audit working papers so that they can be considered for inclusion in the management letter.

Good communication is ultimately a matter of common sense. An auditor needs to be able to react promptly to events, so that his audit is completed efficiently and the client receives good service.

19.3 DOCUMENTATION

19.3.1 *The need for working papers*

The engagement partner has to be satisfied that the work delegated to staff has been properly performed. Generally this can only be done by having available detailed working papers prepared by the persons who performed the work. In effect, working papers provide the principal support for the audit report, including representations in that report of compliance with auditing standards.

Working papers also provide:

● evidence of work performed and the conclusions drawn in arriving at the audit opinion

● a medium for controlling the audit work carried out

● details of problems encountered and their resolution for future reference.

Audit working papers should be sufficiently complete and detailed to enable an experienced auditor with no previous connection with the audit subsequently to ascertain from them what work was performed and support the conclusions reached.

19.3.2 *Working paper files*

Working papers should be indexed. The papers should be presented in a logical format so that the reviewer is able to carry out his task quickly and efficiently. Where information on one schedule is necessary to understand the contents of another they should be cross-referenced.

Working papers can be filed in any one of a number of ways. However, most auditors maintain for each engagement:

● a current audit file or files containing all working papers relevant to the year under audit

● a permanent file or files, containing documents continually referred to over a number of years.

The current audit file is in two parts:

● general working papers covering all aspects of the audit not specific to verification of individual account balances, for example.
  — financial statements
  — sign-off documentation and other completion procedures
  — planning documentation
  — draft financial statements
  — trial balance
  — control and administration papers

● specific working papers containing detailed audit work pertaining to particular account balances.

The permanent file may contain:

● working papers documenting the auditor's understanding of the client's business, organisation, internal control structure, and so forth

● copies of, or extracts from, important agreements that will be relevant from year to year, (eg the company's articles of association)

● details of major fixed assets, such as real estate

● accounting schedules of continuing relevance, such as fixed asset depreciation schedules

- organisational structure and the history of investment in subsidiaries, and other major investments

- back-up copies of audit programmes for use in developing the following year's programme.

Working papers in a permanent file should be designed to allow adequate room for future additions and amendments. If lengthy agreements are filed, a summary schedule of the major points of audit significance should be prepared.

Outdated permanent working papers should be transferred to the rear of the current audit file for the last year in which they applied. This transfer should be noted on the permanent file index and cross-referenced to the relevant year, so that the papers can be traced if necessary.

A client will be unimpressed with an auditor's efficiency if he asks questions the answers to which are already contained in his own records. All staff new to the client should therefore read the sections of the permanent file related to the areas of the audit to which they have been assigned.

19.3.3 *'Lead-Schedule-and-Pyramid' filing*

Under the 'lead-schedule-and-pyramid' filing system, each section of working papers in the current audit file dealing with particular account balances carries a lead schedule at the front of the section. That schedule contains a list (or a summarised list supported by subsidiary lists) of all items in the trial balance making up the amount (or amounts) shown in the financial statements. Each amount in the financial statements should be traceable through the lead schedules to its constituent items in the trial balance and to the supporting working papers that provide audit evidence in support of the constituent items.

If the client presents the auditor with an initial trial balance on which there might be many subsequent adjustments, each lead schedule could be set out in four columns, as follows:

- first column   — amounts per trial balance

- second column   — adjustments

- third column   — final amounts as adjusted

- fourth column   — previous year's comparative amounts.

Any adjustments should also be processed and audited in the working papers supporting the lead schedule, so that any reviewer can easily ascertain the composition of each figure in the published accounts and can be sure that these figures have been audited.

Some advantages of lead schedules are that they:

- break up the trial balance into more manageable components

- provide a clear trail from the working papers to the financial statements

- facilitate working paper review, allowing the reviewer to focus on the more important elements within each financial statement account balance

- simplify the process of keeping track of which adjustments have been made by providing a trail from the trial balance to the final financial statements.

For certain smaller engagements, the auditor might decide to dispense with lead schedules, and have detailed supporting working papers flow directly from the trial balance. This normally would be done if:

- the trial balance is relatively simple, containing few account headings

- the composition of amounts in the financial statements can be easily traced from the trial balance, and

- few adjustments are expected.

In effect, in these circumstances, the trial balance is used as a single 'consolidated lead schedule'. This consolidated lead schedule has to be relatively straightforward for it to serve the same objectives as the lead schedules themselves.

In the pyramid structure of indexing, each schedule is identified:

- first, by the number or capital letter that corresponds to the appropriate section of the audit file, followed by

- numerical indexing indicating the sub-section and sub-division of each sub-section.

The lead schedule represents the top of the 'pyramid.' If lead schedules are not used, the trial balance represents the top.

The indexing structure described above is illustrated by the following example:

- lead schedule — Other current liabilities K

- summary of accruals K-1

- accruals of rent payable K-1.1

- accruals for rent — retail outlets K-1.1.1

- accruals for rent — warehouses and offices K-1.1.2

- accruals for telephone expenses K-1.2

A distinctive index series should be allocated to working papers such as circularisation schedules that do not correspond directly with amounts on the lead schedule.

For example, the summary of the trade creditors circularisation programme should be indexed J100, the control schedule J101 and so on.

As a working rule, all schedules should be properly indexed and cross-referenced as they are completed. This should not be left until the end of the audit. All the adjustments must be fully explained on the appropriate lead or subsidiary schedule.

More elaborate systems of indexing may be necessary or useful when dealing with large and complex areas.

For example, the working papers in respect of a very large client with large and complex stocks might be logically filed by audit objective as follows:

- DA — quantities

- DB — valuation

- DC — net realisable value

- DD — obsolescence

The lead schedule will, of course, be D. The lead schedule for each section (e.g. DA) contains the conclusions reached in that section and the supporting working papers are indexed as DA1, DA2, etc.

The working papers in a section are sometimes filed by audit objective within each major category.

Thus, for example, if three categories of stocks are on the lead schedule D, there will be three main sections (D1 to D3). Within each section the working papers will be filed by audit objectives: D1A (quantities), D1B (valuation) and so on.

19.3.4 *Content of working papers*

All working papers, including papers prepared by the client, should contain the following basic information:

- the name of the client

- the subject, purpose, or content of the working paper

- the balance sheet date

- the index number of the working paper

- the initials of the auditor preparing the working paper

- the date they were prepared

- the initials of the person reviewing the working paper

- the date they were reviewed.

In addition, all computer-generated working papers should show the program name and version number and the disk and/or file reference.

An auditor should document, where applicable:

- the source of information included in the working paper (e.g. from the payroll sheet for a particular week, or from a named member of the client's staff with an identified function), if it is not otherwise apparent

- the audit work that has been performed (ie the extent of the tests, a key describing the audit tick marks used, or an explanation of the audit procedures)

- the findings made, to the extent that they are not otherwise evident

- appropriate cross-references to other working papers

- the audit conclusion drawn (where a judgment significant to that section of the audit has been made).

Most audit programme steps require working papers that identify the items examined. Thus, if a programme step is to review subsequent cash payments, an auditor would either photocopy the cash listing or, if there are only a few items large enough to warrant investigation, list those items. In either case, he would give details of the subsequent verification of payments. If a repetitive audit step needs to be performed on items in working papers, ticks or symbols against the items tested are recommended to evidence the work done. These ticks or symbols should be explained on the working paper or on an explanatory schedule covering a group of working papers.

The person who performs the work should document the conclusions reached as appropriate. Conclusions should not be altered by others: additional comments by the reviewer should be added and signed separately.

In the event that differences of opinion concerning accounting and auditing issues arise among members of the audit team, and these differences cannot be resolved by discussion with the engagement partner or manager, the dissenting staff member should document his disagreement in the working papers. In this situation, the basis for the final resolution by the audit team should also be documented.

19.3.5 *Preparation of working papers*

Working papers should be neat, clear, and concise; they should present the information to the reader in an easily understandable manner. They should be well spaced out, with necessary detail contained in supporting schedules. Excessive detail should be avoided. For example, amounts will generally exclude pence and may in appropriate cases be in round thousands of pounds. Adequate space should be left for conclusions and subsequent additional information and comment. Well-presented working papers generally reflect clear thinking and orderly work.

If a working paper involves nothing more than copying or reorganising data from the client's records, an auditor should consider asking the client to prepare the working paper. This should be discussed and agreed with the client and confirmed, preferably in writing. It may be advantageous to discuss the purpose of the schedules with the client staff who will be preparing them. Schedules prepared by the client should always be tested for accuracy and the audit work done properly evidenced.

An auditor should use all other practical means available for reducing clerical time used in schedule preparation. Extracts of information for the working papers should be photocopied whenever possible. Word-processing facilities should be used where practical to update schedules largely duplicated from one year to the next.

He should also consider the potential for timesaving arising from use of dictating machines, computer spreadsheets and even of rubber stamps for heading up and dating schedules.

Computer models should be tested, documented and reviewed before reliance is placed upon them. This is considered in Appendix 19.1 The scope of such work will depend upon the complexity and purpose of the model and whether it is likely to need subsequent updating.

19.3.6 *Ownership and confidentiality of working papers*

Working papers prepared solely for the purpose of carrying out his duties as auditor belong to the auditor himself. The auditor should adopt appropriate procedures for ensuring their safe custody and confidentiality.

The safe custody of working papers is important because they provide evidence of the nature and extent of audit work performed. If such evidence cannot be produced because the papers have been mislaid or lost, it might be difficult to support a claim that an auditor discharged his responsibilities.

Working papers containing audit evidence or conclusions should not be shown to the client. Also, working papers containing client information to which certain officers or employees of the client would not otherwise have access should not be shown to those officers or employees. If the client requests accounting information that an auditor has extracted, audit evidence should be removed from copies of such working papers or new working papers should be prepared.

The auditor should treat his working papers as strictly confidential and should not normally permit access to them by third parties. Two customary exceptions are noted below.

Holding company auditors Audit files relating to subsidiary companies customarily are made available to the auditors of the parent company if they wish to review them. An auditor should, however, first inform the management of his client subsidiary company that he has received such a request from the parent company's auditors.

Joint audits While the audit is still in progress, the other firm of auditors should be allowed to inspect and/or photocopy his working papers freely. This acknowledges the fact that both firms of auditors have equal responsibility in joint audits.

19.4 TIME CONTROL

The accurate recording of actual audit time is important since it will facilitate the preparation of a realistic budget the following year and will allow the auditor to identify reasons for any legitimate cost increases by comparing actual time with budgeted time.

The preparation of budgets and the monitoring of actual time spent on the audit is greatly eased by the use of standard worksheets.

These may be divided into sections corresponding to the sections of the audit file and further sub-divided for the work within each section. It will generally be necessary to use sub-headings for any section only if the total budgeted time for the section exceeds, say, 20 hours.

It is essential that each member of the audit team maintains a daily record of time spent. Staff must ensure that they are aware of the time budgeted for each area of work allotted to them and should enter the budget on their personal time record. Failure to record time may conceal an overrun of actual time against budget and thus jeopardise the recovery of costs from the client.

On larger audits, time may need to be summarised periodically (at least fortnightly and possibly weekly). In the later stages of the audit the auditor should estimate the time needed to complete each section, add this to the cumulative time to date and compare the total with the budget. This should provide an early warning of any likely overrun in total.

At the end of the interim stage of the audit, the actual time spent must be summarised and reasons for any significant variance on individual work sections must be considered.

At the end of field work on the final stage of the audit, it is most important to make a realistic assessment of the time required for completion so that total actual time can be estimated and finally compared with budget. The assessment should take into account the following:

- the clearance of any outstanding matters
- the finalisation of a post-audit letter to cover points arising during the final stage of the audit
- the completion or updating of the post balance sheet events programme of work
- the supervision of the printing of the accounts and their despatch to the client for approval and signature
- the rendering of the fee.

DEVELOPMENT AND DOCUMENTATION OF COMPUTER MODELS

1 INTRODUCTION

Computerised working papers should always include the following details for identification:

Working paper reference
Name of client
Description/subject
Program name/version number
Disk and/or file reference
Date of printout
Date of period end
Author name
Initials of reviewer
Date of review

Every model should include, or have documented separately, a brief statement of the objectives, operating instructions and details of input expected and output produced. For larger models a contents table or map should also be used.

2 TESTING

Models must always be tested before any reliance can be placed on the figures produced. This will often involve the insertion of test data so that the results of calculations can be reviewed. As well as 'ordinary' test data some of the following items should also be included:

Negative values
Unexpectedly large values
Unexpectedly small values
Alphabetic characters
Zeros

A further quick test that can often highlight simple errors is to put a 1 in every data entry field.

3 DOCUMENTATION STANDARDS

There are two basic categories of model likely to be developed for audit purposes. They are those:

Category I	Prepared by an individual solely for his own use on a one-off basis (i.e. not even saved after being printed out)
Category II	Developed for use on a particular audit which may need to be updated or which may need to be used by staff other than the originator of the program. (This includes models which will be kept for use later in the audit, on the following years' audits, or on other audits).

Where output from a Category I model is to be included in an audit file it should be capable of standing alone. Simply put, it should be sufficiently complete that it is irrelevant to the reviewer whether the schedule has been produced using pen and calculator or by a computer. There is no need therefore for the model itself to be documented.

The documentation of Category II models should meet the minimum standards set for working papers generally. In particular:

- a printout or copy of the details specified in 1 above should be included on the audit file.

- where necessary the preparer of the model should also make notes giving
  — assumptions built into the program
  — limitations to its use
  — an explanation of complicated program areas.

4 REVIEW PROCEDURES

The review of the results of a model should form part of the normal audit review process. The reviewer's objective is to satisfy himself:

- that the answer produced by the model is reliable for the purpose

- that the model has been properly documented.

The level of review will depend upon:

The purpose of the model   — for example, limited review would be needed of a model which calculates a company's depreciation charge if that charge confirms a client's independently calculated charge. However, if the model's answer were to be incorporated directly into a client's accounts then a more detailed review of the model would be necessary.

The complexity of the model — the more complex the model the greater the possibility of an error in the underlying logic and thus the more detailed the review that is needed.

Often it will be clear from the review of the model's printout that the answer produced by the model is correct or reasonable in the circumstances and it will therefore not be necessary to load the model itself.

However, at times, review of the printout alone may not be sufficient to obtain a proper understanding of the underlying logic and assumptions of the model. In such cases it will be necessary to review the model itself, either on screen or, where available, by the use of review software.

The reviewer must be satisfied that he himself has adequate experience to carry out the review. If not, he should delegate the task to someone who has, making it clear to what extent audit reliance is being placed on the model.

5 RETENTION OF COMPUTER MODELS

Unless it is intended that a model will be used again, it will not normally be necessary to keep it once its results have been printed out and the review performed.

In exceptional cases, where a high degree of audit reliance has been placed on the results of a model in drawing conclusions on an item material to the accounts, the auditor should ensure that the underlying logic and formulae of the model have been fully documented on the audit file even though it will not be used again.

CHAPTER 20   COMPLETION REVIEWS

20.1   REVIEW OF POST BALANCE SHEET EVENTS

An audit report is usually issued in connection with historical financial statements giving a company's financial position at a stated date and its results for the period ending on that date. However, events or transactions sometimes occur subsequent to the balance sheet date, but prior to the issuance of the financial statements and the audit report, that have a material effect on the financial statements and therefore require adjustment or disclosure in the statements. These occurrences are referred to as 'post balance sheet' events (PBSEs).

SSAP 17 defines PBSEs as 'those events, both favourable and unfavourable, which occur between the balance sheet date and the date on which the financial statements are approved by the board of directors.'

Prior to issuing his report, an auditor should perform a review of events that have occurred in the period from the balance sheet date to the date of the audit report. His responsibility to the members of the company extends to the date on which he signs the audit report (although he normally plans the work so as to be able to sign the report immediately after the approval of the accounts by the directors). The audit would therefore not be complete without a PBSE review. Furthermore, the auditor retains some responsibility after he signs the report, as described below.

The objective of the PBSE review is to identify events that need to be reflected in the financial statements either as adjustments or disclosures.

20.2   TYPES OF POST BALANCE SHEET EVENTS

20.2.1   *Definitions*

PBSEs are of two types; 'adjusting events' and 'non-adjusting events':

- **adjusting events** are those that provide additional evidence of conditions existing at the balance sheet date and affecting amounts in the financial statements. They include events which, because of statutory requirements or customary accounting practice, are reflected in financial statements (eg proposed dividends and amounts appropriated to reserves).

- **non-adjusting events** are those that pertain to conditions that did not exist at the balance sheet date and therefore do not require adjustment to amounts stated in the financial statements. They pertain to conditions that arose subsequently and require disclosure in the financial statements in order for them not to be misleading.

20.2.2   *Examples*

The differences between adjusting and non-adjusting events are illustrated by the examples that follow. These examples are not, however, intended to be an exhaustive list.

Adjusting Events

- the subsequent determination of the purchase price or proceeds of sale of assets purchased or sold before the balance sheet date

- a valuation which provides evidence of a permanent diminution in value

- the receipt of a copy of the financial statements or other information which provides evidence of a permanent impairment in the carrying value of a long-term investment

- the receipt of proceeds of sales after the balance sheet date or other evidence concerning the net realisable value of stock

- the receipt of evidence that the previous estimate of accrued profit on a long-term contract was materially inaccurate.

- the renegotiation of amounts owing by debtors, the insolvency of a debtor or the receipt of cash or other information indicating that the recoverable amount is not fairly stated, if caused by conditions that occurred before the balance sheet date

- the declaration of dividends by subsidiaries and associated companies relating to periods prior to the balance sheet date of the holding company

- the receipt of information concerning changes in taxation, including rates, if retroactive

- amounts received or receivable in respect of insurance or legal claims which were in the course of negotiation at the balance sheet date

- the discovery of errors or irregularities which show that the financial statements were incorrect

- the resolution of a pending lawsuit where the claim had arisen prior to the balance sheet date

- decisions by the directors on proposed dividends and appropriations to reserves.

Non-Adjusting Events

- mergers and acquisitions

- reconstructions and proposed reconstructions

- issues of shares and long-term debt

- purchases and sales of fixed assets and investments

- losses of fixed assets or stock as a result of a catastrophe such as a fire or flood that occurred after the balance sheet date

- opening new trading activities or extending existing trading activities

- closing a significant part of the operating facilities if this was not anticipated at the year end

- changes in foreign exchange rates

- government action, such as nationalisation

- strikes and other labour disputes

- settlement of litigation when the event giving rise to the claim took place subsequent to the balance sheet date

- augmentation of pension benefits granted subsequent to the balance sheet date

- losses on accounts receivable resulting from conditions arising subsequent to the balance sheet date.

A material PBSE requires changes in the amounts to be included in the financial statements where:

(i) it is an adjusting event; or

(ii) it indicates that the application of the going concern to the whole or a material part of the company is not appropriate. 'Going concern' is considered further in Chapter 23. Changes made to the amounts in the financial statements because a PBSE is an adjusting event ((i) above) do not normally need to be disclosed separately. The fact that changes have been made in respect of (ii) above would, however, be disclosed.

A material PBSE should be disclosed by way of a note to the financial statements where:

- it is a non-adjusting event of such materiality that its non-disclosure would affect the ability of the users of financial statements to reach a proper understanding of the financial position; or

- it is the reversal or maturity after the year end of a transaction entered into before the year end, the substance of which was primarily to alter the appearance of the company's balance sheet. Such alterations, commonly known as 'window dressing', are considered further below.

In exceptional circumstances, to accord with the prudence concept, an adverse PBSE which would normally be classified as non-adjusting may need to be reclassified as adjusting. In such circumstances, full disclosure of the adjustment would be required.

The Directors' Report must also contain particulars of any important events affecting the company or its subsidiaries which have occurred since the end of the year and the auditor is required by law to satisfy himself that this information is consistent with the financial statements.

Occasionally, a subsequent event that requires disclosure in the financial statements occurs and has such a material impact that an auditor needs to consider including an explanatory paragraph in his report to direct users' attention to the event.

20.2.3 *Window dressing*

SSAP 17, paragraph 23, states that a material PBSE should be disclosed where 'it is the reversal or maturity after the year end of a transaction entered into before the year end, the substance of which was primarily to alter the appearance of the company's balance sheet'. Paragraph 10 of the standard states that such alterations include those commonly known as 'window dressing'.

The Technical Release issued by the Accounting Standards Committee to coincide with the publication of the standard concedes that 'window dressing' is not a precise term and goes on to say: 'Some people believe that it encompasses both (a) fraudulent falsification of accounts to make things look better than they really are, and (b) lawful arrangements of affairs over the year end to make things look different from the way they usually are. Fraudulent falsification of accounts is clearly unacceptable and unlawful and it is not a subject for an accounting standard. The term 'window-dressing' as used in the standard is confined to the meaning in (b) above'.

The term 'window dressing' as used in the standard is, however, further restricted in that the definition quoted above does not encompass certain devices found in industrial and commercial companies which are also commonly referred to as 'window dressing'. Examples are a deliberate or accidental delay in the payment of creditors over the year end or an abnormally high level of stock. In neither case is there 'a transaction entered into before the year end, the substance of which was primarily to alter the appearance of the company's balance sheet'.

'Window dressing' in the context of SSAP 17 is therefore confined to matters such as the transfer of funds into a company on the last day of an accounting reference period which are repaid on the first day of the new period. Accordingly it will tend to be restricted to enterprises involved in finance or banking businesses. SSAP 17 does not increase or decrease an auditor's responsibility to identify and consider other forms of window dressing since these will continue to be his concern in the overall context of the true and fair view.

Because of the varied and imprecise nature of window-dressing there are considerable difficulties in framing audit steps to determine whether or not it has taken place.

It is nevertheless a matter to which auditors should be alert in their review of PBSEs.

20.2.4 *Infringement of borrowing powers*

Since borrowing limits are frequently determined by reference to figures contained in a company's latest published accounts, the act of signing the accounts which reveal a deficiency of shareholders' funds may itself cause the borrowing limits to be exceeded. Infringement of borrowing provisions may of course occur even though shareholders' funds are not extinguished.

In all cases where a company's borrowing powers are restricted and the limits will be exceeded as indicated above, an auditor should write to the board drawing their attention to the matter. If the potential infringement is not rectified by subsequent events before the financial statements are signed, for example by the introduction of further share capital or by a temporary dispensation given by trustees of a loan stock, it will be necessary to refer to the matter in the financial statements and perhaps also in the audit report, since in this situation the continued adoption of the going concern basis might be inappropriate.

20.3 AUDIT PROCEDURES

20.3.1 *General*

The audit procedures in a PBSE review should be extended to the date of the audit report.

In addition to the procedures applied to transactions occurring after the balance sheet date to obtain assurance that proper cut-offs have been made and that assets and liabilities in the balance sheet are complete, the auditor needs to perform certain procedures to identify and evaluate events occurring subsequent to the balance sheet date.

The following procedures should be considered:

- read any available minutes of meetings of shareholders, directors and appropriate operating committees. Enquire about meetings for which minutes have not yet been prepared and obtain details about such meetings

- enquire of client's lawyers concerning new or existing litigation, claims and assessments

- read the latest available management accounts or interim financial statements; compare them with the financial statements being audited and make other comparisons considered necessary, including variance analyses. Also inquire of officers and other executives having responsibility for financial and accounting matters as to whether the interim financial statements have been prepared on the same basis as that used for the financial statements being audited

- review the procedures that the company has established to identify material PBSEs

● make specific inquiries of management (see below).

The auditor may ask management for example:

● whether there have been any significant developments relative to
   — items that were accounted for on the basis of tentative, preliminary or inconclusive data
   — risk areas
   — contingencies

● whether any substantial contingent liabilities or commitments have been made, for example by way of new borrowings or guarantees from the balance sheet date to the date of inquiry

● whether the sale of assets or operating units has occurred or is planned

● whether there have been any significant changes in capital stock, long-term debt, or working capital

● whether assets of the entity have been appropriated by government or destroyed, for example by fire or flood

● whether any unusual accounting adjustments have been made or are contemplated from the balance sheet date to the date of inquiry

● whether management is aware of any events that have occurred or are likely to occur that would call into question the appropriateness of accounting policies used in the financial statements. For example, events that might question the ability of the entity to continue as a going concern.

In engagements involving branches, subsidiaries or investee entities, the auditor should carefully determine the locations at which the above procedures should be carried out. If certain entities are audited by other auditors, the auditor should consider obtaining the results of the other auditors' procedures (eg by discussions with the other auditors, written confirmation or review of their working papers).

20.3.2 *Timing of procedures*

The auditor should perform the PBSE review towards the end of the field work, through the date of the audit report. Where appropriate, performance of his procedures should be coordinated with the PBSE efforts to obtain a letter of representation from management with respect to matters relating to the financial statements, as discussed below.

The timing of an auditor's review may have to be modified in situations involving delays between the end of the fieldwork and the issuance of the report. In such cases he should either:

● carry out the review at the end of his fieldwork and update it, or

● postpone the review to approximate the date of signing the audit report.

Either method clearly increases the cost of the audit and this underlines the need to ensure that the financial statements are finalised and approved by the directors as soon as possible after the completion of the field work.

20.3.3 *Management representations*

The letter of representation obtained from management should refer to all significant PBSEs and should include confirmation that there are no other such events which would require adjustment or disclosure in the financial statements. The letter should be dated with the same date as the date of the audit report.

20.3.4 Consolidated groups

Where the PBSE review is performed in connection with the audit of consolidated financial statements, the auditor should perform additional procedures to identify significant PBSEs that have occurred at the subsidiary company level between the date the separate financial statements are approved and the date on which the consolidated financial statements are approved.

Examples of additional procedures to be performed include:

- specifying the dates in the consolidated audit plan to which secondary auditors must complete their PBSE review

- discussions with parent company management

- obtaining formal representations from the management of subsidiary companies, if considered necessary.

20.4 SUBSEQUENT DISCOVERY OF ERRORS IN ISSUED REPORTS

An auditor does not have a duty to search actively for events arising subsequent to the signing of the audit report. However, a problem may arise if at any time before the annual general meeting the auditor receives information which materially affects his view of the financial statements and which, if he had possessed it at the time of the report, may have led to a different opinion. Various courses of action are suggested in the Auditing Guideline 3.402 'Events after the balance sheet date'.

If the directors intend to amend previously approved financial statements after the audit report has been signed but before the financial statements have been circulated, the auditor should ensure that the amendments do not affect the report (apart from the date). He should also extend the PBSE audit procedures described above through the new date of the report.

After the annual general meeting at which the financial statements are laid before the members, an auditor has no duty to consider the effect of subsequent events on the financial statements laid before that meeting. However, if he becomes aware of any information which suggests that those financial statements may have been inaccurate, he will need to consider what steps to take.

In normal circumstances the auditor will seek to persuade management to make appropriate disclosures. The methods used and the disclosures made will depend on the circumstances, as follows:

- revised financial statements could be issued if this can be done promptly. The reasons for the revision should be described in a note to the financial statements and referred to in the revised audit report

- if the financial statements for a subsequent period are about to be issued, appropriate disclosure of the revision could be made in such statements instead of reissuing the earlier statements

- if the effect of the subsequent information cannot be determined without a prolonged investigation and it appears that a revision of the financial statements will be likely, the appropriate disclosure by management could consist of a statement that
  - the original financial statements and audit report should not be relied upon, and
  - revised financial statements and audit report will be issued upon completion of an investigation.

If an auditor does not consider that the directors are dealing correctly with the situation, he should consider taking legal advice on his position.

20.5   OVERALL REVIEW OF FINANCIAL STATEMENTS

20.5.1   *Objectives of the overall review*

An overall review of the financial statements should be carried out at the end of the audit.

Paragraph 6 of the Auditing Standard 'The auditor's operational standard' states: 'The auditor should carry out such a review of the financial statements as is sufficient, in conjunction with the conclusions drawn from the other audit evidence obtained, to give him a reasonable basis for his opinion on the financial statements.'

The review helps in assessing the audit conclusions reached and in evaluating the overall presentation of the financial statements. The overall review includes reading the directors' report, the financial statements and notes and considering unusual or unexpected balances or relationships not previously identified.

The overall review focuses on

- compliance with generally accepted accounting principles
- adequacy of disclosure
- compatibility with the auditor's knowledge of the client's business.

20.5.2   *Compliance with generally accepted accounting principles*

An overall review of the financial statements should be carried out to ensure that the accounting policies adopted are:

- appropriate to the client's business
- consistently applied from year to year
- generally accepted.

20.5.3   *Adequacy of disclosures*

The auditor's overall review of the directors' report and financial statements should ensure that they are compatible with each other and adequately disclose all material information that is needed for the financial statements to be presented fairly. This review should also look to identify any omissions of disclosures required by statute (eg the Companies Acts), regulatory bodies (eg The International Stock Exchange) and SSAPs or SORPs.

A financial statement disclosure checklist is often helpful when reviewing for compliance with generally accepted accounting principles and adequacy of disclosure.

The review should be carried out on the final draft or proof in the form that it is intended to be printed as it is presentation as well as content that is being reviewed. The use of bold or italic type, spacing and insetting can affect the emphasis placed on, and significance of, the information being conveyed.

The review should include a comparison with the previous year's financial statements and careful consideration should be given to the need for any changes in or additions to notes to the accounts.

The overall review also should ensure that financial statements are internally consistent. Questions such as the following should be answered:

- are all dates in the financial statements correct?
- is the nature of each financial statement caption clearly indicated by its title?

- do the financial statements maintain a uniform manner of format, headings and appearance?

- do all amounts appearing in more than one place cross-check to each other?

20.5.4 *Compatibility with knowledge of the business*

The variations and comparability of account balances and key ratios should be considered for reasonableness in light of:

- the company's environment

- its industry

- its business operations

- its other activities

- other evidence obtained in the course of the audit.

Key ratios are listed in greater detail in Appendix 20.1 below.

The appraisal should normally be carried out when the figures in the financial statements have been finalised and the audit work in the main areas has been completed. However, on smaller clients, the work will often be integrated with analytical review work on profit and loss account items.

If an auditor identifies unusual fluctuations and items or relationships that are unexpected or inconsistent, he should investigate them by:

- inquiring of management and evaluating the adequacy of management's responses to such inquiries including obtaining corroborating evidence as necessary

- performing other procedures or obtaining additional evidence as considered necessary to reach a satisfactory conclusion.

Skill and imagination are needed to recognize the matters to be examined in carrying out the overall review. The objective of analytical procedures used in the overall review of financial statements is to help assess the conclusions reached and evaluate the overall financial statement presentation. The review would, for example, include a comparison of material items in the financial statements with previous years and, where applicable, with budgets or forecasts. Such comparisons should already have been made and documented in the relevant sections of the audit working paper files.

KEY RATIOS

Key ratios include general financial ratios that help to confirm an auditor's understanding of the client's business and to view the business from the perspective of a user of the financial statements. Using these financial ratios as part of the analytical review of the financial statements should help to identify possible problem areas in which there may be a need to extend substantive tests.

This Appendix outlines the more common financial ratios that are used in the overall review of financial statements.

Short-term liquidity and debt-paying ability

- **current assets: current liabilities**   (current ratio)
  This ratio is widely used as a measure of liquidity and the financial margin of safety. A current ratio greater than 1.0 (ie net working capital is positive) is indicative of the client having sufficient available assets to pay its immediate obligations

- **cash & marketable securities & net receivables: current liabilities**   (quick ratio)
  A satisfactory current ratio might not disclose that a portion of current assets could be tied up in old or in unsaleable items or in stock that has a lengthy conversion period. The quick ratio eliminates stock and prepayments to provide a better indication of short-term liquidity. In calculating the quick ratio, marketable securities should preferably be included at market value

- **360 × average trade debtors: net credit sales**   (average days to collect)
  The average days to collect ratio indicates the length of time needed to convert trade debtors to cash. Fluctuations in the above ratio may indicate changing business conditions (eg changed terms of sales, change in mix of customers, change in sales volume), potential business problems (eg slow collections either because of poor collecting practices or poor credit policies, credit policies that are too restrictive, deteriorating debts), or even possible errors or irregularities (eg unrecorded sales, improper sales cut-off, lapping, misappropriation of receipts and the manipulation of trade debtor balances)

- **cost of goods sold: average stock**   (stock turnover ratio)
  The stock turnover ratio provides an indication of the quality of a company's stock. It measures the rate at which stock is sold and replaced during a financial period. Fluctuations in the ratio may indicate changing business conditions (eg change in sales volume or change in mix of products sold) or business problems (eg uneconomic purchasing policy, obsolete and unsaleable goods, failure to match stock requirements to the business cycle)

Long-range solvency and capital structure

- **total liabilities: shareholders funds**   (debt to equity)

- **long-term debt: shareholders funds**   (long-term debt to equity)
  A client's long-term solvency depends on the success of its operations and on its ability to raise capital. These two ratios provide some idea of a client's ability to withstand losses without impairing the interest of creditors. The lower these ratios the more 'buffer' there is available to creditors if the company incurs losses. These ratios have a very definite effect on the company's ability to obtain additional financing. If a client is highly leveraged or geared (a high debt to equity ratio), its ability to obtain additional funds for debt financing may be limited. The higher these ratios, the more sensitive a client will be to adverse revenue fluctuations

because of the impact of high fixed interest charges. Prolonged periods in which losses are sustained could lead to default on maturing principal or interest payments.

Performance ratios

A number of operating and performance ratios are used by investors, creditors, and financial analysts. The most widely used of these ratios is *earnings per share,* which is an integral part of the basic financial statements for most public companies. The following ratios may give further insights into operations:

- **net sales: tangible operating assets**
  This ratio (sometimes called the efficiency ratio) indicates the relative volume of business generated from the company's asset base. For this purpose, operating assets are generally determined by removing intangibles and long-term investments from total assets. A low efficiency ratio indicates that additional sales volume should be sought before more assets are obtained. A high ratio may indicate a very efficient use of capital. Alternatively, it may indicate that assets are reaching the end of their useful lives and an investment in additional assets will soon be necessary.

- **operating income: net sales**
  The primary purpose of this ratio (sometimes called the profit margin ratio) is to show the effect on profit of changes in prices or volume. A low ratio is generally an indication that either gross margins are too low or volume is too low with respect to fixed costs.

- **operating income: tangible operating assets**
  This ratio (somethimes called the profitability ratio) indicates the rate of return obtained on operating assets. Note that the profitability ratio equals the efficiency ratio times the profit margin ratio.

- **net income: net assets**
  An important perspective on a company's earnings is provided by the kind of return provided to its owners. This is reflected by the return on investment ratio. If this ratio is below prevailing long-term interest rates or returns on alternative investments, owners will perceive that the company's assets should be converted to some other use, or perhaps liquidated, unless return can be improved.

Income and expense ratios

Analytical review of the relationships between items in the profit and loss account should encompass those items expected to conform to a predictable pattern based on previous years' experience. This review is not, however, intended to be a detailed analysis and should be limited to those relationships capable of being identified as likely to be employed by a user of the financial statements. In other words, an auditor should not at this stage consider ratios involving greater analysis than that available from the financial statements. Examples of income and expense ratios, and possible causes of changes in those ratios, include the following:

- **gross profit: sales**
  changes in the mix of products sold, in unit costs without corresponding changes in sales price, in sales prices without a corresponding change in unit costs, improper sales cut-off and improper stock or purchase cut-offs

- **provisions for bad debts: sales or trade debtors**
  inadequate provision for doubtful debts and changes in the method of determining the provision

- **interest expense: total average indebtedness subject to interest**
  over- or under-accrual of interest, a general change in interest rates and a change in the credit standing of the client

- **maintenance and repairs or depreciation: fixed assets**
  changes in maintenance and repairs or depreciation policies, obsolete or inefficient use of fixed resources and over- or under-accruals of expenses.

CHAPTER 21   AUDIT CLEARANCE PROCEDURES

21.1   OBJECTIVES

Clearance procedures are performed to satisfy the auditor that:

- the audit is complete
- the financial statements and the audit report are in accordance with professional standards, statutory and regulatory requirements and the audit firm's own policies.

Specifically, the clearance objectives in respect of completeness of audit procedures are that:

- the auditor has completed all necessary audit procedures and obtained all necessary documentation
- the evidence he has obtained is sufficient, relevant and reliable
- the accounting and auditing conclusions that have been drawn from the evidence he has obtained are appropriate
- all material and sensitive issues have been brought to the attention of the audit partner and have been satisfactorily resolved
- there are no material open items that remain to be dealt with.

To this effect, the auditor needs to make sure that the working papers have been received in appropriate detail.

In addition, he needs to be satisfied that certain key procedures have been performed, in particular, that:

- a review of post balance sheet events has been carried out (See Chapter 20)
- an appropriate client representation letter has been obtained (see below).

The auditor also needs to be satisfied that the financial statements and the audit report are presented in accordance with professional standards, statutory and regulatory requirements and that:

- reasonable explanations have been obtained for any unexpected amounts or relationships in the financial statements
- such explanations have been corroborated to the extent necessary and are documented appropriately in the working papers
- the information in the financial statements (including the notes) and any accompanying unaudited information is internally consistent and compatible with the auditor's knowledge of the client's business.

To achieve the above objectives, the auditor will normally adopt some form of sign-off documentation or completion checklist together with a strictly regimented sequence of clearance procedures before signing his audit report.

This chapter describes one such set of clearance procedures. They take the following sequence:

(i) Preparation of Points for Partner Attention and Points Forward.
(ii) Review and sign-off by audit manager.
(iii) Review and sign-off by audit partner.

21.2 POINTS FOR PARTNER ATTENTION

The Points for Partner Attention (PPA) form illustrated below is used to document:

- significant items arising from the overall review of the financial statements

- significant audit, accounting or reporting issues that arose during the course of the audit that require the attention and decision of the partner

- the decisions of the engagement partner on those issues.

Points for Partner Attention		Year end	Schedule No.
CLIENT:		Prepared by	Date:
Points		Ref.	Disposal Notes

The PPA form should not be used for general audit queries or outstanding points of a routine nature; such outstanding points should be recorded within the relevant section of the audit file, if still outstanding at the time when initial conclusions on the work in that section are drawn. If the matters require the partner's decision they should be copied onto the PPA forms or if of significance only for the following year, they should be noted as 'Points forward'.

The PPA form is divided vertically into two sides. The left side is used by the manager and senior for noting the matters requiring the attention of the partner. The right side, for use by the engagement partner, documents the decisions on those issues.

It should be emphasised that any contentious point of principle, particularly one that might give rise to a qualification of the audit report, should be referred to the engagement partner at an early stage and not left until the end of the audit.

The points raised should be clearly made and concisely presented. One of the key benefits of using the PPA form as part of the clearance procedures is that it helps partners, in their review of the working papers, to focus their attention on areas of audit significance. In other words, partners reviewing audit working papers will often look first at the draft financial statements and the PPA form so that they can identify:

- the significant financial statement items
- the key audit, accounting and reporting issues

and thereby know where to direct their attention. It often helps if the manager or staff auditor completes the PPA form as if answering the following hypothetical request from the partner 'Briefly and clearly tell me what you believe are the main issues, and where you believe I should be concentrating my review'.

The points drafted for the partner's attention may (but need not necessarily) express an opinion on the the issue. For example, one point might be put in two different ways:

Case I   'Debtors include a long-outstanding balance due from XYZ Ltd. of £53,000. Our understanding of the reason for the delay in payment, based on correspondence we have seen with their customer, is that XYZ Ltd. is currently experiencing cash flow difficulties. The MD does not accept that any provision is necessary as he is adamant that the debt is ultimately recoverable. We are unable to obtain any corroborating evidence to support this'

Case II 'In my opinion, the bad debt provision is underprovided by £53,000, being an amount receivable from XYZ Ltd, a company with liquidity problems. Although the MD does not accept that any provision is necessary and he is adamant that the debt is good, we are unable to obtain any corroborating evidence to support this and all information points to a failure of the debt. The financial statements should be adjusted to reflect this'

Each point should be cross-referenced to the relevant working papers.

The partner should clear each point with a statement as to the resolution of the issue.

Thus, in the example above, the partner may clear the point with a decision such as:

- 'Having discussed the question of this debt with the MD and reviewed the current position of XYZ Ltd. with him, in my judgement there are reasonable grounds to justify the recoverability of the monies due. The item is addressed in the client representation letter'
- 'An adjustment to the bad debt provision of £53,000 has been agreed with the client after discussions with the MD'.

It is not sufficient to clear a point with a request for action.

For example, the following responses by the partner to the example above would not be sufficient clearance:

- 'In my opinion, having discussed this with him, we can accept the MD's view. Please make sure this is included in the representation letter'
- 'We should persuade the client to provide for this'.

Such requests for action are appropriate as partner review points but do not make it clear that the issue has been finally resolved.

If a decision recorded on a PPA form is likely to be of continuing relevance in future audits, a copy should be placed in the auditor's permanent notes file.

21.3 POINTS FORWARD

Points will arise during an audit which need to be considered in the following year's audit. An adequate record of these points should be retained in the current audit file and carried forward to the following year. A review of these points should be undertaken at the commencement of the following year's audit and the action taken to deal with them should be noted.

The auditor should document as Points Forward:

- areas which have caused problems this year, or where problems are envisaged in the following year

- impending changes that will affect audit procedures

- ideas for changing the emphasis or direction or otherwise improving the efficiency of the audit.

This procedure should not be used to defer the consideration of points which ought properly to be dealt with in the current year.

Both the partner and manager should initial a Sign-Off Checklist (see below) to confirm that all Points Forward noted in both the previous year's audit and the current year have been adequately addressed at the current year's audit.

A debriefing meeting involving each member of the audit team held at the end of the audit is a useful way of ensuring that all ideas for improving future audits are collected and noted as Points Forward.

21.4 SIGN-OFF CHECKLIST

The Sign-Off Checklist ('SOC') reproduced in Appendix 21.1 in essence restates the completion objectives outlined in paragraph 21.1 above.

Once satisfied that all significant partner and manager review points have been cleared, and no significant open items remain, the audit manager should sign-off on the SOC and submit it to the engagement partner for signature.

Similarly, when everything has been completed to the partner's satisfaction, the partner too will sign-off on the SOC.

The audit report is only signed after the SOC form is completed.

21.5 LETTERS OF REPRESENTATION

21.5.1 *Requirement for written confirmation*

The auditor should obtain written confirmation of representations made by management during the course of the audit which relate to matters material to the financial statements for which he has been unable to obtain sufficient independent corroborative evidence. Such confirmation may take the form either of individual board minutes or of a letter from the company's Chairman (on behalf of Directors) and Chief Accountant (a 'letter of representation').

Representations by management constitute evidence as to the validity of management assertions in the financial statements, and the purpose of obtaining written confirmation is to document this evidence. Where the auditor has obtained sufficient independent corroborative evidence of particular representations, there is no need for reference to be made to such items in the letter or board minutes.

21.5.2 *Contents of the letter*

The matters to be included in a letter of representation should flow from the audit

223

working papers. They should be specific, not generalisations upon which assurance cannot reasonably be expected. Because the matters included will vary significantly between clients and from year to year, no standard format of board minutes or letter can be suggested. An example of a letter of representation, reproduced from the appendix to the Auditing Guideline 'Representations by Management', is set out in Appendix 21.2.

Where the auditor prepares the financial statements for the company (as opposed to merely auditing them), it may be desirable for the directors to acknowledge their responsibility for the financial statements when confirming their representations in writing. An example of such an acknowledgement is contained in Appendix 21.2.

Where the representations are not recorded by way of individual board minutes, it is good practice to request that the letter be considered at a Board meeting and its approval formally minuted. In this way the letter brings contentious matters and items of subjective opinion to the attention of the whole of the Board of Directors. This is particularly important where reliance has been placed on the representations and opinions of one director, possibly the Managing Director, and where there is some doubt that other directors, including non-executive directors, are aware of, or agree with, those representations and opinions.

If possible a representative of the audit firm, normally the engagement partner, should attend the meeting at which the letter is considered and approved, or at which the individual representations are minuted, particularly if the directors are known to have differing views on any matters included. This procedure should equally be applied to private companies which have 'outside interests' represented on the Board but it is clearly less relevant where this is not the case. The approval of the letter itself should be minuted by the Board.

In all cases where written representations are obtained, the auditor should consider:

- whether or not those representations are consistent with other available evidence

- whether circumstances are such that he might need to refer to reliance on those representations in his audit report.

The letter should be typed on the client's headed notepaper and addressed to the auditor. It normally carries the same date as the directors' signatures on the balance sheet (because both are usually approved at the same board meeting) and is thus usually signed immediately before the audit report is signed. If there is, however, a significant delay between the date of the letter of representation and the date of the audit report the auditor should consider requesting further representations in respect of any post balance sheet events in the intervening period. The letter of representation should not be signed later than the date of the audit report since it is part of the evidence on which the opinion expressed in the report is based.

21.5.3 Groups

The group auditor should ensure that he has any necessary written representations from the management of subsidiaries made at a date as close as possible to the date on which the group accounts are signed. If the management of the holding company is also the management of the subsidiary companies, a single letter of representation covering the group of companies will sometimes suffice.

21.6 ENGAGEMENT ADMINISTRATION

The procedures outlined above are concerned with matters that should be resolved before the audit opinion is issued. There are also a number of completion procedures which relate to objectives of engagement administration and client service. These matters cover:

- the sending of management letters to client
- ensuring that permanent files are brought up to date
- time and cost summaries.

The sending of management letters to clients is the subject of Chapter 22.

21.6.1   Permanent files

Making sure the data in the auditor's permanent files is up-to-date contributes to audit efficiency. This is particularly the case with respect to the documentation of the auditor's understanding of the internal control structure.

The permanent files should be reviewed at the completion of the audit, while the client's affairs are still fresh in mind, to make sure that they have been brought up-to-date in all material aspects.

21.6.2   Time and cost summaries

The use of budgets and time summaries is an integral part of the administration of an audit.

A time budget provides a means of effectively estimating the audit fee, determining staff scheduling requirements, monitoring the time expended in each audit area, encouraging efficient use of time, and planning the subsequent year's audit. However, the primary function of a budget is to monitor and control the time of the staff during the performance of the audit.

Time summaries are useful as an element of control by periodically comparing the actual time spent by audit area (reflected in the time summary) to the expected time (reflected in the time budget).

Staff members should be made responsible for reporting likely budget overruns on a timely basis and for completing and summarising their own audit time records. As the engagement progresses, revisions to the approved budget may become necessary because of unanticipated events. If the field staff become aware of a need for budget revisions, they should alert the engagement manager or partner so that appropriate action may be taken (eg reevaluation of the fee estimates, adjustment of the audit strategy or staffing).

Variances from budget should be investigated as they occur and explanations should be documented in the audit workpapers at the completion of the audit. These may indicate:

- the budget was unrealistic (this should be considered in planning the following audit and should be included as Points Forward)
- the audit approach changed resulting in additional or reduced audit effort (the factors necessitating a change in the audit approach should be considered and may be a factor in adjusting billings to the client)
- problems in terms of the efficiency of the audit staff (this should be considered in preparing staff evaluations for each audit)
- increased audit time by the engagement team due to client's inefficiencies (this should be discussed with management, and consideration should be given to additional billings).

At the completion of the audit, the audit time records should be totalled, compared with budgets (as noted above) and summarised as a basis for producing the fee and to facilitate the preparation of the following year's budget. To perform the comparison with budget, the summary will need to analysed on the same basis as the budget.

21.7 PRELIMINARY ANNOUNCEMENTS

21.7.1 *Introduction*

Listed, USM and 3rd Market companies are required to make a preliminary announcement of the results for the year as soon as possible after draft accounts, even though subject to final audit, have been agreed with the auditors as the basis for completing the annual report. The paragraphs below:

- provide guidance on the work to be completed before an auditor agrees that a preliminary announcement can be made

- explain a suggested additional formal sign-off procedure where the preliminary announcement is dated earlier than the audit report.

21.7.2 *Client categories*

Quoted clients fall into two categories:

- those whose Boards formally approve the financial statements at the same time as they make a preliminary announcement

- those whose Boards formally approve the financial statements at a later meeting.

Auditors normally sign their audit report immediately after (and on the same day as) the financial statements are formally approved by the Board.

For those clients that fall into the first category, the auditor should plan his work so as to be able finally to sign off the SOC form before the preliminary announcement is made. Thus, for example, the letter of representation should be approved by the Board at the same meeting at which the preliminary announcement is agreed, all points for partner attention should have been cleared and the post balance sheet events review completed and, even though the financial statements themselves may be in the form of a printer's proof, all material points of presentation and disclosure should have been discussed and agreed with the client.

In other words, for those clients that fall into the first category, the normal audit completion procedures apply since the date of the preliminary announcement is normally also the date of the audit report. As a matter of good practice the auditor should review the narrative and amounts in the draft preliminary announcement for consistency with the financial statements.

For those clients that fall into the second category, ie where the financial statements are formally approved at a later date, it is good practice to plan the work so as to ensure that the audit work is complete by the date of the preliminary announcement, subject only to points of presentation and disclosure that do not affect the preliminary announcement. In particular, before agreeing to a preliminary announcement:

- the auditor should have completed the overall review of the results/financial ratios/ fluctuations in balance sheet figures

- he should have cleared all points for partner attention other than points of presentation and disclosure

- the Board should be aware of the points on which he will require written representation

- his post balance sheet events review should be brought up to date

- he should have reviewed the wording of the preliminary announcement and checked the narrative (eg for references to 'unaudited', abridged accounts, extraordinary items or post balance sheet events) as well as the figures

- where other firms of auditors are involved, he should have completed his primary auditor reviews.

Where clients fall into the second category, the audit manager and engagement partner should ensure that the completion of these procedures is evidenced on a 'Preliminary announcement — audit clearance' form, which is reproduced in Appendix 21.3.

21.7.3 *Audit timetable*

The auditor should wherever possible encourage clients to formulate an annual reporting timetable that brings them into the first category rather than the second.

In any event, he should agree an audit timetable with the client, in writing, that includes the preliminary announcement date. A detailed audit timetable is an essential planning ingredient. It should help to minimise the pressures for a premature clearance.

21.8 RELEASE OF ACCOUNTS

21.8.1 *Final clearance of accounts*

The initials of the engagement partner on the SOC form authorise the release of the accounts with a signed audit report. Thus the engagement partner must have received the final printed accounts approved and signed by the client and all other necessary written representations and confirmations before signing off.

The SOC form allows for the fact that the date on which the engagement partner signs off the form is often later than the date of the audit report. This may be because there is some delay in the directors signing the balance sheet after the Board has formally approved the accounts or because the signed accounts are returned by post, or because there is some other administrative reason why the engagement partner is unable actually to sign the audit report on the date which is printed on the audit report. Therefore the form requires that both the date the SOC is completed and the date of the audit report should be given.

The accounts do not have to be complete in their final form at the date of the directors' approval for disclosure purposes. The audit report may be given the same date as the date of the directors' approval, provided the audit work is substantially complete at that date and no fresh evidence is collected after that date.

21.8.2 *No release to third parties before signature*

An auditor must make it clear to clients that full accounts must not be released to third parties until both the balance sheet and the audit report have been signed and dated.

Unfortunately there is no foolproof means of ensuring that financial statements, even if on draft paper, are not passed on to third parties with the implication that they can be relied on. As an added precaution in certain cases the auditor may consider it prudent not to include the page with the audit report in draft versions of the financial statements. So that the client knows his intended wording, he should include the text of his report in separate correspondence.

Appendix   21.1

SIGN-OFF CHECKLIST

	Sch. No.
Client:	Year-end:
Partner:	Manager:

Manager Representations:

COMPLETENESS OF AUDIT PROCEDURES

Tick box on completion of work if no exceptions noted overleaf.

1   I have reviewed the audit working papers. In my opinion, except as noted overleaf:

- we have dealt with all matters raised in the audit planning memorandum

- we have completed all necessary audit procedures and obtained all necessary documentation, information and explanations

- the accounting and auditing conclusions that have been drawn from the evidence we have collected are appropriate

- all working papers have been reviewed and all review points and queries have been cleared by the original reviewer.

2   All significant audit, accounting or reporting issues that require the attention and decision of the partner have been:

- noted on Points for Partner Attention

- satisfactorily resolved.

FINANCIAL STATEMENTS PRESENTATION

I have reviewed the financial statements and our audit report thereon. In my opinion, except as noted overleaf:

- the financial statements and our report thereon are presented in accordance with professional standards, statutory and regulatory requirements (see completed Company Accounts Checklist)

- we have obtained reasonable explanations for any unexpected amounts or relationships in the financial statements

- such explanations have been corroborated to the extent necessary and are documented appropriately in our working papers

- the information in the directors' report, the financial statements (including the notes) and any other accompanying, unaudited information is internally consistent and compatible with our knowledge of the client's business.

The audit has been properly completed, all points arising have been satisfactorily cleared, and all exceptions noted overleaf have been resolved.

...................Manager   ....Date

Engagement partner — *to be completed before signature of the audit report*

I have reviewed the financial statements and such working papers as I consider necessary. I am satisfied that the audit has been properly completed, that all points arising have been satisfactorily cleared, that all exceptions noted overleaf have been resolved and that the financial statements with a signed audit report can now be released.

...................Partner   ....Date   (Date of audit report..............)

SIGN-OFF CHECKLIST (continued)

COMPLETENESS OF AUDIT PROCEDURES

Exceptions:

Resolved as follows:

FINANCIAL STATEMENTS PRESENTATION

Exceptions:

Resolved as follows:

EXAMPLES OF REPRESENTATIONS BY MANAGEMENT

The following is the text of the Appendix to Auditing Guideline 3.404 'Representations by management'.

Set out below is an example of a letter of representation which relates to matters which are material to financial statements prepared by an auditor for the company, and to circumstances where the auditor cannot obtain independent corroborative evidence and could not reasonably expect it to be available (see paragraph 4 of the guideline). It is not intended to be a standard letter because representations by management can be expected to vary not only from one enterprise to another, but also from one year to another in the case of the same audit client.

Dear Sirs

We confirm to the best of our knowledge and belief, and having made appropriate enquiries of other directors and officials of the company, the following representations given to you in connection with your audit of the company's financial statement for the year ended 31st December. . . . .

(1)　We acknowledge as directors our responsibility for the financial statements, which you have prepared for the company. All the accounting records have been made available to you for the purpose of your audit and all the transactions undertaken by the company have been properly reflected and recorded in the accounting records. All other records and related information, including minutes of all management and shareholders' meetings, have been made available to you.

(2)　The legal claim by Mr G H . . . . has been settled out of court by the company paying him £38,000. No further amounts are expected to be paid, and no similar claims by employees or former employees have been received or are expected to be received.

(3)　In connection with deferred tax not provided, the following assumptions reflect the intentions and expectations of the company:

(a)　capital investment of £260,000 is planned over next three years
(b)　there are no plans to sell revalued properties
(c)　we are not aware of any indication that the situation is likely to change so as to necessitate the inclusion of a provision for tax payable in the financial statements.

(4)　The company has had at no time during the year any arrangement, transaction or agreement to provide credit facilities (including loans, quasi-loans or credit transactions) for directors nor to guarantee or provide security for such matters, except as disclosed in note 14 to the financial statements.

(5)　Other than the fire damage and related insurance claims described in note 19 to the financial statements, there have been no events since the balance sheet date which necessitate revision of the figures included in the financial statements or inclusion of a note thereto. Should further material events occur, which may necessitate revision of the figures included in the financial statements or inclusion of a note thereto, we will advise you accordingly.

Yours faithfully

Signed on behalf of the board of directors.

The paragraphs included in the example letter relate to a specific set of circumstances. Set out below are some examples of additional paragraphs which, depending on the circumstances, may be appropriate for inclusion in a letter of representation or in board minutes. It is not expected that the auditor will obtain all these written representations as a matter of routine.

— There have been no breaches of the income tax regulations regarding payments to subcontractors in the construction industry which may directly or indirectly affect the view given by the financial statements.

— Having regard to the terms and conditions of sale imposed by major suppliers of goods, trade creditors include no amounts resulting from the purchase of goods on terms which include reservation of title by suppliers, other than £96,544 due to ABC plc.

— With the exception of the penalties described in note 17, we are not aware of any circumstances which could produce losses on long-term contracts.

— DEF Ltd, an associated company, is about to launch a new product which has received excellent test results. As a result, the amount of £155,000 outstanding since 6th January. . . . . , is expected to be fully recoverable.

— The company has guaranteed the bank overdraft of its subsidiary A Ltd but has not entered into guarantees, warranties or other financial commitments relating to its other subsidiary or associated companies.

— The transaction shown in the profit and loss account as extraordinary is outside the course of the company's normal business and is not expected to recur frequently or regularly.

— Since the balance sheet date, the company has negotiated a continuation of its bank overdraft facilities with a limit of £200,000. There have been no other events which are likely to affect the adequacy of working capital to meet foreseeable requirements in the year following the adoption of the financial statements.

— The indices used in the current cost financial statements for the year ended . . . . are, in our opinion, appropriate to the business of the company and have been properly applied on a consistent basis to assets and liabilities.

PRELIMINARY ANNOUNCEMENTS — AUDIT CLEARANCE

Client:	Year-end:	Schedule No:
Manager:	Senior:	

	Initials	Date
Manager's representations		
All points for partner attention on the continuation pages following that affect the preliminary announcement have been cleared.	. . . .	. . . .
All points on which we will require written representation have been brought to the partner's attention for discussion with the Board.	. . . .	. . . .
I confirm that:		
(a) The results, state of affairs and all other information included in the accounts are compatible with each other and our knowledge of the enterprise and its business.	. . . .	. . . .
(b) The draft accounts have been prepared using acceptable and appropriate accounting policies, consistently applied.	. . . .	. . . .
(c) The preliminary announcement is consistent with the draft accounts.	. . . .	. . . .
(d) All post balance sheet events noted to . . . . (date) have been correctly treated.	. . . .	. . . .
All reviews of secondary auditor/other office work have been completed.	. . . .	. . . .
CONCLUSION		
The audit has, in my opinion, been satisfactorily completed, subject only to points of presentation and disclosure that do not affect the preliminary announcement. We have obtained all the information and explanations which we required. All working papers have been reviewed and all review points and queries have been cleared by the original reviewer.		

Engagement partner — to be completed before clearance is given
I have reviewed the draft preliminary announcement and such working papers as I consider necessary. I am satisfied that the audit has been properly completed and that all points arising have been satisfactorily cleared, subject only to points of presentation and disclosure that do not affect the preliminary announcement. I have informed the Board of all matters on which we will require written representation.
. . . . .Partner   . . . . .Date

CHAPTER 22 MANAGEMENT LETTERS

22.1 INTRODUCTION

An auditor normally sends each client a written report, called a 'management letter', containing his observations on matters which have been noted during the course of the audit. The purpose of such letters is to provide constructive advice and assistance in improving the performance of the client's operations, its internal control structure and accounting practices. The auditor's advice will be based on his experience and knowledge of the client's business.

The main objective of an audit is to form an opinion on the client's financial statements and issue an audit report thereon. However, the management letter is sometimes regarded by client management as the major benefit which they themselves derive from the audit.

In addition to demonstrating a positive and responsive attitude to the client's needs a management letter can also protect the auditor against criticism in future years because it provides evidence of matters which he has drawn to management's attention in the past.

The management letter is not the only means open to the auditor for reporting to his clients. Sometimes comments to management would be better presented in another way. In some circumstances (but particularly where he wishes to make, or has been asked to make, comments on individual members of a client's staff) the auditor should consider the use of one of the following:

- an oral report (which should normally be evidenced in writing on the audit files)
- an informal letter from the engagement partner to an individual member of the client's management
- a special report.

The auditor should try to combine a written letter with an oral presentation to the client whenever possible. The presentation may be a meeting held specifically to go through a management letter or may consist of discussing the points raised as part of the post-audit meeting with the client. An oral presentation is important because it enables the auditor to discuss the merits of his recommendations and practical problems of implementation with the client, thus increasing the chance of the recommendations being taken up.

Management letters should not be confused with specific responsibilities which may be imposed on the auditor (by statute, regulation or agreement) to report to a third party on the adequacy of a client's internal control structure. These are matters for specialised guidance.

22.2 STRUCTURE AND CONTENT

22.2.1 *Importance of good structure and content*

Management letters should communicate to clients in a manner that persuades them to accept the recommendations. The auditor should know his audience and tailor the letter accordingly. The letter will usually be read by someone without an accountancy background and it must be capable of being understood by such a person. Jargon should be avoided.

The management letter will normally be more easily understood by the reader if it is well structured. A well structured management letter usually:

- has an effective introduction

- has a body that contains useful and/or cost-saving observations and suggestions

- draws appropriate conclusions

- relegates insignificant matters to an appendix.

There are many ways of setting out a management letter including:

(i) a memorandum in columnar format listing detailed points, together with a covering letter which could highlight the more significant matters raised; and

(ii) a more narrative style of report using separate paragraphs for the different points made, together with a covering letter which could highlight the more significant matters raised.

These two styles are illustrated in Appendix 22.1.

The letter should be concise if it is to be effective. One method of avoiding a lengthy report is to prepare the letter as an executive summary of the most important observations and to deal with the detail in an attachment to the letter.

The format chosen should be the one best suited to the client. For example, if a client has an internal audit department which makes its own recommendations in a specific format, management should be asked whether it would be helpful for the auditor to use that format.

22.2.2 *Introductory paragraphs*

The introductory paragraphs or, where a separate covering letter is sent, the covering letter should normally state the purpose of the management letter. So that the reader is clear about the scope of the work underlying the letter, it is good practice also to:

- state the purpose of an audit

- state that the matters commented upon in the letter are based on observations during the audit.

22.2.3 *The body of the letter*

The body of the letter should contain observations and recommendations which the auditor believes would be helpful to management. The observations should be accurate, specific and precise; the impact of an entire letter may be destroyed if just one piece of information is shown to be inaccurate, if a recommendation is vague or abstract, or if the letter contains trivial or repetitious detail.

The observations and recommendations which are made in a management letter may cover, among other things, the following:

Corporate and financial management

- business strategy and planning

- potential economies, improvements in efficiency or other constructive advice

- opportunities for improving profitability through better financial management

Internal control structure

- weaknesses in the control environment or in the design of accounting systems and internal controls

- systems breakdowns during the period under review, together with a summary of the nature and amounts of material errors discovered

- deficiencies in the operation of accounting systems and internal controls

Accounting practices

- inappropriate accounting policies and practices

- trends in industry best practice in accounting and disclosure

- the presentation, interpretation and analysis of the financial statements

- non-compliance with legislation, accounting standards or other regulations

The material should be ordered in a logical manner which will be dictated by the addressee of the letter and the organisational structure of the client. For example, where different members of management are responsible for different regions, branches or functions (eg information technology, human resource management, marketing, production) the main body of the letter may have separate sections dealing with each area of responsibility.

For each matter the auditor should normally describe:

- his observation, including the symptoms, nature and cause of the problem (or opportunity) and its effect on the client

- his recommendation, which should be practical and tailored to suit the client's specific circumstances (otherwise the letter will lack credibility)

- the benefits and advantages to the client and the feasibility of adopting the recommendation. (The auditor also needs to acknowledge any relevant disadvantages such as cost but should draw a balanced conclusion on the optimum solution to the client's problem)

- the response of client personnel or management (so that senior management can see what action is being taken).

The auditor should use specific examples identified in the audit to illustrate his comments in the letter whenever possible. In some cases, it may be possible to illustrate a point by reference to a trend or relationship in the accounts.

Nothing in the letter should be inconsistent with the audit opinion. An exaggerated criticism may be irreconcilable with an unqualified audit report. There may be cases where the auditor should explain why no audit qualification is required or point out that a qualification may be introduced if the problem or weakness continues in the future.

Matters which should be dealt with in the audit report must not be dealt with in the management letter instead, even if the client's management and its shareholders are the same individuals. For example under the Companies Acts the auditor has a specific duty to report where proper accounting records have not been kept. A management letter cannot be regarded as a substitute for a qualified audit report in this respect.

The auditor's observations and recommendations should be constructive; rather than focusing on the effect on his audit, he should concentrate on the benefits for the client and the possibilities of practical improvements. The commercial value of the comments should be clear to the reader.

Thus the benefit may be a cost saved, a risk averted or additional income, or it may contribute towards other management objectives eg keeping customers, employees or shareholders satisfied.

The benefit should be quantified if there is a reasonable basis for projection, and the auditor should make appropriate qualifying comments about the assumptions inherent in the projection.

The observations and recommendations should be tactful. Although the priority is to inform management of problems, the auditor should avoid making the letter seem to be a personal criticism of certain employees.

It may be that weaknesses which the auditor brought to the client's attention in previous years' management letters continue to exist. He should always consider whether such matters ought to be repeated in his current letter.

Where advice which the auditor has given in the past has not been acted upon by a client, he should consider why his recommendations were not implemented. The advice could perhaps be made in a more effective way such as by arranging a special meeting with the client, or spelling out the benefits more clearly, or it may be that more practical advice is needed.

As an alternative to repeating each point in full or holding a meeting with the client the auditor could consider:

- referring to points in previous letter(s) without repeating them in full

- listing them in an appendix to the letter

- leaving them out altogether.

The appropriate treatment will depend on the significance of the point, the reasons why the client has not acted upon the previous recommendation, and whether there have been changes in management.

In some circumstances the auditor may wish to include additional statements in the letter regarding the inherent limitations of the internal control structure in general, the specific extent and nature of the auditor's review of the internal control structure during the audit, or other matters regarding the basis for the comments made. This could be particularly relevant where regulatory bodies and other third parties will receive copies of the management letters

22.2.4 *Restriction on distribution*

The letter should include an appropriate restriction on distribution which:

- indicates that the letter is intended solely for the information and the use of the client's board of directors and senior management

- specifically refers to any regulatory or other authorities that will be receiving copies because of regulatory or statutory requirements

Points in respect of restriction on distribution or limitation of scope should be made in a location and manner so as not to overshadow the other contents of the letter.

22.2.5 *Concluding paragraphs*

The conclusion to the letter should include an invitation for the client to discuss the letter with the auditor and his offer of further assistance. Where relevant it should also summarise follow-up action agreed with the client. The auditor's expression of appreciation for the cooperation of the client's personnel during the audit could be included here or in the introductory paragraphs.

22.3 COLLECTION OF MATERIAL FOR INCLUSION

An auditor's management letter comments are usually developed from information that comes to the attention of members of the audit team. All members of the audit team should be made aware of the opportunity the management letter provides to improve the quality of the auditor's own performance as a professional advisor to the client.

At the planning stage of the audit, having gained an understanding of the business, the auditor should consider the likely areas for improvements in client profitability and efficiency. Members of the audit team who will be involved in work in those areas can then be briefed so that they are especially alert for specific examples of unprofitable or inefficient practices or for information that will help the auditor to gauge the scale of the problem and to identify its cause and effects.

During the fieldwork, while carrying out analytical procedures or tests of details, the auditor will encounter points which highlight an opportunity for improved performance by the client. Other sources of management letter points include:

- management letters issued by the auditor to other clients, particularly those with similar business activities. He must however always guard client confidentiality and if particular clients are in direct or indirect competition, such exchanges of advice or information would not be appropriate

- discussion with client management on areas giving rise to concern

- matters of concern noted in minutes of board or other management meetings

- discussion with client staff on areas which cause them concern.

This last item, discussion with client staff, is considered in further detail below.

Although the auditor could discuss these matters with client staff within the setting of a formal meeting, it is envisaged that his discussions will be more successful if they take the form of informal interviews during the planning stage of the audit or as he audits the individual detailed areas.

The client staff to be interviewed should be those who play key roles in the company's various operations or have detailed knowledge of its systems. The interviewer should always be an experienced member of the audit team who will ask questions tactfully and sensitively.

The questions asked should be tailored to suit the client's specific business and the individual interviewee. However the following are suggested as examples of questions which might be asked:

- what are the principal responsibilities of your position?

- what are the main tasks you perform?

- of these,
  - which are the most time consuming?
  - which are the most difficult?
  - which are the least difficult?

- are there detailed written instructions that describe the tasks for which you are responsible?
  - if so, how often do you refer to them?
  - if not, how do you know what to do?

- could any of your tasks be eliminated?
  - do they duplicate other people's work?
  - are they unnecessary?

- are you aware of any tasks which are not yet performed but should be?

- could any of your tasks be altered in any way to make them more efficient?

The key to developing effective management letters is the recognition that each phase and area of the audit is a source for potential comment in the management letter.

In developing comments, it is important to focus on underlying causes of problems rather than simply to report the problems and their results. For example, when numerous errors are encountered in the accounting process, the auditor should attempt to determine if they are caused by matters such as lack of supervision, lack of training, insufficiently qualified personnel, or basic systems problems.

The collection of such information should not be left to the end of the audit visit. The member of the engagement team who identifies a matter should immediately draft a point for inclusion in our management letter.

22.4   INPUT FROM THE CLIENT

Before issuing the management letter, the auditor should:

- discuss each observation or recommendation in draft form with the client personnel who are most likely to have to implement it. Such preliminary discussions help to avoid misunderstandings and impractical suggestions that would undermine the credibility of the letter

- obtain the responses of client personnel at the appropriate level of authority to each observation and recommendation included in the letter. Because it provides a good way of confirming to senior management that their staff agree with the comments and of showing what action is intended, the auditor should consider incorporating these responses in the letter.

Frequently, management may request, for a variety of reasons, to have certain comments removed. Sometimes such objections have merit, but if the auditor continues to believe the comment is valid, the comment should be retained in the letter. (He might consider recording management's views in the letter along with his comments.) Omitting a significant comment on the basis of contemplated corrective action may not be appropriate. Also, where the client has corrected a problem which the auditor discovered, he should still spell out in his letter the matter arising and action taken.

After the letter is finalised, but before it is issued, the auditor may wish to arrange a meeting with senior client personnel (eg the board of directors, the audit committee, senior management) to discuss the more important points in the management letter. Such a meeting:

- increases management's awareness and understanding of the points raised

- improves the probability of management acceptance

- increases management's knowledge of the audit services performed.

The auditor should as a matter of courtesy let the client know the timetable for issuing his management letter or alternatively that no letter will be issued.

22.5   OTHER MATTERS

22.5.1   *Addressee*

The management letter should normally be addressed to the Board of Directors or equivalent body. Alternatively, an auditor may agree with the client to address the letter to the client's audit committee.

It is important to establish to whom it is appropriate to send copies. It is important to follow management's instructions carefully; management letters frequently contain sensitive comments and management will wish to control their distribution accordingly.

An auditor should consider sending an executive summary of the main points raised in his management letter to:

- the main board (where the directors are not the recipients of the main letter)
- the chairman or chief executive.

It is very important that such a letter is well-written, picks out only the points which will be of interest to senior management and extends an invitation to the client to discuss its contents with the auditor. The letter should however contain a reference to his detailed management letter.

22.5.2 Other recipients

There is a growing tendency for regulatory bodies and other third parties (such as banks) to request copies of letters to management. Such letters are confidential communications between the auditor and his client. He should not reveal the contents of the letter to any third party without the client's permission. Similarly he should ask the client not to disclose the contents of his letter to a third party without his written consent.

Where the auditor is auditing a subsidiary company, and provided the client agrees, a copy of the letter should be sent to the parent company. If the parent company's auditors request a copy of the letter, he should first check that the client's permission has been obtained before acceding to their request.

22.5.3 Multiple letters

Multiple letters (for example, an interim management letter and a final 'post-audit' letter) may be appropriate on engagements where a large number of matters of sufficient importance come to an auditor's attention at an interim phase of the audit, or where matters of particular urgency arise during the audit.

For clients with tight reporting timetables at the year-end, it is important to deal with as many areas of advice as possible in an interim management letter.

22.5.4 Timing and follow-up

A delay in sending a letter to management reduces its effectiveness because it implies a lack of urgency, de-emphasises the importance of the matters raised and shows a lack of courtesy. It is important therefore that the letter be sent to the client promptly after the completion of the particular stage of the audit. A letter should be submitted immediately if serious weaknesses are discovered which may have resulted, and may continue to result, in losses to the client.

The previous year's letters should be reviewed with the client at the planning stage of the following year's audit. Any remedial action taken by the client should be noted. Amendments may then need to be made to the audit plan and the audit programme.

Appendix   22.1

EXAMPLES OF MANAGEMENT LETTERS

INTRODUCTION

This Appendix illustrates two ways of setting out a management letter:

>   (i) a memorandum in columnar format listing detailed points, together with a covering letter which highlights the more significant matters raised; and

>   (ii) a narrative style, using separate paragraphs for the different points.

Specimen Management Letter (i)

The Board of Directors   [DATE]
[   ] Limited
[address   ]

Dear Sirs,

[   ] LIMITED
REPORT TO MANAGEMENT FOR THE YEAR ENDED [   ]

Following our recent audit, we bring to your attention certain observations on the company's operations which we believe can help you in improving profits and running the business.

These observations have all been discussed with John Smith, your chief accountant, and his comments are noted in the last column of the attached memorandum. We hope to discuss the report with you at our forthcoming meeting.

In particular, we draw your attention to our comments on:

>   ● credit control — we recommend that you consider taking on a full time credit controller; if properly implemented, this could result in a net saving in costs

>   ● [other major recommendations].

We will discuss these with you at our meeting.

These observations arose during the course of our audit which is designed primarily to enable us to form an opinion on the financial statements taken as a whole. Our report therefore cannot be expected to include all possible comments and recommendations which a more extensive special examination might indicate. We should add that this report has been prepared solely for the directors and senior management. Please do not show it to third parties to whom we cannot be responsible.

We take this opportunity of thanking your staff for the help and courtesy shown to us during our audit.

Yours faithfully,

[   ] LIMITED — ATTACHMENT TO LETTER DATED [   ]

CURRENT PROCEDURE [Extracts from report]	AUDITORS' SUGGESTED IMPROVEMENT	CLIENT COMMENTS

1. CREDIT CONTROL

Debtor days have risen from an average of 43 days during 19XX to 54 days during 19XX. Over the same period your turnover has risen from £ak to £bk and the charge for bad and doubtful debts from £ck to £dk (which, in terms of percentage of turnover, represents a rise of e%). We estimate that the additional interest cost of financing the longer credit period during 19XX was £vk.

There are a number of procedural shortcomings, dealt with below, underlying this problem but we believe the root cause is that you do not have sufficient resources devoted to credit control to cope with the increased volume of business.

A full-time credit controller should be employed. Provided a suitably experienced individual could be identified, and the support and commitment of the sales managers assured, the company would gain net savings within a year. The tasks of the credit controller would include those shown below. Should you wish, we would be happy to assist in drawing up fuller terms of reference.

Agreed by J.S. (chief accountant) and FB (sales director).

(a) Credit given to customers

At present credit is given to new customers without adequate references being taken up or adequate authorisation by a responsible official. In addition credit limits are being exceeded, with credit limits unrealistic in many cases.

References such as credit ratings from Dunn & Bradstreet, trade references, and bank references, should be taken up for all significant new customers. All new accounts should be authorised by the chief accountant. Credit limits should be reviewed regularly (at least every three months) by the credit controller in consultation with the sales managers, and all alterations authorised by the chief accountant.

Sales managers should check that credit limits will not be exceeded before authorising sales orders.

Agreed, a review of existing credit limits will be one of the first tasks by the new credit controller.

CURRENT PROCEDURE	AUDITORS' SUGGESTED IMPROVEMENT	CLIENT COMMENTS
(b) Following up overdue debts Overdue debts are not followed up. An aged debtors report is produced monthly and circulated to the sales managers but there is no follow-up or reporting of action taken.	Reminders should be sent within 25 days of the invoice date. A telephone enquiry should follow within 7 days. Sales managers should report to the credit controller on action taken within 14 days of receiving the aged debtors report. A summary should then be prepared for the chief accountant and sales director.	Agreed, initial telephone chasing should be done by the credit controller and reported to the sales managers.
(c) Misposting of cash receipts and sales invoices There have been a number of instances of mispostings of sales invoices to the wrong customer account and of cash receipts not being keyed off against the correct invoices. The two main contributory factors are poor input screed design and the use of temporary operators. These problems lead to delays in settlement and a loss of customer goodwill.	The input screens should be simplified and more clearly labelled. A brief tutorial should be developed for new operators.	JS to look into costs of remedial action.

Specimen Management Letter (ii)

The Board of Directors   [DATE]
[   ] Limited
[address   ]

Dear Sirs,

[   ] LIMITED

REPORT TO MANAGEMENT FOR THE YEAR ENDED [   ]

Following our recent audit, we bring to your attention certain observations on the company's operations which we believe can help you in improving profits and running the business.

Our main observations are summarised below. Attachment 1 sets out these and other observations in greater detail.

A   CONTROLLING THE BUSINESS

- management accounts — we recommend that these should include measures of employee efficiency by branch to improve control over profitability

- computer contingency plans — we recommend an urgent review of the existing contingency arrangements in the event of a computer breakdown, in order to help avoid a potentially serious disruption of the company's operations

- [other points].

B   MANAGING WORKING CAPITAL

- credit control — we recommend that you consider taking on a full-time credit controller. If properly implemented, this could result in a net saving in cost.

- [other points]

All the points made in this report have been discussed with Mr Smith and we have taken account of his comments in drafting it. These points arose during the course of our audit which is designed primarily to enable us to form an opinion on the financial statements taken as a whole. Our report cannot therefore be expected to include all possible comments and recommendations which a more extensive special examination might indicate. We should add that this report has been prepared solely for the directors and senior management. Please do not show it to third parties to whom we cannot be responsible.

May we take this opportunity to express our thanks to you and your staff for the assistance which we received during this year's audit.

Yours faithfully

[   ] LIMITED — ATTACHMENT 1 TO LETTER DATED [   ] *(Extracts)*

A CONTROLLING THE BUSINESS

A.1 Management accounts — employee efficiency

	19X3	19X2	19X1
Turnover per employee £'000	A	B	C
% change from previous year	D	E	F
Operating profit per employee £'000	G	H	I
% change from previous year	J	K	(L)

The above figures for the company as a whole show that reduced employee efficiency is likely to be a principal reason why operating profits of £m, although very healthy, have grown by only N% from last year's profits of £p. Further analysis of these indicators by branch shows that X and Y branches are the main contributors to these declining ratios.

We have discussed this with the sales managers at each branch and have identified two possible causes. First, the more senior employees tend to concentrate on servicing your long-standing clients, leaving the less experienced staff to handle the newer contracts, which tend to be more complex and profitable. F.B is reviewing the allocation of responsibilities at these branches. Secondly, although the volume of new business is rising, the conversion rate of tenders into contracts is falling. F.B. is developing stricter and more formalised criteria for deciding whether to tender in the first place.

In the light of these instances, we recommend that your quarterly management accounts package should include a branch analysis of turnover per employee and operating profit per employee to enable any adverse trend to be highlighted for investigation and corrective action. You may also wish to consider moving, in due course, to a policy of setting targets for these indicators.

A.2 Computer contingency planning

The company is now heavily reliant on its computer systems. As well as the nominal, purchase and sales ledger systems, the computer is used to maintain branch work in progress records and process customer orders. A computer breakdown would so significantly disrupt the company's operations, that it is essential that proper back-up facilities should be in place to cope with such an event. The contingency plans existing at present are not adequate and have never been tested. Although we are not aware of any operating problems with the existing equipment, your hardware is now three years old.

We recommend that the contingency arrangements should be reviewed as a matter of urgency and we would be happy to assist in defining the exercise, should you so wish.

B. MANAGING WORKING CAPITAL

B.1 Credit control

	19X3	19X2	19X1
Debtor days	54	43	40
Turnover £'000	P	Q	R
Bad debts charge £'000	S	T	U
— as % of turnover	v%	w%	x%

We estimate that the additional interest cost of financing the longer credit period during 19X3 was £vK.

There are a number of procedural shortcomings, dealt with below, underlying this problem but we believe the root cause is that you do not have sufficient resources devoted to credit control to cope with the increased volume of business.

We recommend that a full-time credit controller should be employed. Provided a suitably experienced individual could be identified, and the support and commitment of the sales managers assured, the company would gain net savings within a year. The tasks of the credit controller would include those shown below. Should you wish, we would be happy to assist in drawing up fuller terms of reference.

(a) Credit given to customers
At present credit is given to new customers without adequate references being taken up or adequate authorisation by a responsible official. In addition credit limits are being exceeded, with credit limits unrealistic in many cases.

We recommend that references such as credit ratings from Dunn & Bradstreet, trade references, and bank references, should be taken up for all significant new customers. All new accounts should be authorised by the chief accountant. Credit limits should be reviewed regularly (at least every three months) by the credit controller in consultation with the sales managers, and all alterations authorised by the chief accountant.

Sales managers should check that credit limits will not be exceeded before authorising sales orders. JS (chief accountant) and FB (sales director) agree that a review of existing credit limits should be one of the first tasks by the new credit controller.

(b) Following up overdue debts
Overdue debts are not followed up. An aged debtors report is produced monthly and circulated to the sales managers but there is no follow-up or reporting of action taken.

We suggest that reminders should be sent within 25 days of the invoice date. A telephone enquiry made by the credit controller should follow within 7 days. Sales managers should report to the credit controller on action taken within 14 days of receiving the aged debtors report. A summary should then be prepared for the chief accountant and sales director.

(c) Misposting of cash receipts and sales invoices
There have been a number of instances of mispostings of sales invoices to the wrong customer account and of cash receipts not being keyed off against the correct invoices. The two main contributory factors are poor input screen design and the use of temporary operators. These problems lead to delays in settlement and a loss of customer goodwill.

The input screens should be simplified and more clearly labelled. A brief tutorial should be developed for new operators. JS has decided to look into the costs of remedial action.

C ACCOUNTING AND AUDIT ISSUES

C.1 Depreciation
The commencement date on which depreciation is charged on newly acquired fixed assets varies from asset to asset. In some cases depreciation is charged from the month of acquisition, in others for the full year in the year of acquisition. Different individuals have been involved in making the calculations and they have not applied the same basis. The effect on the financial statements this year was not material because the major part of expenditure took place early in the year. We recommend that a policy be set of charging depreciation on all fixed assets from the month of acquisition. This policy should then be adhered to.

CHAPTER 23   GOING CONCERN

23.1   INTRODUCTION

Financial statements are assumed to be prepared on a going concern basis. In auditing financial statements the auditor has a responsibility to evaluate whether there is substantial doubt about the entity's ability to continue as a going concern, at least for a reasonable period of time (normally one year from the date of the financial statements being audited or six months from the date of the audit report, whichever ends later).

In most cases, the auditor will have little doubt on this matter and no specific procedures need be performed. In some cases, however, certain conditions and events may cause concern about a company's ability to continue operations. These conditions and events usually relate to operating performance and inability to obtain adequate financing. Operating problems may manifest themselves as continued losses, doubt as to future revenues, impairment of operating ability (possibly through legal proceedings or unavailability of essential materials), or seriously ineffective management control over operations. In addition, concern might arise from events not relating directly to operations such as loss of key management personnel, labour disputes, uneconomic long-term commitments, and legislative acts.

This chapter deals first with the signs of going concern problems, then with the specific audit procedures that should be performed and, finally, with the implications for the financial statements and the audit report.

23.2   IDENTIFICATION OF GOING CONCERN PROBLEMS

23.2.1   *Red flags*

The auditor should be alert for indicators of possible going concern problems. Examples of such indicators are as follows:

- recurring operating losses or negative cash flows
- failure to make loan repayments
- delay in payments of dividends
- work stoppages or persistent labour difficulties
- dependence on the success of a particular product or customer
- banks refusing to give new or renew existing finance facilities
- technical problems in developing major new products
- suppliers not giving usual credit terms
- uninsured disasters
- risk of significant losses due to legal action
- loss of essential customers, suppliers, employees, patents, franchise
- unplanned build-up of stock
- exposure to political risk or adversely affected by impending legislative changes

- high gearing ratio

- increasing reliance on short-term financing

- imminent or actual breach of borrowing limits or other loan covenants.

It should be emphasised that these are subjective indications and not intended to be comprehensive. Additionally, it must be remembered that some, if not all, of the factors could apply to an enterprise where the ongoing nature of the business is in no way in doubt.

The risk that the occurrence of one or more of these indicators will lead to going concern problems increases during times of high inflation, high interest rates, currency fluctuations and economic depression.

23.2.2 *Infringement of borrowing limits*

Since borrowing limits are frequently determined by reference to figures contained in a company's latest published accounts, the act of signing accounts which reveal a deficiency of shareholders' funds may itself cause the borrowing limits to be exceeded. Infringement of borrowing limits and other loan covenants may of course occur even though shareholders' funds are not extinguished.

Where a company's borrowing powers are restricted and the limits will be exceeded as indicated above, the auditor should write to the board drawing their attention to the matter. If the infringement is not rectified by subsequent events before the accounts are signed, for example by the introduction of further share capital or by a temporary dispensation given by trustees of a loan stock, it will be necessary to refer to the matter in the accounts and perhaps also in the audit report, since in this situation the continued adoption of the going concern basis might be inappropriate.

23.3 AUDIT PROCEDURES

23.3.1 *Preliminary enquiries*

It is not necessary for the auditor to design audit procedures solely to identify conditions and events that indicate there could be substantial doubt about the client's ability to continue as a going concern for a reasonable period of time. Auditing procedures designed and performed to achieve other audit objectives should be sufficient for that purpose. However, the auditor may consider performing the following procedures to identify or confirm going concern problems:

- review management accounts for the period from the financial year end to signing of the audit report

- examine any management profit and cash flow forecasts available for the post balance sheet period

- review relevant board and committee minutes for indications of going concern problems

- review credit terms given by suppliers and look for evidence of late payments

- check whether there have been any breaches of long-term borrowing agreements

- for credit guarantees for the enterprise, obtain written confirmation from the guarantor.

23.3.2 *Consideration of management's plans*

If in the course of the audit, the auditor becomes aware of conditions that lead him to question the ability of an entity to continue as a going concern for a reasonable period of time, he should:

- obtain information about management's plans to deal with the going concern threats, and

- assess the likelihood that such plans can be effectively implemented.

The auditor should ask management to prepare financial and cash flow projections for at least 18 months following the balance sheet date. These 18-month projections are recommended because they extend to the time when he normally will next have the opportunity to issue an audit report on the client's financial statements. He should review these projections and the underlying assumptions to determine that the projections are based on reasonable assumptions.

In reviewing management's projections, the auditor should focus on those assumptions which are material to the projections, especially those that are sensitive to variations, or that deviate from historical trends. Matters to be considered in reviewing management's projections include the following:

- the reasonableness of the assumptions in light of the auditor's knowledge of the client, its business and its management

- a comparison of projected amounts to historical results

- availability of funds from the credit markets that the client intends to use

- plans to draw on unused lines of credit

- the possibility of increasing pressures on cash flow because of
  - acceleration of debt payments due to the inability to comply with restrictive debt covenants
  - rising interest rates in variable rate borrowing

- plans to dispose of assets, given
  - the apparent marketability of assets that management plans to sell
  - possible restrictions on disposal of assets, such as covenants in loan agreements limiting such transactions
  - possible direct or indirect effects of disposal of assets on operating results

- plans to borrow money, restructure debt or extend loan periods, taking into account
  - the availability of debt financing, including existing or committed credit arrangements, such as lines of credit or arrangements for factoring debts or sale-leaseback of assets
  - existing or committed arrangements to restructure or subordinate debt or to guarantee loans to the entity
  - possible effects on management's borrowing plans of existing restrictions on additional borrowing or the sufficiency of available collateral

- the availability of guarantees from third parties

- plans to reduce or delay expenditures, including
  - the apparent feasibility of plans to reduce overhead or administrative expenses, to postpone maintenance or research and development projects, or to lease rather than purchase assets
  - possible direct or indirect effects of reduced or delayed expenses on operations

- plans to increase ownership equity, particularly
  - the feasibility of plan to raise additional equity capital

- the ability of the client to pass on to its customers increased costs in light of competition

- the ability to extend markets, change suppliers, products or personnel

- existing or committed arrangements to reduce current dividend requirements or to accelerate cash distributions from subsidiaries or other investees.

If management's assumptions appear unreasonable, the auditor should ask them to modify the projections using assumptions that he believes (and management agrees) are reasonable.

If management is unable to prepare financial and cash flow projections, the auditor should ask for a written summary of the major courses of action, if any, for dealing with the entity's going concern problems. Appropriate audit procedures should be performed to assess the reasonableness of the courses of action and the likelihood of their being achieved.

The absence of cash flow and profit forecasts may indicate a management weakness necessitating discussion with the directors and senior officials; it will be necessary to decide whether other evidence of viability is adequate and acceptable.

The auditor should evaluate the soundness and achievability of management's plans. For example, if management informs him that it plans to solve its going concern problem by obtaining a new line of credit from a local bank, he should ask management to provide, in writing, details about the new line of credit. He should then confirm these details with the bank and evaluate the reasonableness of the assumption that the line of credit will solve the client's problem.

After the auditor has evaluated management's plans, he should conclude whether substantial doubt still remains about the entity's ability to continue as a going concern for a reasonable period of time.

23.3.3 *Disagreement with directors*

Where the auditor cannot satisfy himself as to the liquidity of the company over a reasonable period, but the directors nevertheless disagree with his conclusions, he should obtain from the directors written confirmation of the reasons why they consider the company to have adequate cash resources. If such a confirmation is not forthcoming (or cannot be substantiated) it will probably be necessary to qualify the audit report.

23.3.4 *Bank and other facilities*

The auditor should check existing facilities to bank certificates or other available evidence and have regard to the date(s) at which bank facilities are to be reviewed. Confirmation should be obtained from the bank or other lenders that further finance facilities will be granted or existing facilities renewed. It should be noted that in practice banks confirm their support in terms which indicate that the bank may, if it so chooses, withdraw its support at short notice. The auditor should be aware that requests for such confirmation may, in themselves, cause banks or other lenders to reassess the credit-worthiness of the company. The auditor may, therefore, wish to discuss the matter with the client before such requests are made. A further difficulty may be that the bank or other lender may be unwilling to consider future support until after the financial statements are finalised and the audit report signed. In this circumstance it will normally be necessary for the auditor to have direct discussions with the bank or other lender.

23.3.5 *Group support*

Where the going concern basis is appropriate for a client company in a group only because of the support of another company or an individual, the auditor should obtain 'sufficient, relevant and reliable audit evidence' (APC Auditing Guideline 'Audit evidence') that the other company or the individual is willing and able to provide such support. [The term 'group' is used in these paragraphs in a loose sense to include companies under common control.]

Given the wrongful trading provisions in the Insolvency Act 1986 (discussed later below), the directors of the company which is being supported will themselves have a positive interest in ensuring that the assurance of support is properly recorded and, if possible, legally enforceable. The directors may wish to take legal advice on their own position.

Where a holding company is acting as banker to a subsidiary, the auditor should bear in mind that the relationship is different from that between a normal bank and its customer. This is because the holding company can, by reason of its control of the subsidiary's board, influence it in ways not open to a bank, eg by coercing a subsidiary into accepting the revocation of a letter of support. The auditor should therefore generally look for a more certain form of commitment that he would accept from a bank. He should also not ignore the possibility of the holding company being taken over with a consequent change of directors, who may adopt a different attitude to the particular subsidiary.

For these reasons, the support should normally be evidenced in writing, oral confirmation being probably insufficient. The document should be signed with due authority and such authorisation recorded in the minute books of both the supporting and supported companies. These procedures help to ensure that the attention of the respective boards has been properly focused on a matter of audit importance. They also provide a formal record of the recognition by the respective boards of their responsibilities and duties in the matter. The further question of the legal enforceability of the document is discussed below.

Only if the auditor is satisfied that the undertaking of support will be implemented should he rely upon it. He should:

● form his own assessment of the persons expressing support and what their intentions really are

● consider the ability of the supporting party to provide support; this will entail at least an examination of the supporting party (and group) forecasts or an enquiry of the supporting party (and group) auditors

● check that the supported and supporting company's borrowing powers have not been and are not likely to be exceeded.

The auditor should consider whether the statement of support needs to be legally enforceable in order to justify audit reliance upon it. His decision will be based on his assessment of the persons expressing support and their true intentions, and the adequacy of references in the financial statements (and directors' report) to those intentions and to the financial problems of the company. Examples of situations where he might not be concerned, from an audit viewpoint, with the question of legal enforceability are where:

● the company needs support, despite being financially successful, only because it is undercapitalised

● the company is of vital strategic importance to the group

● its losses are temporary and planned eg because of a deliberate expansion or a new long-term venture to which the group is clearly committed

● the directors accept that the audit report will be qualified for uncertainty because, for example, the supporting company has an established policy of not giving an enforceable commitment or is prevented from doing so under the terms of its own borrowings, whatever its intentions, or because the directors of the supporting company believe it inappropriate to give an enforceable undertaking.

If the auditor decides that the statement of support needs to be legally enforceable in order to justify audit reliance upon it, he should ask the client to obtain legal assistance in the preparation of a formal agreement (if one has not yet been prepared) and legal advice as to its enforceability. The auditor should examine the document to form his own view, for the purposes of his audit, as to whether the document appears to be enforceable. If a legal opinion is not forthcoming, or where the auditor has reservations about the opinion expressed, he should with the client's permission, take his own legal advice. If such permission is not given, or the second opinion does not resolve his doubts, he should consider qualifying his audit report.

A clear distinction must be made between, on the one hand, assessing the enforceability of a letter of support for the purposes of the audit and, on the other, advising a client on the interpretation of the effect of an existing letter or advising on the form and/ or wording of a letter to be prepared. Auditors cannot give a client advice on legal matters on which the client can rely and should not do so. To attempt to do so would be to extend the auditor's exposure to claims for professional negligence. Accountants Digest No. 154 'Intra-group indebtedness — letters of support and subordination' published by the Institute of Chartered Accountants in England and Wales considers this point and warns that this is a complicated area of law and that auditors should be wary of it. Specimen letters of support are not included in the Digest as differing circumstances may dictate varying wordings. Thus, auditors must avoid interpreting letters for the benefit of clients or involving themselves in their preparation.

However, in those cases where the auditor is not himself concerned from an audit standpoint with the question of legal enforceability, he may give the client a written indication of what he wishes to see in the letter of support (where one has not already been drawn up) provided he makes it clear, in writing, both to the supported company and, if they are also his clients, the companies giving the support, that he cannot advise on the legal effect of these documents or on the adequacy of the protection afforded by them for the boards involved, those being matters for legal advice.

The wording of this statement of audit needs will vary with the precise circumstances. A suggested form of letter is given in Appendix 23.1.

It should be noted that the normal addressee for a letter of support is the board of the supported company and not the auditors.

There is a danger that, even though the auditor may seek to make it clear in writing (see above) that he cannot advise on the legal effects of or the adequacy of the protection afforded by the letter of support, he may, by becoming involved in the preparation of these documents, automatically be drawn into such aspects. He must resist this. For reasons already outlined, he must ensure that his conduct and oral advice reinforces rather than undermines the written disclaimer suggested above.

Where the auditor is placing reliance on a letter of support, he should bear in mind that a holding company and a subsidiary can agree to vary the terms of the agreement or rescind it. In the latter case, however, the subsidiary's directors might, in some circumstances, be in breach of their duty to the subsidiary in so doing (in that they would be relinquishing one of the company's assets). Before signing the audit report, the auditor should therefore ensure that the letter of support has been neither varied nor rescinded.

23.3.6 *Letters of subordination*

In considering the going concern, the auditor may be taking account of the fact that a loan from a holding company has been subordinated to the claims of other creditors and that the subsidiary is thus able to pay those other debts as they fall due. The subordination may be expressed in terms that, while the borrowing company continues to trade, the holding company will not demand repayment unless and until the claims of all other creditors have been met. Alternatively, the letter may be in terms that the holding company agrees that its claim will, in the event of the liquidation of the subsidiary, be subordinated to the claims of other creditors. Furthermore, the letter may include both the alternative terms of expression.

As with a letter of support, the degree of the auditor's reliance on a letter of subordination will depend inter alia on whether it is, on the one hand, a mere statement of intent or, on the other, an enforceable and perhaps irrevocable contract. His approach should be the same as for considering letters of support and is as discussed above. The features of an enforceable letter of subordination are the same as those set out for letters of support in the Appendix 23.1. The same clear distinction should be made between, on the one hand, assessing the enforceability of a letter of subordination for the purposes of an audit and, on the other, advising a client on the interpretation of the effect of an existing letter or advising on the form and/or wording of a letter to be prepared. The auditor must avoid the latter.

Any subordination arrangement should be adequately disclosed in the financial statements. In particular, if a subordinated loan would no longer be subordinated after the commencement of winding-up proceedings, this should be made clear. It is pointed out in Appendix 1 to Accountants Digest No. 154 that what is now section 107 of the Insolvency Act 1986 provides that, in a winding-up, the company's property is to be applied in satisfaction of the company's liabilities pari passu. Therefore, a previously subordinated loan would no longer be so (unless other steps such as are suggested in the Digest had previously been taken). Consideration needs also to be given to the balance sheet format heading under which the creditor should be disclosed — 'Creditors: amounts falling due within one year' or 'Creditors: amounts falling due after more than one year'. The enforceability or otherwise of the subordination arrangements will be a factor. If the arrangement is a mere statement of intent, the legal position is that the holding company could demand repayment at any time.

23.4 DISCLOSURES

Where doubts are raised about the ability of a client to continue as a going concern, as well as carrying out the procedures recommended above, the auditor should consider:

- the adjustments to the financial statements that would arise from the adoption of the cessation basis rather than the going concern basis

- the adequacy of disclosures in the financial statements

- the implications for the audit report

- drawing the attention of the directors to certain statutory penalties.

23.4.1 *Accounting adjustments*

SSAP 17 states that the amounts included in the financial statements should be changed where a post balance sheet event indicates that application of the going concern concept to the whole or a material part of the company is not appropriate. An example of such an event given in the explanatory note to SSAP 17 is a deterioration in the operating results and in the financial position.

If there is a clear indication that the company will shortly cease trading — for example, if the shareholders are intending to wind-up the company voluntarily — the financial statements should be drawn up on a cessation basis. As the circumstances of cessation will be known, the necessary adjustments can probably be estimated with reasonable accuracy.

In most cases, however, there will be considerable doubt as to the likelihood and timing of cessation and consequently of the adjustments required to alter the financial statements from the going concern basis. In these circumstances, the financial statements will continue to be drawn up on a going concern basis, but the auditor may consider it necessary to qualify his audit report. He should consider the extent of the adjustments which would be necessary if the accounts were not to be prepared on the going concern basis. These are likely to include:

- the reclassification of assets and liabilities (for example, a long-term loan could become immediately repayable)

- the recognition of new liabilities (for example, redundancy payments, damages for breach of trading contracts and leases, or unfunded vested pension rights)

- changes in the values of recorded assets (for example, stocks, fixed assets, deferred expenditure and prepayments).

If the view given by the financial statements would be materially affected, then the auditor must qualify. In particular, he should not refrain from qualifying an audit report, if it is otherwise appropriate, merely on the grounds that it may lead to the appointment of an administrator, a receiver or a liquidator.

If the auditor concludes that a departure from the going concern basis would not materially affect the view given by the financial statements, and he therefore does not qualify his report, it should nevertheless be remembered that there is a presumption in both law and accounting standards that the financial statements are prepared on a going concern basis. The APC Auditing Guideline accordingly states 'where there is a significant uncertainty about the enterprise's ability to continue in business, this fact should be stated in the financial statements even when there is no likely impact on the carrying value and classification of assets and liabilities. Where this is not stated in the financial statements, the auditor should refer to it in his report'.

23.4.2 *Disclosure in financial statements*

In evaluating the adequacy of disclosures in the financial statements when going concern doubts exist, the auditor normally considers the following:

- the principal conditions that raise questions about the client's ability to continue in existence

- the possible effects of such conditions

- management's evaluation of the significance of those conditions and any mitigating factors.

If disclosure is necessary and a satisfactory resolution of the question depends primarily on the realisation of particular plans of management, that fact and such plans should be disclosed.

It is important that the accounts explain the use of the going concern basis where the state of affairs and the results shown by the accounts are such as to cast doubt over the validity of the basis. For example, where the company depends on the continued financial support of its holding company, the holding company's expressed intentions or commitment should be disclosed. A suggested accounting policy note is:

'Going concern
The financial statements have been drawn up on the basis of a going concern. The holding company has informed the Directors that it will continue to provide financial support for the company's operations.'

23.4.3 *Going concern audit report references*

The form and wording of any reference in audit reports to going concern uncertainties will depend on the circumstances and the extent to which information is given in the notes to the accounts. In view of the serious effect a 'going concern' qualification could have on a company, and of the need consequently to avoid the accusation that a qualified report in this respect contributed to, or precipitated, the company's eventual failure, it is essential that all proposed qualifications are carefully vetted by the auditor.

As a minimum, the report should refer to the going concern assumption upon which the financial statements have been based and the nature of the related uncertainty.

In the great majority of cases a 'subject to' report will be appropriate. The APC Auditing Guideline 'The auditor's consideration in respect of going concern' states that, in addition to the points mentioned above, the audit report should refer to the nature (but not the extent) of the adjustments that may have to be made to the financial statements. The specimen report included in the guideline therefore includes this information.

In certain cases, the uncertainties concerning the going concern assumption may be so fundamental as to prevent the auditor from forming an opinion on the financial statements. His decision to disclaim will be influenced by the following matters:

- the scale of the adjustments that might be required were the financial statements to be drawn up on a cessation basis;

- the degree of imprecision involved in estimating these potential adjustments; and

- the extent of his doubt as to the sufficiency and reliability of the evidence available in support of the appropriateness of the going concern assumption.

In rare cases the auditor may conclude that the evidence indicating that the company is unable to continue in business is so overwhelming that he will wish to qualify on the grounds of disagreement. In such cases he should give an 'except for' or 'adverse' opinion, depending on the extent of the adjustments that would be necessary were the financial statements not to be prepared on a going concern basis.

If the auditor is satisfied in a particular case that adequate financial support will be forthcoming and this is satisfactorily disclosed in the notes to the account, there is no need to qualify the audit report. However, if the balance sheet shows that the enterprise has negative shareholders' funds, it may help the reader of the financial statements if the audit report includes an emphasis of matter.

23.4.4 *Directors and shadow directors — statutory penalties*

While it must be emphasised that the auditor has no responsibility to do so, it will normally be appropriate and desirable to write to the directors drawing their attention to certain statutory provisions, set out in the following paragraphs, at least in those cases where complete loss of shareholders' funds appears to have taken place and the company may still be trading at a loss. It may also be appropriate to write even in those circumstances where a company's continued trading is supported by its holding or other group company. This is clearly a delicate matter, and the auditor will need to be tactful.

Section 214 of the Insolvency Act 1986, the 'wrongful trading' provision, applies where in the course of an insolvent liquidation it appears that a director, former director or shadow director knew or ought to have realised, at some time before the commencement of the winding-up, that there was no reasonable prospect that the company would avoid going into insolvent liquidation and the person was a director or shadow director at the time. On the application of the court, the court may require the person to make such contribution to the company's assets as the court thinks proper. In reaching a decision the court will assume the person to be a reasonably diligent person having both:

- the same general knowledge, skill and experience that may reasonably be expected of a person carrying out the same functions as are carried out by the director in relation to the company, and

● the general knowledge, skill and experience that the particular director has.

The court will not penalise a person who, having at an appropriately early stage realised that there was no reasonable prospect that the company would avoid insolvent liquidation, took every step to minimise the potential loss to the company's creditors that he ought to have taken.

The court may disqualify a person from acting as a director if he is compelled, under the 'wrongful trading' provision to make a contribution to the company's assets (section 10 of the Company Directors Disqualification Act 1986). Under section 6 of that Act, a person may also be disqualified if:

● he has been a director or shadow director of a company which has at any time become insolvent (whether while he was in office or subsequently); and

● his conduct as a director of the company (either taken alone or taken together with his conduct as a director of any other company or companies) makes him unfit to be concerned in the management of a company.

Reference is made above to a 'shadow director' — a person in accordance with whose directions or instructions the directors of a company are accustomed to act. It should be particularly noted that the directors of a holding company or indeed the holding company itself may be regarded as being shadow directors. If a holding company is so treated and held liable for payments, it thus loses both the benefit of having traded through a subsidiary and any benefit from allowing the subsidiary to go into liquidation.

Section 458 of the Companies Act 1985 makes it a criminal offence for any person to be a party to a company carrying on business with the intention of defrauding creditors — which includes the company obtaining credit when it is clear that it will not be able to pay its debts as they fall due. In addition, under section 213 of the Insolvency Act 1986, such persons may become liable for the company's debts in a liquidation.

A suggested form of letter requesting audit confirmation of support from another company is given in Appendix 23.2.

23.5 CHECKLIST OF PROCEDURES

Audit objective: The going concern basis is appropriate to the accounts

Preliminary considerations

● indications of possible going concern problems

● consider need for preliminary inquiries

Basic procedures

● enquire into conditions, identify and examine mitigating factors

● review management plans including cash flow and profit forecasts

● in case of disagreement with board's conclusions, obtain written confirmation

● confirm availability of bank or external finance

Confirmation of group support

● assess true intentions of supporter(s)

● consider ability of supporting company to provide such support

● check borrowing powers not exceeded

● consider need for enforceability

- obtain written and minuted evidence of support

- if needed, obtain legal advice on enforceability and corroborate by own examination

- check letter of support not rescinded or varied

Disclosure

- consider scale of accounting adjustments required on a cessation basis

- consider adequacy of disclosure in financial statements

- consider need to draw Board's attention to certain statutory penalties.

Appendix 23.1

SUGGESTED WORDING FOR REQUESTING AUDIT CONFIRMATION OF A LETTER OF SUPPORT

Dear Sirs

Your company's financial statements for the year ended. . . . . . .are, we understand, to be drawn up on the basis of a going concern, on the footing that. . . . . . (supporting company) will continue to provide financial support for your company's operations. As part of our audit procedures, we need to see written confirmation from. . . . . . .(supporting company) of its intention to continue to support your company. We would be grateful also for a copy of the board minute from. . . . . (supporting company) approving the giving of this written confirmation of support.

You have asked us to indicate the form and content of a written confirmation that would be necessary to satisfy our audit requirements. For audit purposes, the appropriate form would be a letter addressed to your board of directors confirming the following matters:

(a) there is no intention to alter the ownership of your company;

(b) the supporting company will continue to finance your company at least for the next twelve months, so as to enable it both to meet its liabilities as they fall due and to carry on its business without a significant curtailment of operations; and

(c) an undertaking not to request repayment of the intercompany loan of. . . . . . . (amount) before. . . . . (date). [This confirmation is relevant where an intra-group liability is classified in the balance sheet as a non-current liability and it must therefore extend for more than one year].

We must emphasise that these assurances are being sought purely for the purposes of our audit. If you wish to assess the legal effect of these confirmations or to assess the adequacy of the protection that they afford you as directors of the company, we would strongly recommend that you take legal advice.

Yours faithfully,

Appendix 23.2

SPECIMEN LETTER INFORMING DIRECTORS OF STATUTORY PENALTIES

'Dear Sirs

We refer to/have discussed with Mr. . . . . the draft balance sheet as at. . . . . This balance sheet reflects a materially insolvent position in the sense that there is a substantial excess of liabilities over assets.

No doubt the Board has already considered this situation, but we consider we should write drawing the Board's attention to certain matters. We should be grateful if a copy of this letter is made available to each member of the Board.

A balance sheet insolvency is not the only or even, in particular cases, a relevant test of insolvency. However, it is a question upon which we suggest you should seek legal advice and, in considering the position of your company and of individual directors, you should not rely on the contents of this brief letter.

Under the Insolvency Act 1986, directors, former directors or shadow directors of a company which goes into insolvent liquidation can be made to contribute personally to the assets of a company if they knew or ought to have realised, at some time before the commencement of the winding-up, that there was no reasonable prospect that the company could avoid going into insolvent liquidation. They may also be disqualified from acting as directors of companies. You should note that the term 'shadow director' can include the directors of a holding company and the holding company itself.

Furthermore, under the Companies Act 1985, it is a criminal offence for any person to be a party to a company carrying on business with the intention of defrauding creditors. This may well include the company obtaining credit when it is clear that it will not be able to pay its debts as they fall due.

If you wish to discuss these matters with us in greater detail,. . . . . . . [name], who is a licensed insolvency practitioner, would be happy to meet with you.

Yours faithfully

CHAPTER 24   CONSOLIDATED FINANCIAL STATEMENTS

24.1   INTRODUCTION

Management's assertions in respect of financial statement items are essentially no different in consolidated financial statements to those in a single company. Indeed, in simple terms, consolidation is the presentation of the financial affairs of a group of companies **as if** those companies were one single entity.

The work an auditor performs in respect of consolidated financial statements involves different techniques, since:

- the audit of the underlying information is normally carried out by the auditors of the various companies making up the group

- the consolidation audit must address accounting, auditing and disclosure issues that are unique to consolidated financial statements.

The auditor's overall objective is to make sure that he has obtained sufficient reliable, relevant evidence so that the consolidated financial statements are free of material error. This breaks down into three distinct objectives: to make sure that:

- the financial statements of each member of the group are free from material error insofar as the group is concerned

- those individual financial statements have been consolidated following proper consolidation principles and that all necessary consolidation adjustments have been correctly made

- the consolidated financial statements are presented in accordance with the requirements of the Companies Acts and accounting standards.

Broadly speaking, the audit work to achieve these objectives involves:

- review of the financial statements of each material group member

- assessment of the audit work carried out in respect of group members

- verification of consolidation calculations

- identification and verification of consolidation adjustments, including those in respect of inconsistent accounting policies within the group and elimination of intra-group trading

- audit work in respect of acquisitions and disposals in the period

- review of events subsequent to the balance sheet date

- overall review of the consolidated financial statements.

This chapter looks at the planning, conducting and completion of the audit of consolidated financial statements. It does not give guidance on the particular accounting problems associated with the preparation of consolidated financial statements.

It should be remembered that groups of companies vary greatly in size and complexity — from a simple local 'parent and subsidiary' organisation to large multinational groups where many teams of auditors are involved. It is not necessarily the most complex groups that give rise to the most difficult audit problems, and often it is problems of administration, timing and coordination that can prove more intractible than any other.

More so by far than with single companies, the emphasis in a consolidation audit is on everyone knowing in advance what is required of them — ie careful audit planning.

24.2 PLANNING

24.2.1 *Why the auditor should plan the group audit*

As with single companies, planning is important in the audit of groups to make sure that an effective audit is carried out in an efficient and timely manner. Proper planning ensures that appropriate attention is paid to areas of high risk, auditing difficulty and accounting complexity.

As noted above, groups vary widely in complexity, and the work involved in the planning stage varies accordingly. The degree of detail in which the group audit plan needs to be thought out and documented is a matter of judgement and may vary from:

- a brief paragraph in the audit plan of the parent company (as may be the case in the simplest structure, with just one subsidiary, where both parent and subsidiary are local clients)

- a detailed narrative group audit plan distributed to auditors of all members of the group (as may be the case when dealing with a large multinational group).

24.2.2 *The stages in planning*

The group audit planning process will normally involve the following:

- identify the structure of the group and the nature of the companies' businesses

- assess overall group audit risk and group materiality

- identify areas of high risk, audit difficulty or accounting complexity

- identify group audit requirements, including
  - the sufficiency, reliability and relevance of audit work carried out by secondary auditors
  - any specific requirements in respect of areas of audit difficulty or accounting complexity

- document and communicate requirements to group auditors.

24.2.3 *Group structure*

The first stage in group audit planning is to identify the structure of the group and the nature of each of the component businesses.

For new clients, a chart of the group structure should be prepared or obtained from the client. This chart should be placed in the auditor's permanent working papers file. In the case of existing clients, he should update his chart of the group structure and confirm the updated position (including changes from the previous period) with the client.

The group structure should specify, for each company in the group:

- the nature of the parent's investment in the company (subsidiary, affiliate, investment) giving percentage equity held and indicating expected consolidation accounting treatment

- the nature of the company's business

- its financial year end

- its location

- the auditors.

Particular care should be made at the outset to obtain a clear understanding of the accounting treatment (for consolidation purposes) of each member of the group.

24.2.4 *Assessing group audit risk and group materiality*

The auditor needs to assess group audit risk and materiality at the overall — consolidated — financial statements level. The reasons for this are the same as for a single company (see Chapter 9) since the auditor is reporting on the financial statements of the group as if it were a single entity.

Group materiality will normally exceed materiality in respect of each member of the group, as the group is almost invariably larger than its component elements. It is therefore normally unlikely that the audit of any of the members of the group will have been planned using materiality that is inappropriate from a group point of view. However, care must be taken (especially when dealing with foreign subsidiary auditors or another firm of auditors) that auditors of group members are aware of group planning materiality so that this is not exceeded in their planning process.

With single entities, the assessment of materiality affects both the amount of audit work done in respect of each account balance as well as the overall review of financial statements and the way the auditor deals with errors. However, as noted above, the group auditors would not normally carry out any additional detailed audit tests, over and above the work done on subsidiaries by the subsidiary auditors, and accordingly group planning materiality will normally only affect:

- the level of detail at which the group auditor needs to review the work of the auditors of the group companies, and the financial statements of those companies

- the scope of his overall review of the group financial statements.

The auditor's assessment of group audit risk similarly follows the same process as in the audit of a single entity (see chapter 9). The auditor needs to consider, for example, the operating style and philosophy of group management, the operating structure of the group, degree of decentralisation and methods of control, the accounting environment for consolidated reporting, its frequency, the quality of the systems and competence of the individuals involved, as well as external influences on the group and the auditor's past experience with the audit of its consolidated financial statements.

This assessment of group audit risk need not necessarily affect the assessment of risk at the overall financial statement level for each member of the group. However, the group auditor may choose to inform the auditors of some or all member companies when he has assessed group risk as being high — particularly where the reason for that assessment concerns his identification of one or more high risk members of the group.

24.2.5 *Identification of areas of high risk, audit difficulty or accounting complexity*

Identification of areas of high risk, audit difficulty or accounting complexity at the planning stage enables the auditor to pre-empt problems in the closing stages of the group audit by coordinating the work of each member of the group and their auditors.

Matters that may need to be addressed include:

- areas of high risk within individual member companies

- intra-group trading and intra-group balances

- consistency of accounting policies

- compatibility of business activities

- scope of audit work in member companies/additional audit requirements

- administrative logistics.

24.2.6 *Identification of group audit requirements*

Having established the group structure, assessed materiality and audit risk and identified potential problem areas, the auditor needs to identify group audit requirements. These may be:

- requirements generally in respect of sufficiency, relevance and reliability of audit work carried out by auditors of member companies

- specific requirements in respect of areas of auditing difficulty or accounting complexity.

Normally a full audit of each individual subsidiary will be carried out by its auditors; however, the auditor should suggest that a less detailed examination may be carried out on a subsidiary that is not material to the group accounts if either:

- it is a subsidiary undertaking with no legal requirement for an audit, or

- a full audit cannot be carried out conveniently within the time-limit imposed by the group timetable (in which case the full audit would be completed later).

The auditor needs to consider the audit risks associated with the activities and the materiality of the net assets, results and commitments of the subsidiary in relation to the group as well as the level of intra-group trading and guarantees.

The decision whether or not to reduce the scope of the audit of a subsidiary should be taken in conjunction with the group management since they may themselves wish to rely on the audit.

Where the scope of audit work is to be limited, the group auditor should ensure that the audit objectives are clearly defined and communicated to the auditors concerned. Designing specific procedures to meet those objectives normally requires a knowledge and understanding of local credit and business practices and of the entity's internal control structure, and is therefore normally better left to the local auditors to determine. In some cases, however, the group auditor may have sufficient background knowledge to set out a specific audit programme of tests for each audit objective.

In appropriate cases it may be possible to adopt a rotational approach to the scope of audit work to be carried out by subsidiary auditors.

The reasons for the level of work to be carried out by the auditors of each subsidiary should be fully documented in the group auditor's own working papers, but need not be communicated to the auditors themselves.

Where subsidiary auditors are to carry out a reduced scope audit, the terms in which they are to report should be agreed in advance.

In many cases, the group auditor will need to ask the subsidiary auditors to extend the scope of their work, for example, to review events subsequent to the balance sheet date to a date later than the completion of their local report on the financial statements or to cover special group reporting requirements. Other specific requirements may relate to areas of high risk, audit difficulty or accounting complexity.

24.2.7 *Feedback on work done*

The auditor will also need to consider, at the planning stage, how he intends to satisfy himself about the scope and standard of the audit work actually carried out by the subsidiary auditors.

There is a range of methods available:

- visit the subsidiary and review the auditors' working papers

- ask for a questionnaire to be completed, describing the work done

- ask for copies of key audit documentation eg planning notes and notes of contentious or difficult issues arising during the audit.

In selecting the method, the auditor should consider:

- the materiality of the figures of the company in relation to those of the group as a whole and the nature of, and degree of risk attached to, its business

- knowledge gained through previous experience of the quality of work done by the other auditors

- audit problems previously encountered at the subsidiary

- the assistance that a visit provides in establishing a good relationship and lines of communication with the other auditors

- whether a visit to the client location can usefully add to his knowledge of the group's business.

Requests for feedback on work done and any visits should always be handled with discretion, and the auditor should avoid implying any criticism of the other auditors' competence.

24.2.8 *Integrity, independence and competence*

Before an auditor can rely on work carried out by subsidiary auditors he must satisfy himself as to their integrity, independence and competence. He should therefore:

- ensure that the subsidiary auditors are practising public accountants and considered to be independent within the criteria accepted in the UK (this should be established through written communications with them)

- consider the professional reputation of the subsidiary auditors and their apparent competence to do satisfactory work, for example through previous experience or membership of a professional body of appropriate standing

- ascertain whether the subsidiary auditors have the experience and technical background to carry out an audit in accordance with UK auditing standards.

24.2.9 *Documenting and communicating the auditor's requirements*

It is important that the auditors of each member of the group are given clear, concise and complete instructions as to the group auditor's requirements to enable them to carry out the work required and report before the deadlines set by the group financial reporting timetable. Except perhaps in the case of small local groups, this objective is best met by the preparation of a Group Audit Plan.

Instructions should be sent to auditors of members of the group well in advance of the year end to enable them to carry out their own planning. The group auditor should ask them to acknowledge receipt of the instructions and confirm that they will be able to comply with his requests.

The instructions for each group company's auditor should normally contain:

- the Group Audit Plan, giving general planning details applicable to or of interest to all companies' auditors (see below)

- a covering letter including any instructions specific to that particular group company. This avoids the Group Audit Plan becoming excessively lengthy.

The Group Audit Plan will normally contain:

- general background information on the group, including, where appropriate, a copy of the latest consolidated financial statements

- a copy of the group structure, giving key client and audit contacts for each company and a complete list of group companies

- names of related parties and a note of known types of related party transactions

- an audit timetable

- any general instruction on audit approach

- group materiality (or estimate thereof) and a note of any areas of high risk and any unusual accounting or reporting matters anticipated

- instructions on any additional specific audit objectives

- instructions on forwarding final and, if appropriate, draft financial statements

- instructions on the form of report expected

- instructions for special, non-recurring work, applying to all group companies

- instructions in respect of reviews of events subsequent to the balance sheet date

- procedures for notification of intention or possible intention to issue other than an unqualified opinion

- lists of applicable accounting and auditing standards, including explanations, if applicable, of implications of any new standards.

- instruction on forwarding copies of management letters and, if appropriate, instructions on style and lay-out

- feeing and billing arrangements

Many large groups issue their own standard consolidation package of forms, together with instructions, for completion by members of the group. This will typically include forms for recording the financial statements in a standard layout and supporting schedules specifying information required for the completion of the consolidated financial statements and directors' report.

The package should include a list of all companies. It should require full details to be given of all intra-group balances and transfers of assets, and sufficient information to enable intra-group transactions to be properly eliminated from the consolidated profit and loss account.

The package will normally include a confirmation to be signed by the subsidiary management to the effect that the package has been properly completed following the group accounting instructions, and a preliminary report by the subsidiary's auditors stating that, subject to any specific incomplete or unresolved matters:

- they have examined the package in accordance with Auditing Standards

- in their opinion the package gives a true and fair view of the subsidiary's results and state of affairs.

- they intend to sign an unqualified audit report on the final accounts.

24.3 CONDUCTING THE CONSOLIDATION AUDIT

There are two main elements in carrying out audit work in respect of a consolidation:

- review of the sufficiency, relevance and reliability of audit work carried out in respect of each group member

● work in respect of verifying the validity of the consolidation calculations and the completeness and accuracy of consolidation adjustments.

24.3.1 *Review of working papers*

Before beginning a review of secondary auditor's working papers it is important to review the financial statements (and any completed consolidation questionnaire). The reviewer should then discuss with the local audit partner or manager responsible the audit approach adopted, the particular audit problems that have arisen in the year concerned and how they have been resolved. He should also request them to highlight the significant aspects of both the financial statements and the audit documentation.

In reviewing the working papers, the following areas are likely to be relevant:

● audit planning — the audit files should contain evidence that the audit was properly planned

● knowledge of the client's business — details of the client's business should be documented and an understanding of the client's business should be evident throughout the working papers

● accounting systems — these should be adequately documented

● audit objectives — the reviewer should consider whether all audit objectives have been covered and how they have been achieved. Where reliance is placed on the internal control structure appropriate tests of controls should have been carried out. The degree of reliance on analytical review and the adequacy of sample sizes for substantive tests should also be considered

● the general quality of working papers should be assessed — they should be clearly and logically set out, with adequate conclusions, and should have been reviewed by a senior member of the audit team

● major points arising from the audit should be adequately documented, together with disposal notes

● any reservations or qualifications in the audit report should be fully documented

● letters to management — if major points are included, the reviewer should consider whether the audit approach was suitably modified and he should ascertain the steps taken by management to deal with the matter

● the reviewer may wish to check information for statutory disclosure or adjustment on consolidation back to the detailed working papers; he should also be alert to other matters requiring disclosure or adjustment.

24.3.2 *Review of questionnaire responses and other returns*

The completed questionnaires, audited financial statements and other documentary returns should be reviewed, when received, by the auditor to ensure that no matters are indicated therein that cast doubt on the adequacy of the audit of the subsidiary. At the same time, any matters requiring adjustment on consolidation should be noted. Any information arising from the questionnaire that might be helpful to the holding company should be passed on to the appropriate officer, though the auditor should first ensure that such information is not confidential.

Any uncertainties arising from this review that are of sufficient magnitude to be relevant to the opinion on the group accounts should be discussed with the secondary auditors. Major areas of difficulty can usually be resolved most readily by personal contact, either by telephone or visit; however where additional assurances are obtained these should be confirmed in writing.

Where the subsidiary auditors have qualified their report in any way, this must be noted as group Points for Partner Attention (see below) and the implications for the group carefully considered.

In exceptional circumstances the auditor may not be satisfied by his review of the questionnaire and of the subsidiary auditors' working papers, or may require confirmation of additional accounting information relating solely to the group accounts. In these circumstances he should ask the subsidiary auditors to carry out additional audit tests; only in very rare cases will the group auditor carry out such tests on a subsidiary himself.

24.3.3 *Signed financial statements*

The group auditor should normally expect to obtain signed financial statements of all subsidiaries and associates before he completes his audit report. If signed financial statements are not available for less material subsidiaries by the time the group financial statements are completed and approved, he should obtain an assurance in writing from the directors and auditors of the subsidiaries concerned that the financial statements will be signed as presented and that no amendments or (further) qualifications made. However, only in exceptional circumstances should he be prepared to sign his report on the consolidated financial statements before the financial statements and audit reports of all material subsidiaries have been signed (notwithstanding any assurances given by the directors and auditors in a group financial statements package.) It is important that potential problems with the reporting timetable are discussed with the client at an early stage.

24.3.4 *Events subsequent to the balance sheet date*

The review of events subsequent to the balance sheet date should cover the whole group up to the date of the group audit report. Where a subsidiary's audit report is dated earlier than the group audit report the auditor should consider the need to extend the review for that subsidiary. He should normally request the auditors of each material subsidiary to carry out that extended review. This request should be included in the instructions given to each auditor at the planning stage; he may also request a separate letter from the auditors confirming the results of this review. In addition, he should consider whether to ask the holding company to obtain a letter of representation from the directors of each relevant subsidiary confirming that no material sheet events subsequent to the balance sheet date have occurred which have not been disclosed.

24.3.5 *Checking the validity of consolidation calculations and the completeness and accuracy of consolidation adjustments*

Consolidations should be prepared if possible by the client. If the auditor prepares the consolidation himself it is important that the consolidation schedules be checked or reviewed by another member of the audit staff of at least equal experience to the one who prepared the schedules and that all significant accounting decisions are agreed with the client.

The audit work checking the accuracy of the consolidation includes:

● checking accounts or standard accounting packages to summary schedules for
— balance sheet
— profit and loss account
— notes to financial statements
It is particularly important to check that items from the subsidiary financial statements have been entered under the appropriate heading on the consolidation summary and that transfers from one heading to another have not occurred in the transcription

● checking currency translation rates with published rates or, where it is not possible, confirming with a bank dealing in foreign exchange, and checking arithmetical accuracy of translation

- checking the additions and cross-costs of the summaries
- checking consolidation adjustments to journal schedules and vice versa
- checking final totals on summaries and final figures to the draft consolidated accounts and checking all additions in those accounts.

The scope of such checks will depend on the materiality of the items involved and the extent to which such checks confirm the reliability of the client's own verification procedures.

The auditor must ensure that all adjustments made on consolidation are accurate, and that no material adjustments have been omitted. This involves extensive review and scrutiny of subsidiary financial statements and questionnaires and the consolidated financial statements themselves, as well as direct verification of the adjustments.

Consolidation adjustments arising for the first time, or of a one-off nature, should be verified by reference to the individual company financial statements or standard accounting package, consolidation questionnaire or other evidence. In the case of changes in group structure during the year, the auditor should obtain all necessary relevant documentation, such as a copy of the purchase or sale agreement.

All group member financial statements and consolidation questionnaires should be reviewed, ensuring in particular that:

- all intra-group commitments and contingencies have been eliminated on consolidation
- accounting policies adopted are consistent between members of the group and with previous years.

Important areas where inconsistent accounting policies can arise include:

- the basis of valuation of inventories and work in process (including long term contracts)
- bases of depreciation
- taxation, including deferred taxation
- the classification of items in the balance sheet and profit and loss account
- the treatment of exchange differences
- the treatment of intangible assets and leased assets
- the treatment of pension costs and pension provisions
- the treatment of property revaluations
- capitalisation of interest
- capitalisation of research and development expenditure
- treatment of profits and losses on forward trading.

Where the accounting date of a group member does not coincide with that of the holding company, it may be necessary to adjust on consolidation for transactions in the intervening period. In particular the auditor should consider the effect of:

- inter-company transactions between the two dates giving rise to profits and losses
- losses incurred in a subsidiary between the end of its financial year and that of the group
- remittance of profits during the intervening period

consolidation to bring the accounting policies of all group companies in line with group and parent company practice, has disclosure been made of
— the differing policies?
— an indication of the amounts involved?
— the reason for the differing policies?

24.4.2 *Group Points for Partner Attention*

For each group, the audit manager or senior staff member responsible for the consolidation audit should prepare group points for partner attention (GPPA's).

The objectives for GPPA's are the same as those of PPA's for a single entity (discussed in Chapter 21); the auditor draws together matters significant from a group point of view where a decision is required at partner level.

GPPA's may include:

● issues relating to the group as a whole

● issues relating to the parent company

● significant matters noted in the PPA of subsidiaries (or classes of subsidiaries/ sub-groups) which are material in a group context and therefore require the decision of the group engagement partner.

24.4.3 *Sign-Off Checklist*

A Sign-Off Checklist (discussed in Chapter 21) should be completed in respect of consolidated financial statements prior to the issuing of the audit report. It serves the same control function in the clearance of a group audit as it does in the audit of a single entity.

24.5 CHECKLIST OF ILLUSTRATIVE SUBSTANTIVE PROCEDURES

Audit objective: Sufficient, relevant and reliable evidence has been obtained in respect of the financial statements of individual entities in the group.

● review completed questionnaires or other returns and audited financial statements

● ensure any uncertainties relevant to the audit opinion on the group financial statements are resolved

● consider impact of any qualifications relating to ubsidiary financial statements

● review working papers of subsidiary auditors as planned or where considered necessary

● obtain signed financial statements of all subsidiaries

● ensure that review of events subsequent to the balance sheet date is carried out on all major subsidiaries

Audit objective: The consolidated financial statements have been accurately prepared following proper consolidation principles and all necessary consolidation adjustments have been prepared.

● update and confirm accuracy of chart of group structure

● ensure all subsidiaries are shown and consider whether any should be excluded from consolidation

● consider whether all, but only those, companies within the definition of associated undertakings are treated as such

Consolidation Summary Schedules

- check subsidiary financial statements to summary schedules
- check currency translation rates and calculations
- check additions and cross-costs of the summaries
- check consolidation adjustments with supporting schedules
- check final totals to draft consolidated accounts

Consolidation adjustments

- confirm validity and completeness of recurring adjustments
- agree new or one-off adjustments to subsidiary financial statements, questionnaire or other evidence
- agree details of acquisition or disposal of subsidiary to purchase or sale agreement
- review subsidiary financial statements and questionnaires for necessary adjustments
- ensure intra-group commitments and contingencies eliminated on consolidation
- consider whether accounting policies have been applied consistently
- consider whether adjustments are required for companies with non-coterminous year ends
- check reconciliation of inter-company accounts, ensuring reconciling items properly adjusted
- agree movements on reserves to totals of individual companies
- ensure late adjustments to subsidiaries' financial statements are reflected in consolidated financial statements
- check or prepare group tax reconciliation
- summarise the group deferred tax position
- obtain summary of offset of tax profits and losses if applicable
- ensure other group tax matters have been considered
- review method of foreign currency translation
- review treatment of acquisitions and disposals of subsidiaries
- review treatment of goodwill and period over which it is amortised

Audit objective: The consolidated financial statements are presented in accordance with generally accepted accounting principles and relevant legal requirements.

- review consolidated financial statements using a disclosure checklist
- ensure that, where material, disclosures in subsidiary accounts are repeated on consolidation
- summarise results of reviews of events subsequent to the balance sheet date of holding company and principal subsidiaries
- ensure that adequate information is given of subsidiaries excluded from consolidation or associated companies not equity-accounted
- ensure that adequate disclosures are made in respect of acquisitions and disposals during the year

- ensure that restrictions on the distributions of profits by subsidiaries are adequately disclosed

- ensure that the existence of contingent tax liabilities which would arise on cross-border distributions of retained profits is disclosed

- consider whether adequate disclosure is made where subsidiaries have non-coterminous accounting periods

- ensure that where adjustment has not been made to bring certain subsidiary accounting policies into line with the group, adequate disclosure is made.

CHAPTER 25   THE NEW AUDIT

25.1   INTRODUCTION

This chapter deals with:

- the administrative aspects of the new appointment as auditors
- particular audit considerations in a new engagement
- the administrative aspects of resignation or retirement as auditors

25.2   ADMINISTRATIVE ASPECTS OF THE NEW APPOINTMENT AS AUDITORS

The principal administrative considerations on being approached to undertake a professional appointment for a new client are:

(i) Obtaining clearance from the previous auditors

(ii) Maintaining professional independence, and

(iii) Confirming the terms of engagement in a letter of engagement.

(i) and (ii) are dealt with below; (iii) is covered in Chapter 7.

25.2.1   *Obtaining clearance from the previous auditors*

On being asked to accept a professional appointment as auditors to an established company, partnership or other body the auditor should, in conformity with Statement 8 of the Institute's Ethical Guide (Members Handbook 1.2), request the prospective client's permission to communicate with the auditors last appointed. A specimen letter to a prospective client is set out in Appendix 25.1. If permission is refused the auditor should decline nomination.

When permission is received he should write to the auditors last appointed requesting all the information which ought to be made available to him before deciding whether or not to accept the appointment. A specimen letter to the retiring auditors is set out in Appendix 25.1.

25.2.2   *Independence*

The auditor should at all times ensure that in any professional assignment undertaken he, both in terms of his firm as a whole and in terms of the individuals engaged on the assignment, is seen to be free of any interest which might detract from his objectivity.

An auditor may not participate in the preparation of the accounting records of a listed company audit client save in exceptional circumstances. In the case of unlisted company audit clients, it is frequently necessary to provide a much fuller service than would be appropriate in the case of a listed company audit client and this may include participation in the preparation of accounting records.

In all cases in which the auditor is concerned in the preparation of accounting records of an audit client, particular care must be taken to ensure that the client accepts full responsibility for such records and that objectivity in carrying out the audit is not impaired.

25.3 PARTICULAR AUDIT CONSIDERATIONS IN A NEW ENGAGEMENT

25.3.1 *Background information*

On the first audit of a new client the auditor will need to spend additional time familiarising himself with the client's business and recording background information on his permanent notes file.

Most of the necessary information and documents may be obtained from the client, and these should be asked for well in advance of the commencement of the first audit. It is possible, however, that the client will be unable to provide certain information which will need to be sought from the previous auditors. The previous auditors may well be willing also to supply copies of their notes of background information.

The auditor should also consider the financial statements of the preceding period, in particular:

- the closing balance sheet figures, which affect the reported results for the current period

- accounting policies and the classification of items in the financial statements, which if acceptable will need to be applied consistently.

These are described below.

25.3.2 *Closing figures*

The closing balance sheet figures in the preceding financial statements affect the reported results for the period currently under review. A materially incorrect stock figure, for example, will normally have a serious effect on those results. Any doubt as to the correctness of the closing figures must influence the auditor's opinion on the results for the current period, and he therefore needs to satisfy himself that these figures are reliable. Therefore he should carry out the following procedures:

- an appraisal of the accounts for previous periods, noting trends in profitability, levels of stock, debtors and creditors and, where available, the apparent reliability of management accounts

- consideration of the effect on previously reported figures of matters arising during the course of the current audit.

If the results of the review outlined above cast doubt on any aspect of the previous year's financial statements to an extent that could affect the opinion on the results for the period currently under review, the auditor should consider extending his enquiries to

- an examination of the previous year's figures in conjunction with the company's own records; and

- consultations with the previous auditor. Such consultations may involve discussion and enquiry regarding any material matters arising during the previous audit, and an examination of the predecessor's audit files, working papers and any management letters.

The decision to carry out these additional procedures should be taken after discussion with the client. The client's permission must be obtained before an approach is made to the previous auditors to review their working papers or discuss any points with them.

If, as a result of the auditor's review, he concludes that the previous year's figures might have been materially mis-stated, it may be necessary to qualify his audit opinion. In exceptional cases where, for example, there is a manifest error, a prior year adjustment should be made and the comparative figures corrected; however, in most instances it will not generally be possible to correct previous figures without a complete re-audit.

25.3.3 Accounting policies and financial statement presentation

The financial statements will contain corresponding amounts drawn from the previous period's financial statements either to comply with statutory requirements or as a matter of good practice. Their purpose normally is to complement the amounts relating to the current period and not re-present the previous accounts.

The auditor will therefore need to satisfy himself:

- that the amounts are comparable and consistently presented
- that accounting policies are consistently applied.

This may be achieved by discussion with the client and an examination of the client's year end accounting schedules for the previous period. Questions of accounting policy will normally have been discussed with the client by the auditor, before or shortly after accepting appointment. In certain instances, changes to existing accounting policies may have been a condition of his agreeing to accept appointment.

If insufficient information is obtained from carrying out the procedures outlined above, the auditor should consider discussing the matter with the previous auditors, and reviewing their working papers. As already noted, the client's permission must be obtained before this step is taken.

25.4 RETIREMENT OR RESIGNATION AS AUDITORS

Two principal administrative considerations arise when an auditor resigns or does not seek reappointment as auditor of a company:

- giving formal written notice of resignation
- communication with the proposed successor.

25.4.1 Giving formal written notice of resignation

If an auditor resigns during his term of office as auditor of a company he is required by statute to deposit a notice in writing to that effect at the registered office of the company. The notice must carry a statement which addresses the question of whether there are any circumstances connected with the auditor's resignation which he considers should be brought to the attention of the company's members or creditors. The Companies Act 1989 has introduced a similar requirement for a formal statement in all cases where an auditor ceases to hold office. Provided that there are no circumstances in connection with the resignation which should be brought to the attention of the members or creditors, the letter to the company may take the form set out in Appendix 25.1.

25.4.2 Communication with the proposed successor

The auditor should expect to hear from the firm to be appointed in his place. Whilst every situation must be considered on its merits, in each case he should request written permission of his former client to discuss the client's affairs freely with the proposed successor. Appendix 25.1 contains an example of a letter to a client requesting such permission. If this request is not granted, the auditor should report that fact to the proposed successor.

On receipt of permission from the client the auditor should disclose fully and discuss freely all information needed by the proposed auditors to enable them to decide whether to accept nomination.

The Institute's Ethical Guide (Statement 1.309 in the Members' Handbook) 'Changes in a professional appointment' gives the following guidance of what information should be made available to a successor:

- disagreements with management as to the truth and fairness of the view shown by the client's financial statements

- disagreements with management as to auditing procedures

- disagreement with management on any other similarly significant matter

- any facts which might bear on the integrity of management

- the reasons for the change in auditors if they do not agree with those given to the newly appointed auditor

- any failure or refusal by the client to supply information.

In those cases where there are no matters to be reported, the reply may follow the specimen set out in Appendix 25.1.

SPECIMEN LETTERS — CHANGES IN APPOINTMENT

1.   SPECIMEN LETTER TO PROSPECTIVE CLIENT: PERMISSION TO COMMUNICATE WITH FORMER AUDITORS

Dear Sirs

Following your request to us that we accept appointment as auditors to XYZed Limited, we should be grateful for your permission to communicate, in accordance with professional ethical requirements, with Messrs. ABC, the former auditors, to enable us to determine whether we are able to accept such appointment.

Yours faithfully

2.   SPECIMEN LETTER TO RETIRING AUDITORS

Dear Sirs

XYZed Limited

We understand you have resigned/are resigning/are not seeking re-appointment as auditors of the above mentioned company, and we have been asked to allow our name to go forward for appointment. In order to enable us to decide whether or not we are prepared to accept this appointment we should be grateful if you would let us have all information which ought to be made available to us in these circumstances.

Yours faithfully

3.   SPECIMEN LETTER OF RESIGNATION AS AUDITORS

'The Secretary
XYZed Limited

Dear Sir

This letter is formal notice of our resignation as auditors of XYZed Limited with effect from today's date.

There are no circumstances connected with our resignation which we consider should be brought to notice of the members or the creditors of the company.

Yours faithfully

4.   SPECIMEN LETTER TO CLIENT: PERMISSION TO COMMUNICATE WITH PROPOSED SUCCESSOR FIRM

'The Secretary
XYZed Limited

Dear Sir

Following our resignation as auditors of your company, we have been approached by ABC who, we understand, have been asked to accept appointment in our place.

We should be grateful for your permission to discuss the affairs of your company with ABC, in order to enable them to decide, in accordance with professional ethics, whether they are prepared to accept such nomination.

Yours faithfully

5. SPECIMEN LETTER TO PROPOSED SUCCESSOR FIRM

'Dear Sir

XYZed Limited

In reply to your letter of [. . . .] we confirm that we know of no information which ought to be made available to you in connection with your proposed appointment as auditors to XYZed Limited.

Yours faithfully

Part Three
Suggested Procedures for
Specific Account Balances

INTRODUCTION TO PART 3

Part Two of this book has provided a description of one way of structuring an audit. It gives practical guidance on how an audit should be planned, it discussed the procedures for collecting, documenting and evaluating audit evidence and, finally, it suggested how the process of drawing together findings and documenting major audit decisions in arriving at an audit opinion might be controlled.

This part of the book looks at individual procedures applicable to specific account balances in the financial statements. In order to provide the reader with quick access to the practical steps he might consider in carrying out work in a particular area of the audit, this part of the book is written in the form of a series of checklists of substantive procedures, under a sequence of headings of detailed audit objectives.

Two comments should be made about these checklists. First, they need to be used selectively. They are not a statement of recommended procedures for every audit engagement and an attempt to apply the steps indiscriminately to an engagement would result in an inefficient, and quite possibly ineffective, audit. Before he comes to deciding upon detailed audit steps, the auditor needs to have developed a clear understanding of the business being audited, the industry in which it operates, the objectives, attitudes and ability of management, how the business is run, its internal control structure, the risks that the business faces and the risks of error in the financial statements. Only then can the auditor select steps that properly address the risks of error and avoid procedures that do not make a significant contribution to the process of minimising the risk of undetected material misstatement in the financial statements. This process of audit planning is discussed at length in Part Two of this book.

Second, the checklists are drawn up to address the audit of a general commercial business. It is beyond the scope of this book to give detailed guidance on audits in specialised industries.

The checklists appear in the following sequence:

- Tangible fixed assets
- Intangible fixed assets
- Investments
- Stock and work in progress
- Contract work in progress
- Trade debtors
- Prepayment and other debtors
- Cash and bank balances
- Group and associated undertakings
- Trade creditors
- Other current liabilities
- Taxes
- Borrowings
- Provisions for liabilities, financial commitments, contingencies

- Dividends, earnings per share, capital and reserves
- Income
- Expenditure
- Directors, minutes, directors' report
- Funds statement
- Trial balance, accounting records and the financial statements.

TANGIBLE FIXED ASSETS

Tangible fixed assets stated in the financial statements represent assets that physically exist and that are owned or leased under finance leases by the client

Consider testing recorded existence by one or more of the following methods:

- Physically observe major assets on a cyclical basis and major additions in the initial year of service.

- Make a physical inspection of a sample of recorded items.

- Test a complete inventory of capital assets taken by the client.

- Inspect, or obtain third party confirmation of, documents of title, eg deeds, title policies, vehicle registration documents, as evidence of existence.

- Review property records and make inquiries concerning existence.

- Inspect properties and relate them to the plan contained in the title deeds.

All tangible fixed assets are stated fairly and consistently in the financial statements at depreciated cost, valuation or on some other appropriate basis

- Consider whether changes in income or expenditure indicate changes in assets owned.

- Obtain a summary schedule of tangible fixed assets, by major asset classification, which reconciles the opening and closing balances of both cost and accumulated depreciation and shows the ratio and method of depreciation.

- Check brought forward amounts.

- Agree items on summary schedule to client's other accounting records.

- Check the status of fully depreciated items.

- Test depreciation and amortisation and check that the rates are consistent, correctly applied and continue to meet the objective of writing the assets off over their expected useful lives.

- Ensure revaluations are reliable. Where revaluation has taken place in the year
  — obtain a copy of the valuation, including a note of the basis adopted and assumptions, and file with the permanent notes
  — check that the information supplied to the valuer is reasonable and is consistent with that used in preparing the accounts
  — ensure that the basis adopted and assumptions made are consistent with those used in preparing the accounts and with those used in previous years, where relevant (eg an annual revaluation)
  — assess the overall reasonableness of the valuation, if possible
  — ensure that the valuer's consent to publication is obtained
  — check that the amount of the valuation is correctly incorporated in the accounts, and that revaluation surpluses are properly accounted for

- Where accounts incorporate valuations arrived at in previous years, consider asking the directors to obtain a letter of comfort from the valuers stating whether or not, in their opinion, their professional valuations remain substantially valid.

TANGIBLE FIXED ASSETS (continued)

All acquisitions, transfers, disposals and retirements of tangible fixed assets and related amounts of depreciation are recorded in the financial statements and are valid

- Review board minutes for capital expenditure and disposal plans.

- Obtain a schedule of additions giving dates and referring to invoices etc
  — check authorisation with minutes, capial budgets etc
  — consider disclosure of acquisitions from directors/related parties
  — review additions for evidence of corresponding disposals
  — review repairs etc for capital items
  — ensure capitalisation of expenditures is acceptable by reference to generally accepted accounting principles and is justifiable in terms of the recoverability of the expenditure
  — review hire expenditure accounts for assets held on finance leases and ensure these are capitalised
  — check VAT is properly accounted for
  — obtain evidence as to value of assets under construction
  — check grants are identified and properly accounted for
  — ensure assets held on operating leases are not capitalised.

- Test disposals
  — check authorisation
  — trace to cash book and supporting documentation
  — check accounting entries and treatment of profit/loss
  — consider disclosure of disposals to directors or related parties
  — consider liability to repay grants.

- Enquire what items were disposed of during the year.

- Review interest costs to ascertain whether any amounts capitalised are appropriate.

Tangible fixed assets are properly described and classified in the financial statements in accordance with generally accepted accounting principles and relevant legal requirements and there is adequate disclosure of all capital commitments

- Test consistency and accuracy of analyses for disclosure purposes.

- Review status of capital assets. Pay particular attention to
  — assets not in use
  — assets to be disposed of
  — amounts of interest capitalised.

- For assets stated at a valuation, check historical cost disclosure and tax treatment.

- Review capital commitments — check to orders, accepted quotations, post year-end additions, minutes.

- Review for restrictions and liens.

- Review disclosure of capitalisation, valuation, depreciation and amortisation methods.

- Review disclosure of capitalised leases and obligations.

- Review financial statements for compliance using a company accounts disclosure checklist.

INTANGIBLE FIXED ASSETS

Intangible assets stated in the financial statements represent rights, privileges or earning power owned by the client

- In documents of title and supporting documentation
  - inspect the supporting legal opinion, patent, licence, written assignments or other documentary evidence for major assets on an annual or cyclical basis, as deemed necessary
  - examine certificates of registration and renewal for patents and trademarks
  - obtain legal representation as to the continuing enforceability of contracts or legal rights
  - where the net book values are significant, consider the need to obtain confirmation from an appropriate third party (eg patent agent, licensing authority)
  - check that the terms imposed on the client by agreements have been complied with.

All intangible assets owned by the client are stated fairly and consistently with prior years in the financial statements at amortised cost, valuation or on some other appropriate basis

- Obtain summary schedule and review movements
  - compare year-end balances with those of prior periods and current period budgets and investigate unexpected differences.
  - review relationships between cost, net book value and current period amortisation for the current and preceding periods and obtain explanations for significant fluctuations
  - compute the estimated remaining useful lives using current year's depreciation or amortisation
  - review the levels of profits and losses on disposals and the number of fully amortised assets still in use to assess the adequacy of amortisation rates and residual values.

- Check brought forward amounts to prior period's workpapers.

- Agree items on summary schedule to company's other accounting records.

- Consider possible omissions.

- Test values
  - ascertain whether there is a continuing future economic value by review of management plans and marketing forecasts, assessing whether sales forecasts are attainable and that the necessary finance will be available
  - discuss the position with management and, where necessary, obtain formal confirmation by letter of representation of the forecasts
  - review past periods to assess accuracy of previous forecasting.

- Factors affecting the value of intangibles which the auditor should consider include
  - a change in the client's circumstances, such as disposal of business or change in trade
  - periodic renegotiation of terms of contracts such as licensing agreements
  - operation of law, for example, the expiry of a patent after twenty years
  - changes in the market place, eg competing products.

- Ensure that any capitalised development expenditure continues to meet the criteria (of SSAP 13) for carrying forward rather than immediate write-off.

INTANGIBLE FIXED ASSETS (continued)

- Review for obligations
  - — examine primary and ancillary documents for evidence of liens, restrictions, outside profit participation or other matters that may restrict or limit the client's ownership of the intangible asset.

- Test amortisation
  - — consider whether the asset will generate sufficient future revenues to justify its carrying value
  - — consider over what period the carrying value should be amortised
  - — note that the amortisation period is usually the shorter of the legal life and the benefit period.

All acquisitions, transfers and disposals of intangible fixed assets and related amounts of amortisation are recorded in the financial statements and are valid

- Review board minutes for acquisition/disposals.
  - — check that all decisions recorded in the minutes to make acquisitions or disposals are reflected in the accounting records.

- Test additions — obtain a schedule of additions and, for major items
  - — determine that the addition has been properly authorised
  - — examine such supporting documents as lawyers' letters, patent agents' invoices, covenants, contracts and other agreements with third parties, licences, copyrights, franchises and trademarks received from government bodies or other entities, etc
  - — trace transactions to appropriate entries in the detailed records
  - — ensure that all capitalised expenditures conform with the company's capitalisation policy and generally accepted accounting principles.

- Test disposals to cash book and supporting documentation. Obtain a schedule of disposals and, for major items
  - — determine that disposal has been properly authorised
  - — examine such supporting documents as bills of sale, contracts, cash receipts, etc
  - — trace disposal to the cash book and to the detailed records
  - — determine that reductions in the asset accounts and related accumulated amortisation are correct
  - — determine that net book value at the date of sale and gain or loss on disposal have been correctly recorded and classified
  - — note acquisitions from and disposals to directors and other related parties and consider the need for specific disclosure.

Intangible assets are properly described and classified in the financial statements in accordance with generally accepted accounting practice and relevant legal requirements and there is adequate disclosure of all capital commitments

- Test consistency and accuracy of analyses for disclosure purposes.

- Review financial statements for compliance using a company accounts disclosure checklist.

INVESTMENTS

This checklist covers audit work on both short and long-term investments, including income from investments and disposals. It does not, however, deal with the specific legislative and audit requirements of certain types of businesses such as banks and insurance companies. Nor does it discuss the auditing requirements of such specialised 'quasi-investments' as futures and options. These topics are matters for specialised guidance.

All investments are shown in the balance sheet, they exist and belong to the client

- Obtain an investment schedule reconciling the current and previous balance sheet figures, giving details for each investment (in the form of an investments ledger, printout or other client generated schedules) and showing
  - the brought forward balances (number, nominal value and balance sheet value)
  - the carried forward balances (number, nominal value and balance sheet value)
  - movements in the period (eg additions, disposals, revaluations)
  - a full description of the investment
  - investment income received in the period
  - profits or losses on disposal
  - market value, if recorded at cost (to enable diminutions in value to be identified).

  Agree amounts on investment schedule in total with the general ledger and the accounts

- Where the client has the custody of the investments carry out a sample inspection of the documents of title

- Obtain certificates from all third parties holding the client's investments. These should state
  - that the securities are held for the client
  - in whose name they are registered
  - that they are held free from lien (*see specimen letter below*).

Investments are properly stated at cost or an appropriate valuation and are worth not less than book value

- Determine the appropriateness of the basis of valuation used, by reference to the nature of investment, i.e. long term (fixed asset) or short term (current asset).

- Ensure that the treatment adopted is consistent from year to year and is fully disclosed in the accounting policies notes.

- Test check the carrying value of individual holdings in the investment schedule by vouching changes with contract notes, cash book entries etc. On a partial disposal the book value should be allocated in a first-in-first-out basis (FIFO) or on average value.

- From published sources, check that the client has, on the sample of investments being tested, received all benefits arising from the holding e.g. dividends, bonuses and rights issues etc, and accounted for all liabilities, such as calls etc.

- When investments were not bought or sold through a member of a reputable stock exchange check whether the bargain appears to be at arm's length. Consider the audit implications where this is not the case.

INVESTMENTS (continued)

- Check that investment transactions around the year end have been included in the appropriate accounting period by reference to brokers' statements, contract notes etc. The brokers' statements should be reconciled with the client's ledger balances at the year end.

- Check the valuation of a sample of quoted investments, ie those for which an established market exists, with the published prices.

- Check the valuation of unquoted investments by any appropriate means, including
  — any recent arm's length trades,
  — comparison with similar enterprises for which a value is published
  — a review of the company's most recent audited accounts, noting levels of earnings and distributions, net asset value per share, future prospects, qualified audit report, etc.
  — the investment's intrinsic value to the client's business.

- For both quoted and unquoted investments check that accrued income is correctly treated.

- On the basis of the above valuation work consider whether any provision is necessary for permanent diminution in value.

Investments are disclosed, classified and described in the financial statements in accordance with generally accepted accounting principles and relevant legal requirements

- Check disclosures, using a company accounts disclosure checklist. In particular, consider
  — the classification of investments as fixed (long term) or current (short term) assets
  — investments in subsidiaries and related undertakings or substantial shareholdings (over 10%) which may require additional disclosures
  — uncalled capital, guarantees or other commitments which should be disclosed.

Profits or losses on disposal are accounted for properly

- Confirm or corroborate the completeness of the investment schedule (purchases and sales within the year could have been omitted) by a review of directors' minutes, investment committee minutes, brokers' statements etc.

- Check that the correct calculation of profits and losses on disposals has been tested as part of the work on the investment ledger.

Investment income to which the client is entitled has been properly accounted for

- Review total investment income by reference to the nature of the portfolio.

- Review the investment schedule, where it includes the income on each holding, and enquire into those holdings where there is no income or the stated figure looks incorrect.

- Test income on individual investments by reference to published records of dividend payments.

- Check that any tax credits or tax deductions have been properly accounted for.

SPECIMEN LETTER TO THIRD PARTY HOLDING INVESTMENTS

Dear Sirs

. . . .(name of client)
In connection with our audit of the above company's financial statements will you please check and complete the statement below and return it to us at the address shown on our letterhead.

Thank you

Yours faithfully

[*Name of auditors*]
Reference: [*ie auditor's reference number or initials*].

We certify that, at the close of business on [*insert balance sheet date*], the following securities were held by us on behalf of [*name of enterprise*].
Except where otherwise stated, the securities were registered in the name of [*name of enterprise*]. We have indicated whether or not the securities were held free from lien. There were no other securities held by us on their behalf and details are attached of any other items which we consider to be of relevance to the audit.

Date: Signed . . . .

Particulars of securities held	Securities held free from lien Yes or No	Remarks

The balance sheet includes all and only existing stocks to which the client has good title

Planning attendance at a physical count

● Consider visiting locations before physical count. The auditor should normally first visit the locations where the stock is kept so that when he comes to the review and discussion of stocktaking plans with the client, he will then be more likely to be aware of
  — the nature of the items and any work in progress
  — the layout of the location(s) (it may well be useful to prepare sketch plan(s))
  — whether the stock is kept tidily and is accessible for counting (it is very difficult to count accurately in an overcrowded, untidy warehouse)
  — whether it will be possible actually to count or measure stock or whether some estimating will be necessary
  — the extent to which the individual stock lines are readily identifiable, for example, from bin cards on racks (confusion between lines is a common source of error)
  — the extent to which high value items constitute a substantial proportion of the total value
  — the condition of the stocks (it may be possible to forecast that provisions against certain slow-moving lines will be necessary)
  — the best way of assessing the stage of completion of any work in progress
  — very specialised high value stocks (eg jewellery or precious metals) in respect of which the auditor may require expert help to identify them satisfactorily, to assess their condition and/or to substantiate quantities.

● Review and confirm the physical count instructions well in advance
  — the count instructions should be clear and precise so that they can be understood by the client's staff, who may typically only be involved in such counts once or twice a year
  — the auditor should recommend to the client that such instructions are in writing.

● In particular consider
  — stocks held on behalf of third parties
  — stocks held by third parties (arrange for written certification/inspection as necessary. Depending upon the materiality of the stocks, it may be necessary for the auditor to visit the third party's premises.

● Where independent stock counters are used, obtain the client's permission to communicate with them, and confirm the adequacy of their terms of reference, procedures, competence, independence. Consider attending their count.

● Plan attendance. Brief audit staff involved, and prepare written instructions on the scope of work, form of report required etc.
  — the auditor should plan his own attendance in terms of staff, the locations to be visited, and the timing, nature and levels of test he will carry out.

● The auditor can attend for the whole or for part of the count. Clearly it is preferable that he attends for the whole count but, for example, where the client has continuous stock records which have proved reliable on past audits, attendance for only part of the count may be sufficient
  — all members of the audit team who will attend the counts must be well briefed.

STOCK AND WORK IN PROGRESS (continued)

If they misunderstand their instructions or do not perform the work planned, it will be at best difficult, at worst impossible, to rectify matters later
— written instructions should be prepared for the attendees, to include
— the count instructions
— notes the auditor made on a pre-attendance visit to the location(s) and of subsequent discussions
— the permanent file papers relating to stock
— relevant papers from the prior year current audit file
— a plan of the stock location(s)
— a programme of audit work to be carried out.

Attendance at a physical count

● Observe the procedures adopted during the count.

● Perform and record test counts
— check the counts made by the client's staff by test counting both from the physical items (raw materials, consumables, work in progress, goods for resale and finished goods) to the records of their counts and vice versa. Check that both quantities and descriptions match, including descriptions of condition (old, damaged, deteriorated etc). Particular attention must be paid to high value items. Where the sample includes packaged items or items in containers, some of these at least should be opened for counting. All test counts should be recorded for checking to the final stock sheets at the post attendance stage. Ensure that sufficient information is recorded to enable the test counts to be reconciled with the client's stock sheets eg where identical items are held at several places.

● Work in progress — check the stage of completion
— where a client has work in progress, obtain evidence of its state of completion in as much detail as practicable. This evidence should include the observation of all major items. Further evidence will depend on the client's accounting system and the nature of the product.

● Note cut-off details (purchases, sales, internal cut-off). In checking cut-off, it is far more important to pay attention to high value items so long as these are fairly close to the cut-off point, than to check (without considering value) the last x items immediately preceding the cut-off point and the first y items immediately following the cut-off point
— **purchase cut-off**. List a sample of goods received notes (or other goods received records) for items received in the period immediately prior to the physical count. Verify, by inspection if possible, that these goods have been taken into year end stock. Trace the items to any bin cards or continuous stock records to see that they have been entered in the correct period
— **sales cut-off**. The same methods as for purchase cut-off can be used but should be applied to goods outward or other records of despatches and the financial record of sales
— **internal cut-off**. It may be necessary to check the internal cut-off between departments in the same premises and between geographical locations to ensure that goods are not double counted or omitted altogether. Internal cut-off is also relevant in the classification of items between raw materials and consumables, work in progress, and finished goods and goods for resale.

● Discuss and note damaged, deteriorated or slow-moving items
— hold discussions with management as well as storekeepers and others directly involved with the stocks, to discover the extent and location of stocks which may be damaged, deteriorated or slow-moving

STOCK AND WORK IN PROGRESS (continued)

— during test counts and/or as a separate exercise, note any apparently damaged, deteriorated or slow-moving stocks.

● Note and check serial numbers of used and unused count sheets. Check that the client's staff carry out the planned procedures at the end of the count for ensuring that all stocks have been counted or measured and that all count sheets and cards have been collected. Note the serial numbers of used and unused count sheets or cards, verifying these numbers by inspection where practicable.

● Photocopy or make hash totals of a sample of count sheets to guard against the alteration of count sheets (in particular, the inclusion of non-existent stocks) subsequent to the count. The photocopies or hash totals will be compared at a later stage with the information the client has incorporated into the final stock figure.

Post-attendance follow up

● Review final stock sheets to ensure relevant items have not been omitted and that they include no inappropriate items (eg capital plant, stock held for customers).

● Ensure consistency and acceptability of inclusion/exclusion of non-trading stocks.

● Review final stock sheets for reasonableness.

● Follow up test counts made during physical stock take.

● Ensure all rough count sheets are accounted for and quantities remain unaltered.

● Test check accuracy (including arithmetical accuracy) of compilation of summaries of quantities.

● Compare quantities with continuous records and investigate differences.

● Follow through major WIP items to sales in next year.

● Check that any phased physical counts were properly planned and performed (check instructions, reports of findings etc) and confirm that all major product lines are counted at least once every year.

● Check that continuous records have been amended for phased physical counts and that discrepancies have been properly explained.

● Check movements on continuous records and arithmetical accuracy of records. Checks should be made by reference to goods inwards and outwards notes, internal stock requisitions and returns notes and records of scrappings.

● Check movements of stock to year end if a complete physical count is earlier.

● Follow up work on stocks and returnable containers held by third parties (check certificates/notes of audit visits etc).

● Follow up work on independent stock counters' work. When reviewing the work of independent counters, ensure that
— the assumptions and bases used by them are compatible with those used in preparing the financial statements and consistent with earlier years
— their work has been carried out in accordance with their terms of reference as finally agreed
— their reports contain no obvious errors arithmetical or otherwise, and have been fairly reflected in the financial statements

● Check for any indications that stocks are not owned
— be alert to circumstances which suggest the client does not own certain stocks (eg products returned by customers for repair or servicing, customers' goods held for delivery at their convenience and goods received on sale or return).

STOCK AND WORK IN PROGRESS (continued)

Cut-off

- Purchase cut-off tests. Check
  - items listed at the attendance to purchase invoices and purchase records or year-end creditors
  - a sample of goods received immediately after the count from goods received notes to purchases and stock records to see that they have not been included in year end stocks.

- **sales cut-off tests.** Use the same methods as above but apply them to goods outward or other records of despatches and the financial records of sales.

- Ensure that only direct labour up to the date of the balance sheet is included in work in progress.

- Consider whether cut-off has been applied at the right point and consistently with prior years.

- Consider whether internal cut-off was accurate.

- Ensure that cut-off for phased physical counts was accurate.

Stocks are valued in the balance sheet in accordance with generally accepted accounting principles

General

- Agree valuation principles with client at as early a stage as practicable, paying particular attention to the treatment of overheads.

- Compare the ratios of raw materials stocks to materials consumed and of finished goods stocks to cost of sales and examine the gross profit percentages.

- Compare unit costs with previous year.

- Review final stock sheets for abnormal individual items.

Stocks not subjected to a process

- Compare unit costs with purchase invoice prices, ensuring correct use of appropriate formula (such as FIFO or average cost).

Other stocks — no audit reliance on costing system

- Identify components in finished goods and work in progress.

- Compare the costs of bought-in items with purchase invoices ensuring correct use of the appropriate formula.

- Review estimates of cost of production, labour and overheads.

- Check that internal profits are eliminated, and that standard costs are adjusted for significant relevant variances.

Other stocks — audit reliance placed on costing system

- Check that internal profits are eliminated, and that standard costs are adjusted for significant relevant variances.

- Check validity of costs of materials, labour and overheads recorded in the system.

- Check allocations of materials, labour and overheads to products and thence to finished stocks.

- Check validity of transfers to cost of sales from finished stocks.

- Review standard costs.

STOCK AND WORK IN PROGRESS (continued)

- Check that standard costs are correctly applied at all stages in the system on a consistent basis.
- Check nominal ledger control accounts.

Net realisable value

- Be alert for warning signs in determining nature and extent of tests.
- Discuss values with management and other client staff, and obtain corroboration and representations of opinions
  - fully record all discussions
  - be aware of personal motives
  - obtain adequate management representations in writing.
- Test net realisable value provisions
  - ensure that the basis of the provisions is consistent with that in previous years and compare the provisions made
  - compare cost with sales invoice prices subsequent to the balance sheet date and with current sales catalogues
  - examine continuous records for periods both before and after the year end to assess the movement of individual lines in relation to the quantity held
  - test the arithmetic application of any formulae applied based either on movement or age, ensuring that it has been applied to the correct base information and that the application produces a reasonable result
  - test check this base information to ensure it is correctly compiled (eg, where NRV formulae are applied to an aged stock listing, test check its correct ageing)
  - consider the use of computer interrogation packages to identify slow-moving items and to check the application of formulae
  - ensure that where provisions have been made against finished goods, related stock lines, raw materials and parts have also been considered
  - assess any sales budgets by product to identify whether stock levels are too high
  - follow up any stock lines identified when attending a physical count as possibly warranting provision
  - discuss particular stock lines with production and marketing personnel
  - consider current trends in technology, fashion and the market
  - consider the current position of items stated at less than cost in the prior year's financial statements.

Arithmetical accuracy

- Ensure that the cost figures or net realisable values adopted for individual items have been applied to the correct respective quantities with arithmetical accuracy and that the resultant values have been summarised accurately.

Stocks are disclosed, classified and described in the financial statements in accordance with generally accepted accounting principles and relevant legal requirements

- Review financial statements for compliance using a company accounts disclosure checklist.
- Test accuracy of analyses for disclosure purposes.
- Organise testing to verify correct classification and description, and to identify matters for disclosure, whilst performing fieldwork wherever possible. Pay particular attention to disclosures concerning:
  - accounting policies
  - current replacement cost
  - capitalised interest.

CONTRACT WORK IN PROGRESS

The balance sheet includes all and only valid contract work in progress

- Consider (at the planning stage) the need to inspect contract WIP. If so arrange with client's senior officials; also (if necessary) independent experts to assist the auditor.

- Undertake pre-inspection planning, inspection, follow-up work etc, similar to stocktake attendance (see earlier checklists). Consider taking photographs to supplement written descriptions.

- Check that accounting policy for recognition of commencement and completion of contracts or contract stages is appropriate, and is applied consistently. Ensure the client's policy is
  — clearly defined
  — acceptable practice
  — adopted consistently from year to year
  — still appropriate where the client's circumstances have altered.

- Check a sample of contracts from records of contracts commenced during the year to ensure that they are either included in current year contract WIP or have been appropriately cleared from the contracts ledger (inspect contract documents to ensure cut-off is correct).

- Apply a similar check to a sample of contracts selected from prior year contract WIP. Also, check that balances have been correctly brought forward in contracts ledger
  — refer to relevant documents (eg commissioning certificates signed by customers, architect's or surveyor's certificates of completion, correspondence, minutes) to verify that contracts treated by the client as completed are in fact completed.

Contract work in progress is valued in the balance sheet in accordance with generally accepted accounting principles

Valuation — general

- Check acceptability and consistent application of valuation methods (including criteria for distinguishing long term contracts). Ensure the client's valuation methods are
  — clearly defined
  — acceptable practice
  — adopted consistently from year to year
  — still appropriate where the client's circumstances have altered.

- Assess the client's 'track record' of estimating costs, revenues etc. Select a sample of contracts completed in the year and compare:
  — actual costs (suitably analysed) with previous estimates (including 'cost to complete' estimates and accruals)
  — actual remedial costs with previous remedial estimates and provisions
  — settled claims by customers with previous estimates.

Cost

- Compare key ratios for current year with those for prior years and with budgets

CONTRACT WORK IN PROGRESS (continued)

- Review the contracts ledger for any major apparently abnormal or questionable items. These can include
  - payments made to secure contracts — the client may describe these as 'commission payments', 'agent's fees' or 'sales rebates'
  - pre-contract costs — these can include the above items, and also the costs of feasibility studies, tender costs and pitch costs (eg advertising agency industry)
  - costs incurred because of variation in contract terms, or under guarantee or warranties.
  - if such costs are discovered
    - discuss them with senior client management, and
    - assess whether it is appropriate and acceptable practice to include such items in contract WIP.

- Select a sample of debits in the year end contracts ledger, and check their validity as follows:
  - if the debit is a disbursement charged directly to the contracts ledger carry out tests of validity of the expense (see checklist on 'Expenditure'), and additionally check that charges by sub-contractors were appropriately certified (eg by a third party surveyor) where this is the practice
  - if the debit is a transfer from an account outside the contracts ledger (eg overheads, or transfers from stocks of raw materials), check that the corresponding credit has been posted to the appropriate account and the validity of debt is in this other account
  - if the debit is a transfer between contract ledger accounts ensure that the transfer is valid by examining supporting documentation, checking any calculations and tracing the corresponding credit to the other account
  - if the debit represents a retention by the customer, or a claim by the client against the customer (alternative locations for these items are as 'Debtors'), check to supporting correspondence, contract terms etc to ensure validity.

- Verify overhead absorption rates used — check base data and calculations.

- Verify adjustments to contracts ledger (eg to eliminate 'internal' profits)
  - ie ensure that any profit element included in the contracts ledger or adjustments (eg because recharges from a separate profit centre in the business include a profit element) is eliminated in recording contract WIP in the financial statements.

- Check for any indications that cost is understated (in work on cut-off and liabilities).

- Check that all costs required under accepted practice are included in the cost of balance sheet contract WIP (eg overheads).

Contract provisions and attributable profit

- Coordinate work with work on recoverability of contract debtors.

- Select sample of year end contract WIP biased to high risk contracts or select all contracts in year end contract WIP. High risk contracts include those
  - with unusual profits or losses
  - where liquidity requirements or profits/losses materially affect the client
  - in politically sensitive or volatile areas
  - with a large difference between the gross balance sheet value and any internal or external valuation
  - where costs to date, plus costs to completion, are likely to exceed the agreed price
  - where the work is behind schedule and the contract stipulates significant penalties for late completion
  - with a poor ratio of cash collected to costs incurred

CONTRACT WORK IN PROGRESS (continued)

- — where costs in the year are low compared with costs brought forward.
- Verify contract provisions in the light of the matters set out below.
- Check that contracts are correctly designated as 'long term contracts' or other contracts.
- Check that foreseeable losses/attributable profits are correctly accounted for on long term contracts in the light of the matters set out below.
- Ascertain problems on contracts — refer to correspondence, hold discussions with agents and managers outside the accounting function.
- Compare costs/claims to date plus to complete with total recoveries from customer.
- Check the reasonableness of any estimates.
- Monitor major problem contracts up to the date of the audit report.
- Assess position (stage of completion, balance sheet carrying value) on each individual contract, referring to available evidence.
- Assess reliability/reasonableness of internal or external valuations
  - — when assessing any valuations, review the terms of reference under which they were carried out and bear in mind the competence and objectivity of the valuer. Also ensure that
  - — the assumptions and bases used by the valuer are compatible with those used when preparing the financial statements and, where applicable, consistent with earlier years
  - — the data provided to the valuer by the client is compatible with that used in the financial statements
  - — the stage of completion, according to the valuer's report, is consistent with that ascertained from contract records (and from personal inspection, where performed)
  - — the effective date of the valuer's report is acceptable (it may well not be dated to coincide with the year end, in which case the auditor must take particular care when comparing with cost)
  - — where turnover is measured by reference to work done, the auditor should assess, by discussion with client management and specialists and from his knowledge of practice in the client's industry, whether the methods of measurement used are acceptable. For example, the payment schedule set out in the contract will often be 'front loaded' to improve the client's cash flow, and certificates from internal or third party specialists may simply be confirming that a specific stage of a contract has been achieved and that therefore the contracted sum of cash is due for payment to the client. The payment and certificate may not necessarily provide a reasonable estimate of the value of work done.
- Check contract treatment where recent costs on a contract are low.
- Check that the contract outcome can be assessed with reasonable certainty if attributable profit is taken.
- Verify the recoverability of retentions and claims (if not part of debtors tests).

Payments on account

- For a sample of contracts in progress around the year end, check (by reference to the contract terms and evidence of year end stage of completion) that all (and only) payments on account due under contract terms are accounted for properly.
- Check VAT treatment for payments on account.

CONTRACT WORK IN PROGRESS (continued)

Contracts ledger

- Perform checks of arithmetical accuracy. This includes checking the additions in a sample of individual contracts ledger accounts.

Contract work in progress is disclosed, classified and described in the financial statements in accordance with generally accepted accounting principles and relevant legal requirements

- Review financial statements for compliance using a company accounts disclosure checklist.

- Test accuracy of analyses for disclosure purposes (on sample basis).

- Organise testing to verify correct classification and description, and to identify matters for disclosure, whilst performing fieldwork wherever possible. Pay particular attention to
  - long term contracts (refer to SSAP 9)
  - excess payments on account
  - current replacement costs
  - capitalised interest
  - accounting policy. Review the accounting policy note and any changes in approach to valuation and determine whether these amount to changes in the accounting policy warranting a prior year adjustment or are merely changes in the method of applying the same policy.

TRADE DEBTORS

Trade debtors included in the balance sheet exist, are due to the client and are accurately recorded

- Apply analytical procedures to balances
  - compare balances by customer and in total with prior periods
  - calculate the number of days' credit taken at the year end using the most recent sales and trade debtors figures — compare the number of days' credit with the equivalent figures during the year and for previous years/enquire into the reasons for any significant change
  - consider whether a substantial increase in the credit period indicates poorer credit control procedures
  - identify the general trend in trade debtors over the year and enquire into the reasons for that trend.

- Circularise customers
  - the auditor should ask the client to prepare copies of the confirmation letter on his letterhead and agree the timing of the confirmation with him.
  - where the client objects to the confirmation of any of the specific customers which have been selected, the auditor should record any such objections and make sure he verifies those balances by other methods. He should ensure that the explanations he receives for the objections made are reasonable and not an attempt to cover up problem areas
  - prepare a summary working paper to control the confirmation process, monitor the status of individual requests for confirmation and summarise the results of the process
  - confirmation requests must be mailed by the auditor or under his control and replies must be sent directly to him
  - where cash in transit is a reconciling item, check it to the cash book and to the bank reconciliation to ensure the cash is in fact received
  - where invoices are in transit, check shipping documentation and the terms of the contract to ensure that title passed for the goods before the year end.

- Test cut-off
  - check a sample of entries in the ledger for a few days on either side of the year end with evidence that the goods were shipped or services rendered, preferably with the customer's acknowledgement of receipt of the goods or services or, failing that, evidence of shipment.
  - select material items from evidence of sales returns and allowances (such as goods returned records, correspondence and the relevant sales invoices) for the last few days of the year and the first few weeks after the year end and trace them to the credit of the debtors control account. Ensure that the credit notes (or an equivalent provision for sales returns and allowances) have been recorded in the correct accounting period
  - compare major sales credit notes in the first few weeks after the year end with relevant supporting evidence and ensure that all amounts that should have been provided were provided for at the balance sheet date. Consider whether the level of such credit notes indicates false invoicing prior to the year end
  - examine evidence of receipts from customers (including remittance advices and the cash prelist) in the last few days of the year and the first few days of the following year ensuring that they were posted in the correct accounting period.

TRADE DEBTORS (continued)

- Discuss accounts or items in dispute with client staff.

- Test accuracy of debtors listing.

- Agree or reconcile the total of balances with the control account balance. Where more than one version of the control account exists, all versions should be checked.

- Check a small sample of balances from and to the ledger.

- Test check entries made in ledger accounts. Examine a small selection of ledger accounts by
  - enquiring into any unusual entries, round sum settlements or unpaid invoices
  - checking authority for allowances and amounts written off
  - checking postings to source listings.

- Trace sample of control account entries to source of posting and vice versa
  - examine the control account for a number of months during the year checking postings to and from source listings, and enquire into any entries which appear to be unusual
  - check postings, for two or three months
  - scrutinise the control account for unusual entries for the whole year.

- Investigate credit balances in the debtors ledger
  - scrutinise the receivables ledger for any large credit balances and establish how they have arisen. Consider confirming a sample of these customers to check the accuracy of the balances.

- Investigate debit balances in the creditors ledger.

- Check translation of debtors denominated in foreign currency. Verify the calculation and agree the rates used to published sources. Where a forward exchange contract has been entered into which matches specifically to a debt, that balance should be translated at the contracted rate and not the year end rate.

- Verify validity and accuracy of bills receivable
  - verify the client's title to bills of exchange receivable
  - where they are held by banks for collection or safe custody, ask for confirmation at the year end that the bills are held free from any lien or charge
  - where they are held by the client, inspect them, ensuring that they have been accepted by the customer, are not yet due for presentation and are otherwise in order
  - check that bills that have matured after the year end have been honoured, tracing proceeds to the cash receipts book and bank statements.

All trade debtors are included in the balance sheet

- Review work on completeness of recorded sales
  - where the auditor has not obtained sufficient evidence from completeness tests in other areas, principally revenue, he must consider specifically testing the completeness of trade debtors. The audit work will depend on the individual circumstances giving rise to the needs for further testing.

Trade debtors are stated in the balance sheet at their net realisable amounts

- Apply analytical procedures to balances
  - compare monthly balances on control account
  - compare age profile of debts with prior periods
  - compare number of days' sales in trade debtors with prior periods
  - compare proportion of debts written off with prior periods

TRADE DEBTORS (continued)

- — review movements in bad debt provision.
- Review, analyse and interpret the aged listing to determine adequacy of allowance for doubtful accounts. (If it is impossible to obtain or create an aged listing, the audit work should be extended because of the (potentially) significant weakness in internal control)
  - — examine subsequent period cash receipts
  - — review correspondence, client credit files, reports of external credit agencies and minutes etc
  - — interview client credit and collection officials
  - — for selected items, ascertain whether the debt has since been settled, tracing receipts to remittance advices. If payment has not been received, seek such evidence as is available to judge whether a provision is required. Review customer correspondence files and correspondence with debt collection agencies and lawyers. Discuss the debts with responsible officials and record their views.

- Where the potential loss due to a bad debt is reduced by insurance or guarantee, confirm that the client has complied with all the relevant terms and conditions.

- Consider the following in assessing the recoverability of bills receivable
  - — were any bills dishonoured when the due date arrived
  - — were any bills renewed for a further term
  - — do any bills relate to customers whose ledger balances are judged to need provision against them?

- Consider the need to obtain written confirmation of management representations on specific material debts.

- Review individual items for which provision has been made to check that the provision is not excessive, checking that the amounts have not been settled, reviewing correspondence and discussing the items with responsible officials.
  - — test the calculations of any general provisions, checking the bases used for consistency with previous years.

Trade debtors are disclosed, classified and described in the financial statements in accordance with generally accepted accounting principles and relevant legal requirements

- Review financial statements for compliance using a company accounts disclosure checklist. Pay particular attention to
  - — credit balances in trade debtors
  - — debit balances in trade creditors.

- Test accuracy of analyses for disclosure purposes.

SPECIMEN POSITIVE CONFIRMATION LETTER FOR TRADE DEBTORS

(TO BE TYPED ON CLIENT'S NOTEPAPER)

THIS IS NOT A REQUEST FOR PAYMENT

Dear Sirs

In order to facilitate our annual audit, our auditors, [*name of auditors*], have requested written confirmation of the balance of your account with [*name of client*] as at [*insert date*].

If you are in agreement with the balance entered below, please sign the certificate and return it to [*name of auditors*] in the reply-paid* envelope provided. If however, you do not agree with the balance stated, please enter the balance on the account according to your records, if possible giving details of the difference, and return the confirmation in the same way. We should be grateful if you would also give details of any other accounts between your company and [*name of client*].

Yours faithfully

Chief Accountant

[Our ref]   [*Name and address of auditors*]   **

[Name of customer]

. . . .

The balance of £ . . . . . . due to/from [*name of client*] at [*insert date*] agrees/ does not agree with our records.

The balance according to our records was £ . . . . The difference appears to be made up as follows:

We confirm that there are no other accounts between our company and [*name of client*].

Date . . . .   Signed . . . .

                                            Position . . . .

Notes

*An international reply-paid coupon should be enclosed with requests to foreign customers.

**Control schedule reference number.

PREPAYMENTS AND OTHER DEBTORS

All prepayments and other debtors are included in the balance sheet, they exist, are due to the client and are accurately recorded

- Apply analytical procedures to related balances
  - reviewing costs for material items which might have been prepaid (eg those showing unexpected fluctuations/increases or those such as rent, rates, and insurance where prepayments are expected)
  - reviewing sources of revenue for potential amounts which will be accrued at the year end
  - comparing prepaid expenses and accrued revenues with previous years (taking account of predicted changes) and investigating unexpected relationships
  - consider reasonableness of amounts.

- Trace cash received after the year end, obtain direct written confirmation of the amount recorded as due to the client, or agree amounts to supporting documentation.

- Check grants receivable from the government or any other body by referring to claims submitted by the client and subsequent receipts. A review of the contract with the governmental agency may be needed to determine amounts scheduled for receipt in future periods.

Prepayments and other debtors are stated in the balance sheet at their net realisable amounts

- Assess recoverability and review provisions
  - **accrued receivables;** have these items been subsequently invoiced and paid?
  - **loans or advances;** were any repayments late? Are they still overdue? What security does the client hold? Are any employees with loans still working for the client?
  - **advances to suppliers;** have the goods now arrived? Does the client hold any security or performance bond?

Prepayments and other debtors are disclosed, classified and described in the financial statements in accordance with generally accepted accounting principles and relevant legal requirements

- Review financial statements using a company accounts disclosure checklist.

- Test accuracy of analysis for disclosure purposes
  - ensure that the bases on which prepayments and other debtors have been analysed and classified for disclosure are consistent with prior years and acceptable under legal and accounting requirements

CASH AND BANK BALANCES

Cash stated in the balance sheet exists and belongs to the client

● Compare period end balances
  — compare year end cash balances to those of the previous year end and investigate and obtain explanations for significant changes and fluctuations.

● Review trends and unusual transactions
  — compare monthly cash reports to cash budgets or projections and review monthly cash details for large or unusual transactions.

● Review for window dressing
  — review cash balances and borrowings for transactions whose purpose may be to arrange affairs so that the financial statements give a misleading or unrepresentative impression of an enterprise's financial position.

● Confirm bank balances
  — obtain bank reports from all banks where the client held an account during the year.
  — two copies of the standard letter of request for a bank report for audit purposes should be sent, to arrive at least two weeks before the year end, to all banks with whom the client had an account or an overdraft facility, even if this appears to be unused, during the year. The procedure for standard letters can be found in the Auditing Guideline 'Bank reports for audit purposes'. It should be noted that the guideline requires the bank report to be sent without amendment as this facilitates the extraction of the required information by the bank.
  — check that each bank report received answers all the questions asked, that the answers agree with the details already recorded on the audit working papers (eg bank reconciliation, notes of security, accrued interest and guarantees) and that new information or discrepancies are followed up. It is important that all items on the bank report are either cross-referenced to working papers or cleared by a disposal note.

● Inspect or confirm cash equivalents
  — examine or confirm certificates of deposits, treasury bills and other negotiable cash equivalents held at the balance sheet date. The auditor should normally enquire whether these items are subject to any liens or restrictions.

● Confirm cash in hand
  — care should be taken to avoid over-auditing petty cash, unless
    — there has been material petty cash expenditure during the year
    — cash in hand at the year end is material
    — the client asks the auditor to carry out some specific procedures outside his normal audit work
  — if cash balances are material, they should be counted at the year end in the presence of the cashier. At those locations where the auditor does not attend the cash count, he should obtain a certificate of the year end balance signed by a responsible official (other than the cashier). Arrangements for this should be made in advance of the year end.

All cash owned by the client is stated accurately in the balance sheet at its realisable amount

● Test bank reconciliations

CASH AND BANK BALANCES (continued)

— obtain copies of the client's bank reconciliations at the year end
— check the clerical accuracy of reconciliations
— trace and agree cash book and bank statement amounts to supporting ledgers, statements and confirmations
— check that outstanding lodgements have been cleared by the bank in the new period and examine paying-in slips to ensure that amounts were actually paid into the bank by the balance sheet date or immediately thereafter
— agree year end outstanding cheques to subsequent bank statements and investigate items which remain uncleared. The auditor should ensure that the amounts of cash and creditors in the financial statements are adjusted for any outstanding cheques written back in the cash book in the new year, if material. Where there appears to be a particularly large number of outstanding cheques at the year end, check whether these were cleared within the first few days of the new period. If it appears that the cheques may not have been despatched before the year end, and this is confirmed by the client, the auditor should ensure that an appropriate adjustment is made in the financial statements between creditors and the bank balance
— investigate any other reconciling items where material
— scrutinise reconciliations during the year.

● Test inter-bank transfers
— cheques and documents which support material transfers between bank accounts should be examined for a number of working days on either side of the balance sheet date to determine whether the transactions have been recorded in the proper period and ensure that cash balances are not double-counted. The auditor should pay particular attention to transfers between group companies around the balance sheet date.

● Test accrued income
— determine that accrued interest and dividend income have been properly recorded for certificates of deposits and other marketable cash equivalents at the balance sheet date.

● Review foreign currency translation
— currency and bank deposits are normally valued using the exchange rate at the period-end. The auditor should determine that foreign currency in hand or currency on deposit overseas is properly valued. Consideration should be given as to whether amounts deposited overseas may be freely repatriated, because limitations may affect their realisable amounts and disclosures may need to be made in the financial statements.

Cash is properly classified in the balance sheet in accordance with generally accepted accounting principles and relevant legal requirements and all necessary information about restrictions, liens, and other security interests are properly disclosed

● Review classification
— review cash balances in the financial statements to identify those that may not be freely accessible and those that were created to serve special needs (eg sinking fund accounts or escrow deposits). The auditor should determine whether withdrawal or other use restrictions or currency repatriation prohibitions or limitations are adequately disclosed.

● Review for other disclosures
— bank confirmations, loan agreements, etc should be reviewed for items which need to be disclosed.

GROUP AND ASSOCIATED UNDERTAKINGS

All investments in group undertakings and undertakings in which there is a participating interest are included in the balance sheet, they exist and belong to the client

- Examine share certificates held by client.

- If certificates are held by third parties, obtain written confirmation and consider inspection.

- Review board or operating committee minutes
  - the auditor should be alert during the audit for any indications of a new investment in a related enterprise (eg a new associate or joint venture) or in a group enterprise.

All amounts receivable from or payable to group undertakings and undertakings in which there is a participating interest are included in the balance sheet, they exist and represent rights or obligations of the client

- Update the chart of group structure.

- Review ledgers for balances with group or associated undertakings
  - ensure that, where appropriate, balances with group and undertakings in which there is a participating interest have been correctly identified and extracted for separate disclosure in the accounts. Normally balances with different enterprises would not be netted off whilst balances relating to the same enterprise may be netted off.

- Confirm balances and terms with signed accounts or obtain direct confirmation
  - the value of the balances, terms and due dates should be confirmed
    - by reference to the financial statements of the other enterprise
    - by obtaining direct confirmation from their auditors as part of the consolidation process
    - by obtaining written confirmation from the investee enterprise, or
    - by reference to the other enterprise's records.

- Ensure proper treatment of reconciling items
  - group accounting instructions may dictate that reconciling items be adjusted in a certain manner, for example for disputed items the selling enterprise may be deemed to be correct. The auditor should consider the effect of such a policy on the client's individual financial statements and his audit report thereon.

- Consider treatment of group bank balances
  - consider whether an appropriate policy has been applied where the group operates a composite bank account in the name of the parent enterprise. Normally it is appropriate for each member to show its 'bank balance' as an amount owed by or to the parent enterprise. The parent enterprise then shows the net balance on the composite account in its own balance sheet with corresponding amounts owed to or by its subsidiaries.

- Review intra-group transactions
  - review intra-group transactions during the period for large or unusual items. Consider tax implications, if any. Consider adequacy of disclosure in the financial statements. Where non-trading intra-group transactions (eg

GROUP AND ASSOCIATED UNDERTAKINGS (continued)

management charges or transfers of fixed assets) are material, the auditor should consider whether
  — they are made on a consistent and reasonable basis
  — they agree with normal group terms
  — they have been accepted by the other party
— review cut-off — the auditor should review intra-group transactions around the year end
  — to ensure that cut-off procedures have operated properly
  — for large or unusual transactions after the year end that reverse a transaction carried out immediately before the year end
  — where the client's year end differs from other members of the group, for large or unusual transactions in the intervening period to ensure that they are proper and do not distort the client's results.

● Review intra-group terms of trade
— where the effect is likely to be material, compare the terms of intra-group trading with the standard terms for third parties and note the effect of intra-group trading, otherwise than on arm's length terms. The need for disclosure should be considered.

Investments in and amounts receivable from or payable to group and other undertakings in which there is a participating interest are properly stated at cost or an appropriate valuation and are worth not less than book value

● Consider value of individual investments; consider, for each investment
— the value of the underlying net assets
— profitability
— projected results, if available.

If possible, the auditor should look at the latest audited financial statements of the group or related undertaking. If recent financial statements are not available the auditor should obtain the latest draft financial statements and, if practicable, assurances from its management and auditors that there will be no material adjustments to the stated figures.

● Consider additional provisions where financial years are not co-terminous
— where accounting periods are not co-terminous, and the investee's year end falls before the client's, the auditor should include any further losses incurred by the investee enterprise between its own year end and that of his client in his consideration of whether to provide against the book value of the investment.

● Consider fair value of investee's net assets
— the auditor should consider whether there is any significant difference between the investee's book value of its net assets and their 'true' value. Special attention should be paid to
  — the valuation of land and buildings belonging to the investee enterprise. If these have been owned for several years the market value could be significantly higher than book value (or lower, although this is less likely)
  — the value of goodwill whether or not included in the financial statements of the investee. If the investee is performing poorly and is expected to continue to do so in the future, the value to be put on goodwill will need to be discussed with the client's management for the purpose of assessing the true value of the investment
  — any audit report qualification in the group or related undertaking's financial statements which may call into question the valuation of the investment.

GROUP AND ASSOCIATED UNDERTAKINGS (continued)

- Ascertain recoverability of intra-group balances
  - this is normally dealt with by extending the auditor's review of the valuations of *investments* in those enterprises. In particular the auditor should ensure that, where appropriate, his review includes those group enterprises from which a balance is due but in which the reporting enterprise does not have a direct investment (eg fellow subsidiaries).

- Where there is a deficiency of net assets, consider whether further provision in excess of book value is necessary
  - in making his assessment of the necessary provisions, the auditor should take into account any subsequent increase or decrease in the level of investment and loans to the enterprise since the year end.
  - to the extent that the necessary provision exceeds the book value of the particular investment, the excess should be included under 'other creditors' or, if material, should be separately disclosed under 'provisions for liabilities and charges'.
  - where a provision is made and there are minority shareholder interests in the investment, consideration must be made of the extent to which the minority can be called to contribute to the deficiency. Normally any shortfall in the minority's contribution would need to be provided for by the client.

- Ensure write-back of excess provisions.

Investments in and amounts receivable from or payable to group and other undertakings in which there is a participating interest are disclosed and classified in the financial statements in accordance with generally accepted accounting principles and relevant legal requirements

- Check disclosures, using a company accounts disclosure checklist
- Check completeness of disclosure of commitments
  - the auditor should ensure that any commitments and contingent liabilites that have come to his attention during his work on investments in, and balances with, group and other undertakings in which there is a participating interest are adequately and properly disclosed. Examples are
    - investments in unlimited enterprises
    - guarantees of borrowings or of performance
    - commitments to fund loss-making group or associated undertakings.

TRADE CREDITORS

All trade creditors are accurately included in the balance sheet

- Apply analytical procedures to balances
  - compare the balance on the purchase ledger control account month-by-month throughout the year and the period after the year end; identify the general trend and enquire into the reasons for it (including comparison with the trend expected on the basis of prior years' trends); investigate any material deviations from the trend
  - calculate the number of days' credit taken at the year end using the most recent purchases and the trade creditors figure; compare the number of days' credit with the equivalent figures for previous years; enquire into the reasons for any significant change.

- Reconcile balances with suppliers' statements
  - the sample of suppliers for verification should be selected without regard to whether or not the client has a statement from that supplier
  - reconcile the ledger balance to the statement
  - circularise those suppliers selected for which no statements are available
  - keep a control schedule

- Circularisation of suppliers
  - circularisation letters must ask the supplier to state a balance (not request confirmation of a stated balance) — see specimen letter
  - agree the wording of the letter with the client
  - reconcile the ledger balance to the reply
  - where cash in transit is a reconciling item, check it to the cash book and bank reconciliation
  - check invoices in transit to determine those in respect of goods or services received before the year end
  - for non-replies, cash paid is not an acceptable alternative procedure, for it does not cover the risk of understatement of trade creditors.
  - keep a control schedule

- Check temporary files of goods received and goods returned notes, purchase orders, invoice register and post year-end invoices and payments to ensure that accruals for goods and services received are complete.

- Discuss suppliers' accounts or items in dispute with appropriate staff
  - consider the need to make a provision in the financial statements for amounts in dispute, or the need to note a contingent liability.

- Review results of stock cut-off tests.

- Test cut-off on sales delivered direct from supplier to customer.

- Check 12 months' costs charged for continuous/periodic services.

- Check extraction of purchase ledger balances
  - check the balances from a sample of ledger accounts to a listing of all balances

- Check casts of list of balances.

- Check casts on a sample of purchase ledger accounts.

- Check total of balances to purchase ledger control account — investigate any reconciling items.

TRADE CREDITORS (continued)

- Trace sample of control account entries to posting source.
- Investigate debit balances on the purchase ledger
  - establish how they have arisen and whether they are fully recoverable.
- Examine a sample of ledger accounts for irrecoverable debits within an overall credit balance.
- Check translation of creditors denominated in foreign currency.
- Verify completeness and accuracy of bills payable
  - obtain a list of bills payable at the year end and check:
    - additions of list
    - that the list total agrees to the balance sheet
    - the accuracy and completeness of the list with the bills payable register and correspondence with suppliers and bankers
    - the accuracy of the list with invoices, statements etc

Trade creditors included in the balance sheet are genuine

- Check accruals to relevant supporting evidence.
- Check that invoices in transit (from direct verification/circularisation exercise) relating to supplies received after the year end have been excluded from the accounts.

Trade creditors are disclosed, classified and described in the financial statements in accordance with generally accepted accounting principles and relevant legal requirements

- Review financial statements for compliance using a company accounts disclosure checklist. Pay particular attention to
  - disclosure of security and charges
  - grossing up (inclusion of material debit balances in purchase ledger).

SPECIMEN CONFIRMATION LETTER FOR TRADE CREDITORS

(TO BE TYPED ON CLIENT'S NOTEPAPER)

Dear Sirs

In accordance with the request of our auditors, [*name of auditors*], we are writing to ask you to advise them, in the space provided below, of any amount owed by us to you as at [*insert date*]. If there is a balance owed, it would be helpful if you would also supply them with a statement detailing the items making up the balance.

After signing and dating your reply, please send it direct to [*name of auditors*] in the enclosed reply-paid* envelope.

Yours faithfully,

Chief Accountant.

[*name and address of auditors*]   +

[*Name of customer*]

. . . .

The amount owed by XYZed Limited at [*insert date*] was £ . . . . as detailed in the attached statement.

We confirm that there are no other accounts between our company and XYZed Limited.

Date . . . .   Signed . . . .

                                            Position . . . .

Notes
* An international reply-paid coupon should be enclosed with requests to overseas customers.
+ Control schedule reference number.

OTHER CURRENT LIABILITIES

All other current liabilities are included accurately and validly in the balance sheet

Suppliers of non-trading goods and services

- Carry out an analytical review of expense creditors generally and in particular overheads, royalties, commissions etc (coordinate with tests on profit and loss account charges)
  — analytical procedures may provide significant assurance as to the completeness and accuracy of overhead expense accruals. This work should be linked with the analytical review of expenditure. Review not only the accruals made but also the total charge for the year
  — where the business pays royalties based on sales or commission calculated as a percentage of certain sales categories, an overall comparison between the royalties or commission charged for the year and the level of the relevant sales may provide evidence that the correct accrual has been made
  — similarly, if the company's purchases include the cost of continuous or periodic services, the year-end liability may most readily be verified by ensuring that the profit and loss account has been charged with twelve months' costs.

- Expense accruals may be tested in the following ways:
  — a review of temporary files of goods received notes
  — an examination of orders placed before the year end
  — checking files of unprocessed invoices
  — a sample circularisation of supplies (biased towards suppliers of expensive but irregular goods or services).

- Compare expense accruals with previous years and consider other areas for possible expense accruals (particularly 'one-off' expenses) requiring verification.

- Check accruals for legal and professional fees. Consider writing to the company's solicitors etc for confirmation of work done but unbilled at the year end.

- Enquire into existence of any new agreements with third parties and check accruals for bonuses, commission, profit shares, royalties etc.

Deferred income

- Ensure that:
  — the accounting policy for deferred income is appropriate
  — it has been consistently applied from year to year
  — in particular, no income which should be deferred is included in the profit and loss account.

Payroll and related creditors

- Enquire into existence of any new agreements or regulations concerning remuneration, bonuses, holiday pay, deductions, employers' NI and pensions contributions etc.

- Review payrolls and payroll summaries for evidence that PAYE, NI, pension fund contributions, etc are correctly calculated.

- Check the payroll deductions accounts for the last months of the year and analyse the year-end balance in terms of specific monthly payrolls to ensure all liabilities for deductions are included.

OTHER CURRENT LIABILITIES (continued)

- Check the last monthly/weekly payrolls with the cash book and general ledger to ensure a full year's wages and salaries are included.

- Ensure adequate provision is made for annual bonuses, both fixed and discretionary, and obtain management confirmation of the figures.

VAT

- Review the client's VAT status, obtain copies of any special arrangements, correspondence etc and enquire into the results of any recent inspections.

- Examine the system of accounting for VAT and consider whether specialist assistance is needed in reviewing any special or difficult areas.

- Where all outputs are standard-rated, or the mix between standard and zero-rated output is reasonably constant, some evidence of the accuracy of the VAT due to Customs and Excise at the year end may be gained by comparing the VAT with the sales for the appropriate period.

- Similarly, VAT on inputs may be a reasonably stable proportion of purchases, but care should be taken where the client is partially exempt, particularly where the partially-exempt proportion is liable to fluctuate.

- Where levels of sales and purchases are known to be fairly free from fluctuation, a comparison of input and output VAT for each VAT return for the year and for the previous year may provide additional evidence that VAT has been properly accounted for.

- Verify the year end VAT asset or liability
  - check that it relates solely to VAT on inputs and outputs since the period of the last VAT return, together with any adjustments relating to earlier periods
  - verify the validity of the components of the balance by reference to the books of prime entry and ascertaining the reason for any adjustments
  - reconcile the balance to the next VAT return, taking into account subsequent inputs and outputs if the VAT period does not coincide with the balance sheet date
  - verify subsequent payment or receipt of VAT.

- Consider whether there are any liabilities or disputed liabilities in respect of VAT and VAT penalties which require provision or disclosure in the financial statements.

Other current liabilities are disclosed, classified and described in the financial statements in accordance with generally accepted accounting principles and relevant legal requirements

- Review presentation and disclosure using a company accounts disclosure checklist.

- If it is included in a group VAT registration the client may need to provide for, or to note as a contingency, the liability for VAT due by other companies in the group.

TAXES

Adequate but not excessive provision is made in the balance sheet for all tax liabilities incurred at the balance sheet date.

Tax receivable or recoverable balances recorded in the balance sheet comprise all and only such balances due to the client at the balance sheet date.

The profit and loss account fairly states the charge (or credit) for taxes on the income (or loss) for the year including, if appropriate, adjustments to the charge (or credit) for taxes in prior years.

Tax balances and tax charges (or credits) are disclosed, classified and described in the financial statements in accordance with generally accepted accounting principles and relevant legal requirements.

PLANNING

- Liaise with tax specialists and client — determine who is responsible for preparing and submitting tax computations.

- Obtain previous years' computations and ascertain developments/new problem areas (see table below).

Prior year items

- Check settlement of prior year items to supporting documentation (assessments, receipts, etc)

- Identify over- and under-provisions and ensure correct accounting treatment.

- Verify adequacy of provisions and disclosure of contingencies, where the liabilities are still unsettled at the time of the audit.

- Verify any provision required for interest on overdue tax.

Current year's computations

- Check/prepare provisional computations using appropriate software, standard audit tax forms or checklists
  - these should be cross-referenced to the relevant parts of the audit file.

- Check inclusion of extraordinary items.

- Obtain/prepare supporting analyses (see table of items commonly requiring analysis) — wherever possible the client should prepare these.

- Agree with detailed profit and loss account

TAX ACCOUNT

- Prepare lead schedule (and supporting schedules), noting
  - movements between balance sheet figures for the previous and current years
  - state of agreement of all outstanding assessments
  - due dates of payment of liabilities.

TAXES (continued)

EVENTS AND TRANSACTIONS WITH POTENTIAL TAX EFFECTS

1 The following are examples of events and transactions which might have a significant impact on the client's tax position:

- *leasing, buying or selling a substantial amount of fixed assets*

- *changes in the capital and financing structure*

- *commencing or discontinuing a separate line of business or expanding or altering an existing activity*

- *acquiring, disposing of or transferring any business*

- *ceasing to operate through a particular company*

- *purchasing a major shareholding in another company*

- *large legal disputes*

- *large insurance claims*

- *substantial compensation payable to a director or employee.*

2 The auditor may need to consider in addition:

- *whether the client submits returns and claims on time so as to avoid penalties (eg interest) or loss of reliefs*

- *whether there are any areas of unresolved disputes between the client and the tax authorities, in particular where time limits may be running out*

- *whether the client has entered into any transactions or arrangements which may be artificial, or part of a scheme which may be interpreted as a tax reduction or avoidance scheme*

- *whether the client is subject to special tax regime (eg the close company and close investment company provisions or the provisions relating to unit trusts or investment trusts)*

3 The above lists are not exhaustive. In addition the client will generally enter into transactions for a variety of reasons and not simply to save tax. For these reasons the auditor should discuss any such matters which come to his attention with his own tax and any other relevant specialists before raising them with the client.

DEFERRED TAXES

- Check that all potential deferred tax liabilities are identified and correctly calculated.

- Verify adequacy of deferred tax provision or appropriate treatment of deferred tax asset. Some or all of the following may require consideration when verifying the adequacy of a provision:
  - detailed capital expenditure forecasts for at least twelve months ahead
  - longer term intentions, if no detailed forecast is available
  - cash flow forecastws to indicate availability of funds to finance capital expenditure
  - likelihood of major disposals of plant, particularly if within a comparatively short time of acquisition
  - irregularity or infrequency of spending on major items

TAXES (continued)

ITEMS COMMONLY REQUIRING DETAILED ANALYSIS FOR TAX PURPOSES

The following items commonly require detailed analysis for the purposes of preparing tax computations and agreeing them with the Inland Revenue. The items and amount of detail required should be agreed at the planning stage, both to increase the efficiency of the audit and to minimise annoyance to client staff who will not wish to be asked to explain the same items more than once

- *general/sundry expenses*

- *repairs and renewals, highlighting any items which should be treated as capital expenditure for tax purposes*

- *legal and professional charges, giving sufficient details of the nature of the work undertaken and tax treatment*

- *consultancy fees, indicating purpose and whether paid under deduction of income tax*

- *subscriptions and donations, distinguishing charitable and political donations and those paid under a deed of covenant (indicating the gross, tax deducted and net amounts) and stating whether these items are tax deductible (ie related to the trade)*

- *management charges*

- *entertaining, distinguishing between expenditure on entertaining staff and other expenditure*

- *directors' emoluments, loan accounts, analysed by individual director*

- *lease payments on 'higher cost' cars*

- *interest receivable and payable, noting amounts received and paid in the period and the opening and closing accruals and distinguishing between taxed and untaxed interest, interest on tax reserve certificates or deposits placed with the Inland Revenue and interest paid or received on overdue tax payments or repayments, including any repayment supplement. In each case the date of the receipt or payment should be noted, together with the date of any tax deducted at source*

- *foreign exchange gains and losses, indicating how they have arisen*

- *investment income, together with the related tax credit or, if appropriate, overseas withholding tax*

- *provisions, eg for doubtful debts, reconciling the opening and closing provisions and distinguishing between specific and general provisions*

- *royalties payable and receivable distinguishing between amounts paid and amounts accrued, giving details of tax deducted at source*

- *exceptional and extraordinary items, giving adequate explanations and details*

- *government grants*

- *dividend payments*

- *any other income which might include non-taxable receipts*

- *fixed assets and investments acquired, their cost and the date of acquisition*

- *the cost and book value of assets sold or scrapped, the dates of acquisition and disposal and an indication of their value at 31 March 1982 and any profit or loss on disposal*

- *purchases from and sales to group companies.*

TAXES (continued)

- — the pattern of past capital expenditure compared to depreciation and also to forecasts, which should be recorded in the permanent file
- — the consistency of forecasts with comments in the directors' report and chairman's statement
- — the reliability of previous forecasts
- — the state of, and trends within, the client's industry
- — the trend of creation and absorption of previous deferred tax provisions
- — any plans the company may have for disposal or moving
- — any intentions the company may have for leasing rather than buying assets
- — the likelihood of smaller or larger premises being required due to contraction or expansion of business
- — rollover relief on replacement assets.

- ● Prepare summarising memorandum, setting out to what extent a provision is necessary and concluding whether the provision made is adequate.

- ● Obtain written confirmation of underlying assumptions
  - — ensure that the assumptions made are reasonable.

RECONCILIATION OF TAX CHARGE

- ● Prepare reconciliation of tax charge reconciling tax actually charged in financial statements with expected tax charge, calculated at appropriate rate for period, on net profit shown in financial statements.

- ● Ensure material factors adequately disclosed.

- ● Check calculation of tax on extraordinary items.

ACT

- ● Check computations of ACT on dividends paid or provided in year, vouching to supporting documentation, cash book, etc
  - — agree details to the CT61 returns made to the Revenue
  - — check calculation of provision for ACT payable on distributions proposed at the year end.

- ● Check computations of used and unused ACT.

- ● Check accounting treatment of recoverable ACT

INCOME TAX

- ● Check computations of income tax on relevant payments and receipts, vouching to supporting documentation, cash book, etc
  - — agree details to the CT61 returns made to the Revenue.

- ● Check year end net income tax balance correctly accounted for.

TAX TRADING LOSSES

- ● Check availability and calculation of losses. Ascertain whether
  - — the losses are available to be carried forward
  - — the trade is continuing

TAXES (continued)

— the anti-avoidance provisions cannot be applied to the losses, ie there has been or will be no change in the control of the company and no major change in the nature or conduct of the trade carried on

— the calculation of available losses is correct.

CLOSE COMPANIES

● Check apportionments/clearances/dividends in current and previous years

● Check appropriate tax rate applied to close investment companies
  — for accounting periods beginning on or after 1 April 1989, close investment companies will no longer receive the benefit of the small companies rate.

● Check tax implications of loans to participators or associates
  — consider the need to provide both for tax on the loan and for interest, if the tax is overdue. Consider recoverability of loan (and, hence, tax on loan).

● Consider tax implications of benefits provided to participators or associates.

GROUP COMPANIES

● Ascertain best use of losses, group relief and ACT
  — where credit for group relief has been taken in previous years, confirm that the appropriate written claim has been made to the Inland Revenue within the time limit
  — the auditor should confirm that a 'group election' is in force if dividends are to be paid without accounting for ACT or if other payments are made which are charges on income to the paying company
  — where ACT is surrendered the amount to be received or surrendered must be agreed with the other members of the group.

● Consider client's need for specialist tax advice on management charges or transfer prices.

● Consider impact of controlled foreign companies legislation.

● Consider payment for reliefs.

● Consider best use of surplus franked investment income.

● Ascertain effect on small companies rate of tax of any new subsidiary.

● Ascertain chargeable gains where company has left a group.

PRESENTATION AND DISCLOSURE

● Use company accounts disclosure checklist to verify disclosure.

BORROWINGS

All borrowings are accurately stated in the financial statements

- Obtain/prepare summary schedule of individual borrowings. For each individual borrowing, this should show:
    - brought forward amount at the beginning of the year (principal and interest)
    - repayments during the year (analysed between principal and interest)
    - carried forward amounts (principal and interest) at the year end
    - the key terms of the borrowing agreement, security or collateral given and other salient features.

- Obtain confirmation of amounts outstanding from debenture trustees or other lenders. Request (with the client's permission) each lender to confirm in writing
    - the amount outstanding as at the year end
    - interest charged during the year and interest due but not paid as at the year end
    - summarised repayment and other terms
    - any security granted to the lender

- Compare totals of debentures and other borrowings with previous year and identify and consider movements.

- Ensure all new borrowings are identified and verify details to documentation. Examine
    - board minutes
    - bank reports
    - loan agreements
    - correspondence with solicitors
    - expenditure accounts for issue or interest costs

- Review fixed assets expenditure to identify if funded by borrowings.

- Compare the totals of debenture or loan stocks with the register of debentures or obtain certificates from registrars.

- Check details of secured debentures and other loans against the register of charges. Consider the need to carry out a company search.

- Check the arithmetical accuracy of the schedule of borrowings.

- Compare amounts outstanding on borrowings with relevant agreements.

- Consider if the level of borrowings is consistent with the client's business and future plans.

- Check redemptions of loan stocks by reference to
    - authorisation in board minutes
    - trust deeds
    - cancelled cheques
    - cancelled loan stock certificates.

- Check loan repayments to
    - authorisation in board minutes
    - loan agreements
    - correspondence
    - receipts from lenders, etc.

- Check repayment monies to the cash book and bank statements.

BORROWINGS (continued)

- Check that foreign currency borrowings are translated at appropriate rates.
- Ensure method of allocating finance charges over period of leasing contracts is appropriate and in compliance with SSAP 21.
- Obtain schedule showing balances and movements for each leasing contract.
- Obtain confirmations from lessor and agree/reconcile to schedule. Obtain written confirmation from the lessor or finance company of the following information on a contract-by-contract basis.
  - total instalments unpaid as at the balance sheet date
  - the security (if any) granted to the lessor or finance company
  - (if possible) brief details such as interest rates, lease periods and options under the contract. This can be useful especially where the auditor suspects the parties may have varied the terms of the original agreement without properly documenting the variations.
- For new contracts, check classification of contract and allocation of finance charges.
- Check that contract terms, in particular repayments, have been complied with.
- Check that finance charges for the year are accounted for.

Borrowings stated in the financial statements are genuine

- Check board minutes, loan agreements, etc, to ensure that borrowings are properly authorised.
- Trace receipt of monies from lender to cash book and bank statements.
- Verify all repayments mentioned in board minutes, etc, included in financial statements.

Borrowings are disclosed, classified and described in the financial statements in accordance with generally accepted accounting principles and relevant legal requirements

- Review financial statements for compliance using a company accounts disclosure checklist.
- Check classification of outstanding debentures and loans between those due within one year and those due after more than one year.
- Check that new secured borrowings and other securities given are recorded in the register of charges and registered with the Registrar of Companies.
- Inspect
  - register of debenture holders
  - register of charges
  and ensure that all securities and charges are disclosed in the financial statements.
- Ensure that appropriate details of convertible loans are disclosed.
- Check that the client has complied with borrowing limits and loan covenants in
  - articles of association
  - loan agreements.
- If client is in breach of any loan terms, check for any cross-default provisions (eg default on one loan may automatically trigger default provisions on other loans).
- Consider the need to disclose or provide for the effects of any defaults, or to alter the balance sheet classification.

PROVISIONS FOR LIABILITIES, FINANCIAL COMMITMENTS AND CONTINGENCIES

Adequate but not excessive provisions are made for all liabilities incurred by the balance sheet date and not recorded elsewhere in the balance sheet

- Obtain or prepare a schedule of opening and closing balances of all provisions and movements in the year.
- For each provision, or group of provisions:
    - review, with supporting evidence, the adequacy of the closing provision and consider whether it is, in fact, necessary
    - assess the competence of the personnel responsible for calculating the closing provisions. Consider, for example, the appropriateness of previous years' provisions in the light of subsequent actual events. A 'track record' of reasonable predictions in the past gives some assurance that the current provisions are reasonable also (though changes from prior years in the relevant personnel, the broad nature of the calculations involved and the possibility of management manipulation of provisions can invalidate reliance on a past 'track record').
- Where necessary, obtain written confirmations of representations made by management.
- Identify other areas of potential liability from a review of the audit file, discussions with management and reviews of minutes and correspondence.
- Decide whether provision is required or disclosure of a contingent liability is needed.
- Assess the effect of any pending or threatened legal action.
- Obtain confirmation from lawyers on legal actions by or against the client, discuss with management etc.
- Verify provision for losses on forward foreign exchange or commodity transactions.
- Verify provision for warranty and repair claims.
- Obtain confirmation, in a letter of representation, from management that the auditors have been informed of all pending legal actions and that in management's opinion adequate provision and disclosures have been made.

Provisions for liabilities, financial commitments and contingencies are disclosed, classified and described in the financial statements in accordance with generally accepted accounting principles and relevant legal requirements

- Review financial statements for compliance using a company accounts disclosure checklist.

SPECIMEN LETTER TO LAWYERS

(TO BE TYPED ON CLIENT'S NOTEPAPER)

Dear Sirs

Our auditors, [*Name of auditors*], have requested your written confirmation of the [company's/group's] position with regard to any pending legal action. Would you, therefore, kindly indicate the amounts for which the [company/group] could be liable on the following matters which have been referred to you:

(i)

(ii) [etc]

If there are other matters on which you have been consulted and which, in your opinion, could be material in relation to the [company'/group's] financial position, would you kindly indicate their nature and your estimate of the amount ultimately payable. For this purpose, *a contingent liability in excess of £.......... would be considered material*, whether this arises from a single claim or a series of similar claims.

Would you also indicate any amounts due to you, or accrued but unbilled, for services rendered and costs to [the balance sheet date].

Please send a copy of your letter direct to [*name of auditors*] for which purpose a reply-paid envelope is enclosed.

Yours faithfully

Director

DIVIDENDS, EARNINGS PER SHARE, CAPITAL & RESERVES

Share capital is properly classified and described in the accounts in compliance with the relevant legal requirements

- Check disclosure using a company accounts disclosure checklist.
- Agree the authorised capital with the Memorandum of Association.
- Agree the issued capital with the share register, or obtain a certificate from the registrars.

Movements in share capital are properly authorised and correctly shown and described in compliance with the relevant legal requirements

- Ensure that shareholders' pre-emption rights have been respected.
- Check that the directors were authorised to allot shares, if any were allotted.
- Ensure that there was proper authorisation for any share redemptions.
- Check authority for any share capital reductions.
- Agree all movements to minutes, Memorandum and Articles of Association.
- Consider special rules for allotments of public company shares.
- Test allotments with supporting evidence and trace entries in register.
- Test payments with supporting evidence and trace entries in register.
- Check subsequent receipt of payment on calls due at year end.
- Check additions of allotments list and cash records and agree totals to recorded movements.
- Ensure correct treatment of share premiums—consider share premium account, merger relief and premium paid on purchase or redemption of own shares.
- Vouch issue expenses.
- Ensure that any options granted were in accordance with agreements.
- Check disclosures using a company accounts disclosure checklist.

Reserves are properly classified and described in the accounts in compliance with generally accepted accounting principles and the relevant legal requirements

- Check disclosure using a company accounts disclosure checklist.
- Ensure that it is clear which reserves are distributable.
- Consider additional disclosure requirements, where any allotments in the past two years qualified for merger relief.

Movements in reserves are properly authorised and correctly shown and described in compliance with generally accepted accounting principles and the relevant legal requirements

- Check movements to minutes etc.

DIVIDENDS, EARNINGS PER SHARE, CAPITAL & RESERVES
(continued)

- Check that the movements do not contravene statutory restrictions, Articles, debenture trust deeds or SSAPs.

- Ensure the proper disclosure of movements and the treatment of related tax.

Dividends paid and payable are correctly stated in accordance with the appropriate resolutions and comply with statutory and other restrictions on distributions

- Confirm payment with the registrars and minutes of board and shareholders meetings.

- Check total dividend calculations.

- Agree total amounts to cash book and nominal ledger.

- Ensure compliance with statutory regulations, Memorandum and Articles of Association.

- Check payments to individual members (holdings calculations, returned cheques).

- Check additions of dividends lists.

- Ensure dividend waivers are properly effected.

Earnings per share are fairly stated in accordance with generally accepted accounting principles

- Consider whether the 'nil' basis EPS should be disclosed.

- Consider whether the fully diluted EPS requires disclosure.

- Check calculations.

INCOME

All income is accurately recorded in the profit and loss account

Analytical procedures

- Consider available information and obtain or prepare appropriate analyses e.g.
  - past results, adjusted for known changes in volumes, prices and mix
  - time series trends (the pattern of weekly/monthly sales over a number of years)
  - budgets (depending on their past reliability)
  - cross sectional consistency (e.g. comparison of gross margins at similar retail outlets)
  - a provable figure of sales volumes or quantities evaluated at audited prices.

- Compare actual and expected results, investigate variances and critically assess explanations
  - compare predictions with reported figures
  - investigate material variances with the client's help
  - record and corroborate the given explanations.

Tests of details

- Trace sales from originating source documents to a revenue account in the ledger
  - check that goods shipped/services rendered are invoiced
  - agree invoice details
  - check invoice entered in revenue account in ledger.

- Trace debit entries in sales account to supporting evidence of valid claim or rebate.

- Test cut-off
  - check that shipments around year end are recorded in correct period
  - check that goods returned are recorded in the correct period.

- Check that all other income has been recorded.

All recorded revenues are bona fide income of the client

- Analytical procedures (see above).

- Carry out specific checks, as appropriate (eg consignment sales, agency sales).

- Scrutinise revenue accounts for unusual entries.

Income is disclosed, classified and described in the financial statements in accordance with generally accepted principles and relevant legal requirements

- Check disclosure using a company accounts disclosure checklist.

- Check classification (consistent and acceptable).

- Ensure proper treatment of extraordinary, exceptional and prior year items.

EXPENDITURE

All expenditure is recorded in the profit and loss account

- Consider the need for specific testing, having regard to any specific risks of understatement of expenditure and to audit work carried out in other areas e.g. creditors, provisions, fixed assets etc.

- Where practical, scrutinise the nominal ledger for indications of understatement of expenditure, for example unusual credit entries or credit balances on expenditure accounts or expenditure relating to expense categories, products or suppliers which ought to be recorded, but which in fact are unrecorded.

Expenditure recorded in the profit and loss account is valid

Analytical procedures

- Cost of sales
  - ascertain how cost of sales information is analysed for management purposes
  - identify relationships between different elements of the information available that will enable the cost of sales to be predicted. Where gross margins are predictable, these can be used to estimate cost of sales from sales information, provided that the latter is audited separately. Alternatively, if sales quantities are known (by weight, volume or number of units) this may enable the cost of sales to be estimated
  - compare estimate of the expected level of expenditure for a particular category with the actual figure incorporated in the client's financial statements
  - investigate significant differences
  - obtain adequate explanation and corroboration of material variances.

- Overhead expenditure
  - general method as above
  - try to use actual price increases or those specific to a particular class of expense involved rather than simply a general allowance for inflation.

- Payroll costs
  - general method as above. The information on which the analytical procedures will be based may include
  - analysis of employees by function, department, production area, grade
  - analysis of changes in employee numbers
  - hours worked by factory staff analysed by product type
  - analyses of the effects of strikes, lock-outs, short-time working, etc
  - changes in pay rates
  - changes in shift working
  - changes in production methods, eg introduction of automated machinery
  - productivity and bonus information.

In addition, production and sales information used in analytical tests of sales and cost of sales may be relevant.

Test of details

- External supplies
  - agree sample of entries in the nominal ledger in respect of purchases back to the posting sources.
  - check arithmetical accuracy of sample of nominal ledger accounts and posting sources.

EXPENDITURE (continued)

- — test error-prone items
  - — scrutinise cash book, nominal ledger accounts and purchase invoice batch headers
  - — verify journal adjustments made to the purchases and expense accounts
  - — review cut-off tests on stock and contract WIP.
- — trace sample of recorded purchases from posting sources to
  - — purchase invoices, ensuring correct allocation within the nominal ledger
  - — verify that goods or services have been received for this sample
  - — verify that invoices are correctly priced
  - — check calculations on invoices.
- — consider specific tests on particular expense headings (eg interest payable).
- — where 'true value' of purchase credits is material)
  - — check sample of goods returned notes or other records of disputed or poor quality goods/services to subsequent receipt of credit note and posting to expenditure account
  - — review credit notes received after the year-end for correct treatment.

- ● Payroll and related costs
  - — investigate employee costs in the nominal ledger arising from sources other than the payroll—consider PAYE/NI implications.
  - — check arithmetical accuracy of the payroll (and any payroll summaries relied upon by the auditor) on sample basis.
  - — agree nominal ledger entries to payroll.
  - — tests on representative sample of employees selected from payrolls throughout the year.

Expenditure is measured on an acceptable basis, consistent with previous years, in accordance with the stated accounting principles and relevant requirements

- ● Review acceptability and consistency of application of accounting policies for measurement of expenditure.

- ● Consider if costs and revenues are being properly matched; in particular, consider
  - — research and development expenditure (refer to SSAP 13 for guidance)
  - — long-term construction contracts (refer to SSAP 9 for guidance)
  - — "front-end" fees, for example for financial services
  - — retirement benefit costs (see below)
  - — businesses involved in forward and futures trading, where related contracts may mature in different accounting periods.

- ● Consider if material capital items or prior year adjustment have been incorrectly charged to the profit and loss account.

Retirement benefit costs

- ● Planning matters—review of scheme rules, liaison with actuary, liaison with pension scheme auditor identification of unfunded pension obligations etc.

- ● Unfunded pension obligations—consider whether it is necessary for the existence or otherwise of unfunded pension obligations to be confirmed in the letter of representation. Review the actuarial valuation of any obligation.

- ● Defined benefit schemes
  - — establish whether the actuary has reported in accordance with the agreed terms of reference and guidance note GN9
  - — establish whether the method and assumptions used by the actuary are consistent with the basic accounting objective of SSAP 24

EXPENDITURE (continued)

— ensure that the data, bases and assumptions used by the actuary are compatible with those used for the preparation of the employer's financial statements, appear reasonable and are consistent with those used in prior years. This review should cover
  — membership of the scheme (current and prospective)
  — the anticipated rate of return on the pension scheme assets
  — projected salary increases
— identify the effects of extraordinary/exceptional items (eg closures, early retirement programmes)
— identify the effects of changes in benefits
— consider accounting for and disclosure of pension costs related to directors' emoluments
— ensure that, in broad terms, the information supplied to the actuary by the trustees of the scheme does not appear inconsistent with the financial statements
— establish the effect of any changes in the particular circumstances of the scheme or in regulatory requirements since the full valuation
— ensure that surpluses or deficiencies revealed by the actuarial valuation have been properly accounted for. This will depend on the reason for the surplus or deficiency — refer to SSAP 24 for guidance.

● defined contribution schemes — see checklist on 'other current liabilities'.

Expenditure is disclosed, classified and described in the financial statements in accordance with generally accepted accounting principles and relevant legal requirements

● Review financial statements for compliance using a company accounts disclosure checklist.

● Test the accuracy of analyses for disclosure purposes
  — ensure that the bases on which items have been analysed and classified for disclosure are consistent with prior years and acceptable.

● Check that pensions disclosures in the financial statements are cleared with the actuary.

DIRECTORS, MINUTES, DIRECTORS REPORTS

Directors' remuneration is correctly disclosed in the accounts in compliance with the Companies Act and is in accordance with the company's articles, board or members' resolutions, or any service arrangements

- Obtain written notification from each director to the company setting out his emoluments including:
  - amounts paid other than by the company, which may not be recorded in company's records
  - benefits in kind
  - amounts receivable other than by himself.

- Check details to supporting documentation. The auditor should, consider the following test of details
  - check the rates of salary, profit shares, bonuses, benefits etc, to service contracts and board minutes
  - ensure that directors' fees, salaries, etc. have been authorised in accordance with the company's articles of association
  - check that amounts paid in connection with a director's loss of office have been properly authorised
  - check salary calculations, particularly in respect of profit-sharing arrangements
  - check that the amounts of emoluments agree with the nominal ledger and with payroll sources and cash book payments
  - compare these amounts with the latest P11D forms prepared for the directors
  - check that waivers of remuneration have been properly evidenced (in a deed of waiver); the fact of the waiver should preferably also be minuted.

- Check correct disclosure of amounts paid other than by the client (taking care when client is in a group).

- Ensure all benefits in kind are included.

Transactions or arrangements involving directors, persons connected with them and officers are correctly disclosed in the accounts in compliance with the Companies Act

- Ask each director to confirm the completeness of the disclosures (and consider whether the directors fully understand the statutory disclosure rules).

- Examine minutes of board meetings noting
  - transactions or arrangements in which a director has disclosed an interest
  - the names of persons disclosed as being connected with the directors and bring up to date the information in the permanent file.

- Review relevant ledger accounts, verifying opening and closing balances and movements on accounts with directors, persons connected with them and officers.

- Obtain signed confirmation of ledger account balances and movements.

- Ensure that proper disclosure is made in the accounts.

The information given in the directors' report is consistent with the accounts

- Check accounts and narrative. Review the directors' report and other financial information to ensure that

DIRECTORS, MINUTES, DIRECTORS REPORTS (continued)

— the information given therein is consistent with the accounts
— narrative information relating to the accounts is not misleading
— there are no material omissions or errors of fact.

● Compare the information given in the directors' report with a company accounts disclosure checklist to see that all matters required by law to be stated therein have been included.

● Scrutinise all information to be published with the accounts and ensure that there are no material omissions or errors of fact and that references to figures appearing in the financial statements are correct.

FUNDS STATEMENTS

The funds statement fairly presents the source and application of funds, in compliance with SSAP 10

- Check the calculation of movements and the adjustments made. Ensure that all necessary adjustments have been made. The following points should be considered
  - are all significant movements of funds *separately* disclosed?
  - have adjustments been made for all items that do not reflect a movement of funds?
  - have dividends and taxation been adjusted to reflect payments, not provisions?
  - are sales proceeds of fixed assets shown, if materially different from book values?

- Ensure that it fairly reflects movements of funds for the year. Particular problems may arise with the presentation of
  - acquisitions and disposals of subsidiaries (including piecemeal acquisitions and partial disposals)
  - movements in minority interests
  - foreign operations — eg exchange differences and blocked funds
  - extraordinary items
  - movements related to associated undertakings
  - leased asset movements
  - capitalisation of stocks or other current assets
  - losses on ordinary activities.

TRIAL BALANCE, ACCOUNTING RECORDS AND THE FINANCIAL STATEMENTS

The accounting records required by law (or other relevant regulations) have been properly kept

- Review and conclude on the standard of accounting records in the context of the statutory requirements.

The nominal ledger is properly maintained

- At an early stage of audit, agree nominal ledger brought forward balances with previous year's financial statements.

- Review the audit work carried out in the various audit areas and consider the need for additional tests to confirm that the nominal ledger is an accurate record of all (and only) genuine transactions.

- The nature and extent of these tests will depend on how the work in the various audit areas has been organised:
  - review important suspense accounts
  - review nominal ledger for large or unusual items; verify as appropriate (unusual items could include debits in income accounts, credits in expense accounts, opening balances in income or expenditure accounts, entries that appear inconsistent with the trend and entries not supported by posting references)
  - checks on arithmetical accuracy of nominal ledger.

The financial statements are in agreement with the accounting records

- Confirm that audit conclusions in each area can properly be applied to nominal ledger entries and balances.

- Ensure audit work covers all material nominal ledger accounts and posting sources to the nominal ledger.

- Agree accounts balances from nominal ledger to trial balance, and vice versa (on a sample basis if appropriate).

- Check the arithmetical accuracy of the trial balance.

- Cross refer all trial balance closing balances to relevant audit working papers.

- Process all post trial balance adjustments in relevant audit working papers.

- Ensure that the trial balance figures as finally adjusted have been audited.

- Agree and cross refer all items in the financial statements to relevant audit working papers.

- Review final trial balance figures to ensure all cross refer and agree to relevant audit working papers.

INDEX

Account balance
assessment of risk, 9.4.2
materiality, 9.5.3
Accountability
generally, 2.2
other interests, 2.2.2
stewardship relationships, 2.2.1
Accounting
adjustments, going concern, 23.4.1
estimates,
developing, 17.2
evaluating, 17.4
generally, 17.1
internal control structure, 17.3
policies, disclosure of, 9.6.3
records, Part Three
standards, influence of, 6.7.4
system,
importance of, 10.3.1
legal requirements, 10.3.2
Accounts
final clearance, 21.8.1
release of,
final clearance, 21.8.1
third parties, no release before
signature, 21.8.2
Addressee
management letters, 22.5.1
Administration
engagement. *See* **Engagement**
Advertising
ethical considerations, 3.9.2
Agency
contract, 2.3.1
regulatory, 3.8.3
Aggregation
evidence, problems in using, 5.5.4
Allocation
objectives of audit, 5.6.4
Alloy manufacturer
strategy, example of, 12.4
Analytical procedures
evidence, form of, 5.3.5
preliminary,
documenting, 11.1.4
financial information, examples of,
11.1.3
nature of, 11.1.1
planning, 11.1.2
ratios, examples of, 11.1.3

Analytical procedures—*contd*
substantive test, as. *See* Substantive
test
Appointment
changes in, 3.9.3
App. 25.1
company law, 2.5.1
independence, threat to, 3.5.3
new,
administrative aspects, 25.2
generally, 25.1
particular considerations, 25.3
tenure of, changes in, 3.8.1
See also Engagement
Assets
checklist, Part Three
controls over, 10.4.4
inspection of, 15.2.2
intangible fixed, Part Three
tangible fixed, Part Three
Assistant
staffing audit, App. 13.1
Auditing
clearance procedures. *See* Clearance
procedures
computer. *See* Computer assisted
techniques
environment. *See* Environment
evidence. *See* Evidence
failure. *See* Failure
key components. *See* Key components
meaning, 1.1
objectives. *See* Objectives
planning. (*See* Planning
reasons for. *See* Reasons for auditing
risk. *See* Risk
sampling. *See* Sampling
statutory requirement. *See* Statutory
requirement
strategy. *See* Strategy
summary, 1.5
types of audit. *See* Types of audit
Auditor
appointment. *See* Appointment
behaviour, 3.1
competent, independent person, as,
1.2.3
dismissal, 3.4.1
duties, 2.5.1
fraud, responsibility for, 2.5.3
independence. *See* Independence

333

Auditor—*contd*
internal, use of, 11.3
opinion. *See* Opinion
other, involvement of, 11.2
professional liability, 2.4.4
qualifications, 2.5.1
removal, 2.5.1
remuneration, 2.5.1
3.4.1
resignation, 2.5.1
25.4
retirement, 25.4
rights, 2.5.1
Availability
data, of, 15.6.3
evidence, problems in using, 5.5.1

Balance sheet. *See* Post balance sheet
events
Banks
balances, Part Three
going concern, 23.3.4
Borrowing
checklist, Part Three
going concern, infringement of limits,
23.2.2
infringement of powers, 20.2.4
Budget
time, preparation of, 13.4
Business
failure, 4.3.2
learning about,
assimiliating information, 8.3.3
information gathering exercise,
8.3.1
recording information, 8.3.3
sources of information, 8.3.2
nature of, 8.2.2
operating characteristics, 8.2.3
organisation, 8.2.3
strategy, 8.2.4
understanding,
checklist, App. 8.1
planning, 5.8.1
reasons for, 8.1
what auditor needs to know, 8.2
App. 8.1
Capital
checklist, Part Three
Care
standard of,
audit failure, 4.3.2
audit risk, 4.3.2
business failure, 4.3.2
cases, guidance from, 4.3.1
generally, 4.3
Cash
checklist, Part Three

Cash and carry retail shop
strategy, example of, 12.4
Checklist
accounting records, Part Three
assets,
intangible fixed, Part Three
tangible fixed, Part Three
bank balances, Part Three
borrowings, Part Three
capital, Part Three
cash, Part Three
common control procedures, App. 10.2
contingencies, Part Three
contract work in progress, Part Three
current liabilities, Part Three
debtors,
other, Part Three
trade, Part Three
directors, Part Three
dividends, Part Three
earnings per share, Part Three
environmental inherent and control
risk factors, App. 10.1
expenditure, Part Three
financial commitments, Part Three
financial statement, Part Three
funds statement, Part Three
going concern, 23.5
group and associated undertakings,
Part Three
illustrative substantive procedures,
24.5
income, Part Three
investments, Part Three
liabilities, Part Three
minutes, Part Three
planning memorandum, App. 12.1
prepayments, Part Three
reports, Part Three
reserves, Part Three
sign-off, 21.4
App. 21.1
stock, Part Three
taxes, Part Three
trade,
creditors, Part Three
debtors, Part Three
trial balance, Part Three
understanding client's business, App.
8.1
work in progress, Part Three
Class of transactions
assessment of risk, 9.4.2
materiality, 9.5.3
Clearance procedures
accounts, release of,
final clearance accounts, 21.8.1

Clearance procedures—*contd*
accounts, release of—*contd*
third parties, no release before signature, 21.8.2
engagement administration,
cost summaries, 21.6.2
generally, 21.6
permanent files, 21.6.1
time summaries, 21.6.2
management, representation by, App. 21.1
objectives, 21.1
partner attention, points for, 21.2
points,
forward, 21.3
partner attention, for, 21.2
preliminary announcements,
client categories, 21.7.2
form, App. 21.3
generally, 21.7.1
timetable, 21.7.3
representation,
letter of,
contents, 21.5.2
groups, 21.5.3
written confirmation, requirement for, 21.5.1
management, by, App. 21.1
sign-off checklist, 21.4
App. 21.1
Client
business. *See* Business
categories, 21.7.2
management letters, input to, 22.4
preliminary announcements, 21.7.2
staffing, assistance relating to. 13.3.4
Collecting audit evidence. *See* Evidence
Committee
monitoring, 3.7.4
Communication
control dependent on, 19.2
formal lines of, 6.6.1
Competition
firms between, 3.5.4
Completeness
control procedures, 10.4.8
objectives of audit, 5.6.2
Completion review
consolidation audit, 24.4
financial statement, 20.5
issued reports, subsequent discovery of errors in, 20.4
key ratios, App. 20.1
post balance sheet events,
generally, 20.1
types of,
borrowing powers, infringement of, 20.2.4

Completion review—*contd*
post balance sheet events—*contd*
types of—*contd*
definitions, 20.2.1
examples, 20.2.2
window dressing, 20.2.3
procedures,
consolidated groups, 20.3.4
general, 20.3.1
management representations, 20.3.3
timing, 20.3.2
Comprehensiveness
evidence, quality of, 5.4.5
Computations
reperformance of, 15.2.4
Computer assisted techniques
audit test data, 18.5.1
embedded audit facilities, 18.5.4
flowcharting, 18.5.9
generally, 18.1
integrated test facility, 18.5.3
miscellaneous, 18.5
program,
code analysis, 18.5.7
comparison, 18.5.6
software,
computer audit, 18.2
general purpose, 18.3
special packages, 18.4
system activity file interrogation, 18.5.8
test data generator, 18.5.2
utility programs, 18.5.5
Computer models
development of, App. 19.1
documentation of, App. 19.1
Conclusiveness
evidence, quality of, 5.4.4
Confidentiality
ethical considerations, 3.9.1
working papers, of, 19.3.6
Confirmation
direct, 15.2.3
evidence in form of, 5.3.4
written, requirement for, 21.5.1
Consistency
evidence, of, 14.4.4
Consolidated financial statement. *See* Financial statement
Contract
agency, 2.3.1
work in progress, Part Three
Control
application, 10.4.3
assessment, 10.4.6
assets, over, 10.4.4
communication, need for, 19.2

Control—*contd*

detection, 10.4.7

documentation. *See* Documentation

environment,

dominant individual, effect of, 10.2.2

importance of, 10.2.1

general, 10.4.2

generally, 10.1.1

identification, 10.4.6

internal,

accounting estimates, related to, 17.3

elements of, 10.1.3

evaluation, 5.8.3

structure, documentation of, 10.5

understanding, 5.8.3

10.1.2

walk-throughs, 10.6

prevention, 10.4.7

procedure,

application control, 10.4.3

assessment, 10.4.6

assets, 10.4.4

common, checklist of, App. 10.2

completeness, focus on, 10.4.8

data, security of, 10.4.5

detection, 10.4.7

general control, 10.4.2

identification, 10.4.6

outside service centre, 10.4.9

prevention, 10.4.7

types of, 10.4.1

risk, assessment of,

assessed level, further reduction in, 10.7.3

general principles, 10.7.1

preliminary assessment, 10.7.2

test of,

documentation, 14.5

evidence, 5.9.1

extent of,

evidence,

assurance provided by, 14.4.1

consistency of, 14.4.4

obtained ad interim, 14.4.3

prior audits, from, 14.4.2

sufficiency of, 14.4.5

generally, 14.4

generally, 14.1

objective, 14.2

sampling, 16.2.4

16.6

types of,

enquiry, 14.3.2

inspection, 14.3.3

observation, 14.3.1

reperformance, 14.3.4

Control—*contd*

time, 19.4

Costs

summaries, 21.6.2

Court

professional liability and, 2.4.4

Creditors

trade, Part Three

Criteria

establishment of, 1.2.5

Data

availability of, 15.6.3

reliability of, 15.6.3

security of, 10.4.5

test, 18.5.1

Debtors

checklist, Part Three

trade, Part Three

Decisions

information for, 2.3.2

Demand and supply

factors determining, 2.1

Details

substantive test. *See* Substantive test

Directors

checklist, Part Three

disagreement with, 23.3.3

Disclosure

financial statement, 20.5.3, 23.4.2

going concern,

accounting adjustments, 23.4.1

audit report references, 23.4.3

directors, 23.4.4

financial statement, 23.4.2

generally, 23.4

shadow directors, 23.4.4

objectives of audit, 5.6.5

separate, 9.6.4

Discrepancies

substantive testing, found in, 15.9.3

See also Errors

Dividends

checklist, Part Three

Documentation

analytical procedures, of, 15.8

computer models, of, App. 19.1

controls, test of, 14.5

preliminary analytical procedures, 11.1.4

working papers. *See* Working papers

Documents

inspection of, 15.2.1

testing, as evidence, 5.3.2

Earnings per share

checklist, Part Three

Efficiency

evidence, quality of, 5.4.6

Engagement
administration,
 cost summaries, 21.6.2
 generally, 21.6
 permanent files, 21.6.1
 time summaries, 21.6.2
determining objectives of, 7.5
letters, 7.6
new, particular considerations in, 25.3
partner, App. 13.1
specimen memorandum of terms of,
 App. 7.1
See also Appointment
Engineering company
strategy, example of, 12.4
Enquiry
control, test of, 14.3.2
evidence in form of, 5.3.4
Entity
key component of auditing, as, 1.2.1
Environment
audit firms, 2.4.1
control,
 dominant individual, effect of,
  10.2.2
 importance of, 10.2.1
courts, 2.4.4
generally, 2.4
inherent and control risk factors,
 checklist, App. 10.1
legislation, 2.4.2
parliament, 2.4.2
professional bodies, 2.4.3
professional liability, 2.4.4
regulatory agencies, 2.4.2
summary, 2.6
Errors
cause, investigation of, 16.5.3
dealing with, 15.9
definition, 16.4.1
further undetected, risk of, 15.9.8
implications of, 16.5.3
individual, dealing with, 15.9.4
issued report, in, subsequent discovery
 of, 20.4
keeping track of, 9.5.2,
  15.9.5
kinds of, 15.9.2
nature of, 15.9.1
prior period, 15.9.6
projection of, 16.5.1
tolerable, comparison of projected
 error to, 16.5.2
Estimates
accounting. *See* Accounting
Estimation
degree of, 9.6.1

Ethics
independence. *See* Independence
monitoring. *See* Monitoring
structural proposals. *See* Structual
 proposals
Evaluation
accounting estimates, of, 17.4
Evidence
aggregating, 5.10.1
assurance provided by, 14.4.1
audit process, in, 5.7
auditor-generated, 5.2.3
collection of,
 controls, tests of, 5.9.1
 generally, 1.2.4
 substantive testing, 5.9.2
consistency of, 14.4.4
desired qualities of,
 comprehensiveness, 5.4.5
 conclusiveness, 5.4.4
 efficiency, 5.4.6
 generally, 5.4
 objectivity, 5.4.3
 relevance, 5.4.1
 reliability, 5.4.2
evaluation of, 1.2.4
external, 5.2.2
internal, 5.2.1
need for, 5.1
objectives of audit. *See* Objectives
obtained at interim, 14.4.3
opinion, formation of, 5.10
planning. *See* Planning
prior audits, from, 14.4.2
problems in using,
 aggregation, 5.5.4
 availability, 5.5.1
 inappropriate reliance, 5.5.3
 quantity v quality, 5.5.2
sources of,
 auditor-generated, 5.2.3
 external, 5.2.2
 internal, 5.2.1
sufficiency of, 14.4.5
summary, 5.11
types of,
 analytical procedures, 5.3.5
 confirmation, 5.3.4
 documentary testing, 5.3.2
 enquiry, 5.3.4
 generally, 5.3
 observation, 5.3.1
 physical examination, 5.3.1
 reperformance, 5.3.3
Execution
audit programmes, 19.1.1
briefing, 19.1.2
generally, 19.1.1

Execution—*contd*
supervision, 19.1.2
working papers, review of, 19.1.3
Existence
objectives of audit, 5.6.1
Expectation
precision of, 15.6.4
Expenditure
checklist, Part Three
External audit
nature of, 1.4.5
Failure
business, 4.3.2
standard of care, 4.3.2
Fairness. *See* Truth and fairness
Fees
independence, threat to, 3.5.1
Files
permanent, 21.6.1
Financial commitments
checklist, Part Three
Financial information
examples, 11.1.3
Financial statement
accepted accounting procedures, compliance with, 20.5.2
analytical procedure, 15.6.1
checklist, Part Three
consolidated,
completion review, 20.3.4
24.4
conduct of audit, 24.3
generally, 24.1
illustrated substantive procedures, checklist of, 24.5
planning, 24.2
disclosures, 20.5.3, 23.4.2
going concern, 23.4.2
key ratios, App. 20. 1
nature of, 1.4.1
overall assessment of risk, 9.4.1
overall review of, 5.10.2
20.5
See also Post balance sheet events
Firms
auditing environment, 2.4.1
competition between, 3.5.4
rules, 3.4.3
Flowcharting
computer assisted techniques, 18.5.9
Follow-up
management letters, 22.5.4
Fraud
auditor's responsibility for, 2.5.3
Funds statement
checklist, Part Three
Going concern
bank and other facilities, 23.3.4

Going concern—*contd*
borrowing limits, infringement of, 23.2.2
checklist of procedures, 23.5
directors,
disagreement with, 23.3.3
shadow, 23.4.4
statutory penalties, 23.4.4
App. 23.2
disclosures,
accounting adjustments, 23.4.1
audit report references, 23.4.3
financial statements, in, 23.4.2
generally, 23.4
generally, 23.1
group support, 23.3.5
identification of problems, 23.2
letter of support, suggested wording for requesting confirmation of, App. 23.1
management's plans, consideration of, 23.3.2
preliminary enquiries, 23.3.1
red flags, 23.2.1
subordination, letters of, 23.3.6
Groups
checklist, Part Three
consolidated financial statement. *See* Financial statement
going concern, support for, 23.3.5
letters of representation, 21.5.3
History
statutory audit, of, 2.5.2
Income
checklist, Part Three
Independence
factors strenghtening,
company law, 3.4.1
further suggestions, 3.6
individual firms' rules, 3.4.3
professional recommendations, 3.4.2
factors threatening,
appointment, 3.5.3
competition between firms, 3.5.4
fees, 3.5.1
generally, 3.5
incorporation, 3.5.5
services, 3.5.2
importance of, 3.2
meaning, 3.3
summary, 3.10
Information
assimilating, 8.3.3
auditing and, 1.3
decisions, for, 2.3.2
disclosure of, 3.7.3
financial, examples of, 11.1.3

Information—*contd*
gathering exercise, 8.3.1
key component of auditing, as, 1.2.2
recording, 8.3.3
sources of, 8.3.2
Inspection
assets, of, 15.2.2
control, test of, 14.3.3
documents, of, 15.2.1
Insurance
function of auditing, 2.3.3
Internal audit
nature of, 1.4.5
Internal auditor
use of, 11.3
Internal control. *See* Control
Investments
checklist, Part Three
Key components
competent, independent person, 1.2.3
criteria, establishment of, 1.2.5
entity, 1.2.1
evidence, collection and evalution of,
1.2.4
information, 1.2.2
performance, 1.2.2
position, 1.2.2
reporting opinion, 1.2.6
Letters
engagement, 7.6
management. *See* Management
representation, of,
contents, 21.5.2
groups, 21.5.3
written confirmation, requirement
for, 21.5.1
subordination, of, 23.3.6
support, of, suggested wording for
requesting confirmation of, App.
23.1
Liability
checklist, Part Three
conditions for, 4.2
courts and, 2.4.4
current, Part Three
generally, 4.1
summary, 4.6
third party,
cases on, 4.5
genrally, 4.4
privity, 4.4.1
proximity, 4.4.2
Management
audit, nature of, 1.4.3
going concern, consideration of plans,
23.3.2
letters,
addressee, 22.5.1

Management—*contd*
letters—*contd*
client, input from, 22.4
collection of material for inclusion,
22.3
examples, App. 22.1
follow-up, 22.5.4
generally, 22.1
multiple, 22.5.3
other matters, 22.5
other recipients, 22.5.2
structure and content,
body of letter, 22.2.3
concluding paragraphs, 22.2.5
distribution, restriction on, 22.2.4
importance of, 22.2.1
introductory paragraphs, 22.2.2
timing, 22.5.4
representations, 20.3.3
App.21.1
Manager
staffing audit, App. 13.1
Materiality
assessment of, 5.8.2
consideration of, 9.5
errors, keeping track of, 9.5.2
generally, 9.1
judgements, aspects of, 15.9.7
nature of, 9.3
planning, 5.8.2, 9.5.1
resolving material differences, 15.9.9
Memorandum
planning, App. 12.1
terms of engagement, of, App.7.1
Minutes
checklist, Part Three
Monitoring
audit committee, 3.7.4
disclosure of information, 3.7.3
legal regulations, 3.7.2
professional rules, 3.7.1
New audit. *See* Appointment
Objectives
allocation, 5.6.4
completeness, 5.6.2
disclosure, 5.6.5
existence, 5.6.1
generally, 5.6
obligations, 5.6.3
occurrence, 5.6.1
planning. *See* Planning
presentation, 5.6.5
rights, 5.6.3
valuation, 5.6.4
Objectivity
evidence, quality of, 5.4.3
Obligations
objectives of audit, 5.6.3

Observation
controls, test of, 14.3.1
evidence in form of, 5.3.1
Occurrence
objectives of audit, 5.6.1
Operational audit
nature of, 1.4.3
Opinion
basis of, 6.6.3
content of, 6.6.4
deciding, 5.10.3
forming,
accounting policies, 9.6.3
critical points, 9.6.2
degree of estimation, 9.6.1
generally, 9.6
separate disclosures, 9.6.4
fundamental, 6.8.3
material, 6.8.3
reporting. *See* Reporting
types of,
fundamental, 6.8.3
material, 6.8.3
other than unqualified, 6.8.2
unqualified, 6.8.1
unqualified, 6.8.1
Outside service centre
control procedures, 10.4.9
Packages. *See* Computer assisted
techniques
Parliament
auditing environment, 2.4.2
Partner
attention, points for, 21.2
engagement, App. 13.1
Penalties
directors, 23.4.4
App. 23.2
going concern, 23.4.4
Performance
key component of auditing, as, 1.2.2
Physical examination
evidence in form of, 5.3.1
Planning
analytical procedures, 11.1.2
approach, 5.8.4
communicating plan, 12.5
consolidated financial statement, 24.2
detailed, strategy and, 12.1
engagement. *See* Engagement, 12.1
generally, 5.8
information gathering exercise, 8.3.1
internal control, evalutation of, 5.8.3
materiality, 5.8.2, 9.5.1
memorandum, App. 12.1
nature of, 7.3
objectives. *See* Objectives
phases of, 7.4

Planning—*contd*
procedures, 5.8.4
reasons for, 7.1
risk, assessment of, 5.8.2
scope of, 7.3
segmenting process, 5.8.5
understanding business, 5.8.1
who should perform, 7.2
Plausiblity of relationship
analytical procedures, effectiveness of,
15.6.2
Points
forward, 21.3
partner attention, for, 21.2
Population
completeness of, 16.4.3
defining, 16.4.2
Position
key component of auditing, as, 1.2.2
Post balance sheet events
procedures,
consolidated groups, 20.3.4
general, 20.3.1
management representations,
20.3.3
timing, 20.3.2
review, 20.1
types of,
borrowing powers, infringement of,
20.2.4
definitions, 20.2.1
examples. 20.2.2
window dressing, 20.2.3
Predictability of relationship
analytical procedures, effectiveness of,
15.6.2
Preliminary analytical procedures. *See*
Analytical procedures
Prepayments
checklist, Part Three
Presentation
objectives of audit, 5.6.5
Prior audit
evidence from, 14.4.2
Privity
liability, effect of doctrine on, 4.4.1
Process of audit
evidence in, 5.7
segmenting, 5.8.5
Processing company
strategy, example of, 12.4
Professional bodies
auditing environment, 2.4.3
Professional liability. *See* Liability
Programme
development of, 12.6
Programs. *See* Computer assisted
techniques

Proximity
liability, effect of doctrine on, 4.4.2
Publicity
ethical considerations, 3.9.2
Quality
evidence, problems in using. 5.5.2
Quantity
evidence, problems in using, 5.5.2
Ratios
examples, 11.1.3
key, App. 20.1
Reasons for auditing
accountability,
generally, 2.2
other interests, 2.2.2
stewardship relationship, 2.2.1
demand and supply, 2.1
economic explanations,
agency contract, 2.3.1
generally, 2.3
information for decisions, 2.3.2
insurance, 2.3.3
Reconciliations
reperformance of, 15.2.4
Records
accounting, Part Three
Red flags
going concern, identification of
problems, 23.2.1
Regularity audit
nature of, 1.4.2
Regulatory agencies
auditing environment, 2.4.2
Relevance
evidence, quality of, 5.4.1
Reliability
data, of, 15.6.3
evidence, quality of, 5.4.2
Reliance
inappropriate, 5.5.3
Reperformance
computations, of, 15.2.4
control, test of, 14.3.4
evidence in form of, 5.3.3
reconciliations, of, 15.2.4
Reporting
definition of audit, 1.2.6
directors, Part Three
elements of report,
auditor's opinion, basis of, 6.6.3
communication, formal lines of,
6.6.1
content of opinion, 6.6.4
generally, 6.6
scope of report, 6.6.2
fairness. *See* Truth and fairness
generally, 6.1
going concern, 23.4.3

Reporting—*contd*
judgemental opinion, 6.3
objectives, 6.2
other, 6.9
readership of report, 6.4
standardised report, 6.5
summary, 6.10
truth. *See* Truth and fairness
Representations
letters of,
contents, 21.5.2
groups, 21.5.3
written confirmation, requirement
for, 21.5.1
management, 20.3.3
App. 21.1
Reserves
checklist, Part Three
Review. *See* Completetion review
Rights
objectives of audit, 5.6.3
Risk
assessment of, 5.8.2
9.4
control, assessment of,
assessed level, further reduction in,
10.7.3
checklist, App. 10.1
general principles, 10.7.1
preliminary assessment, 10.7.2
further undetected error, of, 15.9.8
generally, 9.1
inherent, assessment of,
assessed level, further reduction in,
10.7.3
checklist, App. 10.1
general principles, 10.7.1
preliminary assessment, 10.7.2
nature of, 9.2
non-sampling, 16.2.3
sampling, 16.2.2
16.5.2
staffing, 13.3.2
standard of care, 4.3.2
Sampling
background to, 16.2
controls, test of, 16.2.4
generally, 16.1
meaning, 16.2.1
non-sampling risk, 16.2.3
results, evaluation of, 16.5
risk, 16.2.2, 16.5.2
substantive test,
background to, 16.2.4
design,
determining sample size, 16.4.4
error definition, 16.4.1
generally, 16.4

Sampling—*contd*
Substantive test—*contd*
design—*contd*
objective of test, 16.4.1
population,
completeness of, 16.4.3
defining, 16.4.2
selection, 16.4.5
tests of controls, 16.6
when to sample, 16.3
Scheduling of work
procedure, 13.2
Security
data, of, 10.4.5
Senior
staffing audit, App. 13.1
Services
independence, threat to, 3.5.2
other, separation of auditing from, 3.8.2
Sign-off
checklist, 21.4
App. 21.1
Social audit
nature of, 1.4.4
Software. *See* Computer assisted techniques
Sources of Evidence. *See* Evidence
Specialist
use of work of, 11.4
Staffing
allocation, main influences on, 13.3.1
assistant, App. 13.1
audit team, App. 13.1
client's assistance, 13.3.4
complexity, 13.3.2
engagement partner, App. 13.1
manager, App. 13.1
risks, 13.3.2
scope, 13.3.2
senior, App. 13.1
timing factors, 13.3.3
Statutory audit
historical development of, 2.5.2
Statutory penalties. *See* Penalties
Statutory requirement
company law, 2.5.1
fraud, auditor's responsibility for, 2.5.3
generally, 2.5
historical development, 2.5.2
Stewardship
relationships, 2.2.1
Stock
checklist, Part Three
Strategy
decision levels in, 12.2
detailed planning, and, 12.1
developing, 12.3

Strategy—*contd*
examples,
alloy manufacturer, 12.4
engineering company, 12.4
large processing company, 12.4
small cash and carry retail shop, 12.4
travel agent, 12.4
staffing. *See* Staffing
work sheduling, 13.2
Structural proposals
appointment, changing tenure of, 3.8.1
regulatory agency, 3.8.3
separation of services, 3.8.2
Subordination
letters of, 23.3.6
Substantive test
analytical procedures as,
documentation, 15.8
generally, 15.5
significant differences,
identification, 15.7
investigation, 15.7,
when to use,
availability of data, 15.6.3
expectation, precision of, 15.6.4
financial statement item, 15.6.1
generally, 15.6
plausibility, 15.6.2
predictability of relationship, 15.6.2
reliability of data, 15.6.3
details,
assets, inspection of, 15.2.2
computation, reperformance of, 15.2.4
direct confirmation, 15.2.3
documents, inspection of, 15.2.1
generally, 15.2
other procedures, 15.2.5
reconciliation, reperformance of, 15.2.4
selective tests of, 15.3
timing of test,
factors to consider, 15.4.1
year end, extending conclusions to, 15.4.2
errors,
dealing with, 15.9
further undetected, risk of, 15.9.8
individual, dealing with, 15.9.4,
keeping track of, 15.9.5
kinds of, 15.9.2
materiality judgements, aspects of, 15.9.7
nature of, 15.9.1
other discrepancies, 15.9.3

Substantive test—*contd*
  errors—*contd*
    prior period, 15.9.6
    resolving material differences, 15.9.9
  evidence, collection of, 5.9.2
  sampling. *See* Sampling
  types of, 15.1

Sufficiency
  evidence, of, 14.4.5

Taxes
  checklist, Part Three

Testing
  control, of. *See* Control
  data, 18.5.1
  documentary, 5.3.2
  substantive. *See* Substantive test

Third party
  accounts, release of, 21.8.2

Time budget
  preparation of, 13.4

Timetable
  preliminary announcements, 21.7.3

Timing
  control, 19.4
  management letters, 22.5.4
  procedures, of, 20.3.2
  staffing, factors in, 13.3.3
  summaries, 21.6.2

Trade
  creditors, Part Three
  debtors, Part Three

Travel agent
  strategy, example of, 12.4

Trial balance
  checklist, Part Three

Truth and fairness
  accounting standards, influence of, 6.7.4
  establishing, 6.7.3
  fair, meaning, 6.7.1
  overriding requirement, 6.7.2
  true, meaning, 6.7.1

Type of audit
  external, 1.4.5
  financial statement, 1.4.1
  internal, 1.4.5
  management, 1.4.3
  operational, 1.4.3
  regularity, 1.4.2
  social, 1.4.4

Types of evidence. *See* Evidence

Valuation
  objectives of audit, 5.6.4

Window dressing
  post balance sheet events, 20.2.3

Work
  obtaining, 3.9.2
  scheduling, 13.2

Work in progress
  checklist, Part Three

Working papers
  confidentiality of, 19.3.6
  content of, 19.3.4
  files, 19.3.2
  lead-schedule-and-pyramid-filing, 19.3.3
  need for, 19.3.1
  ownership of, 19.3.6
  preparation of, 19.3.5
  review of, 19.1.3

Year end
  extending audit conclusions to, 15.4.2